RESCUED HISTORY Essays on th
Philippine Revolution

RESCUED HISTORY

ESSAYS ON THE NEW HISTORY

OF THE PHILIPPINE REVOLUTION

VOLUME ONE

DOMINGO DC DE GUZMAN

Domingo DC De Guzman

KAIBIGAN BOOKS

Percival Campoamor Cruz

Publisher

Los Angeles, California

January 2018

ISBN-13:

978-1981942282

ISBN-10:

1981942289

Domingo DC De Guzman

TABLE OF CONTENTS

DOMINGO DC DE GUZMAN

Emad: domingodcdeguzman@gmail.com

1. First Prize PALANCA Poetry in English for epic poem, *MOSES,* 1977; 33 pages of the epic excerpted & published by THE MANILA REVIEW 1978

2. Inaugural fellow for Poetry, UP Creative Writing Center 1979-80

3. Fellow for Poetry, Silliman Summer Writers Workshop 1977

4. Contributing Writer of Philosophical Articles, *The Philippines Free Press 1968-70*

5. Published long article (3 spreads) *Art & Revolution*, The Philippine Collegian, 1969

6. Five-hour Lecture on *HEGEL &MARX*, lone student lecturer in a university-wide symposium on Marxism sponsored by the UP History Dept., UP Political Science Dept., UP Philosophy Dept, UP School of Economics, UP Sociology Dept., & the UP Social Sciences Faculty Journal *Pingkian*, Sept. 20, 1970. The other lecturers were: Dr. Zeus Salazar (Sorbonne), Dr. Francisco Nemenzo, Jr., (Manchester), Dr. Ricardo Ferrer (UPSE), Dr.

Felipe B. Miranda, Jr. (Univ. Of Chicago), PhD Candidate Randy David

(Manchester)...The lecture was announced in the Philippine Collegian.

7. Undergraduate thesis in Philosophy: *Can There Be A Presuppositionless Philosophy?*

(booklength) 1974.

8. *Third World Notes On Machiavelli* (political theory, book), 1976

9. Columnist, *Filipiniana* Section, History, Culture, Philosophy, *WHO* Magazine, 1982-85:--Booklength critique of Teodoro Agoncillo's *Revolt of the Masses*;Critique of Nick

Joaquin's theory of Culture & History, Critique of SP Lopez, etc.

10. Designed and gave semester-long seminar to the UP English Dept. Faculty on *Philosophical Introduction to Poststructuralist/Postmodernist Literary Theory & Criticism:Derrida,*

Foucault, Lacan...given every Saturday, 1-5 pm, from November 1985 to February 1986.

11. Columnist, *Malaya*, THE LONGVIEW, 1987 to 1992.

12. Long monographic critical studies of Nick Joaquin, Jose Garcia Villa, Renato Constantino published by *The Review*, 1985-87.

13. Lecture on *Nick Joaquin's Theory of Culture & History* sponsored by the Cultural

Research Association of the Philippines, at the HERITAGE ART GALLERY. The Lecture was announced in 3 national broadsheets and panelled by Conrad de Quiroz

& Alex Magno. (sometime in) 1984.

14. *Praxis & Philosophy*, book published by KALIKASAN PRESS, 1990.

15. Lecture, *Psychoanalysis of Myths*, Recto Hall, UP Diliman Faculty Center, (sometime in)

1991; the lecture was repeated in UP Manila a month after.

16. Columnist, *Philippine Journal*, 1993-98.

17. Columnist, *Philippine Weekly*, Chicago USA, 2000.

18. Lecturer and Panelist for UP Diliman Sociology Dept., *On the Sociology of Power*,

Philippine Sociological Association National Conference, UP Diliman 2009.

19. Lecture on *HOW RIZAL & THE PHILIPPINE YOUTH OF THE 1880s & 1890s BETRAYED THE REVOLUTION & THE FILIPINO PEOPLE*, Philippine Social Science Council 7th National Conference, UP Diliman, October 2013

20. Seminar-Lecture on *The Aguinaldo Counterrevolution*, Balagtas Hall, PUP, Nov. 28, 2013.

WORK EXPERIENCE

Editor in Chief, DAP/Development Academy of the Philippines Publication Center, 1977-79

Professor, Graduate School, Baguio Colleges Foundation 1982-85

Director, Institute of Social History, Polytechnic University of the Philippines, 1986-92.

Editor in Chief, JOURNAL OF SOCIAL HISTORY, PUP, 1986-92

Professorial Lecturer, PUP, 1986-2014.

Lecturer, UP Diliman Political Science Dept. and Philosophy Dept., 1989-93.

Lecturer, UP Manila, History, 1992-93.

OLD & RECENT BOOKS

**THE POWER TO DIE, THE ONTOLOGICAL DIFFERENCE, & THE LOGIC OF ABSOLUTE VIOLENCE, PUP Press, 2007*

**The Evil That Men Do: The Crimes of Rizal & Aguinaldo, the Treason of the Intellectuals, & the Philippine Culture of Corruption, 2010.; Dr. Ed Clemente, Publisher*

**GLORIAHELLOGARCI, Homage to Andres Bonifacio, & Other Poems* 2011; *Dr. Ed Clemente, Publisher*

**Rizal, Nietzsche, Ontological Investigations, The Flowers of Auschwitz,* 2012

**Andres Bonifacio, Or How Rizal and the Ilustrado Youth of the 1880s and 1890s Betrayed the Revolution*, 2013

**The Aguinaldo Counterrevolution & the Letters of Andres Bonifacio and Gregoria de Jesus to Emilio Jacinto, 2013.*

**Book in the Making: EPICHEIREMATA INSPIRED BY NIETZSCHE; Ontological & Existological Investigations 550 pages…*

**Praxis & Philosophy, Kalikasan Press, 1990; 210pp. The publisher, Microbiology Professor Godie Calleja submitted the book for distribution to AMAZON…*

**Heidegger Critique, 700pp.; 1997; unpublished.*

**Anti-Althusser, 1984; 245pp; unpublished*

**Critique of Levi-Strauss, 1987; 200pp; partially published in the Journal of Social History, PUP, vol. 1, 1988.*

**Critique of Reynaldo Ileto's Pasyon & Revolution, 66pp; published in vol. 2 of the Journal of Social History PUP; 1988.*

**The Pre-Socratics and the Origins of Philosophy, Theoretical Physics, and Metaphysics, 1999; Writing grant from UPCIDS (University of the Philippines Center for Integrative and Development Studies); 200pp.*

**Positionings, 250pp; 1993; Critique of Post-structuralism and Postmodernism; unpublished.*

**HEGEL & MARX, 200pp.; 1970; text of a five-hour lecture in a university-wide (UP Diliman) month-long symposium THE MARX CENTENNIAL LECTURES.*

**freedom!--the triumph, tragedy, & death of andres bonifacio & the philippine revolution:--epic poem, 53,000 lines the completion of which for the 1998 centennial literary contest was partly financed by MALAYA editor-in-chief JOY DELOS REYES, and THE PHILIPPINE POLITICAL SCIENCE ASSOCIATION thru its then president FELIPE B. MIRANDA JR.*

FORMAL EDUCATION

BA Political Science, UP Diliman 1967-69

BA Philosophy, UP Diliman, 1969-1974

BS Sociology, Non-Traditional Program, PUP,1990.

*Here is what once upon a time the Cornell philosopher Jonathan Culler who was twice president of the American Comparative Literature Association and afterwards dean at Cornell, in a December 1999 referee's letter to then UPCIDS (University of the Philippines Center for Integrative and Development Studies) director, Prof. Maria Cynthia Rose Banzon Bautista, apropos a writing grant, says of Domingo DC de Guzman's work: "*I am happy to write about the work of*

Dr. Guzman, whom I have never met but with whom I have corresponded about professional matters--principally about his massive work-in-progress. He is clearly a man of great intelligence who has read very widely and perceptively in various schools of philosophy and social and literary theory and is attempting a vast synthesis. It is an extremely ambitious project...He sent me a large section of his project several years ago, and I was very impressed by the quality of his analysis of theoretical issues and the ambitiousness of his undertaking...Dr. Guzman...is certainly a man of wide reading and interdisciplinary reflection and should have things to say to people in almost every field. I recommend him to you."

*Alphonso Lingis, a very distinguished philosopher who teaches at the Pennsylvania State University apropos his referee's letters for two doctoral fellowships at Cornell (an Andrew K. Mellon and a Society for the Humanities…), wrote back to D DC De Guzman in October 2000, to tell him that "*On the basis of your works, I have recommended you for the two fellowships with all possible force*"

ACKNOWLEDGMENTS

In 1983, in the pages of my own column in WHO Magazine, I began, not without a massive and anguishing shock that left me feeling absurd for a long time, to effectively discover and uncover Philippine History--or its core event of truth, the Revolution. The Philippine ruling class and its intellectual-ideological agents, agencies and institutions (what Althusser calls state-ideological agents and apparatuses), always in collaboration with western-global capitalist colonialism/imperialism, had very successfully covered it up (as a criminal and his accomplices would their crime), and almost succeeded in killing, in murdering, the perhaps unkillable thing, which thus remained buried, entombed, in a mountain of lies and downright inversions for almost a century. Interwoven with parallel tasks in poetry and philosophy I have mounted a rescue operation--a veritable war to the death against these ideological criminals and enemies of humanity (they were/are, if you want, ALL the historians so-called, who ever wrote a "history" of it; they're all dead now even as the dead books they had written; kill them all thus is what I have done in these pages; you can, if you want go to the history departments or homes of some of the few surviving dead historians here or in the USA to talk to them about it). I have, if you want, erased them as I have erased Rizal himself, and yes, Aguinaldo, who, in due course, ten to twenty years from now will be remembered only as the cruel jokes and pernicious absurdities of human existence they were/are--and yes, bloody, bloody, bloody, to the point of genocide. This is the 5th in a projected series of six volumes that effectuate this rescue operation.

At this point, when practically all of it is already here, and I mean this truth of this history, beautiful and sad in the clarity of its tragedy, I can now perhaps announce to the whole world that the gift, this gift of their very history to the Filipino people, is here, beautiful and sad and tragic in its truth, for this ceremony of presentation. To pure luck (and I am incomparably lucky for it all) and sheer accident, I owe this unique privilege of being the maker of this gift, of being the giver of this gift of their very history itself, to the Filipino people. I am nearing the close of a life in which through all its tragicomic vicissitudes I have been immensely lucky--as the writer, poet, philosopher, historian and fiery jester I am; being which is all that enduringly matters (and to me, too) anyway. And to great luck and such accidents of destiny, I wish to hereby acknowledge this wholesale indebtedness. I should have said I owe all this to God, as of the fortunate the Romans did to the Goddess of Fortune, but I really don't think there is such a thing...

And who else? I was not lucky in everything, of course! I was so unlucky I did not have intellectual mentors to acknowledge here except foreign ones who are mostly to be encountered only in their already world-famous works; Anaximander for instance, Plato and Aristotle, or Confucius and Lao Tzu and ChuangTzu, or Buddha. Bertrand Russell who was an agnostic helped me become an atheist at the incendiary age of 17; Ivan Karamazov finalized it through his argument from innocent suffering, although Dostoyevski himself remained a believer in the novel itself (The Brothers Karamazov). Because the Holocaust happened where truckloads of babies were burned alive, therefore there is no God and there cannot be. To know and understand what history is about, it is of course absolutely necessary to be an atheist, and, intrinsically connected with this, to believe in freedom, which also means to believe in the irreducibility of the freedom of the will and therefore in the inescapability of moral (and therewith aesthetic, poetic, political, social, historical) responsibility. If there is God, everything is necessarily determined--by Him. And absolutely so. And there is no freedom. And no History; only Nature, only Causality which as such can only be divine, theological, and thus absolute:--absolute determination; such that the determined, in being absolutely determined so, cannot be sufficiently other to be itself, nay, cannot in any way or degree be other to God, and can thus only be God itself, and is thus God determining itself and nothing else besides. Hence, if there is God, only God is and nothing, absolutely nothing else, besides. God is then responsible for everything--absolutely. And the human being, the primordially moral being, the primordially democratic or communistic being, the primordially poetic being, the power to die who had always already chosen to live, and therefore to die,--for the Other, for all the others,--does not and cannot exist. Freedom, as Sartre remarked in, I think, the preface to Search for a Method, is what distinguishes the cultural order from the natural order; it is what separates, or what constitutes the difference that distinguishes, history from nature. To be free is to know the Good--and to choose it, or spurn it, reject it, contradict it, and thus to be evil. Freedom is the specific, the uniquely human, instinct:--the fundamental, the foundational, the onto-existo-logical a priori of human existence, the transcendental a priori of Humanity. S/he who loses it loses her/his very humanity and becomes a monster, a thing, a robot, or regresses to the beast. Always already we are freedom and know it--as it were, instinctively:--a priori. Freedom is a transcendental condition in the Kantian sense. To be free is to know oneself free--and to be ordered, commanded, to the Good, to choose the Good, to be it, to do it; and to know oneself--as it were, instinctively--ordered and commanded thus. Freedom is the primordial foundation of humanity--or of human society. That is why we say there is a primordial democracy at the foundation of society such that the history of any such society is a striving, a struggle, by the people, to concretize and fulfill this primordial democracy which as communal freedom of the power to die for the Other is creative communism. Creative existence which is creative communism is the fulfillment and truth of human society. Creative existence which is creative communism is at once ethical and aesthetic/poetic fulfillment, fullness, exuberance, puissance, brilliance. Creating the beautiful is the superlative of doing the Good, of being good, which is always a form of heroism, of heroic dedication of every moment of existence to the Other, of heroic love, of absolute sacrifice, for all, of expending every moment of existence for the Other so that the self is nothing--i.e., nothing except this heroic dying of each moment for the Other...

The Good and the Beautiful/Poetic are possible only as upsurge of the Tragic. They are possible only where there is no God. Or which is the same thing, it is possible to do the Good and create the Beautiful (i.e., the Tragic) only where the doer, the creator, does not believe in God, forgets totally that there is God, feels and thinks and acts as though there is no God. The good one and the poet who is the best, the superlatively good, one, are atheists, are possible, can happen only, as atheists... The ethical moment is necessarily an atheistic moment. And so is the poetic, the artistic, the aesthetically creative moment.....:--the revolutionary moment in revolutionary times.

The Good is the object of absolute sacrifice, of devotion unto death, that for which, and for the sake of which, one is the power to defy death itself--the power to die.

The Good is to love the Other unto death. The Good is the active loving of the Other--i..e., of all humanity to the point of dying, i.e., of living exclusively, and thus absolutely selflessly, for IT, i.e., for the Good; the Good is the being absolutely, selflessly, devoted to the securing of the free existence and creative, communist, fulfillment of the Other.

The Good is sacrificing everything for love of the Other.

To do the Good is also purest and highest happiness...

The Good is to do the Good... Hence, to do poetry is good, is doing the Good, namely unveiling the beauty of truth, manifesting truth in its beauty, in its purity, in the purity of its tragedy, to the Other, and blessing, exalting, and helping fulfill the existence of the Other thus, that is to say, loving the Other thus... To exalt in beauty and truth which is the tragic itself, the human condition itself, is to console the sad which is humanity itself, tragic humanity...

Heroism is tragic fulfillment--and tragic happiness...the only, the solely true one (happiness and fulfillment) there is...

{And homology is already exemplified--operative--in the praxis of animals...}

To be a human being--the free one--....is to be ordered, to be commanded, to at all times live for the Other, to do nothing else but live for the Other, and thus, to at all times expend one's life, die, for the Other. To live one's life such that it is a constant dying for the Other... Everything else is worthless that is not a dying for the Other--and a guilt...Anything that is not for the Other is of course for the self.

To be ordered, to be commanded to the Good, i.e., to constantly die for the Other, by whom?, by what? By no one. By Freedom. By the non-nature, the supra-nature, that is called Freedom. Which is also to say, by that nothingness which is the self, which is such that it is nothing but existence FOR the Other. The self is nothing but this impulse, this instinct, this existological will to exist FOR the Other; it is as such that the human being is pure freedom.

...and homology, originally purely natural, purely animal, pure life, is infinitely potentiated into creation by the event of death and thus by the advent of the word. Becoming thereby truth-for-the-Other:--poetry and science.

The aesthetics of pure nothingness and thus of the unveiling of pure being in a 70-million -year culture of death, of dying, of becoming nothing, of absolute sacrifice *for the Other* in the African Savannah of our australopithecine ancestors *en route* to humanity --and with it, the ethics of absolute responsibility for the Other, of responsibility unto death for the Other, of absolute sacrifice for the Other...Which gave rise to the primordial democracy of the word, of speech, of language--and poetry is the concrete token and active essence of this primordial democracy, the immortal proof that every human society is a constant struggle to fully realize this primordial democracy which is thus the telic essence of human existence and of history...

Event of Truth... This is redundant. Truth is insistence of the essence, its upsurge, its self-manifestation in its clarity and fullness. Revolution is such an upsurge, such a self-manifestation of the TRUTH of a people...

DEDICATORY

{i}

This volume, together with the four previously published and the two or three to come,

is also the Philippines' HIGH GIBBET TREE OF HISTORY. By way of getting hanged on it in a manner that befits a pernicious enemy of the Filipino People and of Humanity,

this is immortally dedicated to the imperishable memory of the treacherous ingrate and perfidious persecutor of these volumes, Emanuel TAE C. de Guzman…

He among other brutally shameless anti-people crimes

banned these volumes from being used in PUP (Polytechnic University of the Philippines)

and severally terminated from his teaching post this 67-year old author

who had taught there for 30 years; C. TAE, and his compadre criminology graduate

VP for Branches Joseph Mercado and their operator, Sta Maria Campus director

Joey Abat, framed the author up by hiding for two years his UTIMEC

(University Textbooks and Instructional Materials Evaluation Committee) application

in order one day to "discover" that he was using the volumes in his classes

Domingo DC De Guzman

without a UTIMEC permit…They had him denounced as a criminal

and these volumes as contraband by the notorious T3 (Tulfo Tres)

on national TV. The author filed a complaint with CHED (Commission on Higher Education) but the two successive commissioners who were supposed to handle the case, Alex

Brilliantes and a certain Adamat, were TAE C's friends and love TAE so much

and take such great delectation in TAE such that

it's now four years since and nothing has happened except that this Adamat

threatened to sue him for "harassment" when he followed-up the case…

This Adamat is a PUP professor who tries mightily to speak English.

{ii}

Emanuel C. Tae de Guzman--a farcically twisted being

who was able to materially harm this ongoing work in significant ways

and has forced me to revise and expand my concept of ingratitude,

treachery, and overall perfidy…

This is to hang him upside down on this high gibbet tree of history

:--for, injuring and even actively persecuting this work,

his crime thus becomes historical as well,

earning him a place in history thereby as the infamous creeping entity he is,

alongside the likes of Col. Agapito Bonzon, who raped the Mother

of the Revolution, Gregoria de Jesus,

after treacherously shooting down her husband, the Father

of the Revolution and of the entire Filipino Nation, Andres Bonifacio;

forever, that is to say, in the human forever of these words,

of this book, of these volumes of rescued truth, he is going to hang here,

and is already hanging here right now, here, right here,

in the august company of course of the twin leaders of the two,

eventually merged, Counterrevolutions, Rizal and Aguinaldo,

that succeeded in recruiting the entire native colonial middleclass

against the Revolution, and to coup d'etat Andres Bonifacio

and the Katipunan National Democratic Revolutionary Republic

at Tejeros, sell the Revolution twice, precipitate the nation

into the genocidal Philippine-American War

Domingo DC De Guzman

in which the Americans murdered some 2 million Filipinos,

and to superescalate the now globally infamous culture of corruption

of the Philippine ruling class and of almost the entire middleclass

and its intellectual-bureaucrat adjuncts to which the odious

Emanuel C. Tae de Guzman devoutly belongs,

together with Virgilio S. Almario,

Gemino Abad, Ricardo de Ungria, Cirilo Bautista, …, all

the Philippine historians whose total ignorant massmurderous dishonesty

and comprehensive stupidity is proved by their complete ignorance of the above-

mentioned two counter-revolutions, namely,

Apolinario Mabini, Epifanio delos Santos,

Carlos Quirino, Teodoro M. Kalaw, Teodoro Agoncillo,

Rafael Palma, Gregorio F. Zaide, Onofre D. Corpuz, Zeus Salazar,

Reynaldo Ileto, Floro Quibuyen, Ambeth Ocampo,

Milagros Guerrero, Fe Mangahas, Ferdinand Llanes,

Jim Richardson, Glenn Anthony May, John Schumacher,

Miguel Bernad, Pedro de Achutegui, Horacio dela Costa,

Jaime Veneracion, Resil Mojares, Renato Constantino…

and a thousand and one indoctorated other absolutely

insignificant tsismosos and tsismosas, i.e., rumourmongers,

who are hereby hanged upside down too on the HIGH GIBBET TREE

OF PHILIPPINE HISTORY…this:--

THE HIGH GIBBET TREE
OR--THE POET WARRIOR ANDRES BONIFACIO
INVOKES HIS MUSE

{i}

and now you, poet, on the verge of yourself, of the pure event

that will complete you as witness to yourself, and then,

there will only be others, half-blinded ones, from kawit and calamba,

sullied by pigly passions and treacherous designs
preached by these and worked out to ruin a people
and sell a motherland:--none but such as these to see
what happens to your abandoned words and deeds,
thenceforth solely theirs to make anything out of, a pure
public thing, the written. an inch from pure nothingness now

and i must go on speaking if but merely to myself, and in myself to you,
or i go at once…this shattered arm that luxuriates in the pure delirium of pain,

and this, this delicately, this lovingly, putrefying neck—so many alibis to hallucinate to extreme levels of grandeur or madness

the speech of poets...and besides, i really have to make a
summing up,
this summing up dear reader, son, or daughter, of my
revolution
which she must have smuggled from this cell of death
for it has at last reached you, bless your compromised soul!

she has just sneaked this roll of paper in and this beautiful pen,

and by banned candlelight that seems to weep for the
revolution,

i am writing this, and from outside a glimmer like pacific
lightning

of the silvered wrath of the moon... moon and abyss and a
beautiful pen

on a sheet of paper white as milk--i have no other desire
now...

{ii)

on the edge of the edge now, you are absent my pure goddess
queen of my diamond dream which presently i am making
and the dream itself the diamond itself...you are for the first
time
since we were one, quite really absent now; this pure pain
reminds me of it; preparing inside me now, inside my words,
for the real,
the final, nothingness; as i, as my words, rehearse your final
absence now.
and thus i can now, now that from the abyss is where i speak,
now
that, as the living must, you have begun to retreat from deep

inside my words,
now, without too much awkwardness i can begin to name you
by your other, always always other, proper name--name you at all
like others call you, as though we were no longer completely one:-- gregoria,
oriang, my oriang, my mighty river of perfumed waters, my torrent
of pure rose essence, my all-engulfing liquid paradise, my gigantic
unsubduable wave, come, coming always from a deep nowhere,
from one knows not what, from a secret sea, from the hidden sea
of being, deeper, vaster, more powerful, more sea than the seven glorious
seas, more absent, more devastating than the sea of absence
that depopulates the universe in the eyes of sorrow; berserk,
catastrophic wave released in a certain splitting of being,
and one does not merely suspect the immense poverty of man
except that you are, you were, and that is why your sacred waters lap me,
lick me, caress me, inundate me, renew, redeem, rebirth me in the extremest
fecundation, and i rise bearing a universal particle of pure absence
in the crater of my being, centering it for the momentary stand,
the lucky throw of the dice that would redeem the shipwreck,
and for this, for you, i forge these humble tokens in the pure delirium
of the absence of the entire universe, these words of endless gratitude
this gift of no mere things to the adored being...before she blinks me in, my love,

on the eyelids of death now, transparent as the words of the poet

embracing this pure, this unique nothingness now, in fullest clarity

i call your name, gregoria! how strange it sounds hearing yourself calling yourself

Domingo DC De Guzman

by your name for others, for we are, we were, one…this is to practice the abyss

and rehearse pure nothingness…

{iii}

on a bed of the purity of space, of the pure transparencies of time
struck by the true gold of the sun and the true miracles of the silver moon
on a bed of pure coruscating air, entranced, thickened, slowed down
to a self-possession; slipping from itself within itself, seeking

the cradle of the earth, fleeing endlessly into deeper depths…

on a bed of liquid diamonds, cool swirling purity of light

on a bed of liquid sapphire, pure burning blue of caressing coolness

on a bed of liquid turquoise, greenish blue fire coldly blazing

on a bed of liquid amethyst, liquid purple essence

on a bed of liquid roses

on a bed of liquid lilacs

on a bed of liquid rainbow

on a bed of liquid mirrors that devour the sun

the moon the stars the clouds the sky endlessly

on a bed of liquid sky
on a bed of liquid words
on a bed of the words of the poet
on a bed of the words of the love of the poet
on a bed of the love of the words of the poet
on a bed of liquid love
on a bed of my love, liquid, made
of the liquid purity of words for they are a poet's words the poet's sea
of liquid mirrors mirroring the endless sky the clouds the stars the moon
the sun the rainbow of spent sorrow the cool leaves of the rain
the marble of the fled gods the roses of my anguish the amethyst the turquoise
the sapphire the diamond the violet roses of the wind
love words mirrors made of the pure absence of the moon the sun

the pure transparencies of time and space
the leaves that instantly sprout in the blue air
pursuing the fleeing birds, you, my love, asleep, dreaming
summits of blueveined marble crowned by blushing buds of dawn
my gigantic little archipelagic one—they are all here,
the towering peaks of absence that cast
a violet shadow of pain and love, of love and pain, of pained, of painful

love, of loving pain in my words:--we have won, the people

have won, an irreversible victory have we the people won
a triumph of love of freedom of humanity for the coming centuries, for a thousand years, and more, and also have lost much...

{iv}

for those few others, jose rizal,

marcelo del pilar, graciano lopez jaena,

antonio luna, apolinario mabini, pio valenzuela

deodato arellano, edilberto evangelista, emanuel c tae de
guzman

jose alejandrino, and all the others, the rotten, craven,
money-souled,

brown spanishing mental colonial ilustrado assimilationist
sons

of bitches who recruited their likes, the native rich,

against revolution, against independence, against their, our,

having a country of our own, against getting it back from the
white

colonizers at last…and their provincial principalia partners

who joined the revolution to hostage and sell it to the enemy--
emilio aguinaldo, baldomero aguinaldo,
crispulo aguinaldo, mariano alvarez,
santiago alvarez, pascual alvarez,

paciano rizal, miguel malvar,
agapito bonzon, pio del pilar,
ignacio paua, artemio ricarte,
daniel tirona, demonio cuenca,
mariano trias, manuel trias,
demonio de las alas, tomas mascardo,
lazaro macapagal, jose del rosario,
edilberto evangelista, vicente riego de dios,
demonio riego de dios, mamerto natividad,
vicente fernandez, teodoro gonzales,
vicente topacio, demonio topacio,
juan castaneda, juan cailles,
vito belarmino, mariano noriel,
antonio montenegro, clemente jose zulueta,

pantaleon garcia, demonio lipana…they
had violated, they had unspeakably violated,
they had wronged, they had sullied you beyond the reach

of vocables, beyond thinking…you the mother of the people,

you the mother of the revolution, the mother of the nation,

the mother of the freedom, the honour, the dignity, the pride of the people
now and of the coming centuries, and they did that to you…

what they did to me was a risk that had materialized
a debt to fate that i had tempted too much—
for nothing but too much would ever do—
and which had fallen due; and i can say to fate—quits!
for i had cheated her, i had changed, i had diverted her course,
i, more than anyone, i principally, i in the beginning, which was what

mattered most, solely, solitarily, with my poet's words,
with my poet's love, with my poet's anguish, with my poet's hands—quits!
my destiny is mine, i created it myself…
my people's destiny belongs to them now,
they have created it themselves, with me, with you, with all of us
whom the poet can sing without betraying the words, and whom
to fulfill them he must sing…i sing them now, i am singing them now, here,
this triumph of freedom, this newly founded destiny—
for freedom's destiny is the practice of dying for the sake of freedom
which is revolution…i sing them now the heroic ones of the new
nation of the poem…with you, with you, my beloved with your tumultuous
thronging, singing, exulting leaves, so many green, yellow,

pink, red, violet, brown, black, leaves of anguish too, of grief
of sorrow, of heaven-hounding outrage, leaves of berserk

unfathomable anger, of being-annihilating hatred…leaves
bristling

with their unutterable accusations like lightning struck dumb

above the black leaved trees at the unspeakable vileness,

the leprous, pestilent cavitic villainy of emilio aguinaldo

and mariano alvarez, of bonzon, of paua, of ricarte, of
evangelista,
of pio del pilar, of mascardo, of clemente jose zulueta
of trias closas, of de las alas, of riego de dios, of macapagal
gloria of vergalicio almorano of tae c. emanuel de
guzman--leaves

struck dumb, leaves of lightning struck dumb in condemnation
for they cannot bear to speak the name of their crime, the
names
of those criminals, unique and singular in all of history…
flaming leaves, leaves of madness, leaves maddened with
hatred of the criminals
aguinaldo aguinaldo aguinaldo alvarez alvarez alvarez
leaves hallucinating their hatred of them to a depth and a
height

of hatred beyond hatred which still is hatred here right here
unappeasable unforgiving endless crystalline leaves of
unwordable
hatred hatred hatred beyond the term of the human species
hatred beyond the farthest nebulae, utterest hatred that shall
stalk them

beyond the farthest end of being which is endless
beyond the nethermost rim of pure empty space
beyond the most farflung shores of nothingness
beyond every beyond for they did that to you…
they will die in endless ignominy because of it…

{v}

oriang, my love, my blue house of light,
my red rose in the darkness, my ardent unsayable,
my archipelago of summits dreaming summits
of waters mixed with reveries of waters
trees overwhelmed with green sleep
waving in the embrace of a murmured trance,
my dream dreaming itself to sleep…
i want to make of you in me
a diamond dream in the human forever of my words…

i want you in my words in your unforgiving purity
i want in my words' naked twigs of lightning
the unapproachable helplessness of the child in your smile
i want in my words your womb's pitiless innocence
the invincible purity of the dark in which
original incandescence grew wings
dreaming wings of pure light
inside the waters of their dream
dreaming being and absences
inside the waters dreaming
dreaming them into trees of green water
sleeping inventing themselves from inside each leaf
into sierras of blue music, between silence and the sun's metal
asleep on the fatal threshold of being and nonbeing
which each of them becomes in becoming itself
inside your dream dreaming that they are…
thus i want you in the sea of my words
inside the waters of your dreaming sea
inside the sun of your sleeping light
inside the summits of your being and atop them
as the trees that crown them with green sleep…
i want you in the ache of my being which they are
like the dream of trees issuing from each leaf
their roots penetrating simultaneously the pure earth of your dream
dreaming being in the being of your dream
cracking open at once the granite of your sleep
and deeper still to where originate your deepest reveries…
i want in my words your sapphire wind

i want in them your turquoise wind
i want in them your amethyst wind
i want in them the scarlet wind

of your archipelago of being dreaming being
i want in them your unfathomed depths which they are in their sleep
on the threshold of being and nonbeing my words dreaming of you dreaming themselves
into being dream of being dreaming of your little hands and feet
they used to kiss to sleep at night, one by one, slowly, lovingly, lingeringly
that they might dream them into the pure loveache of their lips

which they are and nothing but—
my words, my poet's words,
they that would, if they could
sleep beneath your fingernails
beneath the timid pearls of your tiny feet
to be one with them in the pink blush
of their dream of love...they would, if they could,
sleep there forever, and reinvent you endlessly
in your sleep which dreams them
climbing up or coming down from there
trekking lovely inch by delirious inch
sails unfurled to the four winds
in the vast sea of your dream
wings aflutter in the vertical
luminousity of the air dreaming
the endless sky into being
the archipelago of your dream of being
which you are dreaming
in this ache of being which is me, and nothing but

these words now, dreaming of you into this diamond
dreaming of you as you always did
refashioning me in your great sleep
in which they dream you, and now can only dream you
dreaming them dreaming this diamond
this archipelago, this universe, which you are
inviolate in their shelter of a great poem's light
that is the revolution...in the human forever of my words

Domingo DC De Guzman

which are words of love dreaming you
my diamond, my archipelago, my universe, my little one,
of summits dreaming summits

of waters mixed with reveries of waters
trees overwhelmed with green sleep
waving in the embrace of a murmured trance
my dream dreaming itself to sleep
and from there to pure nothingness now
leaving nothing but these words of love
drawing their unforgiving razors of transparent lightning
from the unapproachable helplessness of the child in your smile
from the invincible purity of the dark which is
the invincible purity of woman
the pitiless innocence of the womb

of my diamond,
of my archipelago,
of my universe,
of my little one,
which you are, and
oriang my love,
these words which dream you

in their human forever
my little one,
my universe,
my archipelago,
my diamond dream,
oriang my love,
they will get the traitors who violated you,
hostaged you, wronged you, sold you
they will get the traitors flush in the face
with their naked razors of transparent lightning
the pitiless innocence of your womb, O
my archipelago of summits and seas and trees of green waves
will rise vertical from the being of your dream
into a towering tree of pure black branches
it will push the sky further up
to give way to its black magnificence
the luminous air will be more luminous
in the clear gold of the sun caressing

Domingo DC De Guzman

its gigantic bronze leaves
whilst the sapphire wind, the turquoise wind,
the amethyst wind, the scarlet wind of your archipelago of being

more brilliantly will be themselves as they linger upon and wave
their appointed branches beneath the silver moon
and the myriad myriad burning eyes of the night
and the unapproachable helplessness of the child in your smile
will twirl themselves into a noose and multiply
until each traitor has its unforgiving grip around his neck, for
my little one, the criminals must be judged and punished
as the criminals they are, as the criminals they are, as the criminals they are
without pity, without forgiveness, if love is to happen, if love is to happen
and love must happen, and my words of your dream dreaming inside you
in your diamond being with their naked razors of transparent lightning
will see to that and will hang the traitors upon the black
branches of that high gibbet tree hang them
till they had bled the last drop of their yellow guilt and
therefore forever forever
in the human endlessness of these words
forever these words of your dream of being
will hang them there forever
the merciless metal of the sun will flay them
will strike them full in the face with their guilt and shame
and the four winds will bear down on them without pity
and their wings will slice into the unpardoning silver wrath of the moon
the acid leaves of the stars will join them in the attack
so that no one will forget
so that no one will forgive
for no one
absolutely no one
has the right to…

Roula Pollard

WARM CONGRATULATIONS, my friend Domingo C. de Guzman,

{iii}
on a bed of the purity of space
of the pure transparencies of time
struck by the true gold of the sun
and the true miracles of the silver moon
on a bed of pure coruscating air
entranced, thickened, slowed down
to a self-possession; slipping from itself
within itself, seeking the cradle of the earth
fleeing endlessly into deeper depths…
on a bed of liquid diamonds
cool swirling purity of light
on a bed of liquid sapphire
pure burning blue of caressing coolness
on a bed of liquid turquoise
greenish blue fire coldly blazing
on a bed of liquid amethyst
liquid purple essence
on a bed of liquid roses
on a bed of liquid lilacs
on a bed of liquid rainbow
on a bed of liquid mirrors that devour the sun the moon
the stars the clouds the sky endlessly
on a bed of liquid sky
on a bed of liquid words
on a bed of the words of the poet
on a bed of the words of the love of the poet
on a bed of the love of the words of the poet
on a bed of liquid love
on a bed of my love, liquid, made
of the liquid purity of words for they are a poet's words the poet's sea
of liquid mirrors mirroring the endless sky the clouds the stars the moon
the sun the rainbow of spent sorrow the cool leaves of the rain
the marble of the fled gods the roses of my anguish the

amethyst the turquoise
the sapphire the diamond the violet roses of the wind
love words mirrors made of pure absence
of the moon the sun the pure
transparencies of time and space
the leaves that instantly sprout in the blue air
pursuing the fleeing birds, you, my love, asleep, dreaming
summits of blueveined marble crowned by blushing buds of dawn
my gigantic little archipelagic one—they are all here,
the towering peaks of absence that cast
a violet shadow of pain and love, of love and pain, of pained,
of painful love, of loving pain in my words:--we have won,
the people have won, an irreversible victory have we the people won
a triumph of love of freedom of humanity for the coming
centuries, for a thousand years, and more, and also have lost much…
{iv}
for those few others,

Like · Reply · Delete · Report · Oct 8, 2015

Roula Pollard

Above poem is an extract from "THE HIGH GIBBET TREE OR--
THE POET WARRIOR ANDRES BONIFACIO INVOKES HIS MUSE " by Domingo C. de Guzman!

Like · 2 · Reply · Delete · Report · Oct 8, 2015

Roula Pollard

" purity of space
of the pure transparencies of time" by Domingo C. de Guzman!
Congratulations Domingo!

Like · 2 · Reply · Delete · Report · Oct 8, 2015

Domingo C. de Guzman

Thanks for this happy moment, Roula Pollard!

Domingo DC De Guzman

Like · 1 · Reply · Edit · Oct 8, 2015

Roula Pollard

You are welcome, dear friend Domingo C. de Guzman, greetings and best wishes from Athens !

Edited · Like · 1 · Reply · Delete · Report · Oct 10, 2015

PREFACE

Revolution, Primordial Democracy, & the People's Right of Sovereignty,

Or Why the People's Right of Sovereignty is the same as the People's Right of Revolution

1.0.) Truth is the insistence of the essence—and its upsurge. This is so at least in the realm of human existence, of the social and the historical, of the political. And perhaps, in the realm of life as a whole. Truth is the insistence and the event of the emergent upsurge of the essence, and of the human. The essence is freedom, or, more concretely, democracy, primordial democracy which at its purest--and mindful of the fact that the root of all sociohistorical inequality is private property and its institutionalization and structuration into social classes--is primordial communism. There is a democracy, a radical democracy, a communism, innate in society and in the human being and which minimally, at the very least, society must be, the human being must be, must *ex-ist,* must go on *ex-isting,* or it is not society anymore, and she, he, is not a human being anymore. This minimal or core infrastructural democracy/communism is inherent and persistent and insistent in the praxis of language; in the ontological/existological democracy and communism, and universalism, of grammar; in every ethical relation and relationship; in the necessarily universalist, egalitarian, communitarian sense, and essence, and grammar of Law, of Right, of Legitimacy (which of course class-division, fascism, tyranny, imperialism, colonialism, and all forms of institutionalized, necessarily evil inegalitarian discrimination pervert and presuppose thus in the perversion); in every instance of the face to face in which spontaneously and willy-nilly the absoluteness of the Other as the *freedom* s/he is, is recognized and affirmed and acted-out…

1.1.) In colonialism where one people subjugates another, there is a danger of utterly destroying this insistent essence itself which is the subjugated truth of the subject people. The European landgrabbers of North America were successful in this kind of destruction in relation to the Indian tribes. And this they did by means of genocide. They physically wiped them out. The few that were able to escape this genocide were too few to be able to re-constitute themselves into that existential-historical unity called *the people*. The other way is the one for vainly trying to effectuate which for his own people Rizal died. It is called *assimilation*. Which in Rizal's case, or rather in the case of the Rizalian-ilustrado Counterrevolution, also eventuated in genocide--the massmurder of some two million Filipinos by the American imperialists.

2.0.) Upon force, no right whatsoever can be founded. This is an existential-, or more exactly, an existological-ontological, law, a law of social-historical being which is as irrefragable and inviolable in relation to this mode of being and existence as any physical law is in the realm of nature.To violate it, to be false to it, is to violate the very essence of the human and to give rise to monsters or debased beings. To contravene it is to contradict the truth of human existence itself which above all is a mode of being free—that is to say, of being democratic/communistic. Existential-ontological laws are laws of freedom.They are laws/principles of democratic existence which is the essence itself of human, social historical existence. Thus, these laws/principles are prescriptions of/by the democratic/communistic essence of human existence. This essence, pre-existent in every human being and in every human society, is in its fundamental form and structure what we call primordial democracy, primordial communism. Truth, the truth of the human being and of human society and of humanity is the concrete, existential, social, historical fulfilment of this primordial essence which is primordial democracy/primordial communism. Hence we have in primordial democracy/communism the concrete criterion by which to measure the truth or falsity, the humanity or inhumanity of any society at any given time. These existential-ontological laws of freedom are at the same time the principles of right. They are also the principles of good and evil.

2.1.) Inviolable: existentially, or rather, existologically-ontologically inviolable, for to violate it is to violate the *ex*-istence itself of the human *ex*-istent, the be-ing itself of the human being, the *be-ing* or the *ex*-isting of the people not as a mere aggregation of human existents but as *the people*, which, as such, is the sociohistorical, the existological, subject/bearer and embodiment of *sovereignty* as the *Sovereignty of the People,* as it was grasped, characterized, analyzed for the first time by Rousseau in his *The Social Contract.* Colonialism is without qualification such a violation. It produces monsters and debased beings like the monstrously debased beings who were the friars in these Islands and yes the Spanish high officials who became the indelible models of presidents and senators and congressmen, and perverted beings like the ilustrados themselves, the *ass*-i-m-ilationists themselves like Rizal himself and del Pilar and Eduardo de Lete, and degenerate and reduced beings like the Guardia Civil or Emilio Aguinaldo and Daniel Tirona and Antonio Montenegro and Agapito Bonzon and Lazaro Macapagal and Ignacio Paua and Pio del Pilar, repressed beings, like the ordinary natives, the ultimate victims of such colonialism, in whom the flower of freedom had had to grow inward and knew only the night of centuries…

2.2.) This then is an existential-ontological law, a law of social-historical being, a law of freedom, a law of being of free beings, a principle of right, a principle of good and evil: Upon force, no right can be founded. This means that colonial force, the force of conquest, does not found any right whatsoever, and that there is no such thing as a right of colonization or a right of slavery, a right to enslave, exploit, dominate, oppress, humiliate--contrary to what the assimilationist colonial ideologist and therefore counterrevolutionary brown Spanish hero, Jose Rizal (the Philippines as an overseas province of Spain--don't ever forget that, you Filipino reader!), or the assimilationist imperialist ideologist McKinley (in his Benevolent Assimilationist Proclamation, remember?,) preached and rammed into the Filipino psyche.

3.0.) Every society is founded upon primordial democracy. It will be immediately seen that this is so once we reflect on the fact that every society is founded upon language—whilst language is primordial democracy at work. The essence of the word is transcendence itself, the being infinitely more than nature, the being infinitely more than the here and now, the being infinitely more than being itself, of the human being. Dignity, the sublime in the human existent, is concrete in the word.The Categorical Imperative, the FOR of the being-FOR-the-Other of the human being is the reflexivity of the word itself. Whilst pure grammar subdues everyone into pure equality, which at the same time constitutes the foundation of the greatest possible freedom. Freedom is not anarchy; lawlessness is the impossibility of freedom itself. Freedom is possible only on the basis of law. That every society is necessarily—with the necessity of the laws of freedom—founded upon primordial democracy is historically supported by the fact that the most primitive societies were without exception democracies, radical democracies, i.e., communisms.

Needless to say, that the foundation, the concrete core of every society is democracy does not mean that every society is a model of democratic existence. What it does mean is that every society, to the extent that in more or less undermined and impaired form its primordial substructure subsists as such, which primordial substructure is precisely primordial democracy--every society, to the exact extent that it remains human, i.e., to the extent that the truth of humanity remains possible and is at work in it, is democratic. And so is it with the human being. The essence too of the human being is primordial democracy…

3.1.) Reflecting on it, and remembering what, curiously enough, and especially amongst moderns or so-called post-moderns, has always already been forgotten, namely that you are free, that as a matter of irreducible fact you are freedom yourself, and society, human society, unlike ant-society, is an association of free beings, one is moved to exclaim, *"Oo nga hane!", "Yes, and how else indeed?"* A free being, because free, is an absolute, a self-determining being, a being whose fundamental relation to being is to totalize it into, yes, a totality, a universe, a world, whose origin in this fundamental sense is it, the free being, itself, herself, himself...An association of such absolutes is bound to be something like democracy, which in its radical purity is communism, which as such would be given in the fact that it is a given that each of us humans constituting it is such an absolute, is such a freedom, is such an origin of the (common) world and is thus at once the co-origin of the world... Meanwhile, the freedom of the individual is given as at the same time the primordial core of her, his social being and is inseparable from it; the individual can only be free and transcendent in society. This being-together of free beings, of transcendences in society is what is called primordial democracy. Primordial democracy is itself the condition of possibility of freedom, of transcendence. One way of confirming this irreducible sociality of individual freedom is to consider how it is that the free being is the being who speaks—which also is why it is self-contradictory sometimes to the point of comedy but also and more often to the point of tragedy, for people to deny freedom *in so many words*.

3.2.) The ultimate proof of this freedom, of this absoluteness, of this being the origin of the world, is the power to die which each of us is...

3.3.) That is why there are heroes, and in revolutions, especially in anti-colonial ones where the people themselves fight to the death to root out and expel a common evil, everybody, staking life itself thus absolutely, proves herself, himself, to be more than mere life, to be beyond mere life by an infinity, i.e., by something that absolutely transcends mere life thus, and which then cannot be measured in terms of mere life, which, being the common good itself makes of this absolute sacrifice a heroism and of each one a hero.. .

4.0.) A human society, properly speaking, is at least a people. And in a people, primordial democracy means first and foremost the sovereignty of the people. Since force does not create right, as long as the subjugated people remains a people with, of course its primordial sovereignty, the colonizing and the colonized peoples are really throughout the period of colonization in a state of war...

5.0.) These are some of the hitherto unexplicated, even unnoted, principles and intrinsic complications which should be considered in analysing questions of colonialism, of colonial assimilation, or its opposite, separation, revolution...We could have said "intrinsic principles and complications" with, of course, a shade of redundance for, of course, if principles are principles then they should be intrinsic to the things themselves. And what we really want to say here is that these principles and laws are intrinsic to the things themselves that constitute that realm of existence and being that is that of freedom, of transcendence, of the power to die, of social-historical existence. *If freedom is to happen and to triumph, then, given any situation in history these are the rules that should be respected, these are the principles that should take effect, these are the laws that should be obeyed and that should not be transgressed. These are the rules, the principles, the laws of freedom*, of the existence of beings whose defining distinction is freedom; these rules, principles, laws, do not apply to animals because animals are not free, are not transcendent beings, are not powers to die. *These then are the rules, the principles, the laws of truth where truth is the essence of human existence—which is freedom, transcendence—happening in conflict, in struggle against forces and tendencies that do not always agree with it, that are indifferent to it, that deny it*. That this structure and dynamic of freedom which we call primordial democracy is primordial, is the always-already there, and is the condition of possibility of human existence, and is thus the persistent, the insistent structure and dynamic of human existence is what we mean by saying that it is the essence of human existence, the vicissitudes of which constitute the truth and falsity of human existence, the triumphs and failures, the fulfillments and deletions of human existence. In radical honesty we can always agree on the present status of this essence, of this truth in conflict, of this truth in struggle, of this truth in the making. Which is to say, it is always, in principle, knowable and objectively formulable whether a society fulfills or not and to what extent either way, the demands of its essence which is primordial democracy. This itself is the principle of social critique—the principle of primordial democracy—intrinsic to every (human) society. At any point in time in the history of a given society, the measures of freedom, of the essence of human existence, of primordial democracy, are in principle determinable for this society; it can therefore be criticized anytime on the basis of it. I say *in radical honesty* it is always possible for us human beings to agree on these measures, on what constitutes this criterion of critique intrinsic to any given society; as usual the charlatans, the relativists, the negative metaphysicians, the opportunists, the fascists, will quibble about what constitutes *radical honesty*. But *that* is quibbling—*not radical honesty*. Radical honesty is self-evident, self-evidentiating. In negative metaphysicians like Derrida, who as the masked Buddhistical capitalist that he is must deny that he is free—and therefore must deny that you are free—he himself is not free because he himself is not; you yourself are not free because you yourself are not; there is freedom or free-ing but no one who is free: *differance with an a* makes sure of that. But if there is freedom or free-ing (though there are no free beings because there are no beings and being itself is mere illusion as Buddha preached) that is itself enough to be itself, i.e., that is itself enough to be not the same as masturbating or traveling (there is a traveling but no traveler, a masturbating but no masturbator, nothing to masturbate…; there is an onanizing but no onanist, no ona, no one...), then masturbating, traveling, free-ing are each of them *one*; which means that (applying the principle of difference with an a to them, there is no doing, or happening of any whatever kind either, no free-ing, no thinking, no masturbating, no dis-semen-ating, no derridaing… In the end, as with the principle of God which must Goddify into pure nothingness everything that is not God including you of course, Godding you too but also of course absolutely erasing you as you, so that then in that there is God there is only God and nothing absolutely nothing else besides, in that *differance with an a* “is”, only “it” “is”. Other relativists like Feyerabend or Rorty are simply too inconsequent and most of the time conceptless in their radical dishonesty to deserve refutation.

6.0.) We point out first of all that sovereignty, not being the same as force, is itself a right. Sovereignty is at the same time, and always, right of sovereignty, and only the people by the laws and principles of freedom which are the laws and principles of human social historical existence and the laws and principles too of good and evil can have that right and exercise it as such, i.e., according to its very essence.

Sovereignty overwhelmed by what by definition, by essence or negation of essence, by essential negation, is evil, is a force of evil, such as a colonial power; sovereignty is then still, as right of sovereignty, sovereignty of the people that bears it—unless if it be that the people themselves that define themselves by means of it have been physically or otherwise eliminated, as in the case of the most successful genocide in world history, namely, the murder of the Indian people by the white settlers of North America.

6.1.) It was this right of sovereignty that Rizal and his ilustrado band of bleeding-in-the-heart defenders of colonialism were seeking to completely surrender and abolish. With it must go the right of the Filipino people to be the people they were. What Rizal and company in their assimilationism were trying to accomplish was the abolition, the dissolution, of the Filipino people.

7.0.) They loved the Filipino people so that they wanted to abolish them. The assimilationists were abolitionists. They wanted to abolish the native land itself; they wanted to abolish the Filipino nation itself; they wanted to abolish the Filipino people itself. That was how they loved their country, their nation, their people.

8.0.) It is only when the people themselves fight to the death that there is revolution. When you fight to the death, protractedly, systematically, it cannot be for mere life, it has to be for something that is more than life, and more than it by something that cannot be measured merely in terms of it. Hence, it is something that is infinitely more than life. In the ultimate analysis, that in the name of which the people fight to the death in a revolution can only be dignity, the human dignity that goes with the transcendence which is the very definition of freedom.

9.0.) Rizal—and with him here were all the ilustrados, all the members of the colonial upper middle-class and for a long, wasted, and perverted time, almost all of the lower middle class during which they together with the above were all severely perverted and corrupted— Rizal thought that the best thing that could happen to his native country, in fact its redemption, its salvation and its apotheosis, was the most thorough hispanization of it possible. Politically, this meant assimilation. He died fighting for it. Or rather—for he was for four long years during his Dapitan exile completely politically silent and passive: as he many times put it, in letter after letter to friends, relatives and selected foes, reiterating the same truculently and quite pathetically in several places during the trial, he had decided to withdraw completely from politics, and had ceased completely to have any political dealings with anyone including himself: he also wrote nothing political during those years—he died because of the less than ten years that he got involved in the politics of assimilationism, getting judicially assassinated thus by mistake: for during those times in friar-infested and therefore medieval Philippines, to be an assimilationist, indeed to be any kind of reformist whatsoever, was to be at once branded a filibustero, an enemy of colonialism, an enemy of Spain, a separatist, a revolutionary. In fact for an Indio of those times to have any opinion at all was to be against Spain. This nasty fact alone should have sufficed to convince them from the very outset of the absolute futility and indeed stupidity of the assimilationist dream. But in the littleness of their souls the band of ilustrados and their colonially favoured rich families at home were simply too desperately attached to Spain, to their Mother Spain, to her culture and civilization, to her white skin and pointed nose, and, of course, to their colonial privileges as the collaborating class, to be able to imagine becoming otherwise, becoming themselves in themselves for instance, becoming separated from her, becoming independent, and free.

9.1.) Perverted and corrupted severely in relation of course to what uncorrupted and unperverted thus by such stupid and antihuman propaganda and activity as *assimilationism*, they would have been able to be and do in connection with the *objective ideal possibilities* of their time and place which was revolutionary time in revolutionary Philippines. And in fact, the colonial middle class, especially its upper stratum to which Rizal and the ilustrado assimilationists belonged, was destined, so to speak, by the social-historical dynamics of their very class-position to play the social-historical role of theoretical and organizational spearhead of the anti-colonial revolution (and this indeed was so in all the other anticolonial revolutions during that century of anticolonial revolutions that was the nineteenth: we were the last, at the very last decade of it, and Rizal thought even then it was not yet time: to such cowards, to such theoretical-intellectual cowards like Jose Rizal, such *not-yet* is eternal). Perverted and corrupted and, in view of such objective, social-historical, class-structural role, *derailed*, too and wasted. And the resources which should have been allotted to revolution preempted too, diverted, wasted, and more importantly, used for the historically opposite purpose, for defense of colonialism! Imagine what would have happened if those fine, talented, necessarily hot-blooded young men whom we encounter in the story of the Propaganda Movement did not have that stupid and contrary thing to derail them and pervert and corrupt and waste them! Imagine if from the very start it was separation, revolution they were thinking and doing! Imagine if from earlier on, the upper middle class had formed instead of an Assimilationist-Counterrevolutionary Propaganda Committee a Revolutionary Committee, and were soliciting contributions to buy arms and defray the costs of underground printing presses...

9.2.) His first publicly relevant political act while in Dapitan was when, surpassing by a new leap of evil his already longstanding treason to his country and people in being the foremost leader of the assimilationist movement, he wrote a letter to Governor General Blanco applying for the post of Spanish military doctor in Cuba to help the Spanish army there kill as many Cuban Katipuneros as possible. This must have been during the last week of November 1895. His bosom friend, the Austrian assimilationist missionary, Ferdinand Blumentritt gave him the information concerning the advertised need for such doctors in Cuba, advising him therewith to apply for the post. In a letter (number 204 in the Rizal Blumentritt Correspondence; see below) to the Austrian assimilationist dated November 20, 1895, Rizal wrote back to tell him that he was going to apply: "Concerning your advice on going to Cuba as a physician, it seems to me most excellent ,and right now I am going to write to the Governor General..." We shall deal with this other crime of Rizal against the Filipino people, against the Cuban people, against humanity, against decency, once more, elsewhere here; we shall not tire of exposing and re-exposing it and with it the tininess of his soul, his exceeding stupidity, his farcical and distorted character—to punish him as his crime and his evil warrants, and to forewarn traitors against the people and against humanity like him to be careful for they could suffer the same ignominious fate as he, Rizal is now suffering it even in death... Elsewhere here we shall demonstrate with new, additional documents, that those undocumented, hearsay stories about his "patriotic", even "revolutionary" motives in going to Cuba –that he wanted to study the revolution there firsthand so that he could become an expert in it when he came back to the Philippines to do it here; that he would very likely shoot General Valeriano Weyler there and thus punish him for being the *Rapist par Excellence* in the October 1891 *Rape of Calamba* in which he cavorted naked with bottomless Dominicans, etc.—were all tall tales and lies. His second... But wait! We have been precipitate! Shadowing in a most macabre way the Pablo Mercado case and that of “”another” supposedly friar-sent spy in late 1892, was that of the man whom he contextually and circumstantially referred to as someone from the KKK and sent to him by Andres Bonifacio, and whom he had “put under the order of the governor”, i.e., whom he reported, betrayed, to the governor, “who sent him to Manila”. That was his first mind-wrecking political act in Dapitan—a direct betrayal of the KKK itself and the murder of its emissary. Pablo Mercado cannot be the same as this man, for from Juan Sitges’ report to Governor General Blanco (see below), we learn that Blanco had given Sitges instructions on what to do “should Pablo Mercado come back”. Here also we have new additional documents to clear things up. Meanwhile, after that betrayal of the KKK in late 1892 (the unnamed emissary must have chosen to die under torture rather than give the Spaniards anything that could lead to the discovery of the KKK because we do not know of any disturbance or complication arising from such a discovery at that time). Rizal’s second political act was his rejection of the plots, one of them already ongoing, to help him escape from Dapitan, condemning himself thus to his own declared abandonment of politics, and directly or indirectly refusing thus to have anything to do with the KKK Revolution about which he must have been pre-appraised by that ill-starred man whom he betrayed to the governor but also a little bit later by his two sisters, Trinidad and Josefa who as early as March 1893 were already KKK members/officers. The Cuban letter of application then would be third in this list; and fourth would be his rejection of the offer from Bonifacio himself through Pio Valenzuela to join and even head the KKK, and his successful attempt to convince the mentally unbalanced Valenzuela to quit the KKK. Treasonous acts which he accomplished doing against the Filipino people on July 1, 1896... The fifth and the last major political act/crime Rizal perpetrated in Dapitan was of course the materialization of the mind-wrecking letter of application for a Cuba military doctor post with which he successfully conferred upon himself the monstrous distinction of being an international counter-revolutionary: receiving on July 31, 1896, Blanco’s letter telling him that if such was his desire still, then he can proceed to assume his new job in Cuba, he abandoned everything at once and sailed to Manila the next morning…

10.0.) Rizal was against revolution, against the idea itself. But in revolutionary times, revolution and freedom which is of course freedom of the people to be the people on one hand, and freedom of the human being to be the human being s/he is, on the other hand, are one and the same thing.

10.1.) But really, revolutions are such, and peoples are such, and human beings are such, that being against revolution in this sense of being against the very idea of it, and thus being against it regardless of time and place, which is to say being against revolution per se, is either an abstract and worthless affectation (it goes by the name of pacifism) or else a wholesale sponsorship of wholesale evil (i.e.,--and this was Rizal's and generally the Propagandists' historical mission and role-- the active, the assiduous advocacy and defence of the wholesale violence of the status quo). It is really always the latter, although it can be also the former when the declaimer of it is an abstract and worthless individual or else when the doing of it is an abstract and worthless gesture because done in non-revolutionary times (preaching peace thus to sheep and kine). As the latter, it is always being against the revolution, always against the radical change demanded by the things themselves as they happen to *the people*, demanded, i.e., by the radical suffering of radical evil by the people themselves which is such that the radical elimination of the radical evil and with it of the radical suffering of the people has become more or less urgently thinkable, and, becoming thinkable thus, has become desirable, indeed radically, uprootingly, incendiarily, revolutionarily desirable.

12.) In being against revolution before the fact of it, before Andres Bonifacio made of it a historical fact, Rizal was really against *the revolution*—against Andres Bonifacio's revolution.

13.) Prolonged radical, mortal denial of and threat against the essence of the human itself which is the essence of the social itself, is what we mean by radical evil and radical suffering. That essence is democracy/communism which concretely-existentially and structurally constitutes the very condition of possibility of humanity and sociality—a concrete-existential-structural transcendental underlying thus and constituting the very foundation of every human society and in general, of humanity itself. Construed as such existential-structural transcendental, it is what we propose to call primordial democracy/communism. Ant society, anthood, does not have it, does not presuppose it; but it would have it and would presuppose it as condition of possibility of anthood and of ant-society if ants were, like human beings, free. Because human beings are free, they can be associated in the form of society only on the basis of structured and lived and existed relations which in being given thus in the very nature of freedom and the way freedom can be structured on the basis of (of course) nature, of biology, of animality, is properly termed primordial. Any and every whatever kind of human society then, as long as it still remains human enough (and we can agree, we can have universal agreement, on what constitutes minimum democracy such that we can say that beyond such minimum democracy human society ceases altogether to exist as such and the human is totally erased, and we do not have human society nor humanity at all) exists, persists, insists, as a form or other of democracy, i.e., a historical concretion on the basis of primordial democracy. In this sense, primordial democracy is the concrete essence of human society and of humanity itself. To succeed in completely destroying it is to succeed in destroying human society itself and therewith humanity itself. Physical elimination of a society, of a people, is of course the easiest and most efficient way to effectuate the destruction of this essence of sociality and of humanity. The genocide of the American Indians by the Western-Christian capitalist invaders was the perfect example of this method of destroying primordial democracy itself and with it the Indians as a people and as a society.

14.) We can have universal agreement on what primordial democracy is and how to measure its fulfillment or denial in a given society because we have the same essence, the same concrete transcendental, the same freedom as our very be-ing. To refuse to acknowledge this universality is fundamental dishonesty. This ultimately ontological--or, mindful of the radical difference between thing-existence and human existence--existological identity, is given in the universal essence of language, the universal essence of the word, which is demonstrated in the fact of translatability. In measuring primordial democracy we are measuring the same thing by the same thing. Only dishonesty, which is extraneous to the thing itself here, can obstruct such universal agreement.

15.) When objective conditions make revolution necessary is when we have what we call revolutionary times--a revolutionary situation.

16.) Revolution becomes necessary when radical evil and radical suffering penetrating and suffusing and threatening to destroy thus humanity and sociality at the very root, i.e., at the level of primordial democracy, has become generally determinable to be unbearable; that is to say, when the objective conditions have reached the point of being such that it has become possible to produce a theory of them which could convince those who suffer radical evil—existing (actively) as their very suffering of radical evil those objective conditions thus--to fight to the death in order to root out such radical evil and put an end to radical suffering.

17.) Before becoming radically thinkable, the rooting out of radical suffering will not become effectively desirable. This is why in revolutions, theory comes first. This is why among the objective conditions for revolution is the intellectual readiness of the people to receive and internalize the theory of the revolution. In fact, this intellectual preparedness is at once theoretical capability. Among the objective conditions of revolution which make for revolutionary times is this intellectual, ultimately theoretical, receptivity of the people for the theory of the revolution. On the eve of the revolution the people shall have become all of them theoreticians of the revolution.

18.) The social-historical essence of humanity is democracy, radical democracy, i.e., communism. For the time being and since the beginning of human history, primordial democracy is bound up with the being of the people, i.e., with the being people of the people. That is to say, the concrete idea of democracy, which we also term primordial democracy, to which Rousseau was referring when he spoke of human beings' being born free in the opening sentences of The Social Contract, has up to now to happen within the concrete form called the people. The nation is a cultural category; the people is a political category. The latter is more fundamental than the former; the former is founded upon the latter. The *right of sovereignty* that makes the people the people…:--it is the be-ing of the people.

This right of sovereignty which defines the being people of the people is always a matter of self-perception, which is to say, of self-esteem, of retaining or losing altogether that dignity which in individuals and peoples is the sublime itself. History has recorded only two instances of an entire people succumbing in such a complete way to colonial brutalization that their being people was completely dissolved, destroyed: the North American Indians and the Jews of the holocaust. Both of them were destroyed physically. In the case of the American genocide, the whites aimed simply to eliminate the Indians physically, which they succeeded to do, of course, and the few remnants were so few that they could no longer constitute themselves into a people. In the latter case, the Nazis, more artful in their evil, endeavoured to destroy first the humanity—the dignity, the right of sovereignty—of their victims and had practically completely succeeded. The extremity of such methods needed to annihilate this peopleness, this be-ing people, this right of sovereignty that goes with the, of course completely reflexive dignity of a people, attests to the near-impossibility of colonially destroying such being people of a people.

19.) Rizal was, from the time he began to write in the early 1880s to his execution on December 30, 1896, the greatest, most perceptive, perhaps even the most intelligent defender of Spanish colonialism and of the idea of colonialism per se in the Philippines and perhaps even in the Spanish metropolis itself. He was also, as far as Spanish colonialism and its antithesis, the Revolution, were concerned, the most successful.

Contrary to the ever-superficial positivist view, Rizal and his band of assimilationist defenders of Spanish colonialism against the revolution-fomenting evil and brutal theological criminality of the friars were not entirely unsuccessful even on the level of piecemeal results (which alone are visible to positivist historiography), as their blow-by-blow monitoring of the vicissitudes of the "great cause" in the Cortes and in newspapers would show: the pages of their assimilationist, anti-friar, anti-revolutionary paper, La Solidaridad would attest to this, as well as Rizal's voluminous correspondence. Their campaign to save Spanish colonialism from the "horrible" and "suicidal" hands of the revolution (which was soon to become the Revolution led by Andres Bonifacio), was in fact enormously successful in swaying and forestalling the main bulk of the colonial middle-class (whose intellectual-ideological representatives they were) against revolution, ultimately against the Bonifacio-led Revolution. It was decisive in corrupting to the core the separatism of the thin stratum of principalia and petty bourgeois professionals (gobernadorcillos like Emilio Aguinaldo, Mariano Alvarez, Malvar, Llanera, Makabulos; elementary school teachers like Ricarte, Santi; justices of the peace like the officious Santiago Rillo...), that joined and eventually officered it, hostaged it at Tejeros, and sold it at Biyak na Bato. The Biyak na Bato Deed of Sale was premised on Rizalian assimilationist demands, and so were the letters of negotiation, manifestoes, protocols, and interviews leading to it and concluding it.

Inside colonialism from the very start and all throughout, the colonial middle class, at the same time that it was collaborating with the friars and the rest of the Spanish ruling class in oppressing and exploiting the masses, was of course fighting against this colonial ruling class, and specifically against the friars for wealth and power. Moribund colonialism meant exacerbated corruption in the colonial administration and escalated friar greed and theologically and ecclesiastically exponentiated inhumanity. The Rape of Calamba by the Dominicans was but the most lurid and publicized (due to Rizal's influence itself) of a system-wide outrage. There was actually, and in the context especially where colonial racism was insuperable, but one historically concrete possibility for this colonial middle class (which was of course Rizal's and the assimilationist so-called ilustrados' class) to triumph over the friars in this struggle, and that was revolution which would of course enable them to overthrow colonialism itself. But they did not want to overthrow colonialism itself. They loved, they were exceedingly devoted to, Spanish colonialism! During those times the Madrid government was dominated by liberals who were themselves anti-friar. This incited Rizal and company's politically naive and shallow imagination to conjure the absurd and stupid and ultimately genocidally bloody delusion of winning this battle against the friars by way of assimilation. They underestimated thereby, too, the truculence and insidious depth of the racism of even those Spanish liberals whom they were beseeching to help them in their hallucinatory project of assimilation. These equations plus their exceeding intellectual poverty (obtrusive in Rizal's philosophical illiteracy) or plain stupidity (nothing can be more stupid and stupidizing than assimilationism ifself) take care of one half of the factors that led Rizal and company pervertedly to advocate assimilation and oppose revolution. The other half was their huge fear and profound distrust of the native masses themselves—a fear and a distrust as huge and as deep as their class's multi-centurial colonial collaborationist crime against them. Rizal never once in his entire writing life mentioned revolution except to denounce and abuse it, and curse and be horrified by it or to horrify the Madrid government with the spectre of it in the facetious hope of successfully terrorizing those "liberals" into granting his assimilationist hallucinations. His horror of revolution, reinforced by his endless love of and devotion to Mother Spain, was one and the same as his horror of the native masses. Whilst every time he professed in the rhetoric of patriotism his burning love for his own people he was burning in the lie of it, for if in this profession of love he truly included the suffering masses, he would have discovered the truth of such love in revolution itself, in rejecting which all his lifelong he to the death rejected the native masses and with the latter his own people themselves.

And thus did he also succeed in disqualifying himself from being *of* the people, from being one of the Filipino people, from being a member of the primordially democratic association called the people, the existological-ontological integrity of which being irreducibly political (the right of Sovereignty), and moral (the Categorical Imperative never to treat the other as mere means to an end but always as an end in itself; which is ultimately the same as the Democratic/Communistic Imperative to never exist for oneself, and to always exist only for the Other, for All the others, for Humanity (which is the morality of the poet as well as of the revolutionary fighter...). In this disqualification he was one with the ruling class which, as such, are as a group, not part of, not one with, and are excluded from, the socio-historical collective, preeminently political subject called, the People.

19.1.) Genocidally bloody delusion, yes, because this would lead to a decisive repression and curtailment of the revolutionary impulse (which was of course already there during those revolutionary times!), the determined opposition of the upper middle class against the revolution and thus the pre-stunted emergence of it, the corruption and enfeeblement of the moral and political fibre of those of the lower middleclass who joined and officered it (think of the gangsterism and vendorism of Aguinaldo and company:--with all of these resulting in the massive delay of the revolutionary process which in turn enabled the Americans to intercept it en route to another colonialism, in which the Americans murdered 2 million Filipinos—a gift of evil, wholesale and world-historical, from Jose Rizal and company…

19.2) Here is an excerpt from a report dated August 30, 1892, by Ricardo Carnicero, the then current military commander of Dapitan to the Governor General (Despujol) on Rizal: "One of the hopes of Rizal is to become deputy at the Cortes so that he can expound there all that happens in the Islands…" Carnicero was too good to Rizal, allowing him even to live with him in his house, that he had later on to be replaced.

THEORETICO-PHILOSOPHICAL INTRODUCTION

ON PRIMORDIAL COMMUNISM

OR, NIETZSCHE ON THE IMPOSSIBILITY OF TRUTH

This essay intervenes in the debates concerning so-called "alternative truths/facts" in a supposedly "post-truth" world by refuting it in its fascist source itself, namely, Nietzsche...

NIETZSCHE ON THE IMPOSSIBILITY OF TRUTH: READING NIETZSCHE'S ESSAY, "TRUTH AND FALSITY IN AN ULTRAMORAL SENSE"

PREPENDIX {i}:--"Ultramoral" here means, as later on Nietzsche himself memorably put it, BEYOND GOOD AND EVIL, i.e., post-moral, and, yes, post-human, beyond humanity; hence, the "post-humanism", the anti-humanism, the inhumanism braggadociously and sneeringly broadcast as such by Nietzsche's post-truth, anti-truth, and therefore nihilistic-fascist disciples, Foucault, Deleuze, Derrida, and sundry other post-structuralists and postmodernists and their proudly immoral, criminal, neither-this-nor-that, sycophantic postmoapes in comp.lit., hum., socio., departments all over the world, and here, mostly in UP and Ateneo…Postmoapes and sycophants because there being no respectable arguments and reasonings in Nietzsche himself as well as in his, mostly French, intellectually dishonest, disciples, there cannot have been anything but academically propagandized and blown-up authority/reputation that impels this motley army of postmoechoes in their echolalic journal essays and books. That also explains why they all end up being fascists and political conservatives.

1.0.) “In some remote corner of the universe, effused into innumerable solar systems, there was once a star upon which clever animals invented cognition. It was the haughtiest, most mendacious moment in the history of this world, but yet only a moment”.

1.1. This is impossible! And the fellow doesn’t know where he is and where he should be. For in the first place, if the same “clever animals invented cognition”, then, by the same token it must have been they who invented haughtiness and mendacity themselves, and surely, the invention of haughtiness—is not haughty? And the invention of mendacity is not mendacious? Moreover, if the invention of haughtiness is itself haughty, is a haughty invention, it must have been because it was invented for haughty reasons—otherwise, granting that it is an invention at all, it would not be the invention of haughtiness but of something else; but a haughty reason presupposes haughtiness which then must already be there for there to be haughty reasons for inventing it. The same for mendacity. And, unfortunately for Nietzsche, the same for cognition, for knowledge, and, therewith, for truth which, among other things, is true knowledge.

1.2. If you are not an idiot like Nietzsche, you won’t put the matter of the emergence of cognition, i.e., knowledge, i.e., truth, like that—you won’t be able to say it is something invented. You cannot invent knowledge without first knowing what it is; that is to say, without knowing, without knowledge being already there. Which then you can no longer invent nor need to. He doesn’t know what he’s saying who says cognition or knowledge or truth was something invented, was something which to be there at all had to be invented, was something which can be invented.

1.3. In the first place, if you do not already know knowledge, you can never know, and therefore can never know it, and therefore can never know anything, can never know at all. For if you do not already know knowledge, both what it is, what it consists in, and how to know, how knowing happens, then you can never know, for nothing can teach it to you, nothing can make you know. To know is to know to know—more.

1.4. Which means that for beings such as we are, who here speak of knowing and not knowing, and have thus a sense of knowing and not knowing, and know how to use the word 'know', to be and to know what it is to know and therefore to know are one and the same thing: to be human, let us say, to be a speaking being necessarily amongst speaking beings, is to know what it is to know, and therefore to know to know, and therefore to know. I am, therefore I know. The human being is the knowing being. Who knows to know...Homo sapiens sapiens...

1.5. To know is to know being—rather than nothing. And this because there is nothing to know in nothing. To know being—what it is to be, what it is to exist, what it is not to be, what it is to no longer exist. To know being—to know the ways of being, to know becoming, to know the ways of coming to be and ceasing to be; doing is being, is a way of being, and to know, which is to know being, is to know doing, the ways of doing, to know agency, to know causality, to know cause and effect...

1.6. Whatever it is that is known in knowing—that is being. Whilst what is known in knowing is what is always already known, is that without knowing which one cannot know. For if you do not already know being, nothing can make you know it. Nothing can teach it to you. For, suppose you do not know being, how can you know it, how can you recognize it, when you encounter it? In fact, not knowing being, you won't be able to encounter—at all.

1.7. And that is because, not knowing being you cannot be at all as the "I", the subjectivity, the agency, the will, the self, the soul, the mind, the ex-istence, the freedom, the mortal being, that you are:-- the dying one who knows herself/himself dying and bound to be absolutely nothing, bound to totally disappear, bound to cease entirely to exist, the power to die, that you are. It is face to face with death that you become the finite infinite, the singular one, the inescapable identity, the nurr, the nuclear-ur-reflection, that you are, and become thereby the power to die. The power to die—to die for the Other: the power of absolute sacrifice for the Other, for the community of human beings, for humanity, the power of communal, of communist, heroism, which, in the truth of your conscience forged across 70 million years of life and death existence in defense of the Other, to take care of the Other, to give her/his very life and existence for the wellbeing of the Other, you of course are:--and that is exactly why always already you are guilty of betraying your charge, guilty of falling short, of never being equal to this infinite responsibility for the Other that you are:--and how else indeed do you explain communist heroism and comprehend the revolutionary fighter—andres bonifacio for instance, or each of the, ultimately millions, who staked all to make the revolution, for instance? The communist revolutionary's love for the people, and indeed for all of humanity, is pure and infinite:--infinite because mediated by the election of nothingness, of death, and due to this mediation also the purest –for what can be purer and more purifying than this passage through death, than this mediation of nothingness? Suppose, as Nietzsche here must presuppose, you do not know being at all such that you do not and thus cannot even know you exist and are the be-ing, the ex-isting, and indeed the bodyself, even the animal that you are, let alone the power to die, the subjectivity whose primordial structure and telos is absolute sacrifice for the Other, is infinite responsibility for the Others? Not knowing being, I would not know I exist and therefore would not know others exist, would not know there is a world out there, would not see, feel, hear, smell, taste, mean anything. I would not be a self at all, there would be no "I" there at all, nor, of course, a "me". Nothing. Only nothing. If I am to be at all then I must at once, I must already, know being; I must already know what it is to be if only in order to be able to identify myself and differentiate myself from the rest of being, from all other beings, from all of being, from being itself as its other, from other human beings, and, from the there of my being there, to respond to them when they call me and identify me to myself... My mastery of the grammar of pronouns as speaker of my native tongue will ensure, nay, necessitate, (in fact, technically necessitate) that I am born into language and thus into society, into humanity, as a primordial, an original, an originary democrat, nay a pure communist (technically, but at one and the same time existologically, because the feat of mastering the pronouns is equivalent to the achievement of the truth of existological, but also technical, functional, better yet, positional equality). This knowledge of being which is immediately given in the evolved human DNA and ontogenetically revived in the many instances of re-exposure to death/nothingness in the trauma of birth and of object loss and of paranoid-schizoid annihilation during the oral and anal sadistic stage, will turn out to be homologically programmed and contains programmatically the knowledge to know—more and more and more. Mathematical physics, is already implicit in it. There is a logos of being and there is a logos of the mind, of thought and language; the logos of the mind/language is homological with that of being,with that of becoming...

1.8. Knowing being thus in, through, as, this passage through death, through, and mediated by, nothingness, is to be without being merely being, to be no longer merely being, is to be free of, from, being to the infinite extent of being able to disown it by owning nothingness, death, instead, necessarily for the sake of what is no longer merely being which precisely is the community of beings who are no longer merely being, and thus for motives, for reasons that are no longer those of being; is to be able at once to mean, to make meaning, to make of being itself a (mere) meaning, to make of it a WORD in the infinite solicitude for the Other—to speak. And this indeed must be why as Wittgenstein found out, a private language is impossible. The essence of language, the truth of language, consists in this mediation by humanity itself as the first, the major addressee, of anything said to anyone, of any communication, of even the most private, minor, communication. Because they show it in their works, they, who are purest in their speech--the poets, philosophers, artists, writers, who address the others through the Other, through humanity itself, first, and then, through that ontologico-existological mediation, the individual others, which is what language, grammar necessarily is in its intrinsic communism:--they, too, are communist heroes. Speech of truth and justice, and, love, which can only be infinite—poetry, philosophy, literature in general in which it is in fact impossible to fashion any direct individual address…:--they are communist heroes too who speak this speech. Speech of infinite responsibility for the Other, of infinite solicitude for the Other, for the community, for humanity itself as ontologico-existological structure and telos of human subjectivity:--the word, language was forged across those 70 million years of purest, intensest, communist heroism from the time our ape-ancestors had had to come down from the trees and attempt to survive on the ground that was the African Savannah--and defend themselves against the constant threat of annihilation from vastly stronger, fiercer predators… Which is why a philosophy of evil such as Nietzsche's would be if it were philosophy at all, is impossible—as impossible as a supposed poem praising Hitler or Marcos or Gloria Macapagal Arroyo or colonialism (as were all the works of Nick Joaquin, for instance), or the Slave Trade, or the Holocaust…For the Nietzschean discourse of evil, being such, is a seduction into evil which as you read it addresses you privately, tempting you with the immanentizing deliriums and perverted delights of the exercise of the will to power, of the perpetration of power as the destruction of the Other and the aggrandizement of the pervertedly beastly "ego" (pervertedly, i.e., evil, pervertedly because this is not a simple return to animality which as such knows no evil in that it knows no freedom either and therewith no transcendence, no True nor Good nor Beautiful to betray: the animal is innocent because unfree, purely immanent, dumb)—it addresses you vis a tergo, secretly whispering such perverted beastly delights in your ear…And this also is why the true writer, poet, philosopher, novelist, artist, who in the truth of being such is necessarily consumed by his work, by his relentless devotion to the Other thus, by liberating and soul-deepening mission of addressing truths and beauties to the Other, is also a communist hero…

1.9. But, to more closely engage Nietzsche here:--Is knowledge/cognition haughtiest to Nietzsche because it pretends to cognize/know when in fact it cannot and is, as he puts it here, all lies? And is therefore in fact most mendacious because the truth is it manufactures its truths and is a lying liar? But how did he come to know this truth about the haughty and mendacious untruth of cognition? Did he not use the same cognition to do so? And proved it capable of truth too and not just mendacities and lies? Cognition's object is being; it is the cognition of being that produces truth, truths—of, about, of course, being—rather than nothing. The cognition of being—and not that of nothingness, yes!; which, if there is being, is what absolutely is not and cannot be. And that is why what cognition must most certainly know is being—and not nothing. For in the first place there is nothing in nothing to know, to cognize, to make true, to nudge a truth of, from, or to falsify or err or lie about. Which means that anyone who claims that this cognition, this human intellect, is incapable of truth and is capable only of lies and errors and falsifications, claims at once to know being completely, and this cognition completely, and therefore everything, absolutely everything, and to have determined that being is such that cognition cannot know it at all, and cognition is such that it cannot know being at all. Nietzsche, Jesus Christ!, is omniscient!

2.0.) "After Nature had taken breath awhile, the star congealed and the clever animals had to die.—Someone might write a fable after this style, and yet he would not have illustrated sufficiently how wretched, shadowlike, transitory, purposeless and fanciful the human intellect appears in Nature."

When it appears in nature thus, to whom does it appear? To nature? And is nature then something to which something can appear? Is nature a subject? And supposing it is to nature indeed and that nature is a subject to which it can appear, how did you come to know that it did? And how dare you take the point of view of nature like that—omnisciently? So it is to you that it appears as such, then? To you only, not to nature? Then you are, once more, a third party here, and moreover, an omniscient one! God… But the ontologically crucial point here is this, namely, that the human intellect, including human feeling, is not nature. Founded upon nature, it is precisely this human intellect that makes the bearer of it no longer merely animal but already human—that is to say, beyond nature. And beyond it, and surpassing it, by an infinity, by the infinite complexity that separates mind from bone, or freedom from causality, or by the infinite leap across such infinite complexity which every human decision is—for instance the decision no longer to be, or else to go on being, which every decision presupposes. In fact, it is in this sense—which is that of the power to die, the power to reject being itself, and thus to affirm it—that this cognition, this intellect, this freedom, this transcendence, this power to die, is beyond even being itself. Freedom, in the ultimate analysis, is freedom from being, freedom from determination by being itself, and is thus in this sense beyond being. Appearing in nature, how dare you compare it with, and denigrate it in relation to nature? In fact, you have of course reduced it into a piece of nature, into a bone, and as such a most insignificant one. And that is why you, Nietzsche, are a most vulgar vulgarizer thus.

3.0.) "There were eternities during which this intellect did not exist, and when it has once more passed away, there will be nothing to show that it has existed. For this intellect is not concerned with any further mission transcending the sphere of human life. No, it is purely human and none but its owner and procreator regards it so pathetically as to suppose that the world revolves around it."

3.1) Only being itself is what cannot not be—being itself, and, in that always already being is beings:--being/beings...Otherwise, everything else can not-be, and everything that can not-be, must end. It is because being cannot come from nothing,--for then it must be nothing but nothing,--that being cannot *not* be, cannot become nothing, cannot cease to be. And is then endless. Because being cannot come from nothing, it cannot have begun; that is to say, there cannot have been a time when it was not; for if there was, there was then nothing but nothing and there must be nothing but nothing now, for being cannot come from nothing.

Beginninglessly being becomes and measured against beginninglessness a sigh and a star might as well have the same duration. There were eternities during which there were no stars. Assuming—with plenty of evidence—that the Big Bang was how this universe began to be, we can theorize, not altogether fancifully, that after the expanding universe is through expanding, having reached the point of return, it then contracts into the same unimaginably dense point which in our quite recent case, i.e., in the case of this universe of ours, exploded some 18 billion years ago, whereupon it again explodes in another Big Bang, and so on...And there must have been infinitely many such Big Bangs already, and there will be infinitely many more...

3.2.) Again, show to whom? To God? Being shown is important only to subjects, and unless you want to be impertinent, not to cats and dogs but only to us, human subjects—with whom the importance of importance itself will end.

3.3.) Why do you talk about missions here at all? Are you a theologian? But you don't believe in God (whom you have pronounced dead)—at least not consciously, for unconsciously, as we have seen, you are to yourself that (tat tvam asi!); you must then be a negative theologian, a negative metaphysician... In any case, who told you that humanity has a mission and that it is purely limited to humanity? How did you come to know that? Do dogs have a mission too and is it or is it not limited to dogship? Naturally, the human intellect is for human use. It is somewhat banal to point that out, is it not? But it does not follow from this that therefore human beings can know nothing except human things—as though human things are not also and at once ontological things, things of being, and as though we can cleanly separate human things from ontological things; nor that such knowledges by humans of human things are for that reason necessarily errors and lies...

3.4.) And yet, not only does the world revolve around it, it originates from it and with it! Without it—the “purely human” “intellect”--there is, in a sense, nothing there but:—being. Being and, entwined with it by the difference called ontological difference, but absolutely indifferently (for what makes different and differential this ontological difference and thus makes it matter in the worlding of the world is the consciousness, the perception, the sensation, the becoming reflexive of it and this precisely in and as, by way of, this “purely human” intellect), those sufficiently delineated particularities called beings—electrons, stars, elephants, ants (although with these last two which, together with dogs and chimpanzees almost already are ex-istences, already, almost, a certain kind of world dawns:--the stark clarity of world as human world separated by an abyss, by an infinity, from the merely animal world of eleph/ants, is due precisely to the unique, the very special, infinitely special quality, and qualification, of this “purely human” intellect in its unique exposure to nothingness/death which gives being, exposing it too, being, yes, in the exposure to nothingness at the species level during the seventy million years of the successful attempt of our ape ancestors to survive on the ground as they were forced by some contingency to come down from the trees thus exposing them to the constant threat of annihilation from beastly predators (it was here too that the heroic a priori structure of absolute sacrifice for the sake of the band, and thus for the sake of all –like you are always already your brother’s, but also of course, and even more so, your sister’s keeper--making each newborn human being the power to die, was constituted and imprinted), and, at the ontogenetic level, in the repetitions of death, in the repeated dying, that the human infant/child is, knowing death thus as absolute nothingness, as its own absolute nothingness by dying it, repeatedly, repeatedly…)

3.5.) “In some remote corner of the universe, effused into innumerable solar systems, there was once a star upon which clever animals invented cognition”. Thus Nietzsche. Clever animals... Invented cognition… In what sense invented? Its “inventors” were animals that must have been clever enough for the feat. Did they remain mere animals afterwards? That is to say: Did they remain the merely natural beings, which as "clever animals" they must be, after the "invention"? Nietzsche's lines here, as elsewhere, look like they are evolutionist; he sounds Darwinian, perhaps Lamarckian. It does look like this "invention of cognition" is meant by him to be an evolutionary event. In Nietzsche, the struggle for existence, the "survival of the fittest", will become a metaphysical theory, a "microphysics of forces" which are at once will-forces or will-points, which to him are the thing in itself:--the will to power; a microphysics then of atomic wills, an eternal struggle amongst innumerable necessarily immortal will-atoms… But there are other Nietzsches…

3.6.) "It was the haughtiest, most mendacious moment in the history of this world, but yet only a moment. After Nature had taken breath awhile, the star congealed and the clever animals had to die.—Someone might write a fable after this style, and yet he would not have illustrated sufficiently how wretched, shadowlike, transitory, purposeless and fanciful the human intellect appears in Nature. There were eternities during which this intellect did not exist, and when it has once more passed away, there will be nothing to show that it has existed. For this intellect is not concerned with any further mission transcending the sphere of human life. No, it is purely human and none but its owner and procreator regards it so pathetically as to suppose that the world revolves around it…" –"Purely human"—what is that? And is there, can there be, such a thing? Can anything in being be separated from anything, from itself, or from another absolutely, as to produce things like a purely this and a purely that? Can anything be more "thingly", and thus less "human", more "unhuman", more neuter, than the absolute neutrality of the abysmal pause that is the hanging in the balance of the next moment of being with the Other and thus of the being with being, in and as which is constituted each moment of being and of ex-istence of that same utterly "pathetic" intellect? In fact, if there is anything purely human, it is this, this pure and absolute neutrality between being and nothingness, between existing and not existing, the or in Hamlet's To be or not to be, this infinite chasm that is the power to die itself. For, fruit of death, fruit of the knowledge of death, fruit of the knowing risking of absolute nothingness in death, this thing, this "unhuman" neutrality and neuterity, this power to refuse or accept being itself which we call the power to die, is unique to those who know death thus and can assume it qua possibility of absolute nothingness, and perhaps only humans are that?

4.0.) "That haughtiness connected with cognition and sensation, spreading blinding fogs before the eyes and over the senses of men, deceives itself therefore as to the value of existence owing to the fact that it bears within itself the most flattering evaluation of cognition. Its most general effect is deception, but even its most particular effect has something of deception in their nature."

4.1.) In real life situations, nay in all situations except that of epistemological squabbles amongst philosophers pseudo or otherwise, there cannot have been, there cannot be even now, such self-overvaluating, self-flattering "haughtiness" that overvaluates cognition and sensation and overvaluates "existence" thereby in at all claiming that such cognition and sensation are capable of laying hold of truth. Nietzsche doesn't know where he is here and naively imputes to those imagined rival philosophers of his who contrary to what he preaches here on the impossibility of truth believe in the possibility and actual happening of truth, this "haughtiness", this self-flattering overrating of the capabilities of cognition and sensation "itself", and vice versa. Which of course begs the question, or is a mere insistence that his doctrine of the impossibility of truth is true true true, is the truth the truth the truth, and therefore true true true and is the truth the truth the truth! Supernaively forgetting awhile that according to him himself right here right here right now right now there is no truth, for truth is, as he on the other hand says, impossible...What Nietzsche is saying here then is, truth is impossible because the human intellect is by nature haughty, i.e., claims to lay hold of, grasp, apprehend, comprehend truth, and deceives itself thus in thus overvaluating its capacities in at all claiming, in at all thinking, in haughtily assuming itself to be such as to be capable of truth. To claim to be capable of truth is haughtiness itself; haughtiness blinds, deceives, self-deceives, ergo it is impossible for the human intellect in its, as it were, intrinsic haughtiness to know a truth:--truth is impossible because the human intellect, haughty by nature is capable only of self-flattering self-deception…This however proves nothing, and is not even an argument; or, construed as an attempt to argue, a petitio…

5.0.) “The intellect, as a means for the preservation of the individual, develops its chief power in dissimulation; for it is in dissimulation that the feebler and less robust individuals preserve themselves since it has been denied them to fight the battle of existence with horns or the sharp teeth of beasts of prey. In man this art of dissimulation reaches its acme of perfection: in him deception, flattery, falsehood and fraud, slander, display, pretentiousness, disguise, cloaking convention, and acting to others and to himself, in short, the continual fluttering to and fro around the one flame—Vanity: all these things are so much the rule, and the law, that few things are more incomprehensible than the way in which an honest and pure impulse to truth could have arisen among men. They are deeply immersed in illusions and dream fancies; their eyes glance only over the surface of things and see “forms”; their sensation nowhere leads to truth, but contents itself with receiving stimuli and, so to say, with playing hide-and-seek on the back of things. In addition to this, at night, man allows his dreams to lie to him a whole lifetime long, without his moral sense ever trying to prevent them.”

5.1.) “The intellect, as a means for the preservation of the individual, develops its chief power in dissimulation…” If this is that at all, which it is not, or is only peripherally so, it does not follow that it is only that; and it most certainly is not the case that the intellect “develops its chief power in dissimulation” (lying, cheating, duplicity…). And here we pin down with, of course, a pin, naked and wriggling like a worm, the most egregious of Nietzsche’s fundamental errors, his most gargantuan stupidity—his atomistic-individualist concept of "man", "man" without the social dimension, a being devoid of primordial or originary sociality and devoid therefore of primordial democracy, an anti-democratic, anti-socialist, anti-communist error produced in him as an ideological reflex by global-intimate capitalism and is thus the determining common feature of all the many variants of capitalist ideology, and a blindness and an absolutely violent perversity then, which he shares with Anglo-American empiricism, behaviourism, liberalism, and generally, capitalist apology. When our ape-ancestors came down from the trees to try to survive on the ground of the African savannah some 70 million years ago, they were already what ethologists and anthropologists call social animals. They were already by then the most intelligent animals in the kingdom. And this great intelligence which had everything to do with their, also most intense, sociality made even more intense by the constant pressure of life-and-death self-defense of the herd and emerging community against throngs of vastly stronger, biologically better equipped beasts of prey, was indeed the chief reason why they were able to survive, thrive, and eventually completely dominate the entire animal kingdom. But they applied, and thereby developed by leaps and bounds that intelligence as a most well-knit social body (and later on with the dawning of true freedom in and as the power to die, as a moral-political body, a body politic, a polis, a primordial democracy), not against each other, not in order to overpower and dominate and cheat each other into defeat, into slavish passivity or working class helplessness as in Nietzsche's and capitalism's nihilistic-genocidal, absolutely violent ideological concept of the human being as will to power, as possessive individual, as malicious pig, which thus aimed to eternalize the regime of fascism/capitalism by naturalizing it. Rather the exact opposite. It was their apprenticeship in death and nothingness, in death as nothingness, as a species—those 70 million years. An apprenticeship in death and/as nothingness which was also the occasion of the dawning of that power to die which was freedom proper as freedom/power to give up on being, to reject being itself for the sake of the life of freedom, i.e., for the sake of the Other, of all the Others. It was in this community of life in death/nothingness, that truth became a life-and-death, an absolute, desideratum, and being true to the Other, honesty, sincerity, fidelity, and beyond all this, devotion to the Other to the point of absolute sacrifice, became virtues of being, ontological virtues, or, more precisely, virtues of be-ing for the human being, and therefore, virtues of being beyond being, virtues of being ex-beings, virtues of ex-isting then, existological virtues, virtues of freedom, virtues of beings who are free in being free of the determining power of being to the infinite extent of being able to choose absolute nothingness over it and thus absolutely to reject it:--virtues, then, of the power to die...All virtues are virtues of self-sacrifice—for the sake of the Other, ultimately of the community of—in the most concrete sense of the concreteness of true heroism—the beloved Others, the heroically loved Others; and virtues therefore of love, of love for all human beings, again in this concrete heroic sense of love. Of tragic love, yes! For everything will in due time perish, and this exactly is why there have to be remembrances of being, of existing, of things past:--and all art is essential remembering, essential re-presenting—of what?—of moments of truth where truth is the truth of essence, the fulfilment of being in beings, of beings, of things in their particular essence. Aesthetics of the tragic--: and that is why all art has an essential depth of sadness and only the sad is beautiful. A picture re-presents being, beings, life, existence in light of death. Whilst only mortals are free, and, being free, demand truth of each other, and equality, and honesty, and justice, and fidelity...Only mortals are by essence moral—truthful by force of essence, or,--essential failure--, lying, deceitful...etc. There is anticipation of essence fulfilled, of essential fulfillment which is truth, the truth of the human existent, in this demand, the way Einstein's equations anticipate truths of the universal process of becoming--a way which presupposes the truth of homology, i.e., of the logic of being and the logic of thinking being homologous with each other, a homologic anticipation which is constantly made and confirmed in its truth in daily praxis, in work and play--think of how a football player or a basketballer anticipates all the time the ball's trajectory, or how a mathematical equation anticipates--and thus predicts--the red shift. For truth is first of all truth of essence and only derivatively true knowledge. All virtues then are moral virtues, and all rights are moral rights, for they are all life and death claims, demands, of freedom on freedom, of free beings on free beings in a community, in a communism, of free beings, who, after those 70 million years of existological apprenticeship in death and nothingness can no longer plead ignorance of the law, of the laws of freedom/morality. The social contract of which most brilliantly and for the first time Rousseau wrote, was also forged across those 70 million years…For the social contract was also the birthing of human society as society of freedoms, of powers to die…

5.2. The ultimate value of existence consists in its absolutization as the object the continuing existence of which, the integrity of which, the wellbeing of which, the consummation of which, the exaltation of which, the love of which, demands of every human individual nothing less than absolute sacrifice:--to die, to sacrifice every moment of one's existence, for this absolute object of absolute devotion, this (one could almost say, Levinasian) Other, is the very structure and telos, the telic structure, of human subjectivity. I used to call this primordial democracy with both its individual and social structuration. I now want to call it heroic communism, primordial heroic communism.

5.3. Heroic communism—primordial heroic communism:--that is the telic structure of human individual and social existence. Levinas calls it absolute responsibility FOR the Other; responsibility FOR the Other to the point of substitution FOR the Other:--to the point of assuming responsibility for the human condition by personifying it in dying for it:--buy assuming the Jesus Christ position in relation to the human condition, but without the theology and the metaphysics of the Christian Jesus. This too is of course the always-already-there foundation and core of conscience…Which is why always already you are guilty, for always already you have fallen short of this imperative of absolute sacrifice, of heroic communism…The poet—every true poet—is a communist hero; as is of course every communist revolutionary. This infinite, this absolute love of the Other as object of absolute sacrifice, of absolute responsibility, of infinite solicitude, of life and death devotion, of endless, of unending, unending love, cannot be merely physical. It is poetic. It is tragic. It gives rise to beauty. Beauty is the telos of language itself, the expression of the internal tension of the tragic which arises from the fact that the absolute—the Other as object of infinite responsibility, of absolute, of insatiable sacrifice--has its origin in death/nothingness. This infinite love, this absolute responsibility, this infinite solicitude, this passion of absolute sacrifice for the Other is not a hypothesis:--it is actual in the being, the existence, the practice, the acts of the communist hero who during the Revolution is each and everyone of the revolutionary people. Every great work of thought, of art, of poetry, of literature, is a concrete expression of it...

5.4. "The intellect, as a means for the preservation of the individual, develops its chief power in dissimulation; for it is in dissimulation that the feebler and less robust individuals preserve themselves since it has been denied them to fight the battle of existence with horns or the sharp teeth of beasts of prey." Nietzsche then, is here one hundred and one percent wrong. The human intellect developed across seventy million years of constant life-and-death challenges, battles, strategies, stratagems in defense of the band, the society, the species, the community, the commune, against stronger, fiercer but less intelligent, less socially emotional predators (these predators but more viciously, nay infinitely more viciously and evilly, and absolutely violently because metaphysically NOW, have for some 500 years been reincarnating originally as Western-European-Christian-Capitalist- global colonialist, man:--in response to their absolutely nihilistic threat, the primordial communist hero in every human being has awakened, has arisen to do battle). The infinite purity and intensity of this communal life-and-death struggle against the mortal enemies of the social body demanded absolute devotion to the Other, to the social body, to the cause of the All, and made truth a life-and-death desideratum, and truthfulness, honesty, a categorical imperative, and absolute sacrifice FOR THE SOCIAL BODY, for the Other, the perfect consummation of individual existence. Misled from the outset by his global capitalist atomistic individualism (supposed humans without the social context, outside of social evolution) Nietzsche's vaunted genealogy of morals and of truth is a total inversion or the real evolutionary-historical process.

5.5. "In man this art of dissimulation reaches its acme of perfection: in him deception, flattery, falsehood and fraud, slander, display, pretentiousness, disguise, cloaking convention, and acting to others and to himself, in short, the continual fluttering to and fro around the one flame—Vanity: all these things are so much the rule, and the law, that few things are more incomprehensible than the way in which an honest and pure impulse to truth could have arisen among men." In man? In petty bourgeois wo/man, such as in Nietzsche, yes!

5.6. "They are deeply immersed in illusions and dream fancies; their eyes glance only over the surface of things and see 'forms'; their sensation nowhere leads to truth, but contents itself with receiving stimuli and, so to say, with playing hide-and-seek on the back of things. In addition to this, at night, man allows his dreams to lie to him a whole lifetime long, without his moral sense ever trying to prevent them." This Nietzsche is a writer you will want to flog for stupidity, for such simplemindedness, for such simpletonism one is astounded that supposed philosophers like Derrida, Foucault, Deleuze, could look up to him as to a master. In the end, one cannot help but conclude that it must be because they are stupider. And if you happen to admire these Nietzscheites? Your stupidity must be as unfathomable as hollow block! He's talking about the human species—of which you and I and he are members. Has he forgotten the fact? Namely that he is a human being like you and I? For if he has not, then he must know that countless, nay infinitely many fundamental sense-perceptual, praxiological, unassailable everyday knowledges and truths are presupposed by all the "illusions and dream fancies" humans are normally capable of being at times immersed in, such as in sleep or in rare fits of clear insanity. They eat things and not merely lick their surfaces; they make and use tools and do not merely imagine or daydream making and using them. They cut up things and organisms and open them up, even disembowel them. And of course, modern science has now known the deepest interior of things such that there is no real interior anymore. As for dreams, can Nietzsche assail them for their supposed falsity without presupposing and implying that people wake up from them as to the reality and truth they seem to hide or dissemble? Nietzsche who was normal enough to function as a professor or even as an ambulance orderly during the First World War or as a compulsive mountain hiker in Sils Maria or as a frustrated lover-suitor to Lou Andreas Salome, knows all these sense-perceptual, praxiological, even scientific-experimental knowledges and truths without knowing which indeed he would not have been able to exist as he did thus. Why then does he here say he doesn't? Why then does he say they—all the other human beings like him—don't? He is a liar then? He is dishonest then? And can he even merely slightly believe anything he says here then? No? Is a man capable of cheating himself so? Of believing his own lie? We really should flog him for the hifalutin imposture more hateful for being so highflown. Calling it philosophy even—bullshit!

5.7. Who, what, the human being is, what a people is, what humanity is, in their deepest, highest, and all-embracing truth, comes out like nowhere else in Revolution, specifically in anti-colonial revolutions, but most purely in the communist revolution--in a revolutionary situation which shows the revolutionary fighter as the exemplar of the deepest, loftiest, grandest and therefore truest human being, namely, the being of absolute sacrifice for the Other, for the people, for humanity, the power to die in pure act, in pure actuality. The communist revolutionary fighter:--for s/he stakes all and gives all, and sacrifices all of herself/himself, for absolutely no consideration save her/his absolutely self-sacrificing love for the Other, for the people, for humanity. That is to say, by way of anything of being or of the world that could accrue to herself/himself,--NOTHING, ONLY NOTHING. Only this love then powering her/him constantly as s/he makes the Revolution—this power to die for the Other which consummates her/his being the power to die that s/he is. This is the primordial telic structure, the deepest, most fundamental nature of human subjectivity which however in everyday humans in everyday situations is mostly covered up, repressed, perverted, sometimes to the point of erasure, of active negation and inversion into evil. This inversion is made into a philosophy by Nietzsche and Heidegger—a philosophy, or, for they are two, philosophies, of evil, the philosophy of the Will to Power or of the Aryan Superman, and the philosophy of the resolute German Nazi Dasein of the Being that Destines…

5.7.1. Writers sacrificing everything in order to write, philosophers, poets, artists consumed by the production of their works which are all for the Other, for the people, for all of humanity and not at all for themselves, for no true writer, philosopher, poet, writes for herself/himself. No one can give herself/himself gifts; all works of art are gifts—for the Other, only for the Other, the people, humanity…Less glorious, less grand, and more compromised, these too are communist heroes who stake all and give all and sacrifice everything for love of the Other, of the people, of humanity…They too act-out, express, articulate and purely attest to this deepest primordial telic structure of absolute sacrifice for the Other of human subjectivity…This of course is the absolute opposite of Nietzsche's will to power, the telic structure of whose subjectivity is the absolute sacrifice of all for the self which is the definition, the essence, of evil itself.

5.7.2. The war of all against all as the original human condition and as telic structure of human subjectivity is utterly false:--the exact opposite is true, namely, that originally, communist heroism and absolute responsibility for the Other is the primordial structure and telos of human subjectivity. Hobbes, the original philosopher of evil, father of British empiricism, theorizer of possessive individualism as the eternal truth of man, father then of capitalist apologetics and justifier of imperialist terrorism was the inventor of that massmurderous notion.

6.0. "What indeed does man know about himself? Oh! That he could but once see himself complete, placed as it were in an illuminated glass case! Does not nature keep secret from him most things, even about his body, e.g., the convolutions of the intestines, the quick flow of the blood currents, the intricate vibrations of the fibers, so as to banish and lock him up in proud, delusive knowledge? Nature threw away the key; and woe to the fateful curiosity which might be able for a moment to look out and down through a crevice in the chamber of consciousness and discover that man, indifferent to his own ignorance, is resting on the pitiless, the greedy, the insatiable, the murderous, and, as it were, hanging in dreams on the back of a tiger. Whence, in the wide world, with this state of affairs, arises the impulse to truth?"—Science has completely refuted this mystification of the unknowable interior of the body:--it has unraveled the DNA which attests to the homological nature of knowledge, praxiological as well as theoretical, mathematical…Let us call it the homological transcendental a priori. Meanwhile, Nietzsche here, following his unnamed teacher Thomas Hobbes, apologizes for global capitalist genocide by naturalizing and in effect ontologizing the will-to-power/money, the infinite greed, the absolute violence, of capitalist man.

6.1. "Whence, in the wide world, with this state of affairs, arises the impulse to truth?"—From nowhere, for, in such an inverted state of affairs truth, indeed, would be impossible. Consequently, and with utmost dishonesty, Nietzsche, answering this his fake question, will have to derive the "impulse" to truth using his calculus of constant overpowering as the subjective telos of being a supposed human being; he will have to invent a necessity, an inveterate desire or will of taking advantage of others as motive for wanting truth, of desiring to be truthful. Correlatively, for of course, to him truth is impossible, truth here to him would be nothing but a convenient convention, namely, whatever it is that is agreed upon by everyone to call truth so that by impulse to truth is here meant impulse to conform—not, for the sake of conforming, of course, but because it benefits one and empowers him to go on doing evil, i.e., to go on overpowering, dominating, trampling, destroying other people, because it gives one power advantages, according to the recipe of the will to power, to agree, to go along, to conform…Writes

Nietzsche towards answering his fake question whence arises the impulse to truth: "This first conclusion of peace brings with it a something which looks like the first step toward the attainment of that enigmatical bent for truth. For that which henceforth is to be 'truth' is now fixed; that is to say, a uniformly valid and binding designation of things is invented and the legislature of language also gives the first laws of truth: since here, for the first time, originates the contrast between truth and falsity..." In Tagalog, we call this kind of thinking, "isip bata". Ganito katanga ang tarantadong ito. At maitatanong mo dahil kakaiba ang katangahan, Seryoso ba ang pasistang Alemang ito o nambobola lang habang alam na nambobola siya?

6.2. "As far as the individual tries to preserve himself against other individuals, in the natural state of things..." This natural state of war of all against all which he got from Hobbes, is not even worth calling a myth. It is much too stupid for that. Even among animals there was never such a thing as a war of all against all within the species. Otherwise, no species would have survived—especially the lions which would all at once devour each other into nothingness. Think of elephants waging such a war against each other! Among animals, the rule within the group is the exact opposite of war of all against all:—it is rather care and protection of all by all, friendship of all with all. And so it must have been among our ape ancestors. Even among animals, mothers take care of their young, sometimes with the active cooperation of the father. How did it happen that Hobbes, or here Nietzsche, was able to forget these facts? The war of all against all however is, in general, with some stageal exceptions pertaining to the care of children, indeed the case for modern capitalist societies...This idiocy therefore must have been a projection on Hobbes' and Nietzsche's part, for, as far as they were concerned as adult capitalist men, it was indeed a war of all against all...Capitalist greed, capitalist inhumanity, capitalist genocide, capitalist evil evil evil was what they to themselves were themselves, and, approving themselves to themselves, they saw their being so as the essential nature of "man". Being petty bourgeois however, Nietzsche quite naturally insinuates into the eternal nature of human being his pure and ugly self thus: "In man"--read "in me"—this art of dissimulation reaches its acme of perfection; in him" (read "in me") deception, flattery, falsehood and fraud, slander, display, pretentiousness, disguise, cloaking convention, and acting to others and to himself" (read "myself"), "in short, the continual fluttering to and fro around the one flame—Vanity..." This is even the perfectest description of Nietzsche's writing style and, of course, its content!!! Thus was that absolute perversion of the originary communist nature of human being that is this evil being called the bourgeois naturalized, eternalized, ontologized. On the other hand, the unique conditions of the starting point of human evolution: their being the most intelligent animal species, their being the most intensely social animals, their being the weakest in terms of physical strength, and the unique contingency of their being forced to come down from the trees to try to survive on the ground of the African Savannah—all these, thrown together into fortuitous combination, involuted and convoluted and revoluted to produce the absolute opposite of the totally dehumanized, completely inhumanized, will to power, absolutely selfish antihuman man, the bourgeois, the capitalist man. .The life-and-death necessity of the constant, infinitely intensified devotion of all to securing the conditions of survival of all, which at the individual level means the constant, infinitely intensified devotion of one to the care and preservation of all, led to the mutational emergence of human subjectivity whose being-for-itself is absolutely the same as, and is thus nothing but its, being-FOR-the Other, such that its self is nothing but infinite, death-defying, nothingness-assuming, infinite responsibility for the Other. Whilst life, mere life, mere animality, withoutn the power to die thus, is necessarily selfish.

6.3.) "As far as the individual tries to preserve himself against other individuals, in the natural state of things he uses the intellect in most cases only for dissimulation; since, however, man both from necessity and boredom wants to exist socially and gregariously, he must needs make peace and at least endeavour to cause the greatest bellum omnium contra omnes (war of all against all) to disappear from his world..." Let us be as clear as possible about this thing for the genocidal stupidity of the Nietzschean, fascistic, liberal, behaviourist, empiricist, atomistic, generally capitalist position hinges on this:-- for both commonsense and uninsane socio-political theory or anthropology or sociology, individuals are at once and irreducibly, social beings, i.e.,they are social individuals—and there is no such thing, there never could have been such a thing nor can there be as the atomic individual that is here presupposed by Nietzsche, and which he got from Hobbes and the Anglo-American empiricist-behaviorist-liberal, ultimately capitalist tradition. As we have already repeatedly pointed out, even amongst animals there are no such atomic individuals; animals, but of course minus the dimension of freedom which accounts for human culture which animals do not have, are already social animals. Animals, including humans, do not give birth to themselves nor nurture themselves nor invent for themselves singly each word of language and language itself, nor is there an individual human being who is not born into a language as into a community of speakers and into a network of public power and into a culture, a morality, a literature, a poetry, a tradition of communist heroism of absolute sacrifice for the Other, the mutational evolution of which stretches as far back as 70 million years… Hence, if there was war of any kind in that supposed "state of nature" it was a war of species against other species but the greatest, closest, bonding and friendship and love and cooperation and heroism for the Other, communist heroism, infinite communist responsibility for the Other, within the species. And this was truest of our ape-ancestors but with the infinite addition of the infinitization of such closeness, such bonding, such friendship, such love due to the truly mortal necessity of defending the commune against the omnipresently threatening annihilation from stronger and more ferocious predators—and this, once more, across some 70 million years! In such a closeness-infinitizing, an emotional bond-infinitizing, a friendship-infinitizing, a love-infinitizing-to-the-point-of-absolute-sacrifice-and-infinite -responsibility-for-the-entire-community, or communist heroic or heroic communist situation, there would have been zero dissimulation, zero dishonesty, zero lying, zero vanity within the species-group or the community:--truth and truthfulness would be the absolute norm. Zero boredom too, and oveflowing gregariousness. Hence this supposed origin of the "impulse to truth" from the wish to shoo away boredom and partake of some gregariousness is egregiously stupid. Only the petty bourgeois intellectual and Dionysiokolakes can need the motivation of the wish or urge to be gregarious or afford to wallow in the luxurious affliction of that absolutely violent viciousness called boredom which must indeed be the absolute antithesis of infinite responsibility for the Other, of absolute sacrifice for the Other, of communist responsibility for the Other, of being one's brothers' and sisters' and people's, and humanity's insatiably, infinitely responsible keeper—

7.0. "This first conclusion of peace" (i.e., the cessation of that capitalist moron's theory of the "state of nature" as bellum omnium contra omnes) "brings with it a something which looks like the first step toward the attainment of that enigmatical bent for truth. For that which henceforth is to be 'truth' is now fixed; that is to say, a uniformly valid and binding designation of things is invented and the legislature of language also gives the first laws of truth: since here for the first time originates the contrast between truth and falsity. The liar uses the valid designations, the words, in order to make the unreal appear as real, e.g., he says 'I am rich,' whereas the right designation for his state would be 'poor'. He abuses the fixed conventions by convenient substitution or even inversion of terms. If he does this in a selfish and even harmful fashion, society will no longer trust him but will even exclude him. In this way, men avoid not so much being defrauded, but being injured by fraud. At bottom, at this juncture too, they hate not deception, but the evil, hostile consequences of certain species of deception. And it is in a similarly limited sense only that man desires truth: he covets the agreeable, life-preserving consequences of truth; he is indifferent toward pure, ineffective knowledge; he is even inimical toward truths which possibly might prove harmful or destroying." 1.) In the first place, there was no such state of nature called "war of all against all," as we have as matter of irrefutable commonsense pointed out; what was there was the exact opposite:--primordial communism each member of which is a subjectivity whose telic structure is infinite responsibility for the Other, i.e., for the entire commune, for all of humanity (because this structure is infinitely mediated by nothingness/death from the perspective of which the subject is able to totalize all of being, and therewith the commune into all of humanity), to the point of absolute sacrifice, i.e., of dying for the commune, for humanity, as especially demonstrated by the poet, the writer, the thinker, the artist who, as we have seen must in her/his work always address first the totality, the all, humanity, and mediatedly thus any sector or individual:--but also of course the revolutionary fighter who achieves universality by mediating his every thought and act with the theory of the Revolution. 2.) It is childish to the point of idiocy to say that the "true" meaning of a word is what people had agreed to designate with it, and therewith that what people sat down and decided to call "truth" is the truth and its opposite "falsity". In the first place, it presupposes that the entire linguistic community sat down and agreed to the designation of every word, which is brainless. Secondly, it amounts to saying that cutting up people is murder because people agreed to call it so, and not because it is murder. It must also mean that people invent the grammar of the language which they totally invent:--they also must have sat down and agreed to call 'a' an indefinite article and 'the' a definite article, and article an article and definite a definite and indefinite an indefinite…Nietzsche is a moron of course but salivating idiots must his French disciples be, namely Derrida, Foucault, Deleuze, all the post-structuralists, all the postmodernists—and dishonest dishonest dishonest for exalting him even…

8.0.) "And, moreover, what after all are these conventions of language? Are they possibly products of knowledge, of the love of truth; do the designations and the things coincide? Is language the adequate expression of all realities?...What is a word? The expression of a nerve stimulus in sounds. But to infer a cause outside us from the nerve stimulus is already the result of a wrong and unjustifiable application of the proposition of causality. How should we dare, if truth with the genesis of language, if the point of view of certainty with the designations had alone been decisive; how indeed should we dare to say: the stone is hard; as if 'hard' was known to us otherwise, and not merely as an entirely subjective stimulus!"

8.1.) But can anything be known without being a subjective stimulus—i.e., without being a percept or a thought? Can I see anything without seeing it? Can I think of anything without thinking of it? Stupid idiot of a moron! Can I perceive without perceiving—i.e., without my sight's being affected by a stimulus from the thing perceived which as it impinges upon my eyes is converted by them and my mind into a percept, into an image of the thing? Can I think of anything without its becoming my thought of it, without the intervention of my idea of it? I can only perceive a thing by reducing it into a percept of it; I can think of a thing, a state of affairs, only by transforming it into a thought of it, an idea, a concept, of it. An exploding volcano cannot be accommodated by my eyes or my mind, a percept of it can, an idea of it can...What then is Nietzsche saying here? That only the volcano itself exploding inside my head is a faithful and true perception of it, thought, idea, of it? No? Then, he is saying that there cannot at all be a true perception, a true idea or thought of anything whatsoever? And why? And, more importantly, how did he come to know that?

8.1.1.) The actually automatic reduction of the exploding volcano into a percept, an image of it, or a concrete idea, a thought of it which my senses and my mind effectuate is a scaling down production of a homology between my perception or my idea of the thing and the thing itself, the exploding volcano. The automaticity testifies to a pre-existing logical sameness or homology between thought and being, between the logic of perception/thought and the logic of being/becoming. The percept is a model, a simulation of the exploding volcano; and so are the mathematical equations of the most advanced physics—which is why they can predict, for instance, the red shift or the existence of hitherto unknown entities...The proof of the truth of perceptual homology is immediately praxiological:--if you doubt that there's an exploding volcano there, go ahead and go there near enough to be also exploded by it:--but only philosophers, solipsistic ones, will be capable of the dishonesty and psychotic effrontery of pretending to doubt it. As for the mathematical homology in physics, the predictions made possible by it are the proof. This homologizing knowledge and truth is in the ultimate analysis what any theory of knowledge/truth must assume which argues for the possibility of knowledge/truth at all. But this is also what any nihilistic theory like Nietzsche must in the ultimate analysis assume in order to deny.

8.2.) According to Nietzsche here, it is wrong and unjustifiable for me to say that my perception of what I am typing on this laptop monitor, and of the monitor itself, and of the keys of the keyboard, and even of my hands as I type, and of the laptop itself and of my writing table and of my body, indeed of myself, as I am typing this right now, are in any way caused by what in all these cases I am perceiving, namely, all of the above out there. Which is to say that it is not true that what I perceive in all of the above cases are out there in the external world. Which is to say that I cannot use my perception of the external world to prove that there is an external world at all. This is the Kantian crime of course which consists in the claim that physical, spacetime reality is nothing but a subjective construct, and the thing in itself, the reality-in-itself, which as such is not spacetime or physical reality, is unknowable—that it is and what it is. And of course, Nietzsche who is a Schopenhauerian idealist is a Kantian. That is to say, in the ultimate analysis, a solipsist. In a word, insane.

8.3.) I grasp a stone—it is hard. Then I touch a piece of cake—it is soft. If I can be certain that stones and cakes exist out there in the external world, then by means of the contrast I can verify and demonstrate that it is true that stone is hard—and cake is soft. If nevertheless Nietzsche here says I can never be certain that stone is hard and cake is soft, because "hard' and 'soft' are nothing but "subjective stimuli", then it must be because to Nietzsche the solipsist, the world which seems to be out there is nothing but a subjective stimulus or so many subjective stimuli. Commonsense realism, the realism of the wo/man in the street, as well as of the mathematical physicist, knows that there is a world out there against which to check and even measure with utmost exactitude that a stone is hard rather than soft, or is in any case harder than a chiffon cake. Diamond is hard not because we say it's hard; we sanely say it is hard because it is hard. It is this everyday realism which is ontologically the same as scientific realism, that here as elsewhere we philosophically defend. It is this philosophical defense that makes of it a philosophy and not a mere hardheaded insistence. Ours is the first everyday realist and scientific realist philosophy ever.

8.4.) Can Nietzsche, according to his own premises, even know that there are subjective stimuli and that they are subjective and not rather "objective" stimulations, frontal or vis a tergo like a knife in the back or from on high like that stimulus dropped singly upon Hirosima and Nagasaki? Because here Nietzsche will be reduced to invoking a certain self-evidence that supposedly pertains to the immediate grasp or reception or impingement of stimuli or sense data. Which self-evidence cannot be more evident than the same kind of self-evidence of perception on the basis of which we immediately know that there is a world out there and what that world is. Can I know what the subjective is without its at once becoming objective? For his experience of his own existence and reality as the "I" he is must also be as a mere subjective stimulus from which, according to his own nihilistic-solipsistic reasoning or "ontology," the existence in itself, the reality in itself, of anything behind the stimulus can only be delusively inferred. From which reasoning it follows that he does not even have the warrant to think himself existing or real.

9.0.) "We divide things according to genders; we designate the tree as masculine, the plant as feminine: what arbitrary metaphors! How far flown from the canon of certainty! We speak of a 'serpent'; the designation fits nothng but the sinuousity, and could therefore also appertain to the worm. What arbitrary demarcations! What onesided preferences given sometimes to this, sometimes to that quality of a thing! The different languages placed side by side show that with words truth or adequate expression matters little: for otherwise there would not be so many languages." There are so many languages because there were and are so many tribes, peoples, nations, and not because "with words truth or adequate expression matters little," which is an atrocious non sequitur. As though a language of pure and absolute truths or of absolute adequation between designation and the infinite details of the designated were possible or even necessary. Such a language, by the way, would be that of omniscient beings, Gods', or God's should he be inclined or should it even be possible for him to talk to himself. In other words, the "canon of certainty" invoked by Nietzsche here in order to judge and disqualify our merely human all too human certainty where there is no absolute correspondence between the words and the infinitely many details of the "things" they designate, is theological, is luridly metaphysical; which at once betrays Nietzsche's reasoning here as that of negative theology or negative metaphysics, which indeed is the standard reasoning of skeptics and nihilists in their self-slapping naivete. Truth is absolute, i.e., Godly, omniscient, certainty; but man is capable only of ungodly, "merely anthropomorphic" certainty; therefore truth is impossible for man; or, there is no God, omniscience is impossible, ergo, truth is impossible... And this negative metaphysical or negative theological reasoning by this negative priest/metaphysician Nietzsche is indeed what is at work here. God is Truth; there is no God, God is impossible; ergo there is no truth, truth is impossible. And this indeed is the reasoning that gave rise to all the rotten egg books of such Nietzscheites as Derrida, Foucault, Deleuze, all the post-structuralists and postmodernists who are all his disciples. Which of course is not original to Nietzsche, for this is the hitherto undisclosed, undescried standard operating procedure, the hidden logic of scepticism and nihilism, from Carvaka to Buddha, to Zeno of Elea and Gorgias of Leontini, to Hume, to empiricism in general (I consider it one of my fundamental contributions to philosophy to have uncovered and exposed this hidden logic of negative metaphysics—and of its positivist correlative). This is the raw nerve of their, of negative metaphysics/theology's, massmurderous because nihilistic, ultimately, world-historically capitalist, globally genocidal capitalist stupidity:--they so desperately believe in God that realizing that there is no God, and acknowledging at last that God is impossible, they have to conclude that therefore there is no true knowledge, there is no truth, and truth is impossible! And no one indeed can believe in God more than that! In light of which we now have to ask, can ask: but why be so perverse as to define knowledge and truth and certainty theologically-metaphysically thus? To which the answer is simply—because metaphysics, positivist (as in Parmenides, Plato, Aristotle, Christianity, Hegel), or negativist, is perversity itself. Globally genocidal perversity, absolutely violent perversity... In both positivist and negativist metaphysics, it is also the perversity of reducing the ontological-existological reality of the human being, of human existence, of humanity itself into a delusive derivative and epiphenomenon of the Divine or of the metaphysical Absolute—of God, Brahma, Nous, the Good, Pure Act, Absolute Spirit, etc., in positivist metaphysics; of Nirvana, of Money-Capital in negative metaphysics. This ultimate negation or denial of the ontologico-existological reality, integrity, dignity of the human being and of humanity per se is equivalent to a denial of the reality of freedom, of human existence itself, of human subjectivity itself, of morality, of the world itself insofar as it is the world affirmed by human beings, and thus of knowledge, certainty, truth, insofar as this is the knowledge, certainty, truth affirmed by these delusive and ultimately unreal subjects who happen to be us everyday, commonsense, flesh and blood social-historical human beings. Thus, all of Nietzsche's ludicrous arguments here are designed to show that knowledge and truth and true certainty are impossible to everyday, commonsense, realist human beings. Metaphysics, positivist or negativist is pure and absolute, absolutist dogmatism (as we have repeatedly demonstrated elsewhere). God or the metaphysical Absolute is the impossible itself and can only be affirmed self-contfradictorily, and therefore blindly, dogmatically. Metaphysicians, and here Nietzsche, must of course not see this dogmatism for what it most stupidly is:--metaphysics, or theology, is naivete itself and stupidity itself; it is even, thus, fascism itself. Instead, the metaphysician automatically declares that it is the realism of the everyday man, of commonsense, and therewith of the physical scientist, that is dogmatic.Circumstantially, Nietzsche repeats this here, as we shall in a while see.

9.1.) Nietzsche says human language does not care for the truth; he says power-opportunism is what rules the invention and use of words and not the desire for truth. And this he purports to show by discovering banal and trivial discrepancies between what the word is able to designate of the thing itself in utter abstractness and skimpiness and the infinite details which true because divine language alone can adequately designate and express. Hence, truth is impossible for mere humans who merely speak this language. Actually, there is implicit in this arrant naivete a claim to omniscience, to being God: this disqualification of the human point of view because it cannot measure up to God's is in effect a claim to know what only God can know (buti na lang walang Diyos!), a surreptitious occupation of his Throne on high. The figure is the same for Kant in his claim that there is a thing-in-itself which is not this spatiotemporal world of everyday existence and of physics, and it is unknowable. To know that there is an unknowable is already to know it. To know the unknowable to be such as to be unknowable is to know it—completely. Only God can say there is an unknowable and that it is unknowable, because only God can know it absolutely as such and know it absolutely completely to be unknowable. Of course, since God is God, he would know it absolutely completely and thus know it to be not unknowable at all.

10.0) "The 'Thing-in-itself' (it is just this which would be the pure ineffective truth) is also quite incomprehensible to the creator of language and not worth making any great endeavour to obtain. He designates only the relations of things to men and for their expression he calls to his help the most daring metaphors. A nerve stimulus, first transformed into a percept! First metaphor! The percept again copied into a sound! Second metaphor! And each time he leaps completely out of one sphere right into the midst of an entirely different one..." Actually, Nietzsche's "thing-in-itself" is what he also calls "Chaos", but he does not mention it here. Chaos is absolute absence of identity; it is pure difference; pure becoming, pure change, and is as such absolutely unlivable. Sentient life, to be able to exist on its basis has to schematize it into a livable environment, into fixed things like food, into beings, into land, sky, sea, rivers, streets, into other dogs, other cats, other people. It is absolutely crazy and unwordably idiotic. To this forthrightly nihilist Nietzsche, even the self, the "I", is nothing but a schematization by, apparently, "itself"! The idiocy is boundless. According to Nietzsche the very being of things is mere construct, mere schematization. When convenient, he descends to this the deepest level of his insanity. But here, he contents himself with an adumbration of the "thing-in-itself" that gets "designated" through the most fantastic transfiguration of socalled "nerve stimulus" impinging upon nerve ends and getting transformed into a "percept"—an "image," apparently? Which, in its second transfiguration becomes metaphorized into a spoken word, a sounded meaning!

10.1.) "When we talk about trees, colors, snow, and flowers, we believe we know something about the things themselves, and yet we only possess metaphors of the things, and these metaphors do not in the least correspond to the original essentials..." So Nietzsche after all knows what the original essentials are! But how? When all all of us can do in being mere human speakers is delude ourselves with mere metaphors that must necessarily miss out on the "original essentials"? The metaphysician is—God!

11.0.) "Let us especially think about the formations of ideas. Every word becomes at once an idea not by having, as one might presume, to serve as a reminder for the original experience happening but once and absolutely individualized, to which experience such word owes its origin, no, but by having simultaneously to fit innumerable, more or less similar (which really means never equal, therefore altogether unequal) cases. Every idea originates through equalizing the unequal. As certainly as no one leaf is exactly similar to any other, so certain is it that the idea 'leaf' has been formed through an arbitrary omission of these individual differences, through a forgetting of the differentiating qualities, and this idea now awakens the notion that in nature there is, besides the leaves, a something called the 'leaf', perhaps a primal form according to which all leaves are woven, drawn, accurately measured, colored, crinkled, painted, but by unskilled hands." Dog perception must at once be able to recognize dogs from cats, from the rest of the animal kingdom. Even more so, the finally evolved human perception must be able to perceive each human individual as a member of the species homo, and therewith each tree as a member of the tree species, each grain of sand as a member of the class of things called buhangin or sand, each patch of cloud as an instance of that general phenomenon called cloud, etc. But even a blur or a splotch or a blot can be perceived by us as a blur, splotch, blot, among other such or in their unlikeness, like many such. There then is no such thing as an "absolutely individualized original experience" of a thing, a leaf, say, or a tree—not even seeing stars after a wrathful bludgeon descends upon your will to power head…

PART I: THE RIZAL-ILUSTRADO COUNTERREVOLUTION & THE PRODUCTION AND REPRODUCTION OF THE MOST CORRUPT RULING CLASS IN WORLD HISTORY

AND ITS PRODUCTION AND REPRODUCTION OF THE PHILIPPINE CULTURE OF CORRUPTION MAKING THE PHILIPPINES THUS THE MOST CORRUPT NATION- STATE IN THE WORLD'S HISTORY

Chapter 1

RIZAL WAS A RACIST AND GENOCIDAL MURDERER OF FILIPINOS IN REJECTING, DENOUNCING AND BETRAYING THE REVOLUTION AND THE FILIPINO PEOPLE…

OR: RIZAL'S SUICIDE MISSION TO KILL ANDRES BONIFACIO AND SUPPRESS THE REVOLUTION…

{To quash confusion, and thin out considerably the expectable disbelief of Filipinos brainwashed by all the lying and perverted historians for 120 years now, this also is what we have discovered, exhaustively documented, and demonstrated beyond any but insane doubt in view of the unquestioned fact that Rizal was against the Revolution, that in all his writings he was directly, forthrightly and even angrily, nay rabidly angry against it, that there is no mention whatsoever of Revolution in his writings in which he did not attack and condemn it: *it was Andres Bonifacio himself who invented the "heroic," "patriotic," "Filipino nationalist" Rizal who supposedly awakened the Filipinos to revolt, etc.; and this he did against the horrified rejection and condemnation of the Revolution by Rizal himself (as Rizal himself testified), in order, by misrepresenting him to be the Revolution's leader and inspiration, to induce the rich Filipinos to join the Revolution--the very same ones whom Rizal through the Assimilationist Propaganda Movement had pre-recruited against the Revolution.*}

***

Quite a number of years ago now, I discovered an ultimate scandal: the Philippine Revolution as depicted in all the textbooks and portrayed in all the films, the plays, the novels, the short stories, the journalistic commentaries, the holiday rituals and government programs on the subject did not exist. That is to say, it never happened. Not merely that it never happened that way, no; but that it "happened" in a violently opposite way.

And in a deviously, invidiously violent, opposite way.

Such that what is there of "revolution" is anything but revolution, and the "history" of it is anything except history.

In all the textbooks and the other media, everything about the Revolution is a lie. But it is not a simple lie. It is an inversion. And it is not a simple inversion either. It is a distorted, perverted, twisted inversion. It is pure fiction. But not a simple fiction. It is a vicious fiction. And the viciousness of the fiction is not all random—it is for the most part systematic. This systematicity was, is, primarily class-determined, and, secondarily, in connection with the genocidal Aguinaldo Counterrevolution, tribally twisted. All the Philippine historians thus far have written and repeated one and the same main narrative as neo-colonial capitalist ideological class-agents and thus as apologists of the most corrupt ruling class in world history, one that had, as former collaborationist native colonial middleclass, betrayed the Revolution and sold the country and the people three times, to the Spaniards, to the Americans, and to the Japanese. National traitors, in other words; the bloodiest and most devious of whom was Jose Rizal, the infamous leader of the assimilationist, necessarily counterrevolutionary, genocidal, "the Philippines as a province of Spain" Propaganda Movement, which recruited the entire colonial middleclass, the entire native rich, against the Revolution:--this explains why after four years of recruiting, and when the Revolution was already archipelagic, the Katipuneros were still practically without guns and bullets and were forced to face the cannons, mausers and remingtons of the Spanish colonial army with bows and arrows, buho spears and boloes. Suppuratingly venal and absolutely unprincipled genocidal traitors against the Revolution, the people, the country, this Rizalianly perverted ruling class is thus the most corrupt ruling class the world has ever seen. Which, as a matter of course, accounts for this world-famous culture of corruption that has made the Philippines the most corrupt country in the world. Thus, Jose Rizal lies at the fount and origin, too, of the Philippine culture of corruption. He is directly responsible for producing the monstrous oligarch and tyrant, the latest version of Emilio Aguinaldo, Ferdinand Marcos, the brigand Erap, and Trump's brown twin of utterest vulgarity and obscenest crudity--Rodrigo Roa Duterte…And Duterte's NCCA (National Commission for Culture and the Arts) Chair, Virgilio Almario… .

It goes without saying that my discovery of this vicious fiction is the same as my discovery that all those vicious fictionists responsible for the production and reproduction of this vicious fiction not only do not know how to use documents to prove a historiographic point—they never used any. For they do not even see the need to prove a point, documentarily, or otherwise. This vicious fiction is all hearsay, tsismis, shaggily proliferant; blown this way or that by class, tribal, regional, clan, personal, even animal, prejudices, and by an all-powerful bêtise.

The new History that, simultaneously with my discovery of this vicious fiction, I of course discovered, is thus the first and only documented Philippine History there is to-date. This new History is, needless to say, absolutely shocking to us Filipinos. That is why we have to document in the most exhaustive way and retrace with utmost critical rigour its every twist and turn.

Shocking—and none more so than this central aspect of it that concerns our former National Hero, Dr. Jose Rizal...

Everything Rizal wrote that bore any connection with the Revolution was a rejection and a denunciation of it. In my classes and in my many lectures in UP Diliman, UP Baguio,

UP Manila, PUP, and in several national conferences and symposia, it has become a habit on my part to challenge the audience to cite even just a single sentence by Rizal that directly or indirectly advocated revolution or Philippine independence from Spanish colonial rule.

Every political sentence then that Rizal wrote constitutes a document that testifies to his rejection and denunciation of the Revolution--and to his unrelenting opposition to, nay, abhorrence of, independence.

From out of that mass of counterrevolutionary and anti-independence documents, four stand out for their insurpassable shamelessness and malevolence. They are, in their order of temporal appearance, 1.) Rizal's Letter of Absolute Sacrifice & of Absolute Spanish Heroism to Governor General Ramon Blanco written and delivered between August 21 and 23, 1896, offering to the Spaniards unconditionally,--as a token of his unconditional love of and devotion to his Mother Spain and therewith his unconditional abandonment and betrayal of his native land and the Filipino people--all his "good services," his very life, and even his name, for them to use "in the manner they might deem best, to suppress the rebellion"; 2.) Rizal's Data for My Defense, written on December 12, 1896; 3.) his December 15, 1896 Fort Santiago Manifesto; and 4.) his Additional Data for My Defense, written on December 26, 1896.

Let us present and analyze them here. But before we make such presentation it will greatly facilitate comprehension if we first make a brief calendar of events in order in its light to more concretely contextualize these documents. Let us begin with the Rape of Calamba by the Dominican friars.

1.) October 1891, The Rape of Calamba—the Dominicans forcibly expropriated the town of Calamba, claiming it to be part of their estate of the diocese of Binan. They assaulted the town at the head of 500 heavily armed soldiers lent them by Gov. Gen. Valeriano Weyler. All the inhabitants were driven out of the town. All the wealthy families were exiled including Rizal's. Rizal himself related in a letter to a fellow reformist the case of a woman named Estanislawa, who was raped and dismembered by the Dominicans. The same Dominicans burned the whole town. This event prompted Rizal's second return to the Philippines. He first stationed himself in Hong Kong and was able within a few months to gather his entire exiled family in a house there.

2.) June 20, 1892, Rizal wrote two letters, one addressed to "The Filipinos," and the other to his family and friends. He told them that he was going home to the

Philippines to die at the hands of the friars, and "to put the finishing touch to my life's work". He was expecting that after killing him the friars would restore his family and his town-mates to their homes. He imagined that his death would create a universal scandal that would impel the Madrid government to expel the friars from the Philippines, expropriate their properties, restore the lands and houses grabbed by the friars to their colonial middle class owners like the Rizal family, and finally assimilate the Philippines as a province of Spain. This was what he meant by his "putting the finishing touch to my life's work." This was his Assimilationist Martyrdom Plot. Needless to say, the whole thing was a grandiose delusion of an irreparable mental-colonial counterrevolutionary agent.

) June 22, 1892, Rizal left Hong Kong for Manila.

) June 26, 1892, Rizal arrived in Manila.

) Between June 26 and July 6, 1892, Bonifacio presented to Rizal what Rizal himself called Bonifacio's "plan" to launch the "rebellion" (Rizal's of course ignorant, disbelieving, downsizing term for the Revolution); Rizal bitterly opposed it and vehemently argued against it. (Bonifacio had actually officially founded the Revolution as early as February 19,

1892, as attested to by The Minutes of the Katipunan.)

6.) July 2, 1892, Rizal launched the Liga Filipina as an integral part of his Assimilationist Martyrdom Plot. In the first place, he wanted to provoke the friars to have him arrested and martyred soon enough. Launching such a suspicious organization as the Liga was such a sure-fire provocation. Secondly, he, in his assimilationist delirium and megalomaniacal self-estimation, was expecting that, as a result of his scandalous murder by the friars, the Filipinos would at last become assimilated Spaniards who would need to unite in order to secure the concrete reality of their formally granted rights as brand-new citizens of Spain. He expertly designed the Liga for that purpose.

7.) July 6, 1892, Rizal was arrested.

8.) July 7, 1892, Andres Bonifacio (supposedly) formally founded the Revolution, supposedly in reaction to the arrest of Rizal . (I have discovered a few months ago however that, according to the MINUTES OF THE KATIPUNAN, Bonifacio formally founded the Revolution on February 19, 1892!)

9.) July 13, 1892, Rizal was exiled to Dapitan.

10.) Sometime in November, 1892, during the (supposed) presidency of Deodato Arellano, the Katipunan sent an emissary to Rizal. He betrayed the Katipunero to the military governor who, according to Rizal, “sent him to Manila”. Needless to say, the Katipunero emissary must have been tortured to death. We can conclude that he died without confessing anything about the Revolution; otherwise, it would have been discovered that early.

11.) During the four years that he stayed in Dapitan, there were attempts by family and friends to "rescue" him or facilitate his escape. He refused all of them. This is important because it confirmed his rejection of the Revolution.

12.) November 23, 1895—In a letter, Blumentritt informed Rizal that the Spaniards needed military doctors in Cuba in order to help them kill as many Cuban Katipuneros as possible. He advised him to apply.

13.) November 25, 1895—Rizal replied to Blumentritt saying it (i.e., the Cuban international counterrevolutionary doctoral project) was an excellent idea and that he was applying at once.

14.) July 1, 1896—Dr. Pio Valenzuela arrived in Dapitan to confer with Rizal concerning the Revolution. Through Valenzuela, Bonifacio invited Rizal to join the Revolution and even offered him its leadership. Rizal refused. According to Rizal, he was able instead to convince Valenzuela to abandon the Revolution, which the latter did. Upon his return to Manila, Valenzuela the traitor surrendered to the Spaniards, begged their forgiveness, and betrayed many of his former comrades.

15.) July 31, 1896—Governor General Blanco's letter accepting Rizal's application and designating him as a Spanish military doctor assigned to Cuba arrived.

16.) August 1, 1896—Rizal in great hurry sailed to Manila to catch the mailboat to Spain.

17.) August 4, 1896—Rizal arrived in Manila but missed the mailboat and had had to wait a whole month for the next boat to Spain.

18.) August 5, 1896—Rizal requested his friend Gov. Gen. Blanco to hide him and hold him incommunicado except to his immediate family. He was evidently afraid of getting into any kind of contact with the Revolution, which, from Valenzuela, he knew, could get exposed anytime.

19.) Night of August 6, 1896—Rizal was transferred to the Spanish warship Castilla; however, before the transfer, Emilio Jacinto was able to climb the boat and offered to take him away. Rizal refused.

20.) August 19, 1896—The Revolution was exposed by Fr. Mariano Gil.

Let us now present the documents.

1.0.) The Letter of Absolute Sacrifice & of Absolute Spanish Heroism.

Of course we have not seen this letter, and it is entirely possible that only three people had read it at all, namely Rizal, Blanco, and the Spanish commander of the warship Castilla, Col. Santalo, who signed it as witness to the great Spanish heroic deed of our foremost national traitor. Col. Santalo (whose first name Rizal neglected to mention in his references to this letter of absolute treason, no doubt because as a Spanish military officer everyone in the Military Court knew who he was) was Rizal's gallant host when for 27 days he, through his own request, was hidden incommunicado on that warship by Gov. Gen. Blanco.

Rizal had hoped to pressure the court enough for it to order the presentation of that letter by no less than its addressee, Gov. Gen. Blanco himself. He was however outmaneuvered once more by his mortal enemies, the friars, who were able to have Blanco removed from office a few hours before he could thus testify on Rizal's behalf. Had Blanco been allowed to testify thus, and still as the Governor General that he was, it was almost a certainty that Rizal would have been exonerated and freed.

Blanco must have known that he was being replaced and sent home, and must have alerted Rizal about it. Rizal made the revelation of that letter of absolute sacrifice to the court on December 12. The very next day, Blanco was, so to speak, terminated, and Polavieja assumed office. The all-important letter was never presented as evidence in court. It is entirely possible that a long long time ago the letter as a material artifact had ceased to exist. Which is not to say—and of course!—that it had ceased to exist as a symbolic, cultural, political, historical, and yes, literary, and, if you want, even a spiritual thing, in that case an evil spiritual thing. A transcendent thing—that is to say, a thing that transcends mere nature, like a smile, for instance, or a kiss, or a work of art, or, in this particular case of Rizal's letter of absolute treason, a work of evil, of moral, political, and historical evil and of unspeakable shamelessness.

We are therefore presenting this absolutely crucial document here in absentia. And that means presenting it in the light of Rizal's own references to it in the self-evidentiating context of the trial. These references can be found, perhaps nowhere else than, in the three other documents.

1.1. In the December 15, 1896 Fort Santiago Manifesto, Rizal wrote: "From the very beginning, when I first learned of what was being planned" (namely, the Revolution), "I opposed it, fought it, and demonstrated its absolute impossibility. This is the fact, and witnesses to my words are now living. I was convinced that the scheme" (namely the planned Revolution) "was utterly absurd and, what was worse, would bring great sufferings. I did even more. When, later, against my advice, the movement materialized, of my own accord, I offered, not alone my good offices, but my very life, and even my name, to be used in whatever way they might deem best towards stifling the rebellion..."(Rizal's Political & Historical Writings, National Historical Institute, 2007, p 350). Rizal did not say, in the eloquent evil and grandiloquent shamelessness of this manifesto, when and where and to whom and how he made his offer of absolute sacrifice. These details he supplied in the two other documents.

1.2. In the December 12, 1896 Data for my Defense, Rizal wrote: "...Nay, when the uprising broke out, I was on the Castilla, incommunicado, and I offered myself unconditionally to His Excellency (a thing I had not done before) to suppress the rebellion. But this was a personal letter and it was witnessed by Col. Santalo. This cannot be used without the permission of His Excellency." (ibid., p. 339) He has here neglected to tell us when his offer of absolute sacrifice was made. This he let us know in the fourth document we are considering.

1.3. In the December 26, 1896 Data for my Defense, Rizal wrote: "When the movement started, I was on board the Castilla and I placed myself at His Excellency's service unconditionally. Twelve or fourteen days later, I sailed for Europe..." (ibid., p. 353). Rizal sailed on September 4, 1896. Counting fourteen or twelve days backwards (he himself was not very sure of the exact date), we have August 21 or 23 as the date of the letter.

2.0.) The December 15, 1896 Fort Santiago Manifesto
"Countrymen: On my return from Spain, I learned that my name had been in use among some who were in arms, as a war cry. The news came as a painful surprise, but, believing it already closed, I kept silent about an incident which I considered irremediable. Now I notice indications of the disturbances continuing, and if any still, in good or bad faith, are availing themselves of my name, to stop this abuse and undeceive the unwary, I hasten to address you these lines that the truth may be known.

"From the very beginning, when I first learned of what was being planned, I opposed it, fought it, and demonstrated its absolute impossibility. This is the fact and witnesses to my words are now living. I was convinced that the scheme was utterly absurd and, what was worse, would bring great sufferings. I did even more. When, later, against my advice, the movement materialized, of my own accord, I offered, not alone my good offices but my very life, and even my name, to be used in whatever way they might deem best towards stifling the rebellion; for, convinced of the ills which it would bring, I would have considered myself fortunate if, at any sacrifice, I could prevent such useless misfortunes. This, equally, is of record.

"My countrymen, I have given proofs that I am one most anxious for the liberties of our country, and I am still desirous of them. But I place as a prior condition the education of the people, that by means of instruction and industry, our country may have an individuality of its own, and make itself worthy of liberties. I have recommended in my writings study and civic virtues, without which there is no redemption. I have written likewise (and I repeat my words) that reforms, to be beneficial, must come from above, for those that come from below are irregular and insecure. Holding these ideas, I cannot do less than condemn, and I do condemn, this savage and absurd uprising plotted behind my back, which dishonours us Filipinos, and discredits those who would plead our cause. I abhor its criminal methods and disclaim any part in it, pitying from the bottom of my heart the unwary who have been deceived.

"Return then to your homes, and may God pardon those who have worked in bad faith!

Signed: Jose Rizal
Fort Santiago, December 15, 1896"

2.1.) In the long essay The Philippines A Century Hence (written at a time when he was finishing the novel El Filibusterismo), revolution was that "unfortunate rupture" which is "an evil for all". Everywhere in his works, the idea of revolution is advanced in order to scare the Spanish ruling class and the Madrid government to grant assimilation status to the Philippines ("the Philippines as a province of Spain," etc.) with all the accompanying "reforms" ("expulsion of the friars," "return to their former Filipino owners," like the Rizal, Del Pilar, Jaena families, of the churchfully and evangelically landgrabbed "friar lands", etc.), at once, very soon, or else—or else, the rapacious and sadistic friars through their unlimited greed and rampant lusts would soon enough push the Indios, the native masses, into revolution.

Here, in this Manifesto, revolution, no longer as mere idea but in its Katipunan actuality, is cursed, insulted, and calumniated as irrational, absurd, impossible, savage, criminal, as dishonour to the Filipinos, and fomented by people who, because undiplomaed and lacking in civic virtues (which, here, is Rizal's way of saying, "uncivilized"), are therefore not true, not real human beings yet and therefore do not yet deserve to be free!

It is not only justice that is denied in its postponement but that of which the active affirmation of justice is but a part, namely, humanity. Whilst he, of course, is a fascist who denies the humanity of human beings anytime, anywhere, and to whatever degree. Colonialism does exactly that, and does it to an entire people, and throughout centuries. Colonialism is fascism, massive, multicenturial fascism. And Rizal the colonialist defender of Spanish colonialism who in that infamous offertory letter of absolute sacrifice considers himself "fortunate" if he could die defending it against the Filipino people's collective attempt to put an end to it, namely the Revolution? Fascist of course!--a multicenturial fascist! Like that (falsely and absurdly) rumoured son of his, Adolf Hitler...

2.2.)"On my return from Spain...":--Rizal was referring here to his final return to the Philippines which must have been sometime in November 1896, in the wake of his foiled attempt to become a national Spanish hero in Cuba by helping mightily kill Cuban Katipuneros there as a most valiant and heroic Spanish military doctor—an international counter-revolutionary and a till-death-do-us-part defender of European global colonialism.

That this avowal of life-and-death devotion to his Mother Spain, and of his martyric, his suicidal, dedication to the cause of eternal Spanish colonialism, of his unwavering readiness to die for the defense of Spanish colonialism whenever that colonialism was being threatened by revolution anywhere in the world—that this Spanish international counterrevolutionary super-patriotism of his was no mere conservationist affectation, or pose, or rhetoric, or opportunist ploy was, as we have already begun to see, even more dramatically demonstrated in the crime of crimes he here boasts about to his Spanish military judges, namely, his "unconditional" offering of himself, of his very life, of his very name, of all his services, i.e., of anything whatsoever that the Spaniards might order him to do, to "suppress the rebellion"—to murder Andres Bonifacio and put down the Katipunan Revolution, for instance.

He was ordered re-arrested on board the Isla de Panay on September 28, 1896 somewhere on the Mediterranean Sea, thanks to the tremendous pressure exerted by the friars on the Spanish government in those days of intense panic and terror, and upon reaching Barcelona was shipped back immediately to the Philippines to face trial. Here he is saying that as he arrived in the Philippines as a prisoner once more, he learned of how his name was being used by, of course Andres Bonifacio and his Katipunero comrades, as a "war cry".

"Countrymen: On my return from Spain, I learned that my name had been in use among some who were in arms, as a war cry. The news came as a painful surprise, but, believing it already closed, I kept silent about an incident which I considered irremediable. Now I notice indications of the disturbances continuing, and if any still, in good or bad faith, are availing themselves of my name, to stop this abuse and undeceive the unwary, I hasten to address you these lines that the truth may be known…From the very beginning, when I first learned of what was being planned, I opposed it, fought it, and demonstrated its absolute impossibility. This is the fact and witnesses to my words are now living...."

3.0.) "The news came as a painful surprise..." Rizal had been forewarned by that other ilustrado traitor, Dr. Pio Valenzuela in Dapitan on July 1, 1896, that the Revolution could break out anytime and that he could get implicated in it. He might not have been primed by this other traitor doctor though that this implication could be as horrible as Bonifacio and company's using his name as a war cry. We can then believe that he was quite surprised when he came to learn about this "war cry" thing. As for its being "painful," nothing could indeed be more painful and absurd to this brown Spaniard of most ardent Spanish patriotism and burning love of Mother Spain (and thus hatred and fear, horror and abhorrence and execration of revolution) than such abuse of his brown Spanish name and such pollution of his brown Spanish honour.

4.0.) "...and if any still, in good or bad faith, are availing themselves of my name, to stop this abuse..." Let us merely point out here that this brown Spanish lover of his very own Mother Spain curses and excoriates Bonifacio and his Katipunero comrades and, in that the archipelagic spread of the Revolution in effect constituted a full ratification of it by the Filipino people who also first became the Filipino people at that exact moment of their unification into such by the Revolution, curses and excoriates thus the Filipino people also, in making use of his name for revolutionary purposes; whilst he here boasts to his Spanish judges of how when the Revolution broke out he spontaneously and unconditionally offered to the Spanish authorities that very name of his, and with it his very life and all his services, for the Spaniards to use in the manner they might deem best to "suppress the rebellion"!

5.0.) "..to stop this abuse and undeceive the unwary, I hasten to address you these lines that the truth may be known..." The "truth", and, but, indeed the truth, namely, that: 1.) even before it was born, he, Rizal, had already done the greatest harm and damage to the Revolution by most powerfully rallying the entire colonial middle class against it; 2.) causing it to be delayed so:--by at least ten years, more than enough time for it to have obviated the encounter with that pestilential pig traitor hostager and vendor of it, Emilio Aguinaldo, and for it to have triumphed before the Spanish-American War, and to have pre-empted therewith the coming of American colonialism and the murder by the Americans of some 2 million Filipinos; 3.) and causing it to be sorely unfunded and practically armless even after its four underground years of archipelagic propagation, so much so that the Katipuneros had had to face the cannons and rifles of the enemy with fewer than five decrepit guns to a battalion and with plenty of buho spears, bows and arrows, and boloes; 4.) and the truth, the glorious and eloquent truth that, if his Spanish military judges did not yet know it, he, Rizal, in actual and demonstrated fact loved Spain better, more ardently, more self-sacrificingly, than any of them, loving her to very death, and that he then was actually a greater Spanish patriot than all of them:--for had he not, sometime between August 21 and 23, 1896, without the slightest compunction stabbed his own native land, his own native mother, in the back, by thus spontaneously and unconditionally offering his very life and his famous and well-palmed name and everything he could do, to the Spaniards, for them to use in whatever way they wished to suppress the Revolution that would liberate his own people from his most dearly beloved Mother Spain?

6.0.) "From the very beginning, when I first learned of what was being planned, I opposed it, fought it, and demonstrated its absolute impossibility..." When was this? Was he referring here to his conference with that other doctor ilustrado traitor Valenzuela on July 1, 1896? Or might this not have been a kind of "slip" on Rizal's part which, if they were subtler, could betray to his Spanish judges that he knew of the "planned" revolution years before, in fact, 4 years and five months before that date? For what he learned about the Revolution in Dapitan from that other ilustrado traitor doctor, Pio Valenzuela, was not a revolution being planned but a revolution which had become so huge and difficult to keep secret that it could be discovered anytime by the authorities and could thenceforth break out anytime. Which, exactly for that reason, did break out a month and 19 days after that Dapitan conference. We can then only conclude that he must have been referring here to that "first", that "very beginning," which was during the ten days from June 26, when he arrived in Manila from Hong Kong to implement his plan of assimilationist martyrdom, to July 2, when, in pursuit of this plan he launched the Liga Filipina, to his arrest on July 6, 1892. And who must have been that fiery one, that super-brilliant one who then must have toppled him and overthrown him, Jose Rizal himself, and his devious doctrine of reformism called assimilation (a synonym for "eternal colonialism" as Rizal himself formulated it in a draft essay) in his own mind and soul, and who sometime between June 26 and July 6, 1892, must have secretly conferred with Rizal to apprise him of his revolution in the making, and without a doubt to recruit him to it? None other than Andres Bonifacio, of course! Who, in founding the Revolution and making of it an archipelagic movement across four underground years, had for the first time united all the hitherto disparate tribes (which the Spanish colonizers had been using against each other) into a nation. And had thereby founded this nation itself called the Philippines. And was thus the father of this nation for being the founder, the father, of the Revolution.

At the transcendent and thus infinite depth of the life-and-death struggle for independence and for the people's sovereignty that was the Revolution itself, Andres Bonifacio and his Katipunan comrades effectively made the different tribes one people first of all and thence a nation. Andres Bonifacio was thus also at the same time the founder, the father, of the Philippine nation-state whose original form was precisely the Katipunan, the revolutionary nation-state which was the Katipunan.

Rizal and Bonifacio then, we have to assume, did confer about the Revolution sometime within those ten days. The younger but deeper, wiser, more intelligent, immeasurably huger man must have passionately argued and pleaded with the older, the tiny, depthless, narrowminded, wealth-and-privilege prejudiced and perverted colonial collaborationist mental-colonial doctoral man—to no avail. What could have happened had the doctor agreed—and accepted the proffered leadership of the Revolution?

This:--Rizal would not get arrested since he would at once go underground and from a mountain hideaway direct the propagation of the revolutionary movement; his ilustrado and other colonial middle-class confreres and sympathizers would very quickly join in; we would then have had a normal anti-colonial revolution led by the most intelligent, wealthy, young intellectuals; it would have been well-funded, and therefore well-armed; and above all, in the unique case of the Philippines, the semi-illiterate vendorial gangster boss Emilio Aguinaldo would from the outset have been stringently excluded from the circle of power—boxed-out culturally, even academically, and yes even linguistically (Aguinaldo's Spanish, as even his hagiographic documentary biographers Achutegui and Bernad could not resist pointing out and testifying to, was crude and ungrammatical) by Rizal himself and the likes of Juan Luna and Antonio Luna, Graciano Lopez Jaena, perhaps even Marcelo del Pilar, Edilberto Evangelista, Jose Alejandrino, Mariano Ponce, Emilio Jacinto, and together with these, by, most certainly, the most intelligent, the one and only genius of the group, Andres Bonifacio.

With Rizal and Bonifacio and the abovementioned ilustrado intellectuals there to organize and lead it, the semi-illiterate Aguinaldo would never have been able merely to imagine to dare what he dared and succeeded to do, namely coup d'etat Andres Bonifacio and the Katipunan, murder him, hostage the Revolution, and surrender it for pay. The uncounted Katipuneros who died by droves as they faced the cannons and remingtons and mausers of the enemy with buho spears and bows and arrows and boloes would not have been massacred thus. The Revolution would have been surer and swifter in its progress and it would have been able to liberate the country before the onset of the Spanish-American War, and the Americans would not even have been able to dream annexing us. The two million Filipinos killed by the Americans would not have been killed, and we would not have been the genocided victims of another colonialism.

7.0) "...From the very beginning, when I first learned of what was being planned, I opposed it, fought it, and demonstrated its absolute impossibility. This is the fact and witnesses to my words are now living. I was convinced that the scheme was utterly absurd and, what was worse, would bring great sufferings. I did even more. When, later, against my advice, the movement materialized, of my own accord, I offered, not alone my good offices but my very life, and even my name, to be used in whatever way they might deem best towards stifling the rebellion; for, convinced of the ills which it would bring, I would have considered myself fortunate if, AT ANY SACRIFICE, I could prevent such useless misfortunes. This, equally, is of record."

"...I opposed it, fought it, and demonstrated its absolute impossibility." Rizal, so he says here, upon learning of the planned revolution from Bonifacio and company (there were then "witnesses now living", he says), when, of course, it was such in its newness and incipiency as to be not much more than a plan, a "scheme" (he later says in this same document), opposed it, fought against its implementation, and tried to convince Bonifacio and company of its "absolute impossibility".

But Rizal, surely, had read and known about the Latin American anti-colonial Revolutions led by, among others, Bolivar through which, in a matter of six years, from 1820 to 1826, all the South American Spanish colonies (except Cuba and Puerto Rico) were able to liberate themselves from Spanish tyranny. How then could he speak here of the "absolute impossibility" of the Philippine Revolution when the equivalent of that revolution had been possible and were victorious 80 plus years ago in South America?

What kind of moral and mental, soul-stunting evil, prejudice, perversity, was it that seeped into his head to enable him to think this supposed "absolute impossibility"?

So he "demonstrated" to Bonifacio and company that it was absolutely impossible. He orates here that he opposed it and fought against it from the very beginning, and added that there were witnesses who at that point in time (December 15, 1896) were still living and could—and should!—be summoned by the Court to testify that he indeed opposed it and fought it and demonstrated its absolute impossibility. This is important. It not only inclines us, it compels us even more to believe what he says here (and elsewhere, in fact everywhere in his works and correspondence) about his being absolutely against revolution in general and the Philippine Revolution in particular:--because he says it in Court and adds that there were living witnesses whom the Court could and should summon to testify to the veracity of his claim.

8.0.) "...I was convinced that the scheme was utterly absurd and, what was worse, would bring great sufferings." "...the scheme...": this is additional indication to bolster our thesis that this first acquaintance with the fact of the Revolution happened not through that other ilustrado doctor traitor Valenzuela in Dapitan in July 1896, but through Bonifacio himself somewhere in Tondo or Binondo (the Liga was launched in the Binondo house of a Chinese mestizo assimilationist supporter, Pedro Ongjunco). Relevant to this important and very interesting chronology is also the fact that when the Liga was reconvened in April 1893, nine months after Rizal's deportation, it was ripped in two six months afterwards, in October of the same year, on the question precisely of the Revolution, and that the counterrevolutionaries (the compromisarios) who of course wanted to go on with the Propaganda Movement for eternal colonialism, i.e., assimilation, counted amongst its leaders Apolinario Mabini, who showed thereby that it was not only his legs that were lame but his mind also, or his soul, or his humanity. Bonifacio of course led the separatistas, the revolutionists who would not compromise with anything or anyone on the question of independence, and were ready to die fighting for the sovereignty of the Filipino people. Let us merely note here that when Bonifacio joined the revived Liga (he was invited as one of the leaders of the revival by Deodato Arellano who was Marcelo del Pilar's brother-in-law), the Katipunan was already fourteen months old, but that neither Arellano nor Apolinario Mabini, nor Don Domingo Franco who became president of it, nor any of the colonial middleclass or native rich members of the old Liga and now involved in the revival, knew of its existence and therefore of Bonifacio's being by then a separatist and revolutionary; this explains why when Deodato Arellano, Mabini, and Franco discovered upon investigation that Bonifacio and his men inside the Revived Liga were in actual fact such dangerous revolutionaries, they were so shocked and terrified that they moved to expel them at once. This means, among other things, that all the historians and all the textbooks are wrong about Deodato Arellano's being the first president of the Katipunan Supreme Council; in fact he might never have been a Katipunero at all. More importantly, this confutes the absurd and invidious claim by all the historians and all the textbooks that the Liga and the Katipunan were one and the same revolutionary organization, or that the latter originated from the former or was an offshoot of it as tendentiously suggested by the same historians and the same textbooks in their blithe matter-of-fact declarations that Andres Bonifacio founded the Revolution on July 7 after learning of Rizal's arrest on the night of July 6, 1892.

9.0.) "...and even my very name...":--For having used the very same name without his permission, and in the service of the Revolution, this evil writer from Calamba excoriates and curses his own Katipunero country(wo)men as criminals and absurd beings, as uneducated (they "lack education") and uncivilized (lacking in "civic virtues"), savages etc.; and now here he boasts of how he had, sometime in August of that year, offered this very name of his for the Spaniards to use in concocting stratagems that would kill as many Filipinos as possible and put down their revolution.

10.0.) "...for, convinced of the ills which it would bring, I would have considered myself fortunate if, at any sacrifice, I could prevent such useless misfortunes...":--At any sacrifice!...Here Rizal repeats his boastful resolve, originally delusively boasted about in the August 21-23, 1896 suicide mission letter to Gov. Gen. Blanco, offering to die and with his name deceive the Katipuneros in order to kill as many of them as possible and thereby "suppress the rebellion."

Can a single counterrevolutionary agent such as Rizal of course was, can a lone national traitor such as Rizal of course was, no matter how charismatic and devious in maskedly perpetrating his special and necessarily massmurderous evil such as Rizal of course was, put down, suppress, defeat, a revolution? And this revolution an anti-colonial one, a rising by a people subjugated for centuries by an alien entity, by, what else indeed but, an alien all-embracing evil, by an evil people, by a rampantly and enduringly evil because colonizing, subjugating, exploiting, oppressing, enslaving, freedom-denying, humanity-negating, necessarily mass-murderous people, such as, of course, the colonizing Spaniards were?

For of all possible kinds of revolution, the anti-colonial one is the purest, the justest; as far as it concerns the affirmation and fulfillment of that essence that sustains and maintains human beings in their humanity, it is the most imperative. In this sense, once sufficiently securely launched—as was Bonifacio's Katipunan Revolution—it is the most irreversible, the most unstoppable in its process of truth which is at the same time a people's practically ceaseless struggle for truth--for its own truth as demanded by the essence of humanity itself. Only human beings revolt; only human beings write poetry. It is for the truth of the poem which is the truth of humanity that there is revolution...

Revolution means a complete turning around or revolutionization of an entire people in their collective will (psyche, soul,) from being pacific slaves or timorous subjects of an oppressive regime into glorious rebels ready to die anytime for something which then is at once fierily demonstrated to be infinitely more important and more desirable than life itself, namely freedom and the sovereign dignity of the free. This is what we mean by human beings' being (by the very principle--which is the principle of freedom, the principle of transcendence--that makes them the human beings they are) the power to die that each of them is.

11.0.) "...I would have considered myself fortunate if, AT ANY SACRIFICE, I could prevent such useless misfortunes. This, equally, is of record.

"My countrymen, I have given proofs that I am one most anxious for the liberties of our country, and I am still desirous of them. But I place as a prior condition the education of the people, that by means of instruction and industry, our country may have an individuality of its own, and make itself worthy of liberties. I have recommended in my writings study and civic virtues, without which there is no redemption. I have written likewise (and I repeat my words) that reforms, to be beneficial, must come from above" (of course, since they are mere reforms!)), "for those that come from below" (which can only be revolution, not reforms) "are irregular and insecure. Holding these ideas, I cannot do less than condemn, and I do condemn, this savage and absurd uprising plotted behind my back, which dishonours us Filipinos, and discredits those who would plead our cause. I abhor its criminal methods and disclaim any part in it, pitying from the bottom of my heart the unwary who have been deceived.

"Return then to your homes, and may God pardon those who have worked in bad faith!
Signed: Jose Rizal
Fort Santiago, December 15, 1896."

12.0.) "...such useless misfortunes..." How utterly and exceptionally perverted Rizal's mind and person was, can be gleaned from this simple observation: Anywhere and anytime in the history of the world, the greatest heroism is universally reckoned to be that of risking life and all to liberate one's own people from foreign tyranny. Rizal did not think so. Rizal was alone (together with his ilustrado assimilationist followers of course) in thinking that such a movement for liberation as the Katipunan Revolution was nothing but an absurd and impossible occasion for "useless misfortunes". And it was not only here that he declared it to be so; for he had written it, and had presupposed and implied it, in all his propaganda works including the two lying and wrong novels. The Revolution to him was, as he put it in The Philippines a Century Hence, "the worst disaster that could befall us" and "an evil for all".

According to Rizal then, Andres Bonifacio and company were farthest from being heroes:--they were execrable villains, absurd and horrible and abhorrent inflicters of "useless misfortunes" upon the Filipino people...

12.0.) "This, equally, is of record..." Equally with what? What else in the declamatory enumeration of Rizal's crimes in this document is "of record"? Answer:--That when he first learned of the Revolution being planned he opposed it, attacked it, and demonstrated it to be "absolutely impossible"; and this because, according to Rizal here, witnesses that he did so were still living at the time of the trial, and should therefore be summoned by the court to testify on his behalf.

13.0) "My countrymen, I have given proofs that I am one most anxious for the liberties of our country, and I am still desirous of them..." Rizal's desire was for "liberties", not Liberty, not Independence, for the Filipinos. Such "liberties" were what supposedly would be granted by the Spanish colonizers to the Filipino natives by way of assimilation, making of them thus refurbished slaves. Necessarily, they were bogus freedoms, fake rights, for by definition they were to be enjoyed by the natives not as free citizens of a free country but as terms of servitude under the same colonial masters. They were not premised on the abolition of the master-slave relationship between Spanish colonizers and Filipino natives. Rather the precise contrary:--they were to be granted, and by Rizal and company were being prayed for, in order first of all to ensure the perpetuity of colonial rule, of the Philippines' remaining, as he himself put it in the draft essay, *The Philippines As A Spanish Colony*, and in the celebrated, lengthy, La Solidaridad article, *The Philippines A Century Hence*, a "Spanish possession", a "Spanish colony", "forever." And even then, sham and duplicitious freedoms and rights as they were, they were *ab initio* made impossible by the inexorable racism of the white man and of the Spanish in particular, the special violence of whose racist truculence was world-embracingly infamous. In other words, even as such bogus freedoms and prestidigitous rights, they were nothing but the wild and insane delusions of such irrefrangible mental colonies and shameless metropolitan social climbers as Jose

Rizal and his ilustrado propagandist company.

It was to secure those "liberties" that Rizal sought martyrdom when he came home on June 26, 1892. The securing of those assimilationist "liberties" by way of his death at the hands of the friars was what he meant by his being able "to put the finishing touch to my life's work" (as he put it in his June 20, 1892 letters of martyrical intent addressed to the "Filipinos" and to his family and friends, which he left in Hong Kong in the care of his friend Jose Ma. Basa, with the instruction that they be published after his expected assimilationist martyrical death—see Letter 321 in Rizal's Correspondence with Fellow Reformists, NHI, Manila.).

Rizal launched the Liga with two aims in mind, one immediate, and the other long-range. The immediate one was to make sure he would get arrested at once and martyrized thus by the friars. The long-range one was to enable the Filipinos through such national native organization to defend and make concrete those expected assimilationist "liberties".

Most importantly, the expeditious securing of those assimilationist "liberties" and therewith assimilation status for the Philippines ("the Philippines as a province of Spain", etc.) was to Rizal and his ilustrado counterrevolutionary propagandist confreres the sole and most urgently needed way to prevent "that unfortunate rupture" and "worst disaster" which was "an evil for all" from breaking out, namely, revolution.

To prevent the Revolution—i.e., Liberty, Independence—thus, was what Rizal, Del Pilar, Jaena, and his ilustrado assimilationist cohorts fought for, and it was what Rizal came home to die for on June 26, 1892. It was what he eventually died for on December 30, 1896.

14.0.) "But I place as a prior condition the education of the people, that by means of instruction and industry, our country may have an individuality of its own, and make itself worthy of liberties. I have recommended in my writings study and civic virtues, without which there is no redemption..." In other words, according to Rizal here, people who have no diploma—like Andres Bonifacio himself and Gregoria de Jesus herself—and are thus far uncivilized or insufficiently civilized in lacking certain "civic virtues" or in being deficient in good manners and right conduct, do not deserve to be free, and are as such irredeemable; in fact, they do not deserve even merely the actually fake "liberties" accorded to assimilated slaves, let alone the genuine freedoms and rights which in a colonial situation can only be had by force of arms, by revolution. In which case, if at all in Rizal's mind an enslaved people could deserve to revolt and thereby be free, they should first have diplomas and "civilized" manners. From which follows that, according to Rizal, Bonifacio and the Katipunan and the Filipino people must not be allowed to gain not only "liberties" but Liberty itself, Independence itself, and should thus not be allowed to revolt, and should be prevented at all costs from making a revolution to gain such Liberty, such Independence...And that no doubt was why he was willing and even most zealous to die to "suppress the rebellion"...

In other words, people without diploma and without "civic virtues", i.e., "uncivilized" (do not forget that he condemned Bonifacio and the Katipunan and therefore the Filipino people as a whole in archipelagic revolt as savages) do not deserve to be free—are not "worthy of liberties," let alone Liberty, Independence, and are thus "without" "redemption":--irredeemable. Does this not mean that according to Rizal, Bonifacio and the Katipuneros and with them the entire Filipino people did not (yet) belong to the human race, for, certainly, anyone who belongs there must by virtue of belonging there be such as to deserve to be free? And with what odious name shall we call this racism of this rabidest of all known and perhaps even unknown mental-colonial sycophants so evilly ignominiously aimed against his very own country(wo)men thus?

Freedom, as Rousseau was I think the first to fully realize and declare and philosophically- theoretically explicate, is every human being's birthright. "Man is born free, and yet everywhere he is in chains..."—so he says in the opening paragraphs of that epochally great and most powerful work, *The Social Contract*. And Kant, his greatest disciple in this line of ethical and political sagacity, concurs. This is true. And not because Rousseau and Kant said so, but because it is true. And that it is true anyone with enough common human sense will, once comprehended in its own self-evidentiating light, at once recognize and acknowledge to be so.

It is freedom—the fact and the principle of it—that separates the human being from the animal, human society from the animal herd. Language is the touchstone. The human being is s/he who speaks. S/he who speaks is free. The human being is above all the being who speaks. The proof and the concrete reality of freedom is language. Human society is the society of beings who speak. The human being is the being who is born into language. Language is the birthright and the primordial condition of the human being. Language is the life and the practice of freedom itself. Born into language in a collectivity of speakers, every human being is born thus into freedom. This is what is meant by Rousseau's saying that man is born free.

Note: It is hardly an exaggeration that the French Revolution was (and is) unthinkable without this little book (Rousseau's The Social Contract). In this work for the first time the thoroughly intellectual, purely philosophical insight and truth was proclaimed—and worked-out!--that the true, objective, original, and originary principle of (socio-) political constitution is not bestial might or divinely ordained power or any metaphysically endowed sovereignty to an individual or party or race or people (not "might is right" or its even more nihilistic and pigly formulation as will to power, not the divine right of kings, or the metaphysical superiority of philosopher-kings, nor the beastly metaphysics of the chosen race, nor the theological metaphysics of the Chosen People) but the freedom of the individual, and therefore the essential, the ontological, the existological equality of all human beings.

And that therefore except as founded upon the solely possible and the solely conceivable mode of relationship of *being-with* amongst free beings, namely original, originary, primordial democracy, no human society and polity can exist.

Without such underlying primordial democracy—which is such that the more profound and vigorous it is in the inevitable anti-democratic errancy and alienation of the given polity/society, the more democratic and thus authentically human such polity/society is—there can only be herds of semi-human beasts lorded over by super-beasts, or, near-future of the global-intimate western-christian capitalist society of walking-talking commodities, a society of the living-dead, a zombie colony...—in which no one, properly, existologically speaking, speaks anymore, for authentically to speak is to be free...

Notes:
1.) See his *The Philippines as a Spanish Colony*, in Rizal's Political & Historical Writings, National Historical Institute 2007; p. 355, in which among other things Rizal wrote: "We therefore say that the modification of the colonial policy in the Philippines is not impossible so that the Philippines can remain a colony as she ought to remain as such. Now we need to find out what kind of colony the Philippines *shall forever* be. For this purpose it is necessary for us to examine the different kinds of colonies..."

2.) In point of fact, and as we have documentarily demonstrated elsewhere here, Antonio Luna, Graciano Lopez Jaena, Edilberto Evangelista, Jose Alejandrino, Mariano Ponce, among others had, prior to Rizal's pre-announced and pre-advertised (by him himself) and much-debated coming home to the Philippines from Hong Kong on that June 26, 1892 day, had written Rizal fiery letters professing separatism and revolution in the mistaken belief that Rizal was going home precisely to found such revolution: in those letters, which also assured Rizal that, as Edilberto Evangelista put it, "the entire Barcelona colony" was with Rizal in finally making the leap to revolution, they volunteered their revolutionary services to their chief, Rizal!

3.) Nothing is more clearly evil than the colonial negation of the humanity of an entire people. Evil is a human being or a group of human beings denying, reducing, diminishing, injuring— negating-- the humanity of another human being or group of human beings.Only free beings can be evil or victims of evil. Nature can neither be good nor evil. Nietzsche, repeating Hobbes in reducing the human into a thing, into a calculus of forces mistakenly named "power", has merely perpetrated such reduction of the human into the natural—into cosmic force, into "life". Which then is spoken of as "beyond good and evil". The "beyond" of this "beyond good and evil" thus is another misnomer. For there is only one possibility (and actuality--in view of ourselves in the daily honesty of our good or evil or half-good half-evil existences) of a beyond here, and that is the being beyond nature of human existence, that is to say, beyond life, beyond mere life. Hence this Nietzschean "beyond good and evil" is nothing but the erasure of the human by reducing it into the natural, the cosmical.

4.) The injury done by centuries of colonial negation of the essence of humanity in the subjugated people does not concern merely and in any whatever sense does not concern mainly, the material sphere of the multi-centurially subjugated people's existence (the centuries of poverty engendered by the centuries of colonial thievery, etc.). What it pre-eminently concerns is rather the long-term injury, the deep and comprehensive harm done by such total, fascistic denial of the enslaved people's very humanity, their centuries of habituation in a degraded existence, in an honourless, dignity-less, beastified existence, engendering in them the habits of unfreedom which are at once the vices of slaves. In short, it concerns the harm done to the subject people's very capacity for humanity, for existence in collective freedom and sovereignty, and their capacity to resume their collective process and struggle for the truth of their own humanity. It is a harm and an injury that can only be reversed and surmounted by the cataclysmic upsurge of the truth of the power to die which is the collective act of defying and fighting to very death the evil, the necessarily evil, the necessarily massively perduring evil, of colonial subjugation.

5.) The power to die is the power to go beyond, to transcend, mere life and the interests of merely living, indeed to transcend being itself and the interests of being, for to risk death is to risk ceasing to be at all, and to choose to die is to reject or abandon being itself. The human being is free because s/he is this power to transcend life itself, being itself; and since this transcending is a willing, i.e., a valuing, it is a transcending towards a meaning and a value that for it is then demonstrated to be infinitely more than life itself, and is beyond being itself. This transcending, this willing, this *be-ing* free, is the origin of meaning itself.

The inability to transcend thus by some former members of humanity, notably the Western, is then a being-reduced into a certain perverse kind of piggity or beastly downfall into thingness that nevertheless somehow senses its own wretched neuterity--a commodity, a thing for sale for instance, a crude, ambiguous form of money, which is the universal instance of global-intimate capitalist man;--which must as such somehow sense its being absolutely futilely so, reflects it in his own diffuse inability to be sad... The somehow of the doing, of the existing, of the be-ing of this being and the sensing of the same as a specimen of absolute futility is what is called nihilism, the state of the total nullity of the human, sensing, feeling itself as such. It is this sensing, this feeling, that separates the nihilist from the robot or indeed this footstool or even that toad over there, no not that one that affects to be able to read but that literal one over there--there; the latter, but not necessarily the former, does not and cannot know itself to be the existence, the fact, itself of absolute meaninglessness.

Chapter 2

RIZAL'S ASSIMILATIONIST MENTAL-COLONIAL SPANISH-PATRIOTIC ANTI-FILIPINO, ANTI-SEPARATIST, ANTI-INDEPENDENCE ANTI-REVOLUTIONARY MADMAN'S FURY...

Philippines! Today, August 19, a hundred and twenty one years ago, Rizal was shocked into assimilationist mental-colonial Spanish patriotic anti-Filipino, anti-separatist, anti-Independence, anti-Revolutionary madman's fury and a true traitor's eye-bulging self-celebration of the intensest hatred of the Filipino people, by the exposure of the Katipunan Revolution, courtesy of Fray Mariano Gil of the parish of Tondo...

Rizal, yes, only in the Philippines, only in the Foaming in the mouth and frothing in the brain, he, Dr. Jose P. Rizal, native of Calamba Laguna of this dreamt-of *Overseas Province of Spain* called the Philippines, began composing a letter of insurpassable Spanish patriotism and unspeakable anti-Filipino and antihuman treachery, an evil unique in the entire history of the world, which, as the now proverbial saying goes, can happen *Only in the Philippines! Only in the Philippines! And only by a Filipino,* and one which but triumphantly concretized in a Spanish-heroic *consummatum est* his lifelong abomination of independence and revolution in all his works and deeds in his and his ilustrado cohorts' entirely successful counterrevolutionary, anti-Independence Propaganda Campaign which resulted in the recruitment of the entire native rich, the Colonial Middleclass, *against the Revolution* (which was exactly why prematurely exposed thus after four years of undergtround recruitment, it was able to raise a measly 161,529.70 pesos for arms and ammunition and was not yet able to consummate a negotiated purchase of the same from the Japanese government)...

In this letter which was signed as a witness by his friend, Col. Santalo, who was commander of the Spanish warship CASTILLA then docked at Manila Bay and on which he was an honoured guest waiting for the next ship to Spain en route to his international counterrevolutionary mission to help kill all the Katipuneros in Cuba and suppress the Revolution there (so massmurderously hateful was REVOLUTION to him anywhere in the world that he was so pure-Spanishly patriotically eager to fight and die anywhere in the world to suppress IT), behosted and betoasted there as an already assimilated Spanish military doctor duly appointed and exalted thus in the name of the Queen by the Madrid government through the gallant sponsorship of his bosom friend, Governor General Ramon Blanco y Erenas, he, according to him himself, repeatedly repeatedly repeatedly, in three extant documents, namely, 1.) the DECEMBER 12, 1896 DATA FOR MY DEFENSE, 2.) the DECEMBER 15, 1896 FORT SANTIAGO MANIFESTO, 3.) the DECEMBER 25/26 ADDITIONAL DATA FOR MY DEFENSE, he, Jose Protacio Rizal Mercado y Alonzo de Realonda, "offered UNCONDITIONALLY my very life, and even my name, and my good offices, for them to use in whatever manner they deem fit to suppress the rebellion"...

THIS LETTER WAS ADDRESSED TO GOVERNOR GENERAL RAMON BLANCO...

All the Philippine historians without a single exception before this author, were immensely successful in NOT NOTICING this letter.

Chapter 3

THE AUGUST 22/24, 1896 LETTER OF UNCONDITIONAL & ABSOLUTE TREASON & RIZAL'S DESPAIR FOR HIS SPANISH HONOUR

When, in the open forum after the UP Diliman 2010 National Conference of the Philippine Sociological Association plenary lectures of Prof. Randy David and Congressman Walden Bello, I exposed for the first time in the history of Philippine historiography the total non-existence and absolute non-mention in the writings of ALL the Philippine historians, of Rizal's LETTER OF UNCONDITIONAL AND ABSOLUTE TREASON AGAINST THE REVOLUTION AND THE FILIPINO PEOPLE, addressed to Gov. Gen. Ramon Blanco and signed as witness by Col Santalo of the Spanish Navy, in which he "unconditionally offered my very life, and even my name, and my good services, for them (the Spaniards) to use in whatever manner they deem fit in order to suppress the rebellion," Walden Bello's quick and obviously unthinking response, seconded and expatiated upon by Randy David, was the scandalously stupid remark that Rizal was then a prisoner on trial for a capital offense and would then do anything to save his own neck and that must have been why he wrote that letter and made that offer; they even took turns reiterating that had I been in his shoes being tried thus for a crime in which I could lose my neck, I would certainly have done the same...They most certainly would have done the same...Cowards mostly end up being traitors and traitors more likely than not are physical cowards...They cannot be dishonoured because to begin with they never had it...But Jose Rizal? That he was no coward was demonstrated by him in a number of instances which canceled completely all doubt that he was a very brave, indeed an exceptionally brave man. When in June 1892 he came back to Manila primarily to redeem with his life the freedom and safety of his exiled family by surrendering himself to the porcinely diabolic wrath of the Dominicans among other friars, and secondarily to martyristically organize the native counterpart of the anti-revolutionary, anti-independence, assimilationist, "the Philippines as an overseas province of Spain" Propaganda Movement, i.e., the LIGA FILIPINA, he knew that what he was doing was suicide, and was told so and argued against with all their might by his entire family and his assimilationist counterrevolutionary ilustrado friends:--it was a double martyrdom plot that he protractedly premeditated there, which he melodramatically spelled out as such in two letters he left in the care of his friend in Hong Kong, Jose Ma. Basa, telling him therewith to publish the letters as soon as he received news of his death (see chapter on RIZAL'S ASSIMILATIONIST MARTYRDOM PLOT in volume 2 of my NEW HISTORY OF THE PHILIPPINE REVOLUTION). In this instance, he proved that he could coolly go to his death not only for his family but also in defense of his ultrabeloved Mother Spain as a death-defying assimilationist counterrevolutionary, sworn to die if necessary in order to ensure that, as he put it in the draft article THE PHILIPPINES AS A SPANISH COLONY," the Philippines "shall remain a Spanish colony forever" (see chapter of the same title in RIZAL'S POLITICAL AND HISTORICAL WRITINGS, published by the National Historical Institute, and translated by Encarnacion Alzona)... And of course, his Cuba international counterrevolutionary mission in which he most sanguinely volunteered to help kill all the Cuban Katipuneros and "suppress their revolution" there, was premeditated suicide too and a most active seeking out of Spanish glory and Spanish martyrdom, so very brave was the brown five-foot two Spaniard from Calamba La Laguna! Whilst, to evade such a super-heroic braving of death in the Cuban battlefields, he, Rizal, Jose P., could have made his escape on the Singapore stopover, as some Filipinos (notably the millionaire Don Pedro Roxas), fleeing from the then already raging Philippine Revolution, did! Finally then, and in the light of all these prior and posterior blazoning of utterest bravery "in order to make a name and undo calumnies" (as he put it in his September 28, 1896 letter to Blumentritt from the Spain-bound Isla de Panay somewhere in the Mediterranean Sea, concerning his reasons for defying and staring death in the eye as a Spanish military doctor), and defend Spanish colonialism and merit a Spanish national hero's monument in Madrid, Rizal's "unconditional offering of my very life, and even my name, and my good services, to be used by them in whatever manner they deem fit in order to suppress the rebellion" was suicidal gutsiness too, for what else was it he was offering the Spaniards but for him to die in killing Andres Bonifacio and all the Philippine Katipuneros, the same as in Cuba, "in order to suppress" the Philippine Revolution? And it could have turned out to be THAT sort of utterest Spanish counterrevolutionary heroism and martyrdom too for the five-foot-two brown Spaniard from Calamba, La Laguna who in point of fact looked very much like Manny Pacquiao, except that his very dear friend Gov. Gen. Ramon Blanco y Erenas to whom he in writing made the offer thought otherwise, quite mercifully...That's settled then:--Rizal was no coward. And Bello and David have no right to insult him so in thus equating themselves with him as a matter of course, automatically. Rizal an automatic coward--imagine that! Like them!--imagine that!!! Ready to betray their own mother or sell her por kilo to save their own necks--imagine that!!!

And for all that, in the automaticity of their stupidity, the same as in ALL the Philippine historians who were able to encounter the three documents concerning that LETTER OF UNCONDITIONAL TREASON, their premise was dead wrong for seeing automatic cowardice and heaping so incredible and so unforgivable an insult on this country's ruling-class' government's US-Imperialist National Hero thus!!!!!! For the occasion of the LETTER was such as to rule out neck-saving cowardice as a motive. For Rizal was then not a prisoner on trial but an honoured guest on the Spanish warship CASTILLA then docked in Manila Bay; he was on his way to his international counterrevolutionary mission in Cuba as a duly commissioned Spanish military doctor appointed thus in the name of the Queen by the Madrid government, and must thus be presumed to have been already an assimilated Spaniard; when his appointment papers reached him on July 31, 1896 in Dapitan, his alacrity to kill as many Cuban Katipuneros as possible was such that he abandoned his Dapitan hospital, house, abaca business, coffee and sugar cane plantations, and even his slew and stun of adolescent boyfriends and took the boat to Manila the very next day, but missed the mailboat to Spain, and had thus had to wait for a whole month for the next one--on board the CASTILLA whose handsome commander, Col. Santalo, the same that signed that LETTER as official witness to the great deed of

Spanish heroism, instantly became his intimate friend (as so he wrote to his mother amid disquisitions re longanizas and short nights upon long days (see esp. His September 2, 1896 letter to his mother in RIZAL'S CORRESPONDENCE WITH FAMILY MEMBERS AND FRIENDS)...He was on that ship from August 6 to September 4, 1896; whilst, on his 13th day there, on August 19, 1896, the Katipunan was discovered and exposed by the odious Fray Mariano Gil and war broke out, and that was when loving to very death Spanish colonialism thus and abominating the Revolution so, and grievously insulted by it in his brown Spanish honour (as he so eloquently denounced Bonifacio and company in his December 15, 1896 Fort Santiago Manifesto), he wrote and delivered the LETTER. "Twelve or fourteen days later" so he wrote in his December 25/26, 1896 Additional Data For My Defense, "I sailed for Spain". We know from the documentary records that his ship, the Isla de Panay, weighed anchor on September 4; counting backwards from there, that LETTER must have been written and delivered between August 22 and 24, 1896...From their automatic response of automatic cowardice, it is plain to see that like ALL the Philippine historians to-date, they have been most intensely brainwashed by the US-Imperialist ruling class government historiographic propaganda machine (today the NHC, the NHI, the NCCA, DEP-ED, CHED, THE RULING CLASS CONTROLLED MASS MEDIA...) that they have completely become unable to read anything by Rizal or on Rizal and did not even notice that Rizal in the December 15 Manifesto was talking, nay bragging, to the Spanish Court Martial officers about a letter, about THAT LETTER, about that unsurpassable feat of Spanish heroism of offering to die in murdering all the Katipuneros in order to suppress the Katipunan Revolution and defend Spanish colonialism thereby; in which conflation the unique in world history shamelessness and treason of the LETTER was suppressed...Hence the monumental scandal of the brutal stupidity or the brutal scandal of the monumental stupidity that in them as in ALL the Philippine historians and in ALL the Philippine History textbooks to-date, there is no cognizance, no consciousness, no mention, let alone an analysis and discussion of the invincible, undethronable in all of world history TREASON and pigly shamelessness of the LETTER...And it is thus too that it is never noticed that in addition to the stoneblind treason rammed mercilessly into the mind of the reader by the December 15 Manifesto's rejection, denunciation and savaging of the Revolution-- (in which Rizal condemned the Revolution as absurd and insane and imprecated Andres Bonifacio and company as "savages," "uneducated" "troublemakers," who "shamed" and "discredited us to our Spanish friends and supporters," as "deceivers of the people", etc…), which shamelessly dishonest and unspeakably brainless historians like Floro Quibuyen are even then able to deny and directly convert into a "hidden" endorsement of the Revolution (dapat pigaan at kaskasan sa mata ng siling palay ang mga ito para makakita),-- two other instances of treason are blazoned in that Manifesto, namely, the LETTER itself and its braggadocious exposure, declaration, and enshrinement there as an act of unparalleled Spanish heroism…

In the first place then, we have to understand that Rizal's despair was neither merely nor preeminently for his life but for the preservation of his self-imagined, most assiduously nurtured, invincibly guarded Spanish honour and reputation as a most devoted son of his ultra-beloved Mother Spain. That honour was absolutely threatened by the accusation of rebellion, i.e., of his being one with the Revolution. And in order to defend that honour against that defamatory accusation Rizal, so he says in this LETTER, and reiterates in his exhibition of IT in the Manifesto and in open court, would do anything, including giving up his very life and allowing the Spaniards to use his name in treacherous stratagems that could lead to the mass-murder of the Katipuneros and thus to the "suppression of the rebellion". That being the case, he could not have needed any other motive to declare the existence of the LETTER (which he did in the two other documents, namely, the December 12 Data For My Defense, and the December 25/26 Additional Data For My Defense--see RIZAL'S POLITICAL AND HISTORICAL WRITINGS, pp 350 et seq.) and expatiate on its contents before the military court, than the preservation of that honour and reputation.

In his emotional letter to Blumentritt dated September 28, 1896, written aboard the boat to Spain as they were crossing the Mediterranean Sea, concerning the telegraphed order for his arrest and confinement to his cabin and for his immediate return to the Philippines for trial, Rizal could not have been anything but absolutely sincere when he circumstantially declared to his Austrian-Spanish assimilationist-counterrevolutionary friend that he was going to Cuba to risk his life and his everything there "to win a name and undo calumnies":--to win a name, that is to say, to shine there as a great Spanish hero fighting and possibly dying in defense of Spanish colonialism; "to undo calumnies", that is to say, to cleanse the dishonour of having been exiled to Dapitan and of thus being branded as a traitor to his ultra-beloved Mother Spain. In his September 2, 1896 letter to his mother, 2 days before he sailed to Spain, he declared that he would do everything there to defend the honour and interests of his ultra-beloved Mother Spain against the Cuban Katipuneros "in order to show" his Spanish friends, Governor General Blanco and Col. Santalo that he was "worthy of their friendship"...

This letter was addressed to Governor General Ramon Blanco y Erenas, and should thus be taken as documentary proof or at the very least very strong indication that even before the exposure of the Katipunan on August 19, 1896, and specifically when he requested Blanco to hide him incommunicado on the Castilla on August 4 or 5, 1896, he had already informed Blanco about the Revolution, details about which having been imparted to him by that other ilustrado traitor and "Only in the Philippines!" chameleon Dr. Pio Valenzuela on July 1, 1896, during their Two Supertraitors Dapitan Conference. For Blanco must have tightly queried him why he was anxious to be hidden incommunicado on the Castilla for the entire month he had to wait for the next boat to Spain en route to Cuba, and specifically of what it was that he so mortally urgently wanted to hide his international counterrevolutionary Spanish military doctor's rotten-to-the-core Calambeno self. And would a traitor who abhorred his own countrywo/men so that he could "unconditionally" offer the Spaniards "my very life, and even my name, and everything I am capable of doing, for them to use in whatever manner they deem fit to suppress the rebellion", would such a racist massmurderer of his own countrywo/men have a thread of humanity and honour left in him to make him withhold the truth from his Spanish military Governor General friend and protect the Filipinos and the Revolution?

Chapter 4

RIZAL'S UNCONDITIONAL OFFER TO DIE FIGHTING THE KATIPUNEROS & DECEIVING ANDRES BONIFACIO TO SUPPRESS THE REVOLUTION-- A TREASON & A PERFIDY UNIQUE IN WORLD HISTORY

In the first place then, we have to understand that Rizal's despair was neither merely nor preeminently for his life (for Rizal is indeed brave, very brave, and those who ignorantly justify his condemnation, his execration, his vilification, his insanification of the Revolution in the December 15, 1896 Fort Santiago Manifesto by saying—as Congressman Walden Bello and Prof. Randolph David did say—that he was then a prisoner under trial and he did it to save his own neck, "as anyone in such situation would" had merely imputed a cowardice to him and a craven soul that without doubt was their own), but for the preservation of his intensely imagined most assiduously nurtured, invincibly guarded Spanish honour and reputation as a most devoted son of his woundingly beloved Mother Spain. That honour was absolutely threatened by the accusation of rebellion, i.e., of his being one with the Philippine Revolution. And in order to defend that honour against that defamatory accusation Rizal, so he says in this LETTER, and reiterates in his exhibition of IT in open court, would do anything including giving up his very life and allowing the Spaniards to use his name in treacherous stratagems that could lead to the massmurder of the Katipuneros and thus to the "suppression of the rebellion." That being the case, he could not have needed any other motive to declare the existence of the LETTER (which he did in the two other documents, namely, the December 12 Data For My Defense, and the December 25/26 Additional Data For My Defense—see RIZAL'S POLITICAL & HISTORICAL WRITINGS, pp. 350 et seq.), and expatiate on its contents before the military court, than the preservation of that honour and that reputation. Meanwhile, all those who seek abominably to justify Rizal's rejection of the Revolution thus are such stupid morons that they either remain blissfully unaware of the abovementioned letter of Rizal's "unconditional offer" to Gov. Gen. Blanco "of my very life, and even my good name, and everything I could do, for them to use in whatever manner they deem fit in order to suppress the rebellion", that they conflate through phantasmatic elision and blindness the Manifesto with the LETTER in such a way that the latter is reduced into the former and is in it erased.

Chapter 5

TESTIMONY FROM *THE PHILIPPINES AS A SPANISH COLONY*

"...colors, would be worth as much or more than the dreamed of independence which, perhaps troubled by internal discords, would place the Metropolis in a favourable situation.

"And let not some people say that because the country and its inhabitants are hated, the latter would pay in excess and in the same coin the insults and injuries they have received, that the feeling of affection (for the Mother Country) is already completely dead. Of course it should be already dead if the Filipino people were not a young people that forgets the harshest offense when it sees that there had been no bad intention and if Machiavelli's keen observation were not true: '*La natura d'oumini e cosi obligarsi per le beneficii che essi fanno come per quelli che essi ricevono.'* ('For it is the nature of men to be bound by the benefits they confer as much as by those they receive.')[1]

---

[1] Here we see Rizal reassuring the Spanish authorities (from whom the assimilationist counter-revolutionary, anti-independence, ilustrado propagandists, whose great leader he was, were begging for assimilationist status, i.e., eternal colonialism), that the Filipino natives, despite the centuries of Spanish cruelty and greed, of "insults and injuries"inflicted by the Spaniards upon them, would not repay them with hatred and ingratitude! For the Filipinos were a young people, so he says here, and were apt to "forget" the "harshest offense" provided they were made to see that there "had been no bad intention" behind it! Which of course is a lie:--for, of course, the intention behind any whatever kind of colonialism can only be bad, nay evil, for depriving a people of their sovereignty and their freedom for whatever purpose is uttermost evil. And

"We therefore say that the modification of the colonial policy in the Philippines is not impossible so that the Philippines can remain a colony ***as she ought to remain as such.*** Now we need to find out what kind of colony the Philippines shall ***forever*** be. For this purpose it is necessary for us to examine the different kinds of colonies…"[2]

Prof. Encarnacion Alzona of UP, who has the additional merit of being Rizal's great-granddaughter, was the editor and translator of *Rizal's Political and Historical Writings* from which we extracted the above passage; she tells us that the thing so titled is "an English translation of a fragment of a Rizal manuscript, without title, apparently a rough draft, for the two pages, whose photostatic copy is before us, have many corrections by him."[3] She adds that "the idea here treated is also found in his published essay, *Filipinas dentro de cien anos* (The Philippines A Century Hence)," which she has likewise translated and included in this same volume. These are not unimportant connections. If there exists an expert on

---

here, Rizal the liar and hypocrite even manages to help himself in such an insinuatingly slavish way to the good esteem of the Spanish colonizers by letting them most suggestively to know that he believes as a matter of course in their ideologically professed enlightementist civilizing and Christian-evangelical soul-saving "good intention", goal, aim, in suffering to colonize those barbaric far eastern natives! In light of which consideration it is revealed to us too that what Rizal farcically meant by the Filipinos being "a young people" is their being an uncivilized one, i.e., naïve, inexperienced in the ways of the world, unlike the Spaniards themselves or the other European peoples who were older peoples and thus in the know about such things.

[2] From *Jose Rizal's Political & Historical Writings*, National Historical Institute, 2007, p 355.

[3] Headnote, ibid., p 355.

Rizal's views who cannot possibly be mistaken about the question of whether Rizal wrote and died for *assimilation*, that is to say *in defense* of Spanish colonialism (and therefore *against* the Filipino people, in hatred and fear and disdain and denigration of the Filipino people, and for till-death-do-us-part love of "the Mother Country", Spain) on one hand, or separatism, revolution, independence, and thus in defense of the Filipino people and for their liberation and independence (and thus *against* Spanish colonialism and for love of native land and of the Filipino people) on the other hand, it would be the renowned Rizal translator Prof. Encarnacion Alzona. Now here she as a matter of course tells us that the idea behind this fragment is the same as that "found in his published essay...*The Philippines A Century Hence*..." And the idea behind this fragment needs no interpretation since Rizal cannot be more brutally direct or more burningly anti-Filipino people, or more ardently a lover of Mother Spain and an uncompromising defender of Spanish colonialism, in declaring it. And the title of this idea is:--*Spanish Colonialism Forever*...

Elsewhere in this volume, namely, in her *Translator's Note*, Prof. Alzona ratifies this view thus: "There are three important political documents in this volume—'Notes for My Defense', 'Additions to My Defense', and 'Manifesto to Some Filipinos'—which throw a bright light on his *infamous* trial and expose the *duplicity* of his enemies. The Constitution of the *Liga Filipina*, reprinted here, was cited in his trial and *utilized by his enemies to bolster their charge that he engaged in revolutuionary activities* "(ibid., xv.).

In other words, in those three additional political documents, the "bright light thrown" upon what without them would not be more clearly demonstrated and evidenced was that of Rizal's *innocence* of the charge of "engaging in revolutionary activities", i.e., of being a revolutionary, of his being a Katipunero leader, member, or sympathizer. In short, the "truth" those political documents more brightly illuminate was, as Alzona sees it, the *glorious and heroic and patriotic* one that Rizal *never* "engaged in revolutionary activities"!:--and was thus never a revolutionary, and was thus never for Philippine independence from his ultra-beloved "Mother Spain"; the "truth" then, namely, that as evidenced by the above fragment, Rizal was for *Spanish colonialism forever* and that he was so until the trial and until death; that he died an anti-revolutionary and a counter-revolutionary *assimilationist agent and campaigner for an eternity of colonialism for his native Philippines* and thus an uncompromising, deadly, bloody enemy of Philippine independence, and thus an uncompromising, deadly, bloody enemy of the Filipino people. And that was why to such as his great-granddaughter Encarnacion Alzona, but also to the Zaide father-daughter tandem who make a lot of money selling the lie that was Jose Rizal, and indeed to almost all the historians who ever wrote on the matter, he was such a great and glorious and patriotic hero! And she was mad, and the Zaides were mad, and all the Philippine historians were, are, mad at Rizal's "enemies" who "infamously", in that "*infamous* trial", showed their "duplicity" in having him convicted of the crime of revolution, of the crime of fighting for Philippine independence, of the crime of choosing the welfare and interests of his own native countrymen over against that of Spain and the Spaniards... This is crazy of course—and stupid beyond measure. Rizal was great, glorious, heroic, patriotic, and to all of these loonies the greatest Filipino hero, *because he was absolutely and to very death against the independence of the Filipinos,* against separation from Spain, against the Revolution, *against the Filipino people*!:--this is crazy of course—and stupid beyond measure. Which can only mean that to Alzona, the Zaides, and to all Filipino historians without a single exception, the Revolution, the Katipunan, was not glorious but rather inglorious, was not great but rather petty, was not heroic but rather anti-heroic and villainous, and criminal and scoundrelly, and traitorous *as Rizal himself orated it was* in his *December 15 Manifesto* mentioned above, that it was not patriotic but rather anti-patriotic, and was evil rather than good! And if nevertheless these writers and vendors of Rizal's lies and the lie that was Rizal are forced in their books to somehow acknowledge and mention that the Revolution was great and heroic and glorious and patriotic as all of the above were in fact in the habit of doing? Well, that means they indeed are *forced*! And supposing some of them felt quite sincere in doing so? In that case, it shows how brutally confused they are and as they are bound to be who have swallowed the lie that Rizal--who from his first assimilationist day to his ignominious and even comical-farcical death had fought against revolution, against independence, and was thus the deadly and utterly bloody enemy of the Filipino people—that this stupid, narrowminded and shallow-souled, ill-educated traitor Rizal was great, glorious, heroic, patriotic, and indeed the greatest, the most glorious, the most heroic, the most patriotic!... This Rizal who was like he was born a natural lie…and natural liar… So good and so smooth was he in doing it, and in being it, in existing it…

Chapter 6

TESTIMONY FROM *THE PHILIPPINES A CENTURY HENCE...*[4]

---

[4]As a whole, the article, actually a series of four published in *La Solidaridad* between 30 September 1889 and February 1890, is a long straightforward argument for assimilation of the Philippines by Spain. It was addressed directly to the Madrid government. It is 33 pages of assimilationism. And Dean Mario Miclat of the Asian Center, who voted inquisitorially to exclude me from the *Rizal Sesquicentennial Conference* says he cannot find assimilationism in Rizal! He has not read Rizal then. He has not read this long, celebrated article. And since all of Rizal's political writings were assimilationist, he must not have read all of them—including the two novels which were in fact *rabidly* assimilationist. Or else, he had been so thoroughly brainwashed like 99.999999 percent of Philippine historians and other intellectuals in this country that he must not know anymore what *assimilationism* means, for to know it is to know Rizal for being the elitist, anti-people, anti-independence, anti-revolutionary traitor who more vigorously and more successfully than anyone of that Europe-based company of upper colonial middle-class scions called (by themselves) *ilustrados*, championed it: he died for it. In his final letter (written in the late afternoon of December 29, 1896) to his Austrian friend Ferdinand Blumentritt, the armchair ethnologist who was able world-famously to specialize on the Philippines without ever visiting it, and who was himself, being of Spanish blood, a most dedicated and fiery campaigner for Philippine assimimilation in the pages of *La Solidaridad* and elsewhere, Rizal wrote: "My dear Brother...When you receive this letter, I shall be dead by then. Tomorrow at seven, I shall be shot; *but I am innocent of the crime of rebellion...* I am going to die with a tranquil conscience..." There.

"...Will the Philippines remain as a Spanish colony, and in this case, what kind of colony? Will she become a Spanish province with or without autonomy? And in order to attain this status, what kind of sacrifices must she make?

And that too by way of letting him, Blumentritt, know that he dies upholding their common ideal, namely, assimilationism, that he was never guilty of that antithesis of assimilationism which was "rebellion", i.e., separatism, revolution, the, to Blumentritt and Rizal, crime of wanting freedom and independence, of fighting for the freedom and independence of the Filipino people from Spanish colonial tyranny. The assimilationist was a horrified abhorrer of revolution because he was the devoted abominator of separation from his ever beloved Mother Spain: the assimilationist native was a favoured (colonial-collaborationist-adopted) son of (a bitch) Spain; no Indio peasant or carpenter or fisherman can fool himself or be fooled by another to join Rizal and del Pilar and the *ilustrado* company in their febrile dream, their ultimately criminal, ultimately massmurderous hallucination of *a necessarily merely quasi hispanity.* Necessarily quasi: the absolutely violent prejudice of race, invented and perfected by the same white men and most insanely intense in the Spaniard of Rizal's time, as he himself attested to in very many words and which his very own personal experience excessively ratified, should have been more than enough to deter him against imagining the desire of assimilation and impede him in the pursuit of it. But such political plots are also at once a question of soul, of the largeness or tininess, of the depth or depthlessness of the soul: Rizal's was small, and shallow and, the sound and fury notwithstanding, shabby.

"Will she eventually separate from the Mother Country, Spain, to live independently, to fall into the hands of other nations[5] or to ally herself with other neighbouring powers?

Rizal then goes on to describe the abuses, the insatiable greed and inhumanity of the friars and the connivance of the colonial authorities with them or their inaction in the face of such abuses, etc., etc...

"If this state of things continues, what will the Philippines be a century hence? The storage batteries are charging little by little, and if the prudence of the government does not provide an outlet, for the complaints that are accumulating, it is possible that one day the spark would fly out. This is not the place to speak of the success that such an *unfortunate conflict* might have; it depends upon fate, upon arms, and on a million circumstances that men cannot foresee; but even if all the advantages were on the side of the

---

[5]She eventually did fall into the hands of America, and for this Rizal himself and the craven bearer of his reformist-assimilationist influence, the Running Man of Asia and vendor of the Revolution at Biyak na Bato, Emilio Aguinaldo, were the two national traitors and criminals who should be held mainly responsible—and with them of course, the ilustrado assimilationists on one hand and their principalia relatives who either remained unregenerate in their colonial-collaborationist corruption or were perverted by the Rizalian assimilationist influence into half-baked separationism which eventually succumbed under the influence of greed into gangsterist vendorialism. They together were the ones most responsible for impeding and delaying the revolution that the Americans were able to catch up with it and overtake it during the Spanish American war which gave the Yankees the perfect alibi to conquer and colonize the country.

government, and consequently, the probabilities of victory, it would be a Pyrrhic victory, and a government should not want that.

"If those who guide the destinies of the Philippines should persist in their refusal to grant reforms, in making the country retrogress, in going to the extreme in its rigorous repression of the classes that suffer and think, they will succeed in making them gamble away the miseries of an insecure life, full of privations and bitterness, for the hope of obtaining something uncertain. What would be lost in the struggle? Almost nothing. The life of large discontented classes offers no great attraction that it should be preferred to a glorious death. *Suicide* [6] can well be attempted; but afterwards? Would there not remain a stream of blood between victors and vanquished, and could not the latter with time and experience become equal in strength, as they are already numerically superior to their rulers? Who says no? All the petty insurrections that had broken out in the Philippines had been the work of a few fanatics and discontented military men who, in order to attain their ends, had to resort to deceit and trickery or avail themselves of the subordination of their subalterns. Thus they all fell. *None of the insurrections was popular in character nor based on the necessity of the whole nation nor did it struggle for the laws of humanity or of justice.* Thus the insurrections did not leave behind them indelible mementos; on the contrary, the people, their wounds healed, realizing that they have been deceived, applauded the downfall of those who had disturbed their peace! *But if the movement springs from the people themselves and adopts for its cause their sufferings?*

"Therefore, if the prudence and wise reforms of our ministers do not find competent and determined interpreters among the rulers beyond the seas and faithful continuators in those called upon by the frequent political crises to occupy so sensitive a post ; if the complaints and needs of the Filipino

---

[6]Revolution is suicide!

people are eternally to be answered with *the petition is denied*, inspired by the classes that thrive on the backwardness of the subject; if all just claims are disregarded and considered subversive tendencies, *denying to the country representation to the Cortes and the right to protest against all kinds of abuses which escape the snare of laws*; and if, finally, the system so effective in alienating the people's goodwill, spurring their apathy by means of insults and ingratitude, will be continued, we can be assured that and within a few years the present state of things will be modified completely and inevitably...

"...Today there is a factor which did not exist before. The national spirit has awakened, and a common misfortune and a common abasement have united all the inhabitants of the Islands. It counts on a large enlightened class within and without the Archipelago, a class created and augmented more and more by the stupidities of certain rulers who compel the inhabitants to expatriate themselves, to seek education abroad—a class that perseveres and struggles thanks to the official provocations and the system of persecution. This class whose number is increasing progressively is in constant communication with the rest of the Islands, and if today it constitutes the brains of the country, within a few years it will constitute its entire nervous system and demonstrate its existence in all its acts.

"...In short, then, the advancement and moral progress of the Philippines is inevitable; it is fated...The Islands cannot remain in their present condition without petitioning the metropolis for more liberties. *Mutatis, mutandis.*(With the necessary changes.)To new men, a new social status....

"...The Philippines, then, either will remain under Spain but with more rights and freedom, or it will declare herself independent after staining herself and the Mother Country with her own blood... As no one should wish or hope for such an *unfortunate rupture* of relations, *which would be an evil for all* and should only be the last argument in a most desperate predicament[7], let us examine the forms of *peaceful evolution* under which the Islands could remain under the Spanish flag

---

[7] Here then, your Dr. Jose Rizal valiantly and with the same omnipresent aura of impending and self-assured martyrdom declaiming that *revolution* was an unfortunate and evil thing, a "rupture of relations" from which only "misfortune" can emerge, and which then all must bewail, oppose, avoid, denounce as he does denounce it here like the monstrosity that it always was for him, dangling and brandishing it as an object of universal horror and abomination in order to scare, to terrorize, to bamboozle the Spanish government into assimilationist reform. The same supposed historians, all of them without a single known exception, who extol Rizal's greatness and at the same time proclaim him the greatest revolutionary in being the supposed inspirer of the Revolution, and who thus acknowledge and proclaim too the glory of the Revolution, fail to notice that in every colonial situation revolution and national liberation were one and the same thing, so that anyone who, like Rizal here and everywhere else opposes revolution must at the same time be against national liberation—and what else could anyone such be, rejecting and fighting against national liberation thus, but a traitor to his own country and people? Positivistic, superficial and vulgar and conceptless and philosophically illiterate without a single exception, these supposed historians are flummoxed en masse by the fact that formalized political independence complete with banners and streamers and brass bands and gun salutes did not cleanly and all at once ensue from the KKK Revolution, so much so that the same conceptless supposed historians are prompted to speak of """the revolution that never was" (this from the most ignorant of the lot), or of the "failure of the revolution" (this of course from one who, so scantily endowed and so unfortunately raised by insubstantial elders as to fail to inherit a thing of joy, is then one in

without injuring in the least the rights, interests, or dignity of both countries.

"...The minister then who would wish his reforms to be real reforms should begin by declaring freedom of the press in the Philippines and creating Filipino deputies...A free press in the Philippines is necessary because rarely do the complaints there reach the Peninsula...But the government that rules from afar, absolutely needs that the truth and the facts reach it through all possible means so that it can appreciate and judge them better, and this necessity becomes imperative when it

---

whom the revolution can only fail, and did fail). But revolution is not as superficial and empiricious as these supposed historians. Revolution—especially one as clearly and decisively delineated as the anticolonial—is the people revolutionized. This is the sense in which revolutions cannot fail. The main object and result of a revolution is the internal liberation of the people from the unfreedom that for centuries had penetrated and determined their very souls, the overthrow of cowardice and the hundred and one pettinesses, venalities, vices injected into them by colonialism, by tyranny and oppression (Tsarism in Russia overthrown by the Bolsheviks for instance, Monarchy and feudalism overthrown in Europe in 1789, in the American Revolution, Southern feudalism and raw and direct negro Slavery). Above all, revolution is the people fighting to the death, ready for absolute sacrifice, in order to wrench from tyranny their right of sovereignty, their freedom, their dignity:--beings who rise to the height of transcendence in thus staking their very lives, affirming their being the transcendent beings, the powers to die that they are, *existing actively* thus their being beyond any mere thing or particularity, their being beyond nature itself, and, positioning themselves thus at the infinite height of the very possibility of absolute nothingness in disdaining death itself, beyond being itself. Revolutions cannot fail, though they can be betrayed—after the success.

concerns a country like the Philippines whose inhabitants speak and complain in a language unknown to the authorities. To govern in another way will also be called 'to govern', as it is necessary to give it a name, but that is to govern badly...It is to administer a house thinking only of giving it lustre and importance without finding out what is in the safe, *without considering the servants*[8]and the family...

"...We say the same thing about Filipino deputies...What danger does the government see in them?...The pacific struggle of ideas, besides serving as a thermometer for the government, has the advantage of being cheaper and more glorious, because the Spanish parliament abounds precisely in champions of the word, *invincible in the field of speeches...* Well now; if the real handicap of the Filipino deputies is their *Igorot smell*...It is useless to refute certain impediments some fine writers have put forth, such as the more or less brown colour of the skin and the more or less large-nosed faces... And as long as the Spanish Cortes is not an assembly ofg Adonises, Antinouses, boys, and other similar angels; so long as one goes there to legislate and not to *socratize* or wander through imaginary hemispheres, we believe that the government should not be deterred by those obstacles.*Right has no skin nor has reason noses...* But we wish to be loyal to the government and we point out to it the road that seems to us best...*so that the discontented elements would disappear...* There being no motive for discontent, with what will the masses be stirred up?... In a similar way, the obstacle that

---

[8]Rizal cannot imagine a household without servants. Assimilationism was possible, was thinkable, was desirable only to natives who in the colonial set-up were permanently, i.e., structurally, the recipients and enjoyers of great privileges. Such was the colonial middle class to the upper stratum of which Rizal and his fellow ilustrado assimilationist propagandists belonged. The same privileges had lulled them to the delusion that the colonial masters could accept them as equals or even as true human beings.

others find in the defective education of the majority of the Filipinos is inadmissible. Besides not being as defective as alleged, there is no plausible reason whatsoever to deprive the ignorant and the helpless (through his own fault or another's) of a representative who can watch over him so that he would not be trampled. He's precisely the one who needs it most. *Nobody ceases to be a man,no onc loses his rights to civilization, for being solely more or less civilized...* The laws and acts of the authorities being watched over, the word *Justice* will cease to be a colonial irony. Justice is the foremost virtue of civilized nations; it subdues the most barbarous nations. Injustice excites the weakest to rebellion.

"The government posts should be filled through competitive examination... We suppose

that Spaniards are not afraid to take part in this competition; thus they can demonstrate their superiority through the superiority of their intelligence. Although this is not done in the metropolis, it should be practised in the colonies, inasmuch as true prestige should be sought in moral endowments, because colonizers should be or seem to be at least, just, intelligent, and upright, just as man feigns virtue when he is in contact with strangers...

"The French colonies have representatives... Cuba and Puerto Rico...have many deputies... What crime has the Philippines committed that she should thus be deprived of her rights?

"In short, the Philippines will remain Spanish if she enters the path of rightful and civilized life, if the rights of her people are respected, if they are granted others they should have, if the liberal policy of the government is carried out without shackles or meanness, without subterfuges or false interpretations...

"No matter how much the Philippines owe Spain, they cannot be compelled to renounce their right to redemption, to let the liberal and enlightened among them roam as exiles from their native land, to let the most common aspirations smother in its atmosphere, to tolerate that the peaceful citizen live in continuous anguish and the fate of the people depend on the caprice of only one man. Spain cannot justify even in the name of God himself that six million men be brutalized, exploited and oppressed, denying them light, the innate human rights and afterwards heap upon them contempt and insults. No, there is no gratitude that can excuse it... No one can demand of the Filipino people the impossible. The noble Spanish people, so devoted to their liberties and rights, cannot tell the Filipino people to renounce theirs...

"Well then; applying all these considerations to the Philippines, we are obliged to conclude...that if her people are not *assimilated*[9] by the Spanish nation...the Philippines one day will declare herself inevitably and unmistakably independent...Neither Spanish patriotism...nor the love for Spain of all the Filipinos...can go against this law of destiny...

"...Let them not say that what happened to the American republics will happen to us. These won their independence easily and their peoples were animated by a spirit different from that of the Filipinos. Besides, the danger of falling again into the hands of other powers, of the English or the Germans, for example, will compel them to be sensible and prudent...

"...Inasmuch as it is necessary to give six million Filipinos their rights so that *they would be Spaniards in fact...*

"...Spain...entreating you *for a loving glance*, for a liberal policy to ensure the peace of our country *and your rule over these devoted but unfortunate Islands!*...Spain... Spain... Spainnnnnnnnnnnnnnnnnnn.....O hu hu hu hu huuuuuuuuuuuuuuuuuuuuuuuuuuuuuuuuuuuuuuuuuuuuuuu uuuuuuuu....

[9]There it is, the word itself.

Chapter 7

TESTIMONY FROM *AN ADDRESS TO THE SPANISH NATION*

(Handbill written by Rizal in Hong Kong, printed November 11, 1891; *Political and Historical Writings*, Appendix A, p 385)

"The Philippines, agonizing in her decadence, is on the verge of complete ruin, because the government, instead of attempting to solve her problems, drags itself behind the friars, laying aside every human consideration, and converts these islands into an inexhaustible lode for their exploitation.

"The friars are the permanent calamity in the Archipelago. The Philippine towns are constantly clamoring against them before the governments at Madrid and Manila. Their complaints are never heeded; on the contrary, their moans, their sighs, are smothered by terrible threats…etc.

"…Of the Nation, of Spain, that during a long time has been equally a victim of the predominance of the same religious communities, whose very powerful influence has been the cause of great havocs…, of Spain who experienced the terrible palsies of the barbarous Inquisition conceived by the same friars…, of Spain who, overcoming her generous and merciful sentiments, her gaze fixed upon the welfare of her children, *decapitated* them in the year '35 in the streets of Barcelona and burned their convents, who, in the glorious revolution of '68 expelled them from her territories and confiscated their properties, *it is asked and it is entreated that she expel likewise those same religious orders from Philippine territory for being troublesome, for being unpatriotic.*[10]

---

[10] The friars, to Rizal's soul, were, *unlike Rizal himself*, unpatriotic. Why? Because by their rapacity and calamitousness they were pushing the natives to separatism, revolution, independence—i.e., to the

"Otherwise, the Filipino people, their calmness lost and their centuries-old patience exhausted, imitating the glorious past of their *Mother Spain* will take justice into their hands...

The *Rape of Calamba* was perpetrated by the Dominicans with the armed assistance of Governor General Valeriano Weyler and his Imelda Marcos wife. This letter-manifesto was Rizal's assimilationist-reformist written response to it. Here he repeats truly *ad nauseam* his standard assimilationist argument, namely, that if the Madrid government does not expel the rapacious and calamitous and lubricious friars soon enough, the Filipinos are about to exhaust their proverbial patience and will in a short while do it themselves—in, of course, a revolution. Here we become aware of a historical detail which must have inspired the social-climbingly deluded ilustrados to sanguinely demand in their assimilationist hallucinations the expulsion of the friars from the Philippines—namely, the fact that the Spaniards themselves had reached a point in their hatred of the friars where they decapitated them in the streets

---

termination of Spanish colonialism in the Philippines. Unlike them, Rizal was *patriotic*. Why? Because in pleading to the Madrid government that the friars be expelled and the Philippines be assimilated, he was protecting in the best way possible Spanish rule in the Philippines against the threat of revolution, separation, independence. In attacking the friars who in endangering Spanish colonialism by being so greedy, bloodthirsty and lustful, were so *unpatriotic* to, of course Mother Spain, *Rizal was attacking the revolution itself as a possibility, and hence was attacking separation from Spain itself as a possibility, and hence was attacking Philippine independence itself as a possibility, and that in his mind and soul was why he was the truly patriotic one—patriotic to, of course of course of course, his ever beloved Mother Spain*. Of course, Rizal in his social-climbing soul was also perfervidly convinced that the best way to love his native land was to attack the very possibility of her independence, and to promote instead eternal colonialism for her...

of Barcelona and burned their convents, and later expelled them from Spain itself and confiscated their properties. Rizal and company were by such details led to the manifest delusion that they could persuade the Madrid politicians to do the same for the Philippines. They forgot that no matter how despicable and swinish the friars were in the Philippines, they were still Spaniards, and to the of course racist Spaniards, Spanish swine were infinitely higher beings than the richest and best-educated Indios like Rizal and company.

Chapter 8

THE CUBA ESCAPADE, OR RIZAL AS INTERNATIONAL COUNTERREVOLUTIONARY

Letter 210. Rizal to Blumentritt, en route to Spain, 28 September 1896.

"Ss Isla de Panay

Mediterranean Sea

28 September 1896

MY VERY DEAR FRIEND,

A passenger on board has just told me news that I hardly believe and should it be true, would bring an end to the prestige of Philippine authorities[11].

---

[11]The trouble with this rabid assimilationist defender of Spanish colonialism against the Cuban Katipuneros and the Philippine Katipuneros was that he even believed in "the prestige" of such as the necessarily, unqualifiedly evil because colonial Spanish "Philippine authorities". Assimilationism was unforgivable because apart from being an impossible, farcical, absurd delusion of kindness and humanity, let alone nobility in, at that point in history, necessarily, irremediably racist conquerors such as were the white race who invented racism itself, it was capitulation to such genocidal evil, a defense of it, and a wish for an eternity of it. Worse, during revolutionary times which exactly was when it could arise at all as a desire, an ideology, a movement, such as were Rizal's and Bonifacio's

You will remember that last year you notified me that physicians were lacking in Cuba; that many soldiers were dying without medical assistance. Instantly I presented myself to the authorities applying for the post of temporary physician for the duration of the campaign. Months and months elapsed and in view of the fact that I did not receive any reply, i started to build a wooden house and a hospital and thus earn my livelihood in Dapitan. On 30 July I received a letter from the governor general of the following tenor:

The Governor General of the Philippines

Manila, 1, July 1896

Mr. Jose Rizal

MY DEAR SIR,

I have informed the government of your desire, and acceding to it, it has no objection to your going to Cuba to render your services to our Army as Assistant Physician in the Corps of Military Health. Therefore, if you still entertain that idea, the Politico-Military Commander of that district will issue a pass to you to come to this Capital City, where in my turn I shall

---

times, it must express itself and effectuate itself and work itself out as counter-revolution, as betrayal of one's own people, as high treason. And yet, such perverse belief in such distorted prestige was precisely the premise behind such evil movement of evil (evil, yes—and we recommend here that the social sciences employ as a matter of principle, of theory, of method, of logic, of the inherence of the concept in the thing itself that should define objectivity itself, knowledge itself, truth itself, science itself, this moral terminology, this language of good and evil) as assimilationism, as the clamour for a reformed, humane, kindly, noble, moral, colonialism, i.e., for a reformed, humane, kindly, noble, moral *wholesale denial of the freedom and therewith the humanity of human beings*!

give you a passport to the Peninsula where the Minister of War will assign you to the Army of Operations in Cuba as assistant in the Corps of Military Health.

On this date, I am writing to the Politico-Military Commander there and you can make the trip immediately.

It has been a satisfaction for me to have been able to please you

Your attentive servant who kisses your hand,
Ramon Blanco.

This letter upset my plans, for I was not thinking of going to Cuba anymore in view of the fact that more than six months had elapsed since i filed my application; *but fearing that they might attribute to something else if i should now refuse to go*, I decided to abandon everything and depart immediately. I went then to Manila with my entire family, leaving behind all my business. Unfortunately, I did noty overtake the mail boat for Spain *and fearing that my stay in Manila for one month might bring me troubles, I made known to the governor general my desire to be isolated from everybody except my family while waiting on board.* Whether due to this or something else, the governor general sent me to the cruiser *Castilla* where I stayed incommunicado except with my family. During this interval, serious disturbances occur in Manila—*disturbances that I regret*—but which serve to show *that I am not the one,* as they believe, who stirs things. *My absolute innocence* has been demonstrated as can be seen in the two letters of introduction in his own writing to the ministers of war and colonies that the governor has given me as well as the accompanying letter which says:

The Commander in Chief of the Army of the Philippines

Mr. Jose Rizal

MY DEAR SIR,

Enclosed are two letters for the Ministers of War and Colonies which I think will be well received.

I have no doubt that you will justify me before the Government by your future behaviour not only for your word of honour *but because the present happenings must have shown you palpably that certain actions which are the product of foolish ideas yield no other result but hatred, destruction, tears, and blood.*

May you be very happy is the wish of your attentive servant who kisses your hand,
Ramon Blanco
Manila, 30 August

The texts of the two letters of introduction are identical and I shall copy only one:

The Captain General of the Philippines

Personal

Manila, 30 August 1896

Most Excellent Marcelo de Azcarraga

My esteemed General and distinguished Friend,

I recommend to you with genuine interest Dr. Jose Rizal who is departing for the Peninsula at the disposal of the Government, ever desirous of rendering his services as physician to the Army in Cuba.

His conduct during the four years that he was in exile in Dapitan has been exemplary and he is, in my opinion, the more worthy of pardon and benevolence as he is in no way involved either in the *chimerical attempt that we are lamenting these days or in any conspiracy or secret society* that they have been plotting.

With this object I have the pleasure to remain, your most affectionate friend and colleague who kisses your hand,

Ramon Blanco.

The letter of recommendation to the Minister of Colonies is identical.

With these two letters I have come, confident that *I would go to Cuba to win a name and undo calumnies*. Now they tell me that they are sending me to Ceuta!!

I cannot believe this for it would be the greatest injustice and the most abominable infamy, unworthy not of a military official but of the last bandit. *I have offered to serve as physician, risking life in the hazards of war and abandoning all my business. I am innocent* and now in reward they are sending me to prison!!!

I cannot believe it!This is infamous, but if it turns out to be true, as everybody assures me, I am communicating to you these news so that you may appraise my situation.

Yours,

Jose Rizal."

In a letter by Antonio Ma. Regidor Jurado to Jose Ma. Basa dated 7 June 1895, which we have partly reproduced above, the subject of which was how to get Rizal out of Dapitan, Regidor remarked in italics: "*All are agreed that the best solution was Rizal's escape; and as you know that I have always been a practical partisan of this solution, I cannot understand why our friend whom I believed courageous and intrepid does not adopt it.*" In a letter dated May 26, 1895, by Rizal's sister, Trinidad, to the same friend and devoted assister of Rizal in propaganda and other matters, Jose Ma. Basa, who was based in Hong Kong (see above, p.), we read of a plot to snatch Rizal away that Trinidad herself, with the help of the mason and propagandist Timoteo Paez was organizing, which, as we know, Rizal himself had rejected. In a letter written two months before Trinidad's, and addressed to Dr. Lorenzo Marquez (see above), Rizal mentioned how: "Some have proposed to me to escape"; he rejected the proposals, he said, because "I have nothing to reproach myself," and did "not want later to be called a 'runaway'". He added that running away thus would prevent him later on from returning to his country. In the same letter by Regidor, the latter wrote that "the sympathetic Mr. Blumentritt" had written to him "that Rizal wanted to leave". Rizal, we surmise, must have told Blumentritt in a letter which we have not located, of his desire to leave Dapitan (or to be released from exile). Accordingly, when Blumentritt came to know of the Cuban opening, he immediately informed Rizal about it. And in the November 20, 1895 letter by Rizal to Blumentritt we have also reproduced above, we find Rizal lauding the "excellent idea" and telling his Austrian friend that he was applying at once. Then, in a letter to his mother dated December 18, 1895 (which we have failed to reproduce here because I can no longer locate the copy of the book *Correspondence Between Rizal and His Family* at the University of the Philippines main library; the assiduous reader can however follow the thing up anytime[12]), Rizal mentioned this project to her, telling her that he had been waiting for Blanco's response, and that he intended to follow it up.

---

[12]It happens that I am in mortal hurry to finish this book on time for the Rizal Sesquicentennial Conference at UP Diliman, it is the 9th of June, and that conference from which the organizers have banned me is on June 22 to 24. My plan is to ambush the participants with this book outside the conference hall…

What all these cross-references tell us should be plain enough and unproblematic—but it is not. And this because Rizal's way of thinking about the matter was very far from being plain and unproblematic. Rizal, at least during his last year in Dapitan, wanted to get out, *but he did not want to escape*[13]. And why did he not want to escape? Because "I have nothing to reproach myself", he said. That is to say: he did

---

[13]We know this—that perhaps as early as April 1895, Rizal had already expressed his desire to leave Dapitan and to be a free man once more but not through anything illegal--from a letter, cited elsewhere in this volume, from Antonio Regidor to Jose Ma. Basa, dated 7 June 1895, the subject of which was the possibilities of getting Rizal out of Dapitan legally or by escaping from the almost unguarded exile, and where Regidor wrote: "The sympathetic Mr.Blumentritt wrote me later that Rizal wanted to leave and much later I received your letter…" In what appears to have been an underscored sentence, Regidor let out his own puzzlement concerning Rizal's refusal to quite simply escape: "All agreed that the best solution was Rizal's escape; and as you know that I have always been a practical partisan of this solution, I cannot understand why our friend whom I believed courageous and intrepid does not adopt it." (*Correspondence with Fellow Reformists*, pp. 721-722.) . We have not located Blumentritt's letter to Regidor, but we know from a letter from Rizal to Blumentritt dated November 25, 1895, that they were indeed writing to each other about this desire of getting out; it was in this letter (see p. 514 of the *Rizal-Blumentritt Correspondence*) that Rizal thanked his good friend for the "most excellent " information about the army doctor post in Cuba: "Concerning your advice on going to Cuba as a physician, it seems to me most excellent and right now I am going to write to the Governor General…"

not want to escape because he was absolutely convinced that he was innocent of whatever wrongdoing or crime it was for which he was banished to Dapitan? This would be curious. For if he was innocent or knew himself innocent, why should he faithfully serve the sentence? In other words, such innocence should rather have constituted (if Rizal were not so intellectually, emotionally and immorally messy) an imperative and urgent ground to escape; and this most especially so if Rizal as alleged by his thoughtless and horrifically brainwashed heroifiers, wanted to do anything revolutionary for his native, Indio, not Spanish, country and native, Indio, not Spanish people. Or else, there really was a pang of guilt in him, but that whatever guilt it was that he himself felt, and which he had duly acknowledged to himself, a guilt to, of course, of course, his utterly beloved Mother Spain of whom he was a most ardent and truly great patriot, a guilt which he could have contracted solely by way of his novels, he must have felt that he had already expiated it and had already atoned for it and paid for it enough by having uncomplainingly and exemplarily served three years of his sentence. Of the reality of this guilt (which would as such be tantamount to acknowledging to its (i.e., this guilt's) exact extent that he indeed had in some way inflicted harm against this utmostly beloved Mother Spain which/whom he loved beyond words, and had in some way hurt her sacred interests, we come most acutely to be aware in his final letter to his brother Paciano written in the late afternoon of the day before he was shot. In this absolutely momentously revelatory letter, Rizal blurted out, and I was amazed when first I opened my eyes to it, and am still quite amazed even now reading it or thinking of it,that he had since Dapitan regretted having written the *Noli* and the *Fili* and the associated works, mostly essays, in that (and to the exact extent that) they "may have contributed" something "to the rebellion"; in other words, Rizal in his Dapitan solitude must have been able to at last imagine the possibility that his attack against the friars and his criticisms of the colonial administration (though in fact too mild especially alongside his fierce exposures of the immoral and insatiable friar piranhas)could be taken in the wrongest possible way by the Filipinos and lead to the promotion of separation/revolution/independence which he of course abhorred unto death, instead of his and his ilustrado confraternity's intensely and protractedly hallucinated ass-imilation and seats for themselves at the Spanish Cortes!

Rizal's love of his Mother Country, which was not the Philippines of course but Spain, Mother Spain, absolutely beloved Spain for which, for whom, Rizal was eager, not merely willing but eager, very, very eager, *to die*, and for whom he indeed died, for he died defending her against the rapacious and lewd and concupiscent friars—Rizal's love and devotion for Spain was such that he would rather be dead than escape or in any way evade the severity of his punishment by her. He so loved Spain that not even the *Rape of Calamba* was enough for him to abandon her and take the separatist revolutionary leap. He so loved Spain that duly chastised by his banishment, he resolved completely to abandon politics and acted politically only from that time on against non-Spaniards, against his perceived enemies of Mother Spain, namely the separatists, the revolutionaries, whether they be Filipino Katipuneros or Cuban Katipuneros or Katipuneros anywhere in the universe (Rizal was an international, a universal, counter-revolutionary and a very deeply disguised enemy of humanity whose mask as such was deftly sewn onto the very linings of his *double entendre* "patriotic" and martyristical face). Not even against the friars did he once again do anything, for, after all, the friars were Spaniards.

When your mother sanctions you and punishes you for something you did not do—and you are that type of person for whom filial piety is absolute because your mother is your absolute and love of her is the absolute principle of your life, you would tend indeed to humbly accept such punishment and not seek to evade it or escape from it. Being a runaway from your mother would mean being unable once again to present yourself to her. There must have been something of this predicament in Rizal's emotional and intellectual and (im)moral condition which determined him to do two things or rather to abstain from doing two things: he abandoned politics altogether, as he often declared to people in his many letters: that is to say, he ceased completely to engage in that kind of activity for doing which he was punished by his mother—his Mother Spain; on the other hand, this despair of having alienated himself from his Mother Spain so, had determined him not merely to distance himself from separatism and revolution as he used to do, nor merely increase such distance, but to absolutely abhor, and detest, and abominate revolution itself. His love and devotion to his Mother Spain was so excessive that he could not bear the thought of being completely banished from her sight, of being a "runaway" from her, and of thereby becoming thenceforth unable to present himself to her. Hence, his refusal to escape, his inability even merely to imagine wanting to escape. He would be able to want to leave Dapitan only if it was because he was released by the authorities, i.e., by Mother Spain herself. Thenceforth, he had only one wish on his mind, and that was to be able to serve Mother Spain so, and do many glorious things for Mother Spain so, that he would thereby be able to redeem himself before her eyes. Hence, the exceedingly great excellence of the idea presented to him by his Austrian-Spanish friend Blumentritt of the fateful chance to leave Dapitan for Cuba in order to fight to the death there in defense of Mother Spain's glorious colonialism and against those abhorrent dismemberers of her, the Cuban Katipuneros! The idea, the opportunity, was indeed made in heaven! Hence, we should really take absolutely seriously what he said in this letter in a matter of course and even almost circumstantial waywhen he said that he was going to Cuba "to win a name and undo calumnies".

If you are a real revolutionary, especially in so brutish a situation as that in which the *Rape of Calamba* could happen, you can at the very most say *only* of the outbreak of hostilities that it is not yet time and that it should as much as possible be prevented from happening so soon. In other words, if Rizal was a real if hidden revolutionary, he would in fact have been doing exactly what Bonifacio and Jacinto and the rest of the of course underground (i.e., real and of course underground) KKK members were doing. You cannot, if you are a sincere and true and unstupid revolutionary of that time postpone underground—necessarily underground-- revolutionary work—and say, it's not yet time, let's wait for the proper time.

In the ultimate analysis, Rizal's complete—except for the three anti-revolutionary crimes he perpetrated there, namely, his betrayal of an emissary from the KKK and therewith his betrayal of the KKK itself sometime in late 1892 during the presidency of Deodato Arellano, his rejection of Bonifacio's offer for him to join and lead the Revolution on July 1, 1896, and his successful attempt to argue the liar and traitor Pio Valenzuela out of revolution and the KKK, and of course his determined refusal to escape, for such refusal must at once be taken as a rejection of revolution—abandonment of politics during his four years of exile in Dapitan must constitute the biggest and most obstreperous demonstration that he was a false patriot and that he could not even have been a hidden separatist revolutionary who was supposedly merely waiting for the proper time to do something about it, i.e., that he must most certainly not be any kind of separatist or revolutionary at all.[14]

Of course, *almost* nothing can be more anti-revolutionary and politically immoral, and politically anti-human, than Rizal's Cuba escapade itself[15]. That he premeditated it, that he

---

[14]Note how even merely to call Rizal a *false revolutionary* must at once feel and look awkward and malaprop. You do not say for instance that Pedro Paterno was a false revolutionary, or that the brothers Trinidad and Felix Pardo de Tavera were untrue revolutionaries: they never had anything whatsoever to do with revolution, i.e., with separatism (during that time they were one and the same thing) except in varying degrees of abhorrence in rejecting it, so that even merely that negative qualification in relation to them could sound like a category mistake.

[15]*Almost*, because his unspeakably immoral and antihuman act of offering himself carrion and stinking pestiferous soul to Governor General Ramon Blanco y Erenas

embarked on it protractedly, even doggedly, and indeed, even ratly, and not with any attempt at secrecy either, should have been more than enough indigestible fact to prevent anyone who is not insanely stupid from regarding Rizal except as a brutish enemy of humanity, a shameless traitor to his own country and people and a conscienceless hater of his own country and people. Anyone not insanely stupid should of course first of all put herself/himself in the shoes or shoelessness of the Cuban revolutionaries, of the Cuban

---

through a letter witnessed by the commander of the Spanish warship *Castilla*, Colonel Santalo, "to be used in whatever manner" the Spaniards "might deem fit, to stifle the rebellion" sometime between August 29 and September 2, 1896, was *mostmost*. And the only thing that could have beaten it in perfidious cravenness and evil treachery against the Filipino people and their revolution and their freedom, was it itself, this unspeakable offering of himself itself *accepted and implemented by Blanco*—Rizal in person at the head of the Colonial Intelligence Agency (CIA) sniffing, ferreting out and exposing and denouncing and executing by droves the revolutionary leadership, hot on the trail of Andres Bonifacio and having Melchora Aquino nailed upon the front door of her house for being hospitable to the Katipuneros, and Dr. Jose Rizal too at the head of the Pacification Propaganda Bureau campaigning mightily to brainwash the Indios against the Revolution, and Dr. Jose Protacio Rizal Mercado too at the head of the Colonial Army massacring the Katipuneros in the of course vain attempt to "stifle the rebellion"... And your national hero Jose Rizal was even able in unwordable shamelessness and utterest cowardice to cite and orate in open court this offertorial crime to save his own scruffy neck (and did not the Spanish soldiers trying him vomit in volcanic disgust upon witnessing him testify thus to his own absolute honorlessness made even more pukegenic by his owning it thus?).

katipuneros themselves, and therewith in the place and situation and position of the Cuban people struggling to liberate themselves from the evil and criminal and anti-human clutches of Spanish colonialism—and from *there* consider what kind of perverted, distorted, farcically and absurdly evil being this Doctor Rizal must malefically be whose mortal concern and dedicated worry was that "soldiers", exclusively Spanish ones of course, whose evil task and criminal, inhuman career was to massacre them and prevent them from being free in their own country, "were dying there without medical assistance", and whom then this scabrously souled Doctor Rizal wanted to keep alive and healthy and strong so that they might be able to kill and maim and torture more of them. How could Rizal have even merely imagined doing it? And yet, we must believe him in his sincerity when he wrote to his Austrian friend that it was "a most excellent idea"!

Will some smart aleck with his brain in his rectum argue that colonialism is not that evil, that it also had contributed many good things, in particular Ingoo de Guzman's English, as Nick Joaquin for instance argued that Spanish colonialism had given us the adobo and roses and pancit guisado and we should then love it and not denounce it as we love adobo and roses and camaron rebosado? Anyone who argues like that is a cuspidor and an inudour. Human beings should, being human, not even be able to imagine making such arguments, thinking such thoughts...You cannot justify colonialism without at the same time justifying Auschwitz. You cannot praise Rizal's Cuban doctoral expedition without at once praising the Nazi doctors who took care of the health of Nazi massmurderers so that they could be more efficient massmurderers... And *that* is that!

To deprive a human being of freedom and the dignity, indeed the sublimity that goes with it, is an absolute evil, is evil without qualification, because every human being is the absolute and is the sublime itself, and s/he is so because s/he is free—a transcendence, a being who is infinitely more than being itself. Colonialism is that absolute evil perpetrated against an entire people, against, say, the 8 million souls, the 8 million absolutes, who were our ancestors during Rizal's and Bonifacio's time. Because the human being is the absolute, s/he is beyond numeration and the utilitarian calculator is a pig.

In fact Rizal showed himself such a monster of immorality here that one feels like retorting *putangina mu* to anyone who defends him here or fails even to see in it his monstrous immorality...

But Rizal wanted to go to Cuba to study the revolution there firsthand so that he would be able to be a better revolutionary leader here when the "proper time" to do it should come? Let us once and for all refute here, now, this witless argument which shames all of us Filipino intellectuals in that it could at all occur here, and in textbooks in history too, and yes even in supposedly scholarly journals, without anyone even noticing that something must be severely wrong in the very concept of it, in the very conceptlessness of it, indeed in the very inconceivability of it..., in the inconceivable stupidity of it.

1.) In the first place, on July 1, 1896, a full month before he received Blanco's letter (July 30, 1896) informing him that his application has been approved by the Madrid government, and that he could at once proceed to Manila for the necessary accreditations (the above-cited letters precisely), he was fully informed by Pio Valenzuela about the by then already four year-old revolution-in-the-making, and was even invited to join it, and even to head it. If he really just wanted to study a revolution firsthand so that he could do it "expertly" here against the same Spaniards when the "proper time" came, why did he not just choose to study this impending one by joining it, or even by requesting observer status while going with the Katipuneros to battlefields and conference rooms/caves? Or did he want to study one that was already at the stage of the shooting war as already the Cuban revolution was? Then why did he not join it instead of going ahead with his Cuba escapade when the shooting war broke out on August 29, six days before his mail boat sailed away? Because he could not escape from the *Castilla*? But he could have made such an escape by simply disembarking and disappearing during the stopover in Singapore, as we know Pedro Roxas and some other Filipinos did who had some apprehensions of getting arrested upon reaching Spain. Escaping thus, he could have secretly returned to the country to join the KKK.

2.) But perhaps, what Rizal wanted was to be able to research a revolution from the vantage point of the enemy of it, namely the colonizers? And that was why he volunteered to die for Spain, in defense of Spain, against the Katipuneros, in that letter which he wrote to General Blanco and which was witnessed by Colonel Santalo[16]? For his offer of his body and

---

[16]Let us cite this document once more in which he owned in writing that he wrote this immoral and swinish letter to Governor General Blanco, let us not tire of exposing it again and again and again for the Filipinos need it as they need to know the very root and origin of the corruption of their souls: "Nay, when the uprising broke out, I was on board the *Castilla*, incommunicado, ***and*** *I offered myself unconditionally to His Excellency (a thing I had never done before) to suppress the rebellion.* But this was a personal letter and it was witnessed by Colonel Santalo. This cannot be used without the permission of His Excellency" (*Data for My Defense*, Rizal's Political & Historical Writings, NHI, Manila, 2007; p. 339.) And let us once more cite the Manifesto of December 15, 1896 which he addressed to the revolutionists and submitted to the military court as another shameless proof of his innocence, of his undying love of and loyalty to Spain, and of his being the mortal enemy of the Filipino people and of their Revolution and of his being the deadly scuttler of their freedom and the dedicated stifler of their desire and their movement for independence: "Fellow countrymen:…Since the beginning, when I heard of what was being planned (namely, the Revolution), I opposed it and fought it, and I demonstrated its absolute impossibility. This is the truth and those who heard me are living. I was convinced that

soul to be used by the Spaniards "to stifle the rebellion" included of course his leading a battalion or brigade or division or even the entirety of the Guardia Civil against Andres Bonifacio and company. But Blanco failed to appreciate the great academic virtues of his research project ha ha ha.

3.) So Rizal wanted to do some field research on revolution in order to prepare himself for his own revolution here in the Philippines "when the proper time comes"! Granted. Although the very idea is incredibly stupid and only in the Philippines by such as the so-called historians here could the idea be taken seriously:--by, in fact all of them without a single known exception before I wrote a word to expose its *only the in the Philippines* stupidity. And was Rizal really that incredibly stupid to even merely imagine entertaining it? But these so-called historians themselves are devoted Rizalists and they maintain like it was a most bright thing that Rizal applied for that Cuban slot in order precisely to do revolutionary field research. So we have to grant it. But why did he not decide to do his field research here, by joining the KKK Revolution? Because he wanted to do the research from the side of the colonial army and that was why he volunteered to Blanco for him body and soul to be used by the Spaniards to suppress the revolution? Unfortunately, Blanco failed to take his offer of absolute sacrifice seriously. Of course, he could not tell Blanco that he wanted to join the Spanish Army against Bonifacio and the KKK because he wanted to study the Revolution firsthand so that he could do it better against the Spaniards later on, "when the proper time comes";

---

the idea was highly absurd and what was worse, fatal. I did more. When later, despite my counsels, the uprising broke out, ***I offered spontaneously, not only my services, but my life, and even my name so that they might use them in the way they deem opportune in order to quench the rebellion***..." (*Manifesto to Some Filipinos*, ibid., 348).

nakakahiya kasi. At tsaka, baka magalit naman yung isa! But why did he want to study the revolution as a Spanish military officer? Type lang nya. Tsaka, me sweldo kaya dun, sa KKK wala. At tyak, maganda uniporme; pagsusuutin mo ba si Rizal ng dinampol? And that's that. Genius kz sya eh...

Chapter 9

TESTIMONIES FROM *EL FILIBUSTERISMO*

It was the narrator speaking. Of course, formally and structurally, the narrator is not the author. The literary form is a crystallization of transcendence, of freedom; it at once imposes an infinite difference, an infinite distance, between the author and the literary voice. However, if it happens that we read elsewhere words by the author unmediated by the transcendentalizing form of literature and thus owned by him/her as such, which words repeat almost verbatim or as the drift goes this narrator of his, we can say that he forgot himself and had usurped completely the place and authority of the narrator and willy nilly had spoken for himself...

Here then are some passages from the novel sequel which, according to the author himself was written by him to cleanse and clarify the non-and-anti-filibusterist, that is to say, the non-and-anti-separatist, non-and-anti-revolutionary, non-and-anti-independence stand, advocacy, and image of *La Solidaridad* in particular and of the ilustrado assimilationist propagandists in general, "bewhitening" the ilustrado propagandists, and he himself with them, as he himself puts it in the several letters we have excerpted above on the matter (to Marcelo del Pilar, Eduardo de Lete, Mariano Ponce, Blumentritt...) by setting them off in lurid contrast with Simoun whom Rizal construed to be the true image of a *filibustero*! (which shows how ignorant and perverted Rizal's view of revolution was...)

Here then are some excerpts from the *Fili* in Virgilio Almario's Tagalog, which presumably he or some other/s translated from the original Spanish or from some English translation/s, we don't know exactly which, for it was *purposely neglected* by Virgilio Almario to tell us exactly from where and how right there in the copies themselves, not on the cover, not on the title page, not anywhere there, so that, puzzling over this mysterious fear and inability to declare the *traduttorial* provenance of the thing, one is left with the only conclusion possible namely, that he must have very solid reasons to be afraid of being pinned by someone to the published claim that he translated the novel/s from Rizal's original Spanish, as though fearful that such a someone might bring the case to the court of law…(for no one knew before the translation/s came out that Almario could speak a word of Spanish)…

1.) *Paghihiganti ni Tales* (pahina 71 at kasunod)

"Kinagabihan, tatlong pagpaslang ang naganap. Sa hangganan ng bukid ni Kabesang Tales, natagpuang patay ang sundalong fraile at ang bagong kasama, basag ang bungo at puno ng lupa ang bibig at may gilit ang leeg. Sa papel na nasa tabi nito ay mababasa ang pangalang 'Tales' na isinulat sa pamamagitan ng daliring isinawsaw sa dugo.

"Pumanatag kayo, mga mapayapang mamamayan ng Calamba! Walang sino man sa inyo ang may pangalang 'Tales', walang sino man sa inyo ang gumawa ng krimen! Kayong nagngangalang Luis Habana, Matias Belarmino, Niceso Eisagani, Cayetano de Jesus, Mateo Elejorde, Leandro Lopez, Antonio Lopez, Silvestre Ubaldo, Manuel Hidalgo, Paciano Mercado, kayong lahat na tinatawag na bayani ng Calamba!...[17] Nilinis ninyo and inyong mga bukirin, ginugol ninyo and inyong mga buhay sa paggawa, pagiimpok, pagpupuyat, pagtitiis, at pagkatapos, inagaw sa inyo, pinalayas kayo sa inyong mga tahanan at pinagbawalan ang ibang kupkupin kayo! Hindi pa sila nasiyahan sa paglabag sa katarungan, nilapastangan din nila ang banal na kaugalian ng inyong bayan… Naglingkod kayo sa Espanya at sa hari, at nang humingi kayo ng katarungan sa ngalan nila, ipinatapon

---

[17] The abovenamed were all Rizal's brothers-in-law and his brother Paciano. And one wonders why they should at all be considered heroes of Calamba—just because they suffered the brunt of Dominican evil? Or they happened to be Rizal's closest relatives?

kayo ng walang paglilitis, inagaw kayo sa bisig ng inyong mga asawa, sa halik ng inyong mga anak... Higit sa tiniis ni Kabesang Tales ang tiniis ng bawat isa sa inyo, ngunit walang sinuman ang nagtamo ng katarungan...Walang habag ni lingap na iniukol sa inyo at inuusig kayo hanggang sa ibayo ng hukay gaya ng ginawa kay Mariano Herbosa...Tumangis o tumawa kayo sa mapanglaw na kapuluang nilalabuyan ninyo ng walang kabuluhan at hindi natitiyak ang hinaharap. ANG ESPANYA, ANG MAPAGPALANG ESPANYA, ANG TUMATANGKILIK SA INYO AT SA MALAO'T MADALI, KAKAMTIN NINYO ANG KATARUNGAN"[18].

---

18 There you have him, the assimilationist-to-death narrator. While Rizal was finishing the *Fili*, the long drawn-out dispossession of the inhabitants of Calamba by the ever-greedy Dominican friars was in full swing; it culminated in the *Rape of Calamba.* The atrocities perpetrated by the friars were able to enter the novel; Rizal's relatives were directly mentioned thus in the narrative. A number of Rizal's fellow reformist-assimilationist crusaders in Barcelona and Madrid were radicalized by it into separatism and revolution, notably Antonio Luna, Jose Alejandrino, Edilberto Evangelista, even Mariano Ponce; there were indications that the entire Barcelona colony was merely waiting for Rizal to tell them to make the leap with him into separatism and revolution; they thought it had become inevitable for Rizal to turn revolutionary at last; they told him they were just waiting for him to lead them, to organize the revolution. Jaena, who was already a separatist even before the Calamba atrocities became known also concluded that Rizal must already be a revolutionary. As we see in one of his letters above, he was waiting for Rizal to lead the way. But no. What the Calamba question was able to push Rizal into was nothing but this more perfervid grovelling and more zealous manifestation of eternal hope that "care-bestowing and

2.) *Rizal summarizes the pink and purple naivete of ilustradist assimilationism which at that exact hour and until death was his, in this passage from El Filibusterismo in which he, or MH del Pilar, or de Lete, was Isagani dreaming (pp 200-201).*

Whilst, according to Rizal himself in several letters and other documents, he made Simoun a terrorist and "true" *filibustero* in order to demonstrate to the Spaniards in Spain, specifically the Madrid government, that they, the ilustrado assimilationists were farthest from being *filibusteros*, for the true *filibustero* is someone like Simoun (see various letters above).

Beneath the moonlight, and suddenly his beloved, the most beautiful girl in the world, Paulita Gomez, and addressing her too, thus, Isagani gushing forth:

"Kung saan mabilis

At lumilipad

Ang pagsibad

Ng mga lokomotora

---

love-giving Spain" (mapagpalang Espanya) "which protects you and promotes your interests" (tumatangkilik sa inyo) "will sooner or later give you justice" (kakamtin ninyo ang katarungan)… Assimilationist to death, Rizal was anti-revolution to death: in his last two letters written in the late afternoon of December 29, 1896, he would re-affirm to the same relatives of his and to his best friend, Blumentritt that: "I will die innocent of the crime of rebellion".

Wika nga ng kung sino.

Sa gayon, mabubuksan para sa lahat ang pinakamagagandang mga sulok ng kapuluan…[19]

Paulita: “Oo nga, ngunit kailan? Kung matanda na ako?

Isagani: “Aba! Hindi mo alam ang magagawa natin sa loob ng ilang taon”, tugon ni Isagani. “Hindi mo alam ang lakas at sigla ng bayang nagigising pagkatapos ng dantaong pagkahimbing…***lilingapin tayo ng Espanya.*** *Araw-gabing kumikilos ang ating mga kabataan sa Madrid* at inihahandog sa *Inang Bayan* ang lahat ng kanilang talino, ang lahat ng kanilang panahon, ang lahat ng kanilang pagsisikap. Nakikipag-isa sa tinig natin ang mga mapagmalasakit na tinig doon, mga pulitikong nakakaunawa na wala nang bubuti pang bigkis kaysa nagkakaisang hangarin at damdamin. Tatanggap tayo ng katarungan at inihuhudyat ng lahat ang isang maningning na kinabukasan para sa lahat!...

“Bukas, [20] magiging mamamayan tayo ng Filipinas” **(sapagkat O hi hi hi, LILINGAPIN TAYO NG ESPANYA, ah ha ha ha, sapagkat ARAW-GABING KUMIKILOS ANG ATING MGA KABATAANG ASIMILASYONISTANG SINA RIZAL, DEL PILAR, ETCETERA, SA MADRID)** “na magiging kaayaaya ang kapalaran sapagkat nasa mapagmahal na kamay” **(ng Espanya, ng mapanglingap**

[19] Tourism ha ha ha. Boracayism, ha ha ha.

[20] Rizal’s assimilationist, eternal colonialist, anti-revolutionary, anti-separatist, anti-independence, anti-Filipino-people hope for a seat in the Spanish Cortes springs eternal indeed in his multi-centurial colonial-middleclass-collaborationist breast…

at mapagpalang Inang Espanya, yeheheyyyy!). Oo, atin ang hinaharap, nakikita kong kulay rosas, natatanaw ko ang pintig ng buhay sa mga rehiyong ito na matagal nang patay, nahihimbing.... Nakikita ko ang pagtindig ng mga bayan kahanay ng mga daangbakal, at may mga pabrika sa lahat ng dako, mga gusaling katulad ng nasa Mandaluyong! Naririnig ko ang silbato ng bapor, ang sagitsit ng tren, ang kalampag ng mga makina... Magtatanod ang ating hukbong dagat sa mga baybayin. **MAGPAPALIGSAHAN ANG MGA ESPANYOL AT FILIPINO UPANG MAITABOY ANG DAYUHANG PANANALAKAY, UPANG IPAGTANGGOL ANG ATING MGA TAHANAN...**

"Malaya sa sistema ng paniniil, walang poot ni kawalang-tiwala, magtatrabaho ang bayan sapagkat sa panahong iyon ay hindi na mapandusta ang pagtatrabaho, hindi na mapambusabos na ipapataw sa alipin. **SA GAYON, HINDI NA PAAASIMIN NG ESPANYOL ANG KANYANG PAGUUGALI SA PAMAMAGITAN NG KATAWATAWANG PAGHAHARIHARIAN..."**

3.) *Simoun. Portrait of the revolutionary as demonic and of the revolution as suicidal destruction: in which Rizal, who had never spoken of revolution except in such terms, indiscriminately lumped revolution with all forms of terrorism and massmurder, with power for power's sake mass-violence, and even with the wholesale violence of colonial conquest! No wonder then that he must die as he did denouncing revolution, cursing the Bonifacio-led revolution, and insisting in his final letters to relatives and friend, that he will die "innocent of the crime of rebellion"*

Simoun speaking to Basilio whom he just yanked out of prison through his political connections and was now persuading to act as his accomplice in the mass-carnage which he planned to turn the wedding reception of Paulita Gomez and Juanito Pelaez into:

> "At sapagkat higit na mabunga ang lupa kapag lalong napapatabaan ng dugo at higit na tumatatag ang trono kapag lalong nasesementuhan ng mga krimen at bangkay, alisin ang pagaatubili, alisin ang pagaalinlangan" (p 263)

And the narrator-Rizal's commentary:

"Ang gayong marubdob na pangangatwiran, ipinahayag ng may paninindigan at lamig ng kalooban, ang lumupig sa binata, na pinahina ang isipan ng mahigit tatlong buwang pagkabilanggo, at binubulag ng silakbo ng paghihiganti kaya't wala siya sa kalagayan upang suriin ang saligang moral ng mga bagay bagay. Hindi naisagot na ang taong pinakamasama man o pinakamahina ang loob ay laging higit sa isang halaman, dahil may kaluluwa at isipan, na gaano man kasama o kababa ay maililigtas pa rin. Hindi naisagot na walang karapatan ang tao na takdaan ang buhay ng sinuman tungo sa pakinabang ng sinuman, at may karapatang mabuhay ang bawat isa bukod sa may karapatan sa kalayaan at kaliwanagan. Hindi nasabing ang Diyos lamang ang *maaaring magtangka* ng gayong pamamaraan, na maaaring *magwasak* ang Diyos sapagkat maaaring lumikha, na hawak ng Diyos ang gantimpala, ang kawalanghanggan, at ang hinaharap *upang bigyan ng katuwiran ang Kanyang mga ginawa, at hindi ito kailanman maaaring hawakan ng tao!* Sa halip na sabihin ang mga pangangatwirang ito, ang tanging naitutol ni Basilio ay isang karaniwang puna:

"Ano kaya ang sasabihin ng mundo kapag nakita ang ganyan karaming pagpatay?"

Simoun's answer to this question completes the Rizalian-theologistic pacifist-opportunist reformist-assimilationist reduction of revolution to terrorism and his condemnation of the former with his condemnation of the latter implicit in his condemnation and refutation of the figure and meaning of Simoun which according to him himself in those abovementioned letters to Plaridel, Lete, et. al., was the main thrust and intent of the novel, namely to demonstrate, by stark contrast with the blackness and (and what else indeed in view of the ultimately theological background and impetus of Rizal's opportunist-pacifist anti-revolutionism, anti-separatism, anti-independence-ism?) *demonism* of the "true *filibustero*" Simoun, the pacifist, theological, God-fearing, even Roman Catholic (note Rizal's emphatic projection of this distinction borne by his Austrian assimilationist co-crusader Blumentritt in his editorial prologue to the latter's review of his *Noli me tangere*), *angelical* anti-separatism, anti-revolutionism, anti-independence-ism, anti-Filipino-pro-Spanish-eternal-colonialism purity and "whiteness" of the *La Solidaridad* and Madrid-based reformist-asssimilationist *crusaders*:

"Papalakpak ang mundo, gaya ng dati, ibibigay ang katuwiran sa lalong malakas, sa lalong marahas!", tugon ni Simoun kalakip ang ngiting malupit. "Pumalakpak ang Europa ng isakripisyo ng mga bansa sa kanluran ang milyon milyong Indio sa Amerika at hindi naman ginawa iyon upang magtatag ng mga bansang higit na moral at higit na mapayapa. Masdan ang Hilaga sa kanyang makasariling kalayaan, sa kanyang batas ni Lynch, sa kanyang mga pandarayang pampulitika. *Masdan ang matahimik-diling mga republika ng Timog, SA KANILANG MABABANGIS NA REBOLUSYON, sa mga digmaang sibil, mga batas militar na gaya sa kanilang Inang Espanya*! [21] Pumalakpak ang Europa ng lupigin ng

---

[21] Here is where the lumping of revolution with terrorism, with unprincipled violence, with absolutely rightless, justiceless, demonic, suicidal, anti-people, anti-social, immoral violence was by Rizal perpetrated in this text—a lumping and dumping into the common/kumon which is in fact everywhere in Rizal's writings and deeds and non-deeds. "Matahimik-dili", "mababangis"—it is in the of course negative use of these adjectives that Rizal betrays

makapangyarihang Portugal ang kapuluang Molucas, pumalakpak ng puksain ng Inglatera ang mga lahing primitibo sa Pasipiko upang palitan ng kanyang mga emigrante. Pumalakpak ang Europa tulad sa pagpalakpak sa wakas ng isang dula, sa wakas ng isang trahedya. Halos hindi pinupuna ng karaniwang tao ang saligan ng mga bagay bagay, ang tanging tinitingnan ay ang bunga. Gawing mahusay ang krimen at hahangaan ito at lalong darami ang mga kapanalig kaysa gawang mabuti, na ginagawa ng mapagkumbaba at nakikimi" (p 264).

And Basilio has now become a mere vengeful terrorist who however, as per the Rizalian theological-pacifistic-colonial-might-is-right recipe has swallowed indiscriminately the Simoun-Rizal reduction of revolutionary violence into terroristic necessarily anti-society violence:

"Tamang-tama", sagot ng binata. E ano ba sa akin kung pumalakpak sila at mamintas? Wala namang malasakit ang mundong iyon sa mga naaapi, sa mga kawawa, at sa mahinang babae? Bakit ako *magsasaalang-alang sa lipunan* samantalang

---

his abhorrence of revolution. Witness the unwordably execrable ideological opportunism behind such theological, angelical, pacifism: he forgot as a matter of the standard colonial perversion of his humanity, of the standard colonial perversion and shrivelling of his soul, of the standard colonial perversion and stunting and dishonestification and tinification of his colonial middle-class colonial-collaborationist mind, the multi-centurial violence of colonialism against the enslaved and dignity-denied native people. And conveniently, he forgot also the deluge-of-blood violence, always of genocidal proportions, of the colonial conquest upon which the always mass-murderous dignity-denying and exploitative quotidian "peace" of colonial domination was founded.

wala naman itong pagsasaalang-alang munti man ukol sa akin?"

"Why should I take into consideration society at all when to me society shows no consideration whatsoever?" If Rizal had been careful enough to make and underline the difference, a whole world of it, and thus an infinity of it, between terroristic violence and revolutionary violence[22]—a carefulness he had

---

22 Revolutionary violence, especially anticolonial revolutionary violence which is the clearest and purest kind of revolutionary violence there is, the all-the-time perfectly justified and urgently necessary kind of violence, is of course *violence*, and therefore *tragic*. Were not evil *evil*, there should never have been such violence. Whilst than colonial evil, than evil perpetrated by a people against another of such a scale and depth as to directly and irremediably deny the victim people's humanity, freedom, dignity, nothing is eviler—as most horribly demonstrated by the Nazi holocaust, and by the Turks' murder of two million Armenians in 1915:--of course there was the most successful genocide to date perpetrated by the white race against the Indians of North America, let no one forget that. Class-violence comes a very close second of course and is very close indeed to eclipsing the evil of the first: the Gulag, Pol Pot's Killing Fields… The point is revolutionary violence in this its purest form of anti-colonial violence is the violence exercised by the entire society, in fact, by the people themselves against the unqualified and unqualifiable evil of the colonialists, and Rizal cannot be more wrong in simply treating it as a form of violence against society itself as undoubtedly terrorism is; whilst, more evilly violent *against society, against of course native society*, is colonial violence in its quotidianity (an everydayness that makes evil a banality and for such beneficiaries of it as Rizal and his colonial middleclass collaborator family, virtually imperceptible), and for being permanent and long-term…

never in any case shown anywhere in his works and deeds—he would have avowed right here, and blazoned in clear logic and distinct passion that as antipodally against terroristic or unprincipled violence such as Simoun was about to attempt to consummate with his macabre trinitrotoluened wedding gift of a wondrously nihilistic lamp, revolutionary violence in its inevitability and its urgent necessity, far from being premised on a total disregard of human society, was to the exact contrary founded upon the absolute valuation of it, in the sense of the being absolute of every human being in her/his freedom, in her/his transcendence, in her/his dignity, *and* in society's being the existing-together of such ontological-existential absolutes:--and founded therefore upon the absolute consideration for human society, for its integrity, for its transcendent well-being, for its fulfillment, for the realization of its in fact democratic, primordially democratic (and therefore anti-colonial), promise.

Chapter 10

REPORT ON RIZAL TO THE GOVERNOR GENERAL BY THE DAPITAN COMMANDER COL. RICARDO CARNICERO, DAPITAN, 30 AUGUST 1892

"...One of the hopes of Rizal is to become deputy at the Cortes so that he can expound there all that happens in the Islands..." (Appendix iv to the *Miscellaneous Correspondence of Dr. Jose Rizal*; p. 358.)

Chapter 11

RIZAL'S DEDICATION OF EL FILIBUSTERISMO TO THE PRIESTS GOMEZ, BURGOS, & ZAMORA, HIS FOREWORD, HIS WARNING, & BLUMENTRITT'S INSCRIPTION ON THE NOVEL'S TITLE PAGE

All the abovementioned documents are cited here from translations reproduced by the father-daughter tandem of so-called "historians", Gregorio and Sonia Zaide, in their multimillion-earning Rizal course textbook whose literarily and even grammatically crude title betrays at once the creeping level of intelligence of its authors: *Jose Rizal: Life, Works, and Writings of a Writer, Genius, Scientist, and National Hero*—an utterly informative title indeed! Not all writings are necessarily written by a writer, of course! A cobbler could have cobbled some of them. And could such an insight be whipped into our astounded eyes by anything less brilliant than this by the enterprising genetic duo? And, but, no, wait, wait!—we have misplaced two words in that fateful title which correctly ordered now reads: *Jose Rizal: Life, Works, and Writings of a Genius,* ***Writer****, Scientist, and National Hero…*

1.) ***The Gomburza dedication.***

To the memory of the priests, Don Mariano Gomez (85 years old), Don Jose Burgos (30 years old), and Don Jacinto Zamora (35 years old). Executed in Bagumbayan Field on the 28th of February 1872.

The Church, by refusing to degrade you, has placed in doubt the crime that has been imputed to you; the Government, by surrounding your trials with mystery and shadows causes the belief that there was some error, committed in fatal moments; and all the Philippines, by worshipping your memory and calling you martyrs, in no sense recognizes your culpability[23]. ***In so far, therefore, as your complicity in the Cavite Mutiny is not clearly proved***, *as you may or may not*

---

23 This means that, according to Rizal, had "all the Philippines" thought them *instead* to be guilty of fomenting or being involved in the insurrectionary event called the *Cavite Mutiny*—which involvement and thereby guilt would have made them precursors of the Revolution and therefore *Filipino heroes, anti-Spanish heroes, anti-colonial heroes*—then "all the Philippines", *instead* of "worshipping" their "memory" "and calling" them "martyrs", would have execrated them, *as of course Rizal would have*, as traitors to his/their ever-beloved Mother Spain, calling them villains *instead* of heroes and evil agents of anti-Spanish revolt, hence, true *filibusteros*, *instead* of martyrs defending Spanish colonialism against—whom?:--against the friars, against the revolution-fomenting friars, as Rizal and his fellow ilustrado assimilationists standardly, repeatedly, nauseatingly put it in their pleadings and beggings for the assimilation of the Philippines as an overseas province of Spain. And Rizal could dedicate his novel, his assimilationist novel, his despairing, bleeding-in-the-heart-Spain-loving novel, his bleeding-in-the-brain-for-too-much-love-of-Mother-Spain novel, his novel of undying loyalty to Mother Spain, his anti-revolutionary, revolution-cursing, revolution-abhorring novel, to the three priest-victims of friar injustice and abuse, of revolution-fomenting friar rapacity, venality and inquisitorial licentiousness *because* he does agree here with this "all the Philippines" of his sick and craven and perfidious imagination… He does agree with "all the Philippines" that—*what*?:--that the three priests, in being in fact leaders of the anti-friar movement for the secularization of the parishes which would thus detract by so much against friar-power and curb significantly the revolution-inciting abuses of the friars against the natives, were in fact anti-revolutionary,

have been patriots, and as you may or may not have cherished sentiments for justice and for liberty, ***I have the right*** *to dedicate my work to you* ***as victims of the evil which I undertake to combat.*** *And while we wait expectantly upon Spain someday to restore your good name and cease to be answerable for your death*[24]*, let these pages serve as a tardy wreath of dried leaves over your unknown tombs, and let it be understood that every one who without clear proofs attacks your memory*[25] *stains his hands in your blood!*

---

anti-separatist, anti-independence heroes and martyrs, were in fact great defenders of Spanish colonialism against the revolution-fomenting friars, were in fact such great Spanish heroes in being such great *proto-assimilationist* martyr-heroes! Rizal then can, so he says, dedicate his novel –his of course anti-revolutionary, anti-independence novel—to the three martyr priests because they were martyrs *for* assimilationism, for eternal colonialism, for the ideal of *the Philippines as Spanish colony forever!*

24 This, circumstantially and therefore all the more conclusively, is the proof that this dirty, stupidly conceived, evilly designed, melodramatic novel carries the anti-revolutionary, anti-Filipino people, anti-independence *assimilationist* intention: You can wish for this restoration and await it only within the framework of an assimilated Philippines.

25 In light of the above-delineated logic, and in the textual-ideological context, of the situation, to "attack" thus the "memory" of the three *proto-assimilationist, anti-revolutionary, anti-independence, anti-Filipino people, pro-Spanish colonialism priests* is to accuse them of being the opposite which to Rizal and his ilustrado cohorts is most execrable, namely, of being instead proto-revolutionary rebels fighting against and seeking to overthrow and expel not only the friars but Spanish colonialism itself—which is to say, *of being guilty as charged.* For exactly the same reason,

This dedicatory slab, a twisted document by a twisted mind, was Rizal's forthright attempt to appropriate the three priests as proto-assimilationist *and therefore* anti-revolutionary (anti-separatist, anti-independence, anti-Filipino-people), Spanish colonialist heroes—*anti-filibusterist* heroes! The novel *El Filibusterismo* is against *filibusterismo*, against *revolution*, against *separatism*, against Philippine

---

Rizal, if he could, would have risen from his polluted grave in being thus *attacked* by all the Filipino historians and other intellectuals and politicians and professors and teachers and the entirely brainwashed Filipino race together with the Philippine government and state—staining their hands thus with his blood in scandalously mistaking him for a Filipino hero who died fighting for Philippine independence when the holy truth is he was a most pure and burningly ardent Spanish hero who died fighting for everlasting Spanish colonialism in the Philippines, for "Spanish colonialism forever", for, in a word, *assimilation*, and thus against revolution, against Philippine independence, against the freedom and humanity of the Filipino people:--against the friars who were greatly endangering Spanish colonialism with their holily inspired lubricity and divinely intense omnipresent rapacity which was steadily pushing the natives toward revolution, on the one hand, and against the revolution itself, against the revolutionaries themselves, against Bonifacio and his Katipuneros whom he had rejected, denounced and betrayed and had not ceased denouncing and excoriating as backstabing criminals, savages, dishonourable and discrediting and absurd and bloody criminals who "lacked education and civic virtues" and who therefore "did not deserve to be free" let alone to rise in arms to try to free themselves from the "enlightening" and "civilizing" and holy colonial Spanish embrace on the other hand. (See his *December 15, 1896 Fort Santiago Manifesto* below, p.)

independence, against the Filipino people and their sovereignty. This ideologico-political assimilationist, anti-revolutionary dedication then is as it should be and sits perfectly well with what Rizal intends to effectuate in writing the novel and with what it actually succeeded to do, namely, 1.) attack in rabid fashion the very idea of revolution; demonstrate dramatically (it was actually melodramatically as it came out because no doubt of Rizal's deficient capability as a writer of literature) its "utter absurdity" and the "needless sufferings it would bring", as well as its "criminality" and "barbarism", as he later put it in his *December 15, 1896 Fort Santiago Manifesto*, and earlier in such documents as his celebrated assimilationist, anti-revolutionary *La Solidaridad* article, *The Philippines A Century Hence*, and in a hundred and thirty seven other places; and 2.) brainwash still more and convince even more firmly the colonial middle class[26] against revolution, against separatism, against independence, and instigate them even more fervently to band together and work, agitate, and fight for *assimilation*, which to him and his propagandist friends in Madrid meant fighting principally and almost exclusively against the friars who by means of their rampant greed, their unbridled cruelty and their fanatical lubricity were actually the most active and most potent sowers and fomenters of filibusterism, i.e., of separatism, of revolution, of independence. Two other intentions of his which might not have been as clearly, if at all realized to some effect, must be mentioned here, namely: 3.) exhibit before the eyes of the Spanish authorities in Madrid the revolution-fomenting dogmatic lechery and illimitable greed of the friars in order to incite them to the fury of their

[26] the ilustrado-principalia strata of the native population who alone were the intended readers of the novel in the Philippines: the Filipino masses, ignorant of Spanish were not meant by Rizal to cast a glance at a page of his there:--he was making assimilation *not* revolution and did not need nor want to speak to the Filipino masses—and that was the forthright, vulgar, criminal, anti-Filipino reason why he chose to write exclusively in Spanish.

somewhat liberal sentiments against those agents of God, and scare those Spanish authorities with the spectre of revolution to which by their Godful evil the friars were without fatigue pushing the Filipino masses; and 4.), as he himself put it in a letter to Mariano Ponce[27], and which he repeated in another

[27] In a *La Solidaridad* article entitled *Iluso* which came out in the April 15,1892 issue, Eduardo de Lete attacked an unnamed Filipino propagandist for crazily contemplating to go home to the Philippines to start making a revolution there. Rizal felt alluded to; indeed, he at once concluded that the Don Quixote dela Mancha of the Philippines being ridiculed so was none other than himself. He also made the conclusion that it was Marcelo del Pilar who was behind the scandalous piece, that as editor in chief of the paper he assigned De Lete to write it. He first wrote and complained to everybody except De Lete and Del Pilar about it. Hence this letter to Ponce who was known to have been very close to Del Pilar. When the outcry reached them they wrote Rizal denying it was him that they had thus mocked. Although it was not impossible that Rizal was really their intended victim, it could with equal probability have been Jaena instead. Jaena went home to the Philippines sometime in February or March, 1892, with the announced intent to start a revolution. After four days in Manila, he hastily fled when he sensed that he could be arrested anytime. (To the eternal discredit of the dishonest editors of the English translation of the *La Solidaridad*, the De Lete article was by them deleted! Filipino intellectuals will do anything to protect the reputation of this traitor from Calamba, and, but also, that of the traitor from Bulacan, Bulacan!) But to Rizal's letter to Ponce now: "Perhaps they are also pursuing a more profound policy, *and they are pretending to go against me and attack me furiously in order to play better the role of pro-assimilation partisans. In this regard I praise them*, but in that case, I believe they ought to attack me strongly, mentioning my name, because many Spaniards who are not well informed about our inside

letter, this time to that other wasted and pernicious because ultimately evil effort Marcelo H. del Pilar, to paint filibusterism in the figure of Simoun in the "dark" and sinister aspect that he did in order, in pursuit of the same assimilationist delusion, to loudly display to the same Spanish authorities by the stark contrast, that the assimilationist propagandists in Madrid were, to the precise contrary, immaculately "white"[28].

The assimilationist, anti-revolutionary, anti-separatist, anti-independence, Spanish colonialist, anti-filibusterist logic of this document is nothing less than transparent, and, as in all the other documents we have elsewhere cited to prove Rizal's

---

affairs do not understand Lete's allusions and the article does not achieve its purpose. I only warn them that the idea is somewhat risky, but if it were thus, they may believe that I sincerely applaud them and they can increase the attack with my secret congratulations. Only I observe that in following that policy, Lete sells himself and sells us. *On making my enraged Simoun speak, I have wanted to pursue the same end, setting a darker background so that the Filipinos of Madrid may appear white, but in doing so, I did not sell any secret.*"

[28] See Letter 313, p.160 below, dated Hong Kong 23 May 1892. "Had I not told you before leaving Europe that I would never undertake anything against you? What animal has bitten you that you attack me when here I do not meddle at all in politics and I work only to prepare a free place for refuge for the Filipinos, devoting the rest of my time to writing some books? Have I not told you that I was leaving you in politics so that you may earn much prestige? Do you need to attack me for that? I cannot explain myself. So that I say to myself: If you have acted for political reasons, I applaud you and I should like you to continue, for it seems to me that *you are on the right road. That was my purpose in making Simoun a dark figure in order to show that those of* La Solidaridad *are not* filibusteros".

abhorrence of revolution and horror of independence, it makes this dedicatory defense of Spanish colonialism self-explanatory.

Here is the logic: 1.) The friars are the worst and deadliest enemies of Spanish colonialism in the Philippines because 2.) they are so excessive, so lacking in restraint, in their rapacious, venal and licentious abuses against the natives that 3.) they are actually irresistibly pushing the natives to the desperate recourse of revolution, and are thus the most powerful inciters to, and fomenters of, revolution; 4.) the three priests were enemies of the friars: they were leaders of the movement for the secularization of parishes which would mean the expulsion of the friars from the parishes, which as such would curtail so much of their power and deprive them of their most lucrative and most comprehensive arena of fiduciary and carnal abuse—i.e., their most potent and far-reaching posts as objective fomenters of and inciters to revolution; 5.) hence, the three priests, in being, like Rizal and his assimilationist fellow ilustrados, the enemies of the friars in thus attempting to disempower them and neutralize their revolution-impelling abuses, were actually the great friends of Mother Spain and were the dedicated defenders of Spanish colonial rule against the revolution-fomenting friars and thus against the very possibility of revolution—against the evil natives' being pushed into the evil proposition called revolution which would put an end to beloved Mother Spain's loving and caring and noble rule; 6.) far from being traitors against Mother Spain then—which they would be if it was true that they were the patriotic plotters of that revolt, that insurrection in Cavite (and that was why it was important to Rizal that the charges were never proved), they were great Spanish heroes and martyrs who died fighting against the very possibility of revolution by fighting against the abusive and revolution-fomenting friars; 7.) and that was why Rizal was mad against those who would go on accusing the three anti-revolutionary Spanish hero-martyr priests of being guilty of being proto-revolutionaries in being the plotters behind that Cavite revolt, of being Filipino patriots, of being Filipino rebel-heroes desiring and fighting for insane Filipino liberty and deluded justice thus, and those perverted ones who would go on insisting that the three great Spanish-colonialist-hero-martyr priests were guilty of the charge of rebellion thus and of the unforgivable, the heinous crime of being Filipino rebel heroes thus, would *stain their hands in your blood O Gomez, O Burgos, O Zamora, O, O!*

The Foreword: *We* [29] *have often been frightened by the phantom of filibusterism that from only a nurse's narration it*

[29] "We"—who? We already know, like we should really at this point in the demonstration, *always already have known*, that this"we" who were Rizal's exclusive readers and exclusively intended audience were, and can only have been the Spaniards in Spain, the Spaniards here, and *their*, i.e., Rizal and company's "our" *government*—in Madrid and here in Manila:--but to abrade further and scoop out the forgetting and the ignorance imparted by the national, ruling-class sponsored, state-sponsored, governmentally enforced brainwashing by all the so-called historians and intellectuals in the Philippines for more than a century now concerning this fact and its presuppositions and implications, this bears repeating. Let us repeat it here then that this false patriot was a stinking rotting zombie of a fish for he it was who said—and all the brainwashed Filpinos therafter have repeated, are repeating him, for a century and more now—"Ang hindi marunong magmahal sa sariling wika, higit pa sa hayup at malansang isda", and his whole lifelong, truncated that it was, he never really wrote anything in his native Tagalog, and instead wrote all his works in Spanish, in the language of the colonizer, which he showed thus to most ardently, burningly love, and in loving which so so very much he had devoted all his energies to secure its eternal sway in this archipelago, and had offered "spontaneously" and "unconditionally" his very life and even his name and all he can do to murder Andres Bonifacio and "stifle", "quench", "suppress" the "rebellion" thereby (see his *December 15, 1896 Fort Santiago*

has become a positive and real being whose name alone (in depriving us of our serenity) makes us concoct the greatest myths in order not to meet the feared reality. Instead of fleeing, we shall look at its face, and with determined if inexpert hand we shall raise the veil to uncover before the multitude the mechanism of its skeleton[30].

Manifesto and his December 12, 1896 *Data for My Defense* below, p), making the "spontaneous", "unconditional" offer to Governor General Ramon Blanco himself, in "a personal letter witnessed by Col. Santalo":--whilst he did die defending this holy Spanish language against the Tagalog and Kapampangan and Visayan and Ilocano speaking revolutionaries. And let us also once more repeat here that loving so intensely and all-consumingly his Mother Spain thus, this absurdly evil and lying wretch and massmurderous criminal had had to write exclusively in the language of the evil colonizers because he was importuning them his whole short lifelong to please please please make the Philippines the eternal colony of Spain by *assimilating* it as an overseas province and so that he could become a congressman in the Spanish Cortes thus; and that he did not write in his native Tagalog nor in any of the dialects of the Filipinos masses because he had absolutely nothing to say to them except to insult them—as he did in the abovementioned *Manifesto* which was the one single attempt he made to address his own countrymen—with their "lack of education and civic virtues" (i.e., with their illiteracy and their uncivilized ways) and with their "savagery" and "absurdity" and their continuing failure thus to "deserve to be free", i.e., to qualify as human beings, tanginang 'to!

30 Filibusterism is here of course the synonym for revolution which, however, for extreme fear and hatred of the thing Rizal became severely incapacitated to comprehend as such, refusing unconsciously thus to recognize it for what it was—for instance, for what it was,

for what it did, for the Latin American colonies which revolutionarily were able to liberate themselves from Spanish rule in 1820-26--so that he could not even call it by its proper name, and had at all times referred to it as "rebellion", castrating and downsizing it thereby. Whilst here he boasts of staring it in the eye and of anatomizing it—here, in this novel-sequel called *El Filibusterismo*, dedicated as such, by its very name, to its unblinking, undaunted, unflinching exposure, and, in this foreword boastfully telling, assuring, the reader—that is to say, the Spanish reader, namely and solely the Spaniards here in the Philippines and the Spaniards there in Spain and the "government", i.e., the Spaniards in their colonial government here and the Spaniards in their government in Europe—that such as they conjure and picture and imagine it here in the Philippines and amongst the likes of Rizal himself, namely the colonial middle-class, especially the ilustrados so-called, the in fact *assimilationist* (and therefore eternal colonialist) propagandists, it is nothing but a phantom, a ghost, an insubstantial object of groundless fear; telling the Spaniards thereby, from whom they, Rizal and company, were most assiduous and obsequieous in begging for assimilation status, that they have nothing to fear from these so-called ilustrados who like him want nothing but, and nothing short of, that eternal colonialism that is assimilation. Later in this same preface the assurance of nonfilibusterism becomes a warning that, should those Spanish readers persist and even be aggravated in their fear and suspicion of revolution amongst the assimilationists, then nothing anymore can be done for them but to abandon them to the fatality of what, in their failure to recognize where the real threat of revolution is coming from-namely, from the friars whose abuses exacerbate the sufferings of the masses and push them into revolution--

If, upon seeing it, ***our country and its government*** [31]*reflect, we shall consider urselves happy no matter whether they censure us for the audacity, no matter whether we ay for it*

---

31 "our country and our government":--to a severe mental colony like Rizal, his native country is always automatically, subconsciously subsumed under his "Mother Country", Spain; whilst, of course, the Philippines being a colony of Spain, the government of this farflung colony is in point of fact a subordinate part of the Spanish government. This novel-sequel and the one before it, have in Rizal's mind no other audience, no other readers, but the Spaniards and their government. The Filipino people are excluded. Rizal is not talking to them, nor for them:--to the precise contrary, Rizal, while talking about them, and specifically about the threat of revolution they pose, and which he uses to scare the Spaniards and their government to grant assimilation status to the Philippines plus the expulsion of the friars and the return of the friar lands and other properties to their rich Filipino owners (to Rizal precisely, and Del Pilar, and Jaena…) from whom the same rapacious friars had expropriated and thieved them (which before such divine expropriation and thievery were of course thieved and expropriated by Rizal and company, i.e., by the colonial middle-class collaborators, from the people, just as the entire country was expropriated and thieved by the Spanish colonizers, by Spanish colonialism as a whole, from the people)—Rizal is thereby talking and working against them in thus leading the propaganda campaign towards their eternal colonization—i.e., assimilation—by Rizal's beloved "Mother", Spain. While lying and without cease professing his burning love for them, Rizal was from first to last the deadly enemy of the Filipino people—all the deadlier and eviler in that he apparently believed that he truly loved them in doing everything to have them eternally enslaved thus by his ever beloved "Mother", Spain.

like the young student of Sais who wished to penetrate the secret of the priestly imposture. (On the other hand, if in the face of reality, instead of being soothed, one's fear is increased and the trepidation of another is aggravated, then they will have to be left in the hands of time which educates the living, in the hands of fatality which weaves the destinies of peoples and their governments with the faults and errors that they are committing everyday.[32])

THE WARNING

They are going to waste their time who would attack this book by holding on to trifles, or who from other motives, would try to discover in it more or less known physiognomies. True to his purpose of exposing the disease of the patient and, in order not to divert himself nor divert the reader, whilst he narrates

---

[32] Here, parenthetically, is the warning, and it is addressed to the only people Rizal and his fellow assimilationist campaigners had been exclusively addressing (these brown aspiring Spaniardlings who really should be numbered amongst the most dedicated Spanish patriots, intense lovers of their Mother Spain and therefore therefore therefore intense haters of their very own native country and people, the socalled ilustrados, the socalled propagandists): Spain herself, i.e., "our country", i.e., the Spaniards themselves, "and its government":--here Rizal is warning them once more, cajoling them once more, half-threatening, half-imploring not to commit the error of waiting for the "disaster" of the revolution until it is too late, and therefore imploring them to assimilate the Philippines at once, and expel the friars at once, and return the lands and other properties of Rizal and company at once, which, of course—and how else?—they, these colonial middle-class agents,these Rizals and Del Pilars and Jaenas and Aguinaldos and Malvars and Lunas and Alejandrinos and Ponces etc., had themselves thieved and expropriated from the Filipino people…

only real facts which happened recently and are absolutely authentic in substance[33]*, he has disfigured his characters so*

---

[33] In letters to MH Del Pilar and Eduardo de Lete (see below), Rizal was categorical in declaring that his two novels, and specially this last one, were assimilationist works. Ibarra of the Noli has here been "disfigured" into the *terrorist* Simoun who to the politically naïve, sociologically uneducated, and historically ignorant Rizal was supposed to personify the *filibustero* whose *filibusterismo* is supposed to be the "rebellion", the "revolution", Rizal is boasting here to stare in the eye and anatomize. In the abovementioned letters, Rizal emphasized that he had made Simoun a "dark figure" in order by the contrast to demonstrate to the Spaniards in Spain how utterly "white" the *La Solidaridad* assimilationist propagandists were. In concrete terms pertinent to the historical conjuncture of Rizal's colonial Philippines, to be an assimilationist was to argue for reforms as the only way, and a most urgent one, to prevent the impending destruction of colonial rule, namely, revolution. It meant ignoring the general evil of colonialism, and indeed to represent colonialism as a general good but, in the case of the colony, a still incomplete one: it was to agitate and argue for its completion that the assimilationist was the assimilationist he was, for this completion of the general good of colonialism was none other than—*assimilation.* But a concrete feature of the 19th century world-conjuncture was revolution, specifically, anti-colonial revolution. Although terribly belated (the Latin American colonies had successfully revolted in the first half of the twenties—1820-26), revolution as a concrete possibility had at long long last arrived in the Philippines. Assimilationists like Rizal, Del Pilar, Jaena, the Lunas, were dyed-in-the-hide mental colonies; to become fullfledged Spaniards was their dream of dreams; such dream would be aborted by revolution, separation, independence; hence,

that they may not turn out to be the typical pictures some readers found in his first book. Man passes; his vices remain, and to accentuate and show their effects, the pen of the writer aspires.

THE INSCRIPTION BY FERDINAND BLUMENTRITT ON THE TITLE PAGE

It can easily be supposed that a rebel (filibustero) has recently bewitched the league of friar-zealots and retrogrades[34]

---

they dreaded, they feared, they hated the revolution as "the worst disaster" that could befall them. In arguing for assimilation as antidote to revolution, they would of course fail to consider that it was colonialism in general, colonialism per se with its overarching and profound evil perpetrated *for too long now* that was the one true cause of revolution; nor could they be expected to pinpoint their very own criminal colonial collaborationist selves as a, let alone the, cause of it: they would thus accuse their bitterest class-enemy, the friars, of being it. Of course, the friars were thinking the same of them! It was to defend colonialism against the now urgent eventuality of revolution that they were arguing for assimilation whose most egregious feature was the expulsion of the friars from the colony and the return of their lands and other properties which they had originally expropriated and thieved from the people but which the friars had recently thieved from them.

[34] "Friar-zealots and retrogrades…": this is a rhetorically guarded reformulation of the main campaign idea and argument of Rizal and his fellow assimilationist propagandists that in their insatiable rapacity and unappeasable cruelty towards the Filipino natives, the friars are actually pushing them towards the last resort of revolution:--that is how they, the friar-zealots, the retrogrades, are supposed to spread ideas of rebellion"

so that, unwittingly following his incitements[35]*, they should favour and foment that policy which pursues one sole end; to spread ideas of rebellion throughout the length and breadth of the land, and to convince every Filipino that there is no salvation except through separation from the Mother Country.*

---

throughout the archipelago ; hence, to obviate this "greatest disaster that could befall us" (as he describes revolution in, among other places, his longish essay, *The Philippines A Century Hence*), the Spanish government should hasten to grant assimilation status to the Philippines and expel the friars and return to their true owners—most especially Rizal and his colonial middle-class assimilationist friends--those friar lands and other properties thieved by them who thieved them from the Filipino people...

[35] Incitements to revolt…:--the friars once more, egged-on and abetted and whetted in their sadisms, rapacities, and lusts in lacerating the humanity of the people, in abusing and thieving and raping them, and thus in precipitating the people into revolution, by the terrorist (and therefore actually anti-revolutionary) Simoun…

Chapter 12

BLUMENTRITT'S REVIEW OF THE NOLI ME TANGERE[36]

Let us say it at once: the great virtue of Rizal's two novels, outside of the question of their literary merits, and their political premise and implications was, and is, to have documented in a graphic and most compelling manner the evil of the friars. One could say that as such historical documents they were great and valuable works. Their glaring defect however was, and is, that of being too kind to Spanish colonialism in particular and to colonialism in general. Colonialism per se is a form of radical evil, being a form of radical denial of the freedom, specifically of the *right of sovereignty,* of an entire people; it is a radical denial of the transcendence, the dignity, the humanity itself of the subject people; it is truly a wholesale, protracted, and profoundly destructive crime perpetrated by a nation, a people, against the humanity itself of another nation, of another people. It is as such always, wherever and whenever it happens, an absolutely unjustifiable outrage against humanity. Any attempt to mitigate it is a crime worse than it. Any description of whatever supposedly good or beautiful thing it had given rise to in the subject country and people should always begin and end with an exhibiting of the radical evil of its premise and presupposition, of its very condition of possibility which is this wholesale denial and suppression and protracted undermining and destruction of the subject people's *humanity.* An honest novelist who would not pervert the truth and would not apologize for evil must never praise the grandeur and the beauty of a colonial cathedral without at the same time exhibiting the anguish and pain of the native slaves and peons who built it, and the fact that such beauty and grandeur, which of course are truly there too, are at once the permanent occasion of an eclipse of humanity and a darkness of the mind. Truth itself demands it of her/him; to fail which is to lie. In

---

[36]Pp 546-569; *Miscellaneous Correspondence,* Appendix.

Rizal's novels, this lie, this falsification, this ultimately criminal mitigation of an absolutely unjustifiable evil was an angling of the work towards assimilationist hope[37].

Let us exhibit at once the anatomized heart of what the document in question attests to, namely, Rizal's decisive, determined, and unwavering assimilationism and anti-separatism, i.e., his being anti-revolution, his being anti-Philippine-Independence, and his devotion to an eternity of Spanish colonialism as expressed in the conception and writing of the *Noli me tangere*. This was a book review published by *La Solidaridad* itself. The beautiful thing about it is that Rizal had enthusiastically endorsed what Blumentritt had to say there of his first novel not only in letters to fellow reformists and sundry friends like Blumentritt himself, but in an *Editor's Note* which he, Rizal himself had written. The fundamental and central thing that the review brings out and exposes was precisely the assimilationism, anti-separatism, anti-liberationism, anti-independence-ism, anti-revolutionism of the novel; whilst the main thrust of the *Editor's Note* written by Rizal himself was—as the document itself will show—to concur with and fully endorse this political evaluation of the novel. Concerning this political heart of the matter then, it was like Rizal himself telling us that he wrote the novel to promote assimilationism, to oppose separatism, to reject revolution, to defend Spanish colonialism against it, and combat all likelihood and possibility of Philippine independence. Here then, the review's heart:

"The novel was not written in order to separate the Philippines from Spain, but to call the attention of all the Spaniards of the Mother Country who are noble not only by lip service to the misrule that has reigned, reigns, and can reign in the country *in order that Spain may be able precisely to retain the Philippines by introducing the necessary reforms...*"

---

[37]Assimilationism is necessarily an asshole's hope.

There. And this by way of summing it all up, occurring as it did at the review's end. The novel was reformist, assimilationist; it was not separatist, not revolutionary, and its author was not a *filibustero*. Rizal in his *Editorial Note* writes:

"The opinion, however, that the professor emits about the *Noli me tangere* might perhaps raise protests from those who pretend to have been born infallible—stainless white sheep—from those who accuse every adversary of being a *filibustero...*"

That is, from those who are wont to accuse me, Jose Rizal, of being separatist and a hater of Spain and of things Spanish when the truth is no Spaniard could possibly love Spain more... But to the document now.

A. Rizal's Editorial note to the Review

"In the present struggle between the Filipino people, avid for education, and certain classes which endeavour to perpetuate ignorance in the country, the learned Philippinist[38], the Austrian professor Mr. Ferdinand Blumentritt intervenes... The opinion however, that the Professor emits about the *Noli me tangere* might perhaps raise protests from those who pretend to have been born infallible—stainless white sheep—*from those who accuse every adversary of being a filibustero*, and describe every opinion contrary or different from his own as heretical or protestant ...[39]—Namely, the

[38] This "learned Philippinist" *ethnographer* was so learned indeed that he never set foot on Philippine soil and had for anthropological specimen no one except Rizal himself and his devoted travelling companion Maximo Viola, whom Rizal had seduced into the beautiful idea of paying for everything in their continental trips.

[39]That is to say, from those who are wont to accuse Rizal of being separatist and a hater of Spain when the truth is

friars. But, says Rizal, "they would have no reason to say so", because "Professor Blumentritt is a fervent Catholic, an obedient son of the Roman Church, which he considers the only true one, the only one that can redeem mankind."

Rizal's major anxiety here was of course to project to the whole world and especially to the Spaniards in the Peninsula, particularly those in the Madrid government, the, in any case, glaring anti-revolutionariness and anti-separatistness and anti-independenceness of his novel—in a word, its reeking *assimilationism*. Which also was why it had to be reviewed thus by the Austrian-Spanish ethnological Philippinist assimilationist journalist crusader Blumentritt, which review Rizal now endorses here and commends for telling the truth about the reeking assimilationism, the stinking anti-independencism, the perfidious anti-separatism, the malevolent and actually genocidally criminal anti-revolutionism of his novel. Hence his repeated insistence that Blumentritt was no *filibustero* was equivalent to his own insistence that he, Rizal, himself, in his novel as elsewhere, was no *filibustero*: "Neither can he be branded a *filibustero*, despite the cheapness of this term, because not only has he Spanish blood, but he is besides a devoted champion of Spanish rights, defending them in all questions, in those of Tawi-Tawi and Caroline Islands for example, in periodicals, books, treatises, lectures, etc., with such ardour that he was considered deserving of a decoration by the Madrid government, which also awarded him a prize for numerous works exhibited at the Philippine exposition..."[40] Published by *La Solidaridad*, Rizal must have considered this review as a major assimilationist propaganda coup: so highly regarded was Blumentritt by the Spanish government and the Peninsular political public in general!

---

no Spaniard could possibly be blamed for loving Spain more: he is in fact willing to die defending Spain against the (objectively) separatist friars! As in fact he did.

[40]P. 147.

In other words, Rizal was saying, if the world-renowned ethnologist and naturalist German-Spanish professor had any bias on the matter, it would be in favour of Spain, i.e., against filibusterism, against revolution, against separation, against Philippine independence from Spain. And in fact, here as in all his many articles published by *La Solidaridad*, and elsewhere, Blumentritt was himself directly arguing for the assimilation of the Philippines by Spain. We may add that in many of his letters to Rizal, especially during the critical period of the *Rape of Calamba* in October 1891, Blumentritt was anxious and empathic about cautioning Rizal against jumping into separatism and revolution. He was worried that the outrage inflicted upon Rizal's family[41] could so distract his mind and

---

41 And also upon his own town-mates though this was always, of course, of incomparably lesser moment in this reckoning: as his letters and other manifestations of the period demonstrate, in addition to the main, secret, but delusional motive, it was ultimately because he wanted to suffer in lieu of his parents, perhaps more in lieu of his mother than his father, and of his brother too, and his "friends" (he forgot the sisters!), that he finally decided to go home and risk death; in fact, if one did not already know of the abovementioned main and secret motive, one would tend to conclude (although a certain fuzziness would invade his/her mind later on)—that that was the one and only motive, as he exposed it nakedly in several parts of his infamous twin letters, one addressed to "My Beloved Parents, Brothers, and Friends", and the other "To the Filipinos", which he entrusted to his friend and fellow assimilationist reformist Jose Ma. Basa before he embarked for Manila from Hong Kong: he wanted to be able to save them by surrendering himself; read thus, it was a purely family affair, as he also was, at the same time that he seemed to be gesturing towards his other, bigger, secret, motive and contemplated spectacular act (something about "putting the finishing touches to his (life's) work"!—which is to say, to his short lifelong assimilationist project)

avowing it to be nothing but: "I have my duties to my conscience *before all*", he says there, "I have moral obligations to the families that suffer, to my aged parents , *whose sighs penetrate the heart*, I know that I alone, *even with my death*, can make them happy, return them to their native land and to the tranquillity of their home...*I do not have anybody except my parents; but my country still has many sons who can take my place*..." But alongside such unguarded or poorly guarded exposures, he would be lapsing into the rhetoric of patriotism, of love of his countrymen and native land, allowing himself thus to wax heroic (and not merely filial), and, as was his wont standardly self-sacrificingly grandiose, helping himself thus to the, for him in his profound and undescried fakeness (assimilationist fakeness of course, the sham heroics of the assimilationist traitor who for all that could be honestly imagining himself truly in love with his country and people in the very act of betraying them), ultimately somewhat tergiversant feelings (for did he not know that every true native hero in the colonial world of that century of revolutions that was the 19th was a revolutionary, a separatist, a liberator, a bestower of the gift of independence upon his people?) of pre-savored martyrdom and national—and, but, *Spanish national too, and above all and especially for him Spanish Spanish Spanish*—holification. In all humility, he declares himself to be one who knows "that the destiny of my country gravitates around me". Elsewhere there he declares that he is going home not to expiate any faults "of which I don't have any", "but to put a finishing touch to my work" (which of course was assimilationist work, not revolutionary work, for, he was risking ending his life's work now by getting himself killed and until now he had never done anything except assimilationist work which at such historical juncture was of course the diametrical, and certainly—as exhibited by Rizal himself in his ultimate historical effects—deadly, bloody, in fact mass-murderous as it were unhinge it and precipitate him thus into the "despair" and the "disaster" of that "unfortunate rupture" that to him, Rizal, in his lying and badly conceived and poorly written and of course (how else? How else in its assimilationism?—theoretically uneducated essay, *The Philippines A Century Hence*, was called revolution, which, the colonial-revolutionary situation and times being such there then, should at once be spelled thus:--***I N D E P E N D E N C E***. The despair, the "counsel of despair" called ***i n d e p e n d e n c e*** (ibidem, locus citatus), the disaster, the "greatest disaster" "that could befall all of us" called ***I N D E P E N D E N C E*** (ibidem, locus citatus), the terrible "misfortune" the "unfortunate rupture" called ***INDEPENDENCE*** (ibidem, locus citatus). Knowing this Jose Rizal thus, how could anyone, Filipino or not, fail to execrate him? This messy, inverted-heroic exhibitionist and true Spanish martyr who died defending Spanish colonialism against Padre Damaso and Andres Bonifacio, and could have earlier died defending the same against Jose Marti and Camilo Cienfuegos and the Cuban KKK...

"...And if any of the contending parties would doubt his impartiality in Philippine questions, *it would not be in truth the ruling class*, because Blumentritt is steeped in and nourished with all the books that the friars and the Peninsular Spaniards had written, depicting the country according to their whim;[42]and if the judgment of the learned professor did not

---

opposite of revolutionary work, and was thus farthest from being involved in any revolutionary work), "and to witness by my example what I have always preached". In short, his other main, secret, motive and project was to die an assimilationist martyr—in the delusional hope that such death would force the Spanish government to grant his assimilationist demands!

[42]Rizal is referring here to the liberal politicians of Spain and the Madrid government itself. Both were anti-friar. In all his works Rizal can be seen to be addressing directly or else implicitly the Madrid government and the liberal

fall victim to their prejudices and calumnies, as did that of so many others, it is due solely to his sane commonsense and to his solicitude to study things carefully.[43]

"On Philippine questions Blumentritt has read not only all the Spanish authors but also foreign ones who, in general, it might be said, do more justice to the inhabitants of this country than those whose duty is to defend them and who are the very ones responsible for the many vices and defects of their present state. Unfortunately, Filipinos write few books, and still those that come out are prohibited.

JOSE RIZAL"

---

politicians of Spain. Which was logical, because it was from them that he was begging that the Philippines be *assimilated.*

43 Here, Rizal should have mentioned what apropos of ethnologists is the most important qualification, namely fieldwork, actual research contact with the tribe and indeed a long enough period, lasting usually a year or two, of habitation in their midst. He however could not mention it because it never happened: Blumentritt, the world's foremost etnological authority on the Philippines and the Filipinos was never able to do it. This is important, for this Austrian scholar-journalist was Rizal's true partner in the latter's lifelong struggle for *assimilation.* Anyone engaged in so heinously criminal and delusive-deluding undertaking cannot be a sound human being. Blumentritt confirms that crack which in each other he and Rizal confirm and reinforce. This Austrian-Spanish Roman Catholic crusader for eternal colonialism for the Filipinos has also become a national hero in the Philippines which he had by way of that Rizalian association and through his copious *La Solidaridad* journalism mightily helped to make the world's most corrupt country now.

B. Blumentritt's Review of the *Noli me tangere*

"In that distant corner of the globe, known under the name of The Philippines, the state of things today is such that it recalls to us the past centuries. The administration of the country, thoroughly military and bureaucratic, is subordinated to the interests of the omnipotent friars. Without representation in the Cortes and without freedom of the press, there abuses are the order of the day…

"…But alas, the times have changed. While the Philippines, like a Spanish China fearing the contact with the foreigner, remained isolated and slumbered in soporific lethargy, everything remained at peace. But the movement that conquered Japan itself and stormed the legendary walls of the Celestial Empire, would not stop before Spanish China. Neither customs nor processions could frighten Progress… Progress came with slow but sure pace. First, Manila was opened to foreign commerce; then other ports were afterwards fitted out, and with commerce came new ideas for the beautiful though unprepared country. The ideas spread slowly; but with the opening of the Suez Canal, with the entrance of Japan in European culture, and with the shipping lines of the Pacific, from the distant corner that it was, the Far East was converted into an animated rendezvous of the numberless lines—carriers of the world's commerce—and then the light shone[44] definitively for the Philippines…

---

[44] "The light", indeed! The light of the En*light*enment. Enlightenmentism was progressivism. It was the effective ideology of Western-Christian-capitalist global colonialism. It was the same evil doctrine as the *White man's burden* bluff. It was Rizal's, and all the ilustrados', fighting credo as reformist crusaders in the Spanish metropolis; it was the social-historical lie that *La Solidaridad* was propagating among the Filipinos—i.e., among the colonial middle class which in the colony was after all the only section of the natives it was able to reach; it was a veritable religion, the *religion of progress*; with it, the priests and other ideologists of

"Then not only the Spaniards and the half-breeds, but also the Indios began to awaken from their mental lethargy...Then they felt the need to learn...Thus, it is not to be wondered at that the most avid for instruction, the most able sons of the country, should have gone to the best schools in Spain and abroad. From those points they returned to their homes with new ideas and they saw with different eyes the state of their native land: *Here in the Philippines censorship and bailiffs.*

---

western-christian capitalist global colonialism had sanctified and validated colonial oppression, domination, exploitation, and the mass-murders that went with every colonialism; with it the colonizers had sought to appease their conscience and boost up their criminal self-righteousness; it was the opium of the colonial middle-class, the collaborationist class; and in the case of Rizal and company, it was the opiate that gave them and sustained in them that delusive, nay hallucinatory, hope of colonial redemption called *assimilation*, which as such would be redemption from colonialism within colonialism! Which, spelled-out and articulated socio-politically within the turn of the century socio-historical conjuncture proved to be, in the unique case of the Philippine colonial situation, the most effective and necessarily deadly, in fact genocidally deadly, counter-revolutionary strategy possible. With it, and thanks to it, Rizal and company, together with their principalia disciple and effect, Emilio Aguinaldo, the co-authors among others of the two million murders perpetrated by the Americans against the Filipino people: for, among other things, it was this *assimilationism* that from the very start had injured the revolution so that it was born an injured revolution (for Rizal and company had swayed the colonial middle class away from it and against it, and had so retarded it and made possible the very selling of it to the Spaniards by Aguinaldo at Biyak na Bato, and had thus paved the way for the coming of the massmurdering Americans.

There in Spain liberty and liberalism! In Spain they were free citizens; in the Philippines their category was lower and they were reduced to submission. *As a natural consequence of that, the educated Filipinos endeavoured that their needy homeland share in the privileges granted to her sons by the metropolis*[45]. Previous censorship prohibited, however, all free discussion of the multiple mistakes and the frequent abuses committed by some members of the government. And not only were they compelled to keep silent, but also they were accused of treason to the mother country for every patriotic desire they manifested for a radical change in the system of government, because, since the emancipation of the American continent, *the Spaniards in their colonies imagined seeing separatist ideas behind every liberal movement.*

"Inexpressible mourning the country suffered when the garrison at Cavite mutinied. In truth it was nothing more than a plain mutiny that was swiftly suppressed…with the help of native troops! The Spaniards however harbored the conviction

---

45 And such indeed was how it happened that the so-called *ilustrados*, led by Marcelo del Pilar, Jaena, Rizal, came upon their assimilationist conservative, anti-revolutionary, counter-revolutionary, anti-separatist, anti-independence destiny which, such as it was during that century of anti-colonial revolutions, the 19th, was a necesarily bloody, even genocidal perversion of their true destiny, their revolutionary destiny—as it was that of all the other colonial middle classes in Latin America (Bolivar and company) and elsewhere-- which of course was to theorize the anti-colonial revolution, organize and lead it and risk all in the fight to the death for the independence of their native country. What Blumentritt was trying to sketch out here was the genealogy of the Philippine Assimilationist movement in general and that of the assimilationist work of Jose Rizal in particular, of which the book in question, the *Noli me tangere*, was the outstanding instance.

that this mutiny was a frustrated attempt to declare the Philippines independent.[46] The friars and those Peninsular

---

[46] This is valuable testimony to what must certainly have been the real nature of that non-heroic event projected otherwise by the paranoia of the colonial power and picked up later on by the necessarily lying and opportunist (in that sense schizoid and schizophrenogenic) historiography of the colonial middle class now become since 1946 the official ruling class. Only full democracy, where in the fullest possible sense sovereignty resides in the people, is fully legitimate. And this according to the essence, which is primordially democratic, and which then is always conflicted-conflictual, a conflicted-conflictual essence in the making, a conflicted-conflictual essence in becoming or becoming essence, of the social and the political itself. In this sense, every ruling class, in that it is merely a class and not the people itself, is to that extent, and by virtue of that difference, illegitimate. Illegitimacy is always a point, an element of weakness, of political vulnerability. It is always at such points that the threat of revolution-- which then is always by force of essence interpreted as the more or less violent act of self-defense by an oppressed people and a re-appropriation of its usurped sovereignty—is located. By virtue of the same force of essence then, every ruling class is constrained to *misrepresent* itself as the legitimate bearer and executor of the will of the people and, in being to that extent the same as the people, in being *authentically* sovereign. The force of essence, hence of democracy intrinsic to the political and the social, is such that even the most blatantly despotical regimes must invent myths that purport to show how they rule on behalf of the people and are therefore the true bearers of the will of the people, and are then legitimate sovereigns. The heroification of the Cavite Mutiny and of Jose Rizal were of the same kind of self-legitimizing

mythologies, lies, invented and propagated and even by law enforced by the Philippine ruling class.

The underlying, foundational essence of every society then is democracy; in its originariness we call it primordial democracy. This is to be expected since unlike any other association or aggrupation of beings, human society is an association of free, of transcendent, beings. By human society's being always in its underlying essence democratic is meant precisely this:--that it is not unfree beings, not mere animals, but rather free beings, beings who transcend mere animality, mere nature, mere life and are thus *transcendent*, that constitute it, and that free, transcendent beings cannot otherwise be associated in the form of society except as foundationally and also in a sense, one thart dialectically conforms with the necessity of conflict, and is as such also open to the possibility of total defeat, as in the case of genocidal denial (the North American Indians for instance), teleologically democratic. This democratic essence in the making is always conflicted because there are always forces inherent to being human that thwart it; the ineradicable animality of the human species is one fundamental source of such conflicting, anti-democratic forces. Metaphysics—including the metaphysics of the reduction of the human to the merely animal as in Nietzsche for instance or in Hitler (they are one and the same)—is another, where always an absolute is conjured in the name of which the human, specifically the transcendent in the human, and therefore the democratic in the human, is more or less deviously but always deviously denied.

Notice how the mythological or ideological, lying, opportunistic, schizophrenogenic heroification and holification of the "martyrs" of the Cavite Mutiny and of Jose Rizal exhibit the same element of a forcible invidious linking of both to that undeniably democratic project and

Spaniards who had material interests in the perpetuation of the obsolete system of government utilized *this natural apprehension of the good Spaniards, which at bottom was quite laudable.*[47] This mutiny furnished them with a propitious occasion to accuse all liberal Filipinos of *filibusterismo*, a *filibustero* being understood to be a traitor to the mother country, who attempts at the emancipation of a Spanish colony, or sympathizes with the idea.

---

expression of the will of the people which was the revolution, forcibly and violently—with the violence peculiar to every lie private or public—converting both of them into great and grandiose contributory factors, in the case of Rizal even as the central factor, in the making of the revolution. We speak of the democracy of nations and of the democracy of humanity as a whole: the essence both of every concrete society and of humanity as a whole is the same conflicted-conflictual teleological (a teleology without guaranties except the resurgent tenacity of the forces of democracy inherent in language itself, in art, in literature, in the face of the Other) democracy. Every ideology lies about this essence. Every ideology is a lie where the liar gets to believe in the lie itself.

[47] As a matter of course, and quite nonchalantly, this "natural apprehension" of the necessarily evil and necessarily massmurderous colonizers, was to such as this evil because *assimilationist (i.e., colonialist)* Blumentritt to be "át bottom quite laudable"! And the necessarily evil because assimilationist, i.e., colonial apologist and defender and conservationist, Jose Rizal concurs, as we have seen in his total endorsement of this review. In fact the "natural apprehension of the *good Spaniards* " spoken of here by Blumentritt was raised into a metaphysical argument and a method of colonial *assimilationist* self-defense by Rizal: in the assimilationist tracts he wrote—and he wrote nothing else--

"Then there began an era of persecutions beside which appears like child's play the drive against the demagogues that Germany witnessed at one time...

"...Rizal has been accused of things that make us doubt the judgment of his accusers, or prove at least their lack of serenity. He is accused that all the Spaniards in his book arc rascals, slanderers, intriguers, venal, etc. and this is deduced as the principal proof of the anti-Spanish character of the book. That the majority of the Spaniards in the book are not or ought not to be models of virtue is already inferred from the tendencies of the prologue to the book. However, there are also honorable ones among the Peninsular Spaniards in the *Noli me tangere*, like the lieutenant of the civil guard who appears from the beginning. And even granting that the Peninsular Spaniards of Rizal are all wretched, is the book thereby anti-Spaniard, **a book written with ardent patriotism[48] in order to call the attention of the rulers to**

---

48 "ardent patriotism":--ardent *Spanish, NOT indio, not native* patriotism, make no mistake about it!!! For, of course, unless you are anti-Filipino, anti-separatist, anti-revolution, anti- Philippine-independence, and thereby an enemy of humanity like Blumentritt, like Rizal, like Marcelo del Pilar, like all the ilustrado assimilationist-reformist crusaders in Spain and their Manila funders, indio, native, Filipino partriotism can only have one uninsane, honest, meaning during those times, namely, precisely, separatism, revolution, independence. Whilst, as Rizal argued indefatigably in all his works, the best way, the surest and most secure way to prevent that "greatest of all disasters" (see *The Philippines a Century Hence),* namely, *Philippine independence* from happening, the best, the surest, the most secure way to destroy separatism and pre-empt the revolution that necessarily was one with it, and thus the best, the surest, the most secure way to conserve and defend Spanish colonialism was **ASSIMILATION.** In other words, if working and fighting for revolution,

the cancer that gnaws at the heart of the country? Had there been or is there perchance corruption in the Philippines? Why is the present captain general, Weyler, so much praised? Why? Precisely because he wants to eradicate the evil. Ought I to cite names? I do not want to wash dirty linen. Rizal then had sufficient reason to paint in the *Noli* black what is black. *But it is ridiculous and infamous to suppose in him hatred of the Spaniards because he is Indio or because he represents all the Spaniards as wretched men...* His heart does not harbor the slightest spark of racial hatred. He loves every Spaniard who is really noble and brave…He does not look at the color of the skin or at the difference in language, but at the character of the man. Is this to be anti-Spaniard? Is this not rather to be Spanish in the sense of the noble quality that the nation attributes to itself? *That he is not benevolent toward the friars, he should know why and it is explained by the present troubles he and his country are having;* **but in no sense is he anti-Spaniard.**

"…I believe that had Rizal been a Peninsular Spaniard his *Noli me tangere* would not have encountered so many enemies…The misfortune of Rizal is to have come to the world *on a Spanish island* [49]and in addition to be an Indio! There is his principal crime!

---

separation, independence was truest Indio, native, Filipino patriotism, working and fighting for ***assimilation*** was, truest *Spanish patriotism*, as without a doubt Blumentritt meant to say in the above passage.

[49] "Spanish island" nonchalantly, as a matter of course, almost; almost like saying Rizal was born in Spain itself! As though this Austro-Spanish Spanish patriot, by the Royal Crown decorated lavishly for his of course Spanish patriotic deeds, did not know that the Philippines, never Spanish was a colony colony colony colony colony colony colony colony colony colony. And the net effect, the subtle ideological result, was that such pro-Spanish, colonial defense of colonialism as assimilationism was *naturalized*,

and separatism, revolution, advocacy of independence, became *unnatural acts!*

And this indeed is how an *ass*-i-m-ilationist *ass*-hole must always apologize for colonialism, for colonial evil than which no worse evil exists. No worse evil, yes! For the holocaust was colonial, and so was the genocide of the North American Indians (the most successful genocidal project in history thus far); and the genocide of the Armenian Christians by the Muslim Turks in 1896 and 1915 (in which close to two million human beings were colonially destroyed); and so, of course, was the genocide of more than 2.5 million Filipinos by the same North American enemies of humanity during the Philippine-American War between 1899 and 1906 made singularly possible and historically facilitated in the most efficacious way by Rizal himself and, by way of that same partnership, by Blumentritt himself, by what Rizal and Blumentritt and the *La Solidaridad* company did to the Philippine colonial middle-class as a whole and specifically to the upper stratum of the same with his charismatically powerful *assimilationism*, pulling away the colonial middle class from the revolution and most effectively pre-judicing and pre-disposing them against it, forcing Bonifacio and company to launch a most severely handicapped revolution both in terms of leadership and finances, making the revolution make do with quasi-illiterate tribalist-gangsterist vendoristic provincials like Emilio Aguinaldo:--pre-creating a vacuum of intelligence and competence into which the likes of those Caviteno gangsters could, and as they must, did rush: suppose it was Rizal himself, together with Antonio and Juan Luna, Jose Alejandrino, Edilberto Evangelista, Mariano Ponce, Marcelo del Pilar, Graciano Lopez Jaena, and thirty other ilustrados, together of course with the ilustrado Andres Bonifacio, and yes, Apolinario Mabini, who were from the very start there to found and lead the revolution: would

"...And I still wish to mention something that characterizes the state of the Philippines. No sooner than was my intention to translate into German the *Noli me tangere* known in the Islands, I received letters from Filipino and Peninsular Spaniards entreating me to desist from carrying out my plan. And why? *The Filipinos fear that I, who have always fought for the integrity of Spain with the ardor of a patriot* would gain the reputation of a *filibustero* by the mere fact of having translated the *Noli me tangere,* which would endanger my Filipino friends, because there (Philippines) not only the

---

such quasi-illiterate racketeers like the Aguinaldos and the Alvarezes, Pio del Pilar, Ricarte, Rillo, Trias, the two Riego de Dioses, Daniel Tirona, Tomas Mascardo, Antonio Montenegro, de las Alas, Lumbreras, Antony, Zulueta, Vicente Fernandez, Ignacio Paua, Noriel, Cuenca, Belarmino, etcetera, be able to insinuate themselves into the national revolutionary leadership enough for them to be capable of betraying and selling it as they did?:--hindi makakaporma si Aguinaldo kay Rizal, o kay Antonio Luna:--whilst months before, in letters we have cited in this documentary, almost all of the above had expressed to Rizal their eagerness to join him in the revolution they all imagined Rizal would be going home to precisely found. Which is to say, Rizal's and Blumentritt's *assimilationism* was chiefly responsible—and Rizal and Blumentritt with it—for all the negative effects of the prejudicial relationship between the Rizalistically brainwashed colonial middle-class and the revolution which led directly to the slaughter of thousands of buho-spear-and-bolo-wielding Katipuneros rushing headlong against Remingtoned and Mausered Civil Guards and Spanish regulars, the retardations, the betrayals, all resulting in the absolutely fatal *delay* that left the Philippines unliberated when the Spanish-American War broke out, leaving it free to be seized thus and genocided by the North American massmurderers.

filibustero is punished but also his friends… I had to laugh aloud when I received the first of such letters. I, the most faithful partisan of the Queen Regent, of her late husband and the young innocent king, I who by word of mouth and in writing have defended the honor and flag of Spain am a *filibustero*!...[50] On the other hand, what do my Peninsular Spanish friends say? They implored me not to publish the book in German so that its contents would not be known in Austria or Germany, and so that I might not lose the sympathy so many times I had won in Spain. This argument gives much food for thought and this request speaks eloquently in favour of the *Noli me tangere*, because from these requests that have come from different quarters can be deduced a multitude of marvelous considerations.

---

[50] This then, for the purpose of this historical documentation, is the most important truth to which this review of Rizal's *Noli* testifies, namely, that the most zealous, the most faithful, the most celebratedly loyal, the best-decorated veteran Austrian-Spanish defender of Spanish colonialism is doing it, and Rizal is absolutely unanimous with himself in endorsing what it says here about **his and his novel's being the purest and most intense manifestation of *Spanish* patriotism—*Spanish patriotism*, note well, and make no mistake about it, Spanish, *not* Indio native patriotism!!!**--about his and **his novel's being the purest and most intense expression of *Spanish colonial conservation and self-defense*** against, of course, separatism, against revolution, against independence which the brown savages might soon be prompted by the abuses of the friars and of inept Peninsular colonial administrators to ***savagely perpetrate*** (as Rizal himself put it most ignominiously in his *December 15, 1896 Fort Santiago Manifesto*, but also in his egregiously infamous *The Philippines a Century Hence*, and elsewhere).

"For the present, I deduce from these that the majority of the peninsular Spaniards have not the least notion that the situation in the Philippines is wellknown in foreign countries. Those suppliants, moved undoubtedly by a noble patriotic sentiment, implored me not to translate the book because they feared that the *Noli me tangere* might expose in Austria and Germany all the wretchedness of monasticism and the pompous administration of the Philippines. However, I pointed out to these friends that the Germans, in taking up the Philippines, read not only German books but also Spanish, French, English, and Dutch, and *in this rich bibliography there are accusations against friars and government employees,* ***beside which the*** **Noli me tangere** ***appears like the defender of paternal government.*** The publication of the book neither would teach the Germans anything new, and I even dare to believe that, the misrule in the Philippines being already known as it is in all Europe and profoundly felt by the friends of Spain—I dare to believe that ***the Noli me tangere*** **would only serve the good name of Spanish colonization, because this book proves that colonization has borne fruits, inasmuch as it has imbued a young and noble native with that aversion to the immoral in whatever form, activity or garb it may manifest itself, which is undoubtedly the surest sign of perfected morality and civilization...**

"...The native who has incurred the hatred of the friars is found there without protection and without a right, *inasmuch as the government is only an executive arm of monasticism*, which places the interests of its order ahead of the interests of the state.

"While Plaridel, defender of Rizal, refutes word for word the accusation of *filibusterismo*, the detractors only lose time in vague accusations. I don't wish to take up the booklet of Father Jose Rodriguez, because every word he dedicates to Rizal is merely filth. I only wish to inform the German readers of the following so that they may know with what ignoble adversaries Rizal has to fight...[51]"

---

[51] On page 564 of this volume, right below what we are exposing now, we find the following footnote by Blumentritt himself: "A determined adversary of Rizal writes: 'How can I deny that there is much good, however in the novel *Noli*? Some excellent descriptions; passages of much merit...the novel is well studied and it has passages which are really vivid. As with the rest, I do not understand why Fr. Rodriguez wrote that booklet that concedes to its readers 80 days of indulgence, for the *educated Filipinos* would undoubtedly prefer the interesting perusal of *Noli me tangere* to the insipid offspring of the Father, *and the ignorant among the Indios* will not read it, written as it is in Spanish, a language they do not understand.'" But the ignorant among the Indios will not read the *Noli* either, written as it is in Spanish, a language they do not understand. This simple reflection should have alerted all those brainwashed historians, writers, teachers, media people, intellectuals of all sorts, who do not tire in repeating that it was Rizal, through his works, and especially his novels, who awakened the Filipinos into revolution, to the glaring improbability of such claim. Of course Bonifacio who founded the revolution read him, read his *Noli* and the *Fili* also (together with *real and true and tested revolutionary literature* on the French Revolution , on the Lives of the American Presidents, etc.). But it is simply facetious to conclude from this that he became the revolutionary he was because of such Rizalian readings. And it is not the least of the reasons for this facetiousness, this ridiculousness and absurdity that the writer himself failed to be converted into revolution by those supposedly revolutionary texts. To this failure of Rizal himself to be convinced by himself in writing the *Noli*, let alone the *Fili*, to found or join the revolution should be added the fact that all those who were able to read it, namely his fellow

Filibusterismo, note, is the same as being *anti-Spanish* by way of advocating or sympathizing with *separatism, revolution, independence.* There is *nothing* anti-Spanish, nothing of separatism, revolution, independence, in Rizal, in the *Noli*, insists Blumentritt; Plaridel, eleven years older than

---

ilustrado assimilationists and their colonial middleclass families and friends, likewise failed to be made revolutionaries of by it. It did not make of Antonio Luna a revolutionary—or Marcelo del Pilar who also wrote a review of it for *La Solidaridad,* or Jaena, or Ponce, or Edilberto Evangelista, or Jose Alejandrino, etc. Although of the abovenamed ilustrados, only del Pilar did not later on and for reasons other than reading the *Noli* or the *Fili,* profess at least a readiness to jump into separatism and revolution, sounding off, challenging, inviting Rizal to found the revolution which with him as leader they were all eager to join. But really, the matter should have been a lot simpler (had not these people come to be so perverted by a century of state-sponsored ruling-class buttressed brainwashing): read the novel—and the *Fili* also—with enough intelligence and honesty and discover for yourself that what Blumentritt, Plaridel, de Lete, were here and elsewhere passionately arguing, demonstrating, illustrating, namely that far from advocating Philippine independence, far from being separatist-revolutionary (or *filibusterist*), the *Noli* was a most vivid and powerful manifestation of purest *Spanish patriotism* in its impassioned preaching *to the Peninsular Spaniards for whom solely it was written* that the best way to conserve Spanish colonialism in the Islands and pre-empt that greatest of all evils, that "worst of all disasters", that "most unfortunate rupture" (as he put it in *The Philippines A Century Hence* and everywhere else) that was revolution was to expel the friars and *assimilate* the country as an overseas province of Spain…

Rizal and the original Indio assimilationist chief crusader can only concur, and proceeds to refute word for word the absurd and ignorant charges of separatism, revolution, independence, being anti-Spanish leveled against Rizal and his *Noli me tangere.*

"...Let us now take up the question whether the *Noli me tangere* really solves as anti-Spanish propaganda, although I have before me a series of magnificent articles that prove brilliantly that Rizal does not write against but for the interests of Spain." Footnoting this sentence, Blumentritt continues: "I refer to the series of articles of Plaridel (Marcelo H. del Pilar): '*Noli me tangere* before Monkish Hatred in the Philippines', published in *La Publicidad*, Barcelona, 10, 13, 18, and 22 July 1888. See the last." Here we see that had those ilustrado propagandists like Plaridel, and Blumentritt himself, lived long enough to hear later perorations by Filipino intellectuals and necessarily dishonest and stupid Rizalists that it was Rizal through his novels that awakened the Filipinos to revolt, they would have been scandalized or would at the very least have smiled knowing smiles, because they were intimately in the know that and how Rizal was a most impassioned lover of Mother Spain and of everything Spanish, and was the most brilliant and uncompromising defender of Spanish colonialism amongst them, the most tenacious, the most truculent advocate of eternal colonialism for the Philippines under the heading and the banner of *assimilationism.* In particular, they most closely knew and would of course recall that his novels were rabidly anti-separatist, anti-revolutionary, anti-independence in being, precisely, assimilationist, and more pointedly, that none of those who were supposed to have been awakened by them were able to read them for they did not know any Spanish if they knew how to read at all, whilst those Filipinos who were able to read them, namely, mainly the same assimilationist anti-revolutionary propagandists and their anti-masses, anti-people families, were merely and expectably confirmed in their assimilationist anti-separatism and anti-revolution and anti-independence: for the truth was Rizal wrote them for the sole consumption of the Peninsular Spanish government and politicians whom the propagandists were trying to persuade to have the Philippines assimilated. And thus did Eduardo de Lete with acid irony put the matter when in his 1929 manifesto concerning his quarrel with Rizal over the *La Solidaridad* article *Iluso*, put it (see below).

"...I say moreover that in Philippine literature there is no other book as the *Noli me tangere* in which so ardent a love of country is manifest. Written with the blood of the heart of *a patriot, who harbors no mortal hatred whatever of Spain*[52], but only a just aversion against anyone who abuses selfishly and scandalously the power bestowed on him by the State or the Church...

"The novel was not written in order to separate the Philippines from Spain, but to call the attention of all the Spaniards of the Mother Country who are noble not only by lip service, to the misrule that has reigned, reigns, and can reign in the country, **IN ORDER THAT SPAIN MAY BE ABLE PRECISELY TO RETAIN THE PHILIPPINES BY INTRODUCING THE NECESSARY REFORMS...**The peaceful evolution that Spain is now undergoing, after a period of numberless revolutions, thanks to the high administrative ability of Alfonso II and to his august widow, gives hope that Rizal's wishes might be faithfully fulfilled. And I myself believe that the energetic campaign now being waged in the Philippines against corruption by General Weyler is a consequence of *Noli me tangere*. And if I am not mistaken, at least I would say that Weyler acts on this problem wholly in accord with Rizal..."

---

52 A Filipino patriot in the 1890s "who harbours no mortal hatred whatever of Spain"!?? What kind of an animal was that? As much as a square-circle such spineless creature or toad must contradict itself.

Chapter 13

TESTIMONY FROM THE CORRESPONDENCE WITH BLUMENTRITT

Nor should the German ethnographer's enthusiasm for, and recognition of Rizal be exaggerated, so that Rizal appears like some great and world renowned scholar being welcomed and toasted by European anthropologists. In connection with this, the following anecdote told by Rizal himself in the first letter to Blumentritt that we are considering here is apropos: "I have already visited Mr. Jagor who was very affable towards me. He invited me to attend a meeting of the Geographic Society and introduced me to the most famous professors and scholars. He made me join their monthly dinner where I met the famous Virchow. *The scholar told me jestingly that he wished to study me ethnographically*. I replied that i was willing to submit to his study for the love of science and I promised to introduce to him also another example, my compatriot (Viola)". (Letter 13; Rizal, Berlin, 12 January 1887; p 39)

An informant who can discourse with the ethnographer must indeed be quite amazing. He would be most welcome then too as source of information on things tribal. And this most happily to such an armchair ethnographer as Blumentritt, who had never even once set foot on his country of world-renowned expertise, the Philippines. Moreover, towards setting the perspective correctly on this matter, let us not forget that it was not the *German Society* (of literary writers), or some group of German philosophers (including Nietzsche for instance who was moving about in those places then), not a Humboldt or a Goethe that waxed enthusiastic over him. Only the Far Eastern section of German ethnography. Moreover, Rizal as ethnographer had his most important work in his *Annotations On Morga*. And what he supplied there were *annotations* on Morga, *not Morga* itself.

(1.)

Letter 15; Rizal, Berlin 26 January 1887.“**Under the present circumstances, we do not want separation from Spain...**”

“...I agree with you concerning the independence of the Philippines. *Only, such an event will never happen.* A peaceful struggle shall always be a dream, for Spain will never learn the lesson of her former South American colonies. Spain cannot learn what England and the US have learned. But, under the present circumstances, we do not want separation from Spain. All that we ask is greater attention, better education, better government employees, one or two representatives, and greater security for persons and property. Spain could always win the appreciation of the Filipinos if she were only reasonable! But ‘those whom Jupiter wishes to destroy, he first makes mad.’” (italics supplied) (p. 45)

We do not have Blumentritt’s letter to which this one by Rizal was a reply. We have then to content ourselves with a reconstruction of what exactly Blumentritt said about the “independence of the Philippines” to which Rizal here says he agrees. What I think Blumentritt was saying was that independence should finally be had by the Philippines *but only by way of a “peaceful struggle”*. It was liberation without revolution. Blumentritt was never for revolution; never once in his letters here did he endorse the idea; whilst from Rizal’s letters to him we can always glean that the Austrian Roman Catholic ethnographer remained a passionate journalistic crusader for the assimilation of the Philippines to Spain. Even during the traumatic aftermath of the *Rape of Calamba* in October 1891, Blumentritt was emphatic, in fact grew even more emphatic , even anxious, in counselling Rizal against reacting to the outrage revolutionarily or separatistically. Blumentritt was half or one-fourth Spanish and loved Spain and Spanish culture with passion; he had had a number of commendations and decorations conferred by the Spanish government for services rendered towards promoting Spanish glory and interests. Perhaps then Blumentritt was saying that after assimilation the Philippines should eventually win independence, one that would be freely granted by the Mother country herself. And to this kind of independence beyond and by way of assimilation, Rizal says he agrees. Blumentritt might have said it as he was thinking about the fact that perhaps no complete assimilation between such races was possible. Rizal then says he agrees to this kind of independence, but adds that it is in fact impossible. A peaceful struggle leading to independence has no chance of succeeding. And this because Spain is incapable of learning those lessons of history which she should have learned when she lost all her Latin American colonies violently, revolutionarily. Moreover, Rizal is saying, he, and his Filipino confreres do not really want separation, independence, under the present circumstances, even should it be freely and peacefully granted. Why? Rizal did not directly say why, but we can deduce from the context that, as he put it a little less than ten years later in that infamous *Fort Santiago December 15 Manifesto*, and which many, many times he repeated before that, it was because the Filipinos *did not yet deserve to be free* as they "still lacked education and civic virtues," etc. Everytime we encounter this metaphysical argument in him or in McKinley (that other *ass*-i-m-ilatorist) or in anyone else, we should always see in it a species of racism, of, as we put it elsewhere, *metaphysical racism*. A metaphysical *not-yet* metaphysizing or, if you want, *theologizing, religionizing* human temporality thus is imposed upon, is inflicted against, the subject race, the colonized native, *postponing therewith her/his humanity*. At the same time, a metaphysical, a theological, an absolutist, a religious value, substance, essence, numen, mystic potency, is thereby conferred upon *that* the not-yet-having of which renders the native, the subject race un-human, pre-human, not-yet human, like a child, or like Aristotle defines the slave in a fit of epochal (for the epochal Aristotle himself was the one doing it) dishonesty and blindness in the first pages of the *Politics*, or the way Western-Christian-Capitalist global colonialism with its *Enlightenmentist metaphysics* as panoptical and cutting-edge (in fact genocidally decapitating) ideology defines the "savage", who then is properly, rightly, legitimately, even, as the friars put it, and yes McKinley also (who must have read Rizal!) (think of his *Benevolent Assimilation Proclamation*), *holily* subjectible to tutelage, supervision, guidance, instruction, educative and civilizing subordination—i.e., domination, oppression, exploitation. Meanwhile, the colonizer into whom Rizal and company wished with all the might of their colonial being to be assimilated, is metaphysically exalted into an absolute being, conferrer of the numen, bearer and injector of the essence (education, civic virtue, civilization, science, progress, reason...) the not yet having of which renders the native, the savage, not yet human. Rizal himself would understand this because, without having formulated the thing this way, he knew it. He knew, and he said it in various places, that if there is an essence of humanity (an essence which as modern philosophy has taught us, and especially existentialism, is not a substance in the traditional, Aristotelian or Platonist or even Hegelian sense), it is freedom, and the rest, culture, civilization, are, so to speak, superstructures founded upon it. He knew that regardless of the quality and quantity of whatever distinguishes a nation from another, they are both associations of free beings. He knew that every human being is a free being, that each of them is, as Rousseau put it, born free. Knowing this, he should have known, and he knew, that this freedom cannot be postponed without postponing the humanity of the human being itself. He knew it but forgot it. Was it lack of human depth and largeness, was it cowardice that precipitated him into the genocidal, ultimately genocidal, abyss of that forgetting? For that forgetfulness meant that he would be assimilationist instead of separatist, that, instead of revolution and national liberation, he would be the great champion of colonial reaction and counterrevolution which, immensely successful, would eventually lead to the counterrevolution of the upper strata of native society and the thoroughgoing, fatal ideological corruption of the *separatism* of those of the lower middle class that would join and eventually officer and hostage and betray and sell it. A corruption (of separatism) that would go all the way to necessarily double-faced political brigandage: Aguinaldo the coward, the craven Emilio Aguinaldo y Famy, the Running Man of Asia, was a Rizalist when, smelling death close by during the Spanish retaking of Naic, he resolved right then and there to quit and slide back to assimilationism and the expulsion of the friars or at least the return to the Filipino owners of the friar lands. Such Rizalistically corrupted separatism would spell itself out in the exact wordings of the terms of sale in which was sold the Revolution to the enemy at Biyak na Bato. Genocidal influence: it would injure and delay the Revolution so much that the Americans would catch up with it and murder 2 million Filipinos thanks to the breach, the, in the ultimate analysis, *Rizalian Aguinaldian breach.*

(2.)

Letter 17; Rizal, Berlin 7 February 1887. **"Good news"—A Spanish deputy pleads for Philippine representatives to the Spanish Cortes.**

"...I'll give you good news; Deputy La Guardia recently presented three proposals to the Congress pleading for representatives for the Philippines. I have already written to him expressing my gratitude[53]..." (p 47)

---

[53]I'll tell you something, come closer, I'll whisper it to your ear: Dean Mario Miclat, one of the three chiefs of the UP Diliman Rizal Sesquicentennial Conference to be held on June 22-24, 2011 told me point blank that he cannot find any assimilationism in the writings of Jose Rizal! He is dean of the Asian Center where the conference will be held. He, together with the other two (Dean Michael Tan of the College of Social Sciences and Philosophy, and Dr. Marot Flores of the Filipino Department), voted to block me and prevent me from reading a paper in that conference. I don't know if it is true, but there are allegations and whisperings that the National FF Artist for Literature Virgilio Almario lobbied against me here and exerted tremendous pressure to exclude me from that conference. Was Virgilio Almario afraid I might ask questions concerning the Tagalog translation of Rizal's *Noli* and *Fili* by, *supposedly, allegedly, absolutely unbelievably* a certain Virgilio Almario who could be for the graphic similarity the same Virgilio Almario who was once dean of

(3)

Letter 19. Rizal, Berlin 21 February 1887. "**Spain, not the Philippines, should want assimilation...**"

"Mr Quioquiap is somewhat more blunt than Canamaque, Mas, San Agustin, etc., but more sincere. He wants political distinction and he is right. The Philippines had long wished for *Hispanization* and they were wrong in aspiring for it. *It is Spain and not the Philippines who ought to wish for the*

---

the College of Arts and Letters at UP Diliman? Who cannot possibly be mistaken for Rio Alma Coroza who knew Spanish enough to at all imagine being able to translate such delicate historical works? And meanwhile, do you know that he, Virgilio Almario has always owned, has always already owned, that his supposed translation of the two novels was not by someone named Virgilio Almario? Why? How come? Because the Virgilio Almario—I do not know if he is the same who was dean of UP Diliman CAL—who certainly cannot be Michael Coroza Almacen—who "translated" the two novels did not have imprinted right after the titles on the title pages and on the front covers that the books have been "***translated from the original Spanish***". Now anyone who translates a thing, a literary work, as completely linguistically imbricated as a novel who nonetheless cannot at once claim that it has been ***translated from the original*** must not have translated it from the original at all—or else, or else, must not have been the real translator!!! In both cases, the *cabron* in question cannot be a translator; the one being a literary murderer, the other being a plagiarist, a thief, a..., in the Philippines, only in the Philippines...

assimilation of the country. Now we receive this lesson from the Spaniards and we thank them for it."[54] (p 57)

(4)

Letter 23. Rizal, Berlin 21 March 1887. "Here (in the Noli) I answer all the false concepts which have been formed against us and all the insults which have been intended to belittle us..."

"...I send you a book; it is my first book, though I have already written much and received some prizes in literary competitions. It is the first impartial and bold book on the life of the Tagalogs. The Filipinos will find in it the history of the last ten years. I hope you will note how different are my descriptions from those of other writers. The government and the friars will probably attack the work, refuting my arguments, but I trust in the God of Truth and in the persons who have seen our sufferings at close range. Here I answer all the false concepts which have been formed against us and all the insults which have been intended to belittle us. I hope you will understand it well..." (61-62)

The novel as history... As such, the *Noli* and the *Fili* are great works; of art, yes—and history. Being an assimilationist work, it was written in Spanish for purely Spanish readers, specifically the Madrid government, the liberal politicians and intellectuals in the peninsula on one hand, and the colonial middle class, the literate, Spanish-speaking upper crust of native society whom Rizal and company were recruiting to the assimilationist crusade, on the other hand. As history—and

---

[54]There is no assimilationism in Rizal, no! And for that exact reason, Mario Miclat cannot see it. There are no eyes in Mario Miclat to see it...Eyeless thus, Mario Miclat who banned me from the Sesquicentennial Rizal International Conference (June 22-24, 2011) whose venue is the patient of his deanship, will of course not see it here...Turbid eyes, eyes perturbed by stupidity...

art—liberated for a hundred years now from the defining socio-historical context and exigency of the Revolution which it did not intend to promote, and which indeed, it intended to thwart, to prevent, to pre-empt, it has become greater and more powerful. Today, reading it in Tagalog or English translation, the Filipino youth and even the Filipino olds, learn from the novels of the abhorrent evil of the friars and they come to hate them so, and they become so hateful to them they cannot hate them enough, and they are quickened to the desire of having joined the Revolution against them, against Spanish colonialism per se whose hatefulness, whose immeasurable evil has now come to be epitomized by those endlessly execrable friars...This effect on them of the novel/s is the prime cause of the misunderstanding and the peddled lie that it must have been responsible, that it was responsible, that it was *chiefly* responsible for inflaming so many Filipinos into revolution. You read it today, you are inflamed into retrospective revolutionary fervour by it, and you conclude automatically that so must your ancestors have been inflamed reading it. But if your ancestors were not Spanish, or mestizo, or did not speak Spanish, or were not even very literate like the Filipino masses that massively joined the Bonifacio-led Revolution, they would not have been able to read it. The novel, or novels—they are really one—was assimilationist. It was intended primarily to influence the Spanish government in Madrid to grant assimilation status to the Philippines, to make of it an overseas province of Spain, and of the Filipinos Spanish citizens. And that was why it had to be written in Spanish and by someone who was master of the Spanish language. Being assimilationist thus, it was also intended for Philippine readers who could be recruited to support the "Great Assimilationist Cause", the Spanish-speaking upper stratum of the colonial middle-class to which Rizal and his *La Solidaridad* hispanizers belonged.

(5)

Letter 24. Blumentritt, Leitmeritz, 27 March 1887.(p 63) Blumentritt prophesies that someday Rizal would for his own people become "one of those great men who will exert a definite influence on their spiritual development..."

"...Your work has exceeded my expectations, and I consider myself lucky that you have honoured me with your friendship. But not only I but your people also can be called lucky for having in you a son and a loyal patriot[55]. If you will continue

---

55 A loyal patriot! Before you jump into conclusions concerning this seemingly disinterested testimony, bear in mind first of all that Blumentritt was a part-Spanish Austrian *Spanish patriot* whose chief preoccupation throughout his life was ethnographically, journalistically, and otherwise, the defence of the colonial interests of his dearly beloved Mother Spain: as an ethnographer, his specialization was the Philippines, which however he never visited—an armchair anthropologist then (which anytime it happens is a dishonesty), who must have been very glad to meet in Rizal a live ethnographic specimen and by that much conduct a kind of exalted portable fieldwork. And that, concerning the Philippine question, his staunch, his immovable stand and advocacy was—*assimilationism.* This was the common bond which explains why they instantly evinced such attraction to each other and were moved instantly to praise each other to the highest empyrean. As a matter of fact, as a crusader (literally for the fellow was a most devout Roman Catholic like his Spanish forebears) for *Philippine assimilation,* he had published more articles in *La Solidaridad* than even Jose P. Rizal. Here is Rizal himself testifying to Blumentritt's undying Spanish colonial patriotism and, for the sake of the former, his equally immortal desire for Philippine assimilation, as he, Rizal, was introducing him editorially in his, Blumentritt's, infamous review of the *Noli* which also came out in *La Solidaridad*: "In the present struggle between the Filipino people, avid for education, and certain classes which endeavour to perpetuate ignorance in the country, the learned Philippinist, the Austrian professor Mr. Ferdinand

Blumentritt intervenes. We do not need to give here his biography, which has already been published in various periodicals of Spain, Especially in *Espana en Filipinas*. All those who are interested in geography, ethnography, and linguistics, all orientalists, all those who are engaged in the study of the Philippines, know his name, respected and honoured in the civilized world of Europe. The opinion, however, that the Professor emits about the *Noli me tangere* might perhaps raise protests from those who prertend to have been born infallible—stainless white sheep—from those who accuse every adversary of being a *filibuster*, and describe every opinion contrary to or different from his own as heretical or protestant. And they would have no reason to say so. Professor Blumentritt is a fervent Catholic, an obedient son of the Roman Church, which he considers the only true one, the only one that can redeem mankind. Neither can he be branded a *filibuster*, despite the cheapnewss of this term, because not only has he Spanish blood, but he is besides a devoted champion of Spanish rights, defending them in all questions, in those of Tawi-Tawi and Caroline Islands, for example, in periodicals,, treatises, lectures, etc., with such ardour that he was considered deserving of a decoration by the Madrid government, which also awarded him a prize for numerous works exhibited at the Philippine Exposition. And if any of the contending parties would doubt his impartiality in Philippine questions, it would not be in truth the ruling class, because Blumentritt is steeped in and nourished with all the books that the friars and the Peninsular Spaniards had written, depicting the country according their whim; and if the judgment of the learned professor did not fall victim to their prejudices and calumnies, as did that of many others, it is due solely to his sane common sense and to his solicitude to study things carefully. On Philippine questions, Blumentritt has read not only all the Spanish authors but also foreign ones who, in general, it might be thus, you can become for your people one of those great men who will exert a definite influence on their spiritual development..."

And so he did. And all at once he became responsible for three fatal crimes against his own people: 1.) He was responsible for making possible through his reformist-assimilationist anti-revolutionary and later on counter-revolutionary activity and powerful leadership of the colonial middleclass the swaying away of the latter from revolution and later on against the Revolution, whilst sociohistorically this class should have been the most advanced and the most radical, as it in fact was in all the other European colonies around the world during those revolutionary times, and should thus have theorized, organized and spearheaded the Revolution as it did in all those other European colonies; 2.) he did not sway them into revolution, he wasted the chance to sway them into revolution; and 3.) those of the ilustrado propagandists in

---

said, do more justice to the inhabitants opf this country than those whose duty is to defend them and who are the very ones responsible for the many vices and defects of their present state. Unfortunately, Filipinos write very few books, and still those that come out are prohibited." (Appendix to *Rizal's MiscellaneousCorrespondence*, Manila, 1961, pp 547-548). Needless to say, Blumentritt's review was a long, impassioned defense of the *Noli* as an *assimilationist* novel whose main objective was to defend Spanish colonialism in the Philippines by exposing the friars as the main revolution-provoking threat to Spanish rule in the islands. (We shall take up this review itself below.) In short, Rizal's being a "loyal patriot" here means his being a do-or-die defender of the Mother Country, Spain, into whose bosom Rizal wanted his native country assimilated: hence the profound ambiguity of this "loyal patriotism" which is at once interpreted as truest loyalty to and love for the native land in its being against separatism, revolution, independence!

Europe who, in the wake of the *Rape of Calamba* had concluded that separatism and revolution had become the only hope and credible response for them and the Filipino people, and had told, had written, Rizal so, and were waiting for him to signal the leap for they were sure too that it had become Rizal's inevitable stand now, were criminally failed by him. This was during the last three months of 1891. I am referring to Antonio Luna, Graciano Lopez Jaena, Edilberto Evangelista, Jose Alejandrino, Mariano Ponce, and perhaps the great majority if not all of the members of the Barcelona colony. Had he made the leap with them, they could have, with Andres Bonifacio in the Archipelago, formed the truly national nucleus of the revolution which as such would have pulled into it to lead it the entire colonial middle class with its influence, intelligence, and great resources.

(6.)

Letter 41. Rizal, Geneva, 19 June 1887. Rizal is all set to go home to the Philippines. In view of this, Blumentritt is admonishing him *against* revolution. Rizal answers that he has no desire for conspiracies which seem premature, implying that he could perhaps be interested in mature ones, but Rizal was fond of talking like that: revolution to Rizal is self-destruction, suicide, and forever premature.

"...I assure you that I have no desire to take part in conspiracies which seem to me too premature and risky. But if the government drives us to them, that is to say, *when no other hope remains to us but seek* ***our destruction*** *in war*, when the Filipinos would prefer to die rather than endure longer their misery, then I will also become a partisan of violent means.[56]

---

56 Rizal must be bragging here, and this in view of everything that Rizal wrote and did not write, and of everything that Rizal did and did not do, and specifically in view of the fact that despite the extreme provocation of the *Rape of Calamba* Rizal failed to "become a partisan of violent means", and in view most emphatically of the fact that he could at least have pleaded guilty of rebellion and

defied his military judges and dared them to sentence him to death during the trial (that is of course if he was really some kind of revolutionary, if he was not in fact the addict of assimilation, the assimilationist-to-death he was!). But no. And we know that it was not out of cowardice that he did not do so, for we believe that Rizal was brave, very brave (he proved this beyond any shadow of doubt when he came home the second time on June 26, 1892, literally inviting death as a martyr of assimilationism). Rather, it was because as a matter of fact he not only would be a liar if he did so:--he hated, he abhorred, he abominated the Revolution, as he himself declared it in no uncertain terms, and even in terms that courted eloquence in his *December 15 Manifesto* in which he excoriated Bonifacio and company as "backstabbing" "barbarians", "savages", "uneducated", "uncultured" ("lacking in education and civic virtues") "troublemakers" "working in bad faith" who "discredit" him and his countrymen and "shame" him to those Spaniard friends of his who were supposedly helping them in their assimilationist project, etc... He hated, he abominated, he abhorred the Revolution, and that was why in his last two letters written a few hours before he was shot, the one to his brother, Paciano and the other to, precisely, Blumentritt, he reaffirmed as he said his last goodbye that he "will die innocent of the crime of rebellion": we have to believe him in these re-affirmations:--there was absolutely no reason, barring insanity, for him to lie to them about it in those final letters. Meanwhile, Rizal's supposed secret, ultimate revolutionariness has here been made to hinge by all the historians who ever wrote on the matter on the phrase: "too premature and risky"; they take this to mean that Rizal was merely biding his time, was waiting for time to ripen. But, aside from the fact that he, as we are saying, must be bragging to his Austrian-Spanish friend here, he himself, in his own words, and thanks to his rhetorical

> The choice of peace and *destruction* is in the hands of Spain, because it is a clear fact, known to all, that we are patient and peaceful, mild, unfeeling, etc. But everything ends in this life; there is nothing eternal in the world and that refers also to our patience. I cannot believe that you, as a free man, as a citizen of Europe, would like to advise your good friend to endure everything and behave as a pusillanimous man, without courage... Be assured that I desire the happiness of my country and so long as I believe that the evil is *only in the system* of Spanish government, *I will combat everything that may be planned against Spain.*[57] I thank you for your

---

tendencies, betrayed his own real stand on the matter by defining revolution as self-destruction and as suicide:--not a fight to the death for liberty, for independence, for the transcendent good of the country, for freedom and dignity, no, no, no, no, no, but—*self-destruction, suicide*! Nor was this but an adventitious formulation, a rhetorical flourish: in *The Philippines A Century Hence*, published in *La Solidaridad* in September 1889 to February 1890, he defined revolution as "the greatest disaster that could befall us", etc...Now, for anyone who thinks of revolution that way—as suicide, as of course insane self-destruction—the proper time for it can never come.

57 That is to say, as long as Rizal believes that *colonialism can be good, and is good,* that is, as long as he is convinced that *Spanish colonialism* is good and the only evil lies in the system of its Spanish administration, he will combat any plan for revolution that he may find afoot in his coming home to the Philippines. As we have been saying, colonialism per se is evil per se and there is absolutely no valid justification for it. This is what the (anti-colonial) revolutionary first of all realizes; this was what Rizal died without realizing. He would not have wanted at all to go to Cuba to help the Spanish army defend colonialism there against the Cuban Katipuneros if he had had any glimmering of a realization that colonialism per se is evil.

recommendations but pardon me if I believe that a recommendation for me in my own country sounds dismal. Recommendations can be useful abroad, but in the native land of the recommended person, they are a bitter thing. It is true that they are useful, but I am ashamed to deliver such letters. I thank you and happen what may, I trust in God.

"I believe that you put on enchanted spectacles when you read something about me, and that is my luck. I tell you this because you like my writings. Your advice that I remain in Madrid and there write is very kind; but I cannot and ought not to accept it. I cannot endure life in Madrid; there we are all a voice crying in the desert. My relatives want to see me and I want to see them also. In n o other place is life for me so pleasant as in my native country, beside my family..." (pp105-107)

(7)

Letter 68. Rizal, London, 23 June 1888. Assimilationists are also human; they too have emotional ups and downs. Today they are jubilant that a liberal-minded deputy has spoken for representation of the Philippines to the Cortes (see letter ...above); tomorrow they despair at the seeming impossibility of ever becoming brown Spaniards. Here, Rizal, very low in criminal assimilationist zeal rests his case on God and seems to gesture towards doing something which does not rely on begging freedom and dignity from the racist Roman Catholic colonial master. Separatism? Revolution? Or brave and standardly empty rhetoric? But it was rhetoric like this to which Rizal by way of bragging not infrequently resorted to, that encourages the uniformly dishonest and unbright Filipino writers on the history of the revolution to go on insisting that if not already a secret revolutionary, Rizal

---

And, of course of course of course, he would have accepted instead Bonifacio's invitation for him to join and even lead the revolution here if he knew that colonialism was evil per se.

was on the verge of almost being potentially one! Empty rhetoric in any case, for did he do anything to follow it up? Nay, did he not do everything to refute it? Nay, did he not do everything to fight against the very idea of it, to betray it when it was already there, and to denounce it till death?

"You say that you are fighting for me and my fellow countrymen. I thank you for it. But I beg you not to fight for me and my countrymen but for truth, because, after all, my countrymen and I will soon perish, and you ought to work for the imperishable" (These—we cannot restrain ourselves—are cheap rhetorical ideas:--hilaw na hilaw si Rizal!) "But you will gain the fame of having had the boldness to defend the weak and the defenseless, which is very infrequent" (And here he contradicts what he just said on fighting for the truth only and the imperishable.). "Keep yourself always impartial, as until now: raise or knock us down as we may deserve" (Anong kalandian ito?). "Forget that you are my friend, because I would be very sorry if you would suffer anything ***for our cause***" (bakeet?, why?). "I believe that it is already late; the majority of the Filipinos have lost already the hope they have pinned on Spain! Now we await our fate from GOD" (anu ito?) "and from ourselves, but never anymore from any government." (p. 172)

(8)

Letter 74. Rizal, London, 7 August 1888. Rizal asks Blumentritt somewhat rhetorically not to intervene anymore in the "violent fight"...

"I believe that you ought to withdraw from this violent fight which poisons your gentle heart and embitters your beautiful character, because politics, when it blazes between tyrants and oppressed peoples, has no heart nor brains, but fangs, poison, and vengeance. In the past, you lived always quietly and in peace. Continue living thus and do not go down to the burning arena on which we fight[58]. Leave us alone to settle our affairs" (Huuu, daming clichés...) "We are struggling for our rights, for the rights of humanity[59], and if there is a God, He will have to help us." (Oh my God!) "We are still few and weak, but we shall be stronger and more numerous. Your life and the peace of your family are sacred to me and I fear that our situation may bring them misfortune. You have to write our history, you ought to remain impartial[60]. Stop all your correspondence if you do not want to wage a pitched battle for us. As for me, the struggle is different. Nature, if I am not mistaken, gave me a tender and delicate heart. I am inclined to be friendly and I should like to be everybody's friend" (???), and despite this I have to hide my sentiments, I have to scold and even hate and I make a hundred enemies for every friend! If I were a free European, I would be married by now, I would have a family, and I would live beside my parents, devote myself to science, and with my friends contemplate and love in peace and

---

58 If one did not know that Rizal was such a...--but this burning arena was simply hyperbolical, for assimilationism was not a burning thing at all; skirmishing by way of the bimonthly pages of *La Solidaridad* with expectably fifth-rate Spanish journalists of anti-assimilationist, and in fact racist persuasion in a relatively liberal and tolerant metropolis like Madrid...

59 Struggling? For "rights of humanity" indeed? Are "assimilationist rights" rights? Are they in any case human? Nay, are they real? Are they not mere illusion, delusion, hallucination?

60 How pedantic! And what would constitute impartiality in the writing of such a history? Why should involvement of this armchair ethnographer in the journalistic crusade for Philippine assimilation injure his historiographic balance and overthrow his impartiality? And why indeed was Rizal proposing that task of writing our history to the foreigner? Why was he not proposing it to himself instead?

tranquility this beautiful world. If you know how I envy the last clerk of London!"[61]

(9.)

Letter 101. Rizal, Paris, 4 June 1889. Blumentritt is embroiled, fighting for Philippine assimilation. When they triumph in this fight and the Philippines gests assimilated, there will be more liberties in the Philippines; then, Rizal is inviting Blumentritt to live with him there.

"I have received your letters as well as your manuscripts. They are for the Philippine youth like an admonition of an old wise friend, for we are here fighting for our native country entirely without protection. You alone lend us strength and courage and you also admonish us when we depart from the path... When we shall have more liberties in the Philippines in a way that you and I may be able to live there, then we shall go. There is God for honorable persons..." (pp 259-60)

(10.)

Letter 102. Rizal, Paris, 19 June 1889. Blumentritt—Champion of Philippine Assimilationist Reformism.

"The Philippines can and ought to cherish hopes when she can count on such champions of her cause."

---

[61] No revolutionary, and certainly and even more empathically, no anti-colonial revolutionary, would envy the British prime minister or the King of Spain. And I am absolutely certain Andres Bonifacio did not. Of course Rizal was no revolutionary—in fact, he was the polar opposite; as chief assimilationist crusader, he was evil spearhead of colonial conservatism; which, Indio colonial social-climber that he was, was exactly why he could envy the last clerk of the British East India Company.

(11.)

Letter 114. Blumentritt, Leitmeritz, 10 Sept. 1889. Peninsular Spaniards defend Blumentritt; they are also reformists but do not favor the expulsion of the friars.

"The Peninsular Spaniard who defended me in *La Solidaridad* must be Colonel Pio A de Pazos y Vela Hidalgo, because he and Engr. Ramon Jordana are the only peninsular Spaniards I know and *who are completely with us* (only they are opposed to the expulsion of the friars because no Spanish government for many decades will permit it)."[62]

(12.)

Letter 118. Blumentritt, Leitmeritz, 12 Oct. 1889. What is an *assimilated Frenchman*?

"I suggest that you look up in the legislation for French overseas colonies what is an *assimilated Frenchman.* I recall that in French Cochinchina, every native who pays a certain amount of taxes is granted all the rights of a French citizen, including the right to vote. It would be very useful to publish it in *La Solidaridad.*"[63]

---

[62] That is to say, they are assimilationists too, like the two of them (except that they do not think it feasible to have the friars expelled from the country and that's why they are against it!).

[63] There! And do we even need to explicate anything here to add anything to what we here seek to exhibit to the brainwashed Filipinos, namely that Rizal was an assimilationist assimilationist assimilationist and *La Solidaridad* was an asshole assimilationist asshole newspaper

(13.)

Letter 124. Rizal, Paris 22 Nov. 1889. Rizal tells Blumentritt that he is editing Blumentritt's prologue to Morga. He admonishes him for advocating a begging, whining kind of *assimilationist embrace* from the Spaniards. This means, of course, that—and here it is for those who like Miclat "cannot find any assimilationism in Rizal"—he, Rizal, was for some less humiliating form of assimilation and therefore for assimilation.

"...I have also taken the liberty of striking out some portions referring to *fraternity*. You harbor the best intentions; you

---

fighting for eternal asshole colonialism for the Filipinos? Unfortunately yes, we have to, the Filipinos being so thoroughly brainwashed and into their brains have been crammed to bursting point so much lies and direct inversions by the ruling class and its government, its education system, its mass media, its "organic" intellectuals. **What is an assimilated Spaniard? An Indio who...is granted the rights of a Spanish citizen, etc...** :--Rizal, for instance, and all those ilustrado assimilationist campaigners in the Peninsula who only lacked the right to vote in liberal Spain, assimilated thus already into liberal Spain:--and that was how they were able to hallucinate the hallucination of such assimilation extended to the Indio farmer, fisherman, carpenter, weaver, etc... A most laudable hallucinatory intention indeed! And, but, therefore, hallucination—only! And, being a mere hallucination—a malevolently twisted abstraction and as such malevolently twistedly *violent*—a most bloody one, in fact, as history has demonstrated by producing and holding up at least two million Indio corpses, compliments, chiefly, of Chief Assimilationist Counter-Revolutionary Dr. Jose Rizal, and with him, the money obsessed Biyak na Bato Vendor of the Revolution and the Motherland, Emilio Aguinaldo (and the Americans), even a genocidal one...

want the Spaniards to embrace us as brothers; *but we should not ask for that imploring and repeating it all the time, because it is somewhat humiliating for us.* If the Spaniards do not want us as brothers, neither are we anxious for their affection. We do not look for fraternal love as *charity*. I am convinced that you like us much *and that you also wish the good of Spain*, but we do not solicit Spain's *compassion*. We do not want compassion but justice. All our efforts tend to educate our people—education, education, education of our people—education and enlightenment. Fraternity as the alms of Spanish pride—that we do not ask. I reiterate that you alone have the best intentions; you wish to see men embracing one another for love and reason, but I doubt if the Spaniards like that." (pp 305-6)

(14.)

Letter 162. Rizal, Biarritz 29 March 1891. Rizal lamenting over the persecution of his family by the rapacious and lustful Dominicans because of him (partly true); but he is "not repenting... having undertaken this campaign"—this *assimilationist campaign* of course in which his closest and most indefatigable fellow campaigner was no other than this letter's addressee, Blumentritt. He looks upon assimilationist campaigning as his lifelong duty, and should he be reborn to the same situation he would as in Nietzsche's Eternal Recurrence of the Same, do it again, repeating everything he had done assimilationistically including writing this letter in which he affirms his eternal assimilationism despite those persecutions to which it must once more expose his family, and despite the repetition of Leonor Rivera's abandonment of him, martyring thus for the second time and ad infinitum even his love because of it, too, because he had to be so far away from her for so long because of it, so unfathomably devoutly assimilationist was he, O, O!!! And he believes in God too, quite astonishingly. And fervently even, as it appears here and in various other communications, it is quite an astonishment, really, really.

"...What has happened to my family? When I think of my family, I am overcome by such sorrows that if my faith in God[64] had been less, I would have committed a folly. I am not repenting[65] for having undertaken this campaign[66]. If I were now in the beginning of my life, I would do the same that I

---

64 Rizal really believed in God—if ever *that* was in doubt.

65 The proof, or at least textual indication that as early as February 1892 Rizal was already contemplating ***assimilationist martyrdom*** **by going home to the wrath of the friars and the enactment of the spectacle of his death at their malefic hands which he was expecting would focus the attention of the Madrid government on the Philippine problem and whip up such liberal fury and outrage against the friars that the Spanish liberals would be moved to move for their expulsion and for the final assimilation of the Philippines (!!!),** was this: he will repeat almost verbatim what he is saying here about not repenting anything as far as the campaign for assimilation is concerned, and how if time would be repeated he would do exactly the same things he had done as central figure in this anti-revolutionary, counter-revolutionary, anti-separatist, anti-independence campaign *for eternal colonialism* for the Philippines *in his two pre-departure Hong Kong letters* of the last week of June 1892 (one addressed to the Filipinos in general, in fact even to posterity in general—he also mysteriously and vaingloriously asked them in the same letter to have these published "after my death", and the other addressed to his family and friends)--*adding moreover and in an even more mysterious tone that he was going home "to put the finishing touches" to this error-free, unrepented, and unregretted work of his.*

66 *"this campaign"*: and what else indeed but this assimilationist campaign to which second only to Rizal or Marcelo del Pilar, Blumentritt the Austrian-Spanish ethno-journalist had contributed so much.

have done, because I am sure that I ought to do it, it was the duty of everyone; and God could ask me, Why did you not combat the evil and injustice when you saw them? But when I think that all—parents, brothers, friends, and nephews have to suffer *on account of my name*, then I feel that I am immensely unfortunate and I lose my good humor. When I find myself alone and I meditate, I ask myself if it is better to be a good relative than a true Christian[67]. When my fiancee' abandoned me, I realized that she was right, that I deserved it, but nevertheless my heart was bleeding. Recently I received her letter announcing that soon she would marry. She was always very much solicited by Filipinos and Spaniards. I have also received letters from my countrymen in which they tell me about their sufferings and persecution, saying that they would remain firm and that they do not fear the tyranny of the powerful. *At times I wish that a volcano would erupt in the Philippines and devour all sufferings and injustices so that all of us may be able to sleep the sleep of death!*[68]

"...I have finished my book (the *Fili*). Oh no, I have not written in it my idea of revenge[69] against my enemies, but

---

[67] And assimilationism is even a matter of being a true Christian to him! How could Dean Mario Miclat of the UP Asian Center have failed to find "any assimilationism" in Rizal? A former Marxist become a bourgeois apologist for bourgeoisedom now. Of course I too am no longer a Marxist. And that is because I discovered that Marx was not enough of a communist, was in fact not a communist at all, was in fact a disguised prophet of that terminal world religion called capitalism.

[68] Such a volcano must be something like a revolution; why cannot Rizal even name it directly thus? Whilst, here as elsewhere, such a revolution can only mean Filipino native self-destruction—"the sleep of death"—to him.

[69] Before you entertain what is usually and in course of time—more than a century of brainwashing and lying and stupidizing time perpetrated by the state itself and its of

only what is for the good of those who are suffering, for the *rights* of the **Tagalog race**[70], though brown and may not have good features!"

---

course Rizalistical ruling class itself and the mass-media, and 999.99 of every 1000 Filipino intellectuals (an underestimate actually)--inevitably entertained by all Filipino readers of Rizalian declarations such as this, I want to inform you that this Rizalian "idea of revenge" was NOT revolution but, and what else indeed but, assimilation—the assimilationist expulsion of the friars, the same as befell them in Spain itself when, on two almost revolutionary occasions, in 1835 and 1868, friars were beheaded right in the streets of Barcelona, and were banished from Spain itself and their properties expropriated by the State (see *Address to the Spanish Nation* below, and in *Rizal's Political and Historical Writings*, NHI 2007, Appendix A, p 385.). And that, as we shall show in tireless detail and unrelenting logic below, this idea of revenge of his became concrete in and as the idea of *assimilationist martyrdom* which he attempted to actualize on his June 26, 1892 return to the Philippines via Hong Kong:--it was in fact in order to spectacularly implement and stage this idea that he went home at all and surrendered himself to the wrath of the cormorant and Godful friars, inviting them thus to martyr him! Needless to say, the idea was a flop. The friars failed to martyr him; farcically, Governor General Despujol, somewhat of a liberal and a mason and duly impressed with him, saved him from the otherwise martyrizing bloodthirsty Godfulness of the friars by smuggling him out of their sight and reach to Dapitan before they could even begin to clamour for his head.

[70] Here, the unconscious speaks: he wrote his novels, and no doubt all his other works, "for the rights of the Tagalog race"—only. In any case, and this in a letter to his

(15.)

Letter 163. Blumentritt, Leitmeritz, 1 April 1891. Blumentritt proposes what never ever crossed Rizal's mind, namely, that vernacular versions of some articles in *La Solidaridad* be circulated in the Philippines . And yet, the fellow was of course a mere assimilationist and, from the looks of it, never could become a separatist and advocate of Philippine independence. And of course, such assimilationist articles can only lull the Filipinos into assimilationist patience and deluded assimilationist hope...

"...It would be very good if some of the articles in *La Solidaridad* were translated into Philippine languages. I figure the thing in this manner: *La Solidaridad* publishes a sheet as supplement to each issue as the Manila newspapers do with Reyes' writings."

This can only mean one thing, namely, that unlike Rizal, Blumentritt could want to recruit some native Filipino mass support for the assimilationist crusade; unlike Rizal, he wanted to also address the lower classes; unlike Rizal, he could imagine that those of them who can read in the vernacular were worth talking to: unlike Rizal, he was not contemptuous of the Indio native peasant and worker. Blumentritt did not know that to the contrary, Rizal's contempt of them was bottomless... What would he have finally thought of Rizal had he got to know how he betrayed a Katipunero to death and the Revolution therewith in Dapitan in 1892?; and how when Patino and Fr. Mariano Gil uncovered the Revolution on August 19, 1896, Rizal, like a vile and creepingly venomous zoologic specimen made that written offer of himself, his very life, his name, all he could do, in a letter to Governor General Blanco (officially witnessed even by the commanding officer of the Spanish cruiser *Castilla* aboard which he hid himself

---

ethnographer friend who specializes on races, tribes, nations, here he forgot the Igorots, the Pampangos, the Ilocanos, the Cebuanos, the Bicolanos, the Warays, etc...

from the about-to-explode Revolution in full view of the Governor General and the Spanish military), for the Spaniards to use him "in whatever manner they might deem fit to suppress the rebellion"?; and how during the trial, he in utmost shamelessness, and in order to save his own neck, alerted the court and everybody concerned who could read it, to the great Spanish loyalty and Spanish anti-revolutionary ardour and unfathomably deep Spanish patriotism of that *offering of his all to suppress the rebellion*, making this alerting by way of that indescribably ignominious *December 15, 1896 Fort Santiago Manifesto* which he addressed to the Filipinos and which he requested the Spanish authorities to publish for dissemination to the Filipinos especially to those who were already in arms ?; and how in and by means of this very same manifesto he in effect repeated the same offer of absolute sacrifice for the sake of preserving Spanish colonialism against Andres Bonifacio and company, proposing once more to allow him to persuade those natives who were already in the Revolution to abandon it and those who had not yet joined to desist from joining it, proposing implicatively thereby that he be allowed to lead an army to pursue Andres Bonifacio and company and murder all of them…?; and how in that same manifesto he called Andres Bonifacio and company savages and barbarians lacking in good manners and right conduct, regressive troublemakers who stabbed him in the back and shamed him to his Spanish friends…?

(16.)

Letter 164. Rizal, Brussels, 23 April 1891. Rizal lies about his "countrymen" who want to go on fighting for their "rights" in the face of growing persecution. Such "countrymen" of his were actually members of the colonial upper middle class who were clamorous for their *assimilationist* "rights".

"…My father and my entire family remain courageously united and faithful to the Filipino party, and my brother is even braver in his exile than he was before. All my family now bear the name *Rizal* instead of *Mercado*, because the name *Rizal* signifies persecution! Good! I want also to join them and be worthy of the family name. My countrymen are obstinately persisting in their *rights*, and with *Bimentrit* and their Rizal they want to continue fighting[71]".

"For this reason, I believe that now is the opportune time for me to return to the Philippines *and share with them all the dangers*. For I have always been of the opinion that I can do more in my country than abroad[72]. What good have I done

---

[71] His countrymen? His family perhaps, and the ilustrados and their families at home; but the main bulk of his countrymen, the working classes, were hardly aware of their rights as human beings, and were certainly completely ignorant of what *assimilationist* "rights" they were that Rizal and company with the able help of Blumentritt the half-Spanish or one-fourth Spanish Austrian ethnographer were "fighting" for. Soon enough, in a little more than a year, they, the native working classes, would begin to know in a most fiery way their birthright as human beings and as a people: Andres Bonifacio would teach it to them by founding the Revolution with them; and that revolutionary birthright was the exact, the antipodal, opposite of Rizal's assimilationist "rights" for which as he reports here, his family and his collaborationist "countrymen" were supposed to want to continue "fighting".

[72] This was a lie! A bragging lie, an opportunistic lie... Since when did this "always" begin? Before he began writing the *Noli*? Sometime during the writing of it? Before its publication? For during those times, he was free to come and go without political harassment. Why then did he not come home and stay here and "do more"? Nor was money a problem then, for he had enough all those years to tour Europe, Japan, the US. But the fellow was a terrific liar; and more terrific and terrible in that he lied mostly to himself or by way of first convincing himself of his own lie and then announcing it for the consumption of others afterwards. Moreover, in that his lying, his supposed,

in these three years and what evil had occurred because I was in my country?...

"...I have finished the second part of the *Fili*... (399-400)

(17.)

Letter 165. Blumentritt, Leitmeritz, 26 April 1891. Blumentritt dissuades Rizal from going home. He must not go home until

---

opinion did not in fact mean wanting to stay home to make what cannot be made by one who does not stay in his homeland protractedly enough to make it, namely revolution, for making it means addressing one's own people themselves, waking them up, instigating them, inflaming them, recruiting them, organizing them, leading them...:--since, in point of fact, what he was doing all those years and was continuing doing right now was the exact opposite of revolution, was in fact assimilationist crusading which to the precise contrary was then *the most effective way to pre-empt revolution and to counteract and defeat the very idea of it by pulling away from it the Spanish-speaking colonial middleclass and predisposing them against it,* whilst addressing themselves propagandistically to the Madrid government and the metropolitan political public, it was not true either that in pursuit of such counter-revolutionary, anti-separatist, anti-independence, anti-Filipino goals, the best place to be at was *not* in Spain but in the Philippine islands. A liar then; and all because he wanted to put across a memorable romantic image of himself! And to congratulate himself for the bravery of braving the brave fangs of the rapacious and mass-murderous and lustful and Godful friars by staying at home without staying at home at all! How to shoot that in a movie...? In a movie which I am going to write... And direct, or at least be a consulting director to... Two movies, one of them a comedy... Suggested title for the latter: ***LAZIR....***

Assimilation Day. For only then would it be safe for such as him.

"...I'm by no means in favour of your going to the Philippines now. You expose yourself to great perils *and your native country needs your intelligence and your freedom.* I believe that better times for the Philippines are approaching. The struggles of *La Solidaridad* are not useless. I would not dare such optimistic opinions only from my head, but some Spaniards who from the beginning of the campaign fled from me as from a heretic, have written me again, telling me that they have found out that I was right.

"Don't go to the Philippines *yet*; it is better for you to go to Leyden and see Prof. Kern and you study the scientific basis of the Malayan language. Then prepare for your people a dictionary like the one Littre has given the French, and even had you done nothing more than this (even if you had not written *Noli me tangere*), your name would be immortal, not only in your native country and among your people , but in the whole world." (401-2)

(18.)

Letter 166. Blumentritt, Leitmeritz, 20 June 1891. The *Fili*, a thunderbolt!

"I'm curious about your new work...I know your second novel will be a thunderbolt that will knock down the enemies." (401-2)

(19.)

Letter 168. Blumentritt, 5 July 1891. Blumentritt is trying very hard to dissuade Rizal from going to the Philippines. He cites how Graciano Lopez Jaena (who wrote him about it) had to flee Manila after just four days.

"...Lopez himself writes: 'I was in Manila only four days, I left hurriedly to come to this place (Hong Kong) because I had a suspicion that if I would stay longer in the Philippines as I wished, I would be in Bilibid or Marianas, as our friends the friars are persecuting me.' I beg you to abandon such an idea (of coming back to the Philippines)". (407-8)

(20.)

Letter 172. Rizal, Gand, 22 September 1891. Rizal insists: he will have to return to the Philippines, to—certain death… This means that his truly melodramatic plot to commit assimilationist martyrdom was fully hatched as early as the writing of this letter…

"…I have to return to the Philippines. Life is becoming a burden to me here. *I have to give an example not to fear death* even if this may be terrible. Besides, many are complaining against me that I am doing this and that to the Filipinos. *I have some secret enemies*. I want to go there so that I shall not hear anything more. I have had enough with my political enemies; *I do not want to have them within the party.*[73] ***I AM GOING TO MEET MY DESTINY.*** It is better to die than to live miserably. I expect to finish my third novel during the trip. If I receive money, I shall leave on 4 October."

(21.)

Letter 173. Rizal, Paris, 9 October 1891. Rizal does not want to write for *La Solidaridad* anymore. He remains committed to assimilationism however, and confirms this anew by saying that he agrees completely with what Blumentritt writes there. Swears that he will continue to faithfully but quietly work for assimilation and against separation, against revolution, against independence.

---

[73] "…within the party"—make no mistake about it, this *party* was, but of course of course or course!, no revolutionary, no separatist party but, and of course of course of course, an assimilationist, i.e., anti-revolutionary, anti-separatist, anti-independence party.

"...You would like me to write an article for *La Solidaridad.* Unfortunately, I have to confess that I am not thinking of writing any article anymore for that periodical. I could have told you this before but I wanted to hide from you the unpleasant attacks against me. Many things occurred between us. You already write, ***and I am completely in accord with what you write*** [74]. What Blumentritt and Rizal can do, Blumentritt can do alone. I have suggested many projects; they engaged in a secret war against me. When I tried to make the Filipinos work, they called me 'idol, they said that I was a despot, etc. They wrote to Manila twisting facts and they said that I liked this and that, which was not exactly the truth. Through some persons, I learned that before my *Fili* had gone to press, they already said that it was worthless and it was very inferior to the *Noli*[75] . Secretly they were scheming against me here as if they wish to destroy whatever little reputation I may have. ***I withdraw in order to avoid quarrels*****. Let the others guide the policy.**

They said that Rizal is a very difficult person; well, Rizal clears out. The obstacles ought not to come from me. It is very possible that they tell you a very different story of what happened, but you have a clearer vision and you will understand more than you are told. For my part *I shall work*

---

74 What Blumentritt was writing from first to last and quite voluminously for *La Solidaridad* was *pure assimilationist* counter-revolution, pure ssimi8lationist anti-separatism, pure assimilationist ant-independence, *pure assimilationism.* And Rizal as he says here, was in full accord with all of it.

75 Marcelo H. del Pilar will tell him this directly in a letter later on, and he will agree with him in a reply letter, telling del Pilar that he knew all along that that was the truth (namely that the *Fili* was inferior to the *Noli*), and that he was happy to be so confirmed by del Pilar in his judgment of his own worth, adding that those who said that the *Fili* was even better than the *Noli* were merely being too kind to him and that's why they could not see the truth.

faithfully[76] and quietly; I shall devoted my strength to the Motherland. It does not matter what they may say about me; ***I have done my duty, I envy no one, I TRUST IN GOD* and in the fate[77] of my country.**

"I don't know yet exactly whether I have to go to the Philippines or establish myself in Hong Kong. My country lures me, I want to embrace my parents and brothers[78], but my friends and countrymen are opposed. At any rate, I have to leave Europe. Life here is becoming unbearable for me.

"Had I the means, I would have gone there in order to embrace you *for the last time, for it seems to me that I shall not see you anymore.*

"My future appears terribly arid to me. It seems that I shall never marry.[79]"

(22.)

---

[76] That is to say:--he continues to be committed to the assimilationist cause and will go on working for its anti-revolutionary, anti-separatist, anti-independence ideals, and will do everything to foil any attempt at revolution, separation, independence.

[77] Assimilationist fate—make no mistake about it!

[78] Curious, but Rizal always forgets his sisters. An especially glaring case of this forgetting happened in his twin letters which he wrote prior to his departure from Hong Kong to the Philippines, dated 20 June 1892. The first of these was addressed thus: **TO MY BELOVED PARENTS, BROTHERS AND FRIENDS.** Here, the brothers he wanted to embrace were, in addition to Paciano, his brothers-in-law, the husbands of his sisters!

[79] There! Leonor Rivera's marriage to someone else was a determining factor....

Letter 174. Rizal, Mediterranean Sea, 22 October 1891.

"...The nearer I get to my country, the more vehement is my desire to return to the Philippines. I know that everybody considers it folly, **BUT SOMETHING IS PUSHING ME ON.** Is this fate or a misfortune?[80] I cannot give up my desire to see my native land."

(23.)

Letter 175. Rizal, Hong Kong, 10 December 1891. The *Rape of Calamba* happened in October of that year, while Rizal was at sea for Hong Kong. The Rizal family, and the rest of the Calambenos, were totally dispossessed. Many were exiled. No data on the murdered but 500 soldiers fully armed were let loose upon the unarmed populace. A warship was deployed; cannons were unloaded. Cavalry attacked from Manila. The Dominican friars were seen totally naked chasing ricecakes across the paddies and in the violated streets... But, although everybody, perhaps even his family, was expecting that the last straw had thus been loaded to break Rizal's assimilationist back and turn him into an avenging revolutionary, nothing of the sort happened. It did make of him a "separatist" though: he hatched the insane project of colonizsing North Borneo in order to transfer there his family and the dispossessed Calambenos—Viva *La Nueva Calamba*!

"...Just a few lines to inform you that my father, brother, and brother-in-law have arrived here fleeing from Manila. My aged mother, blind, is in the hands of the Spaniards!... My sisters are also coming..."

(24.)

---

[80] Let us not forget that, as he mysteriously intimated in his September 22, 1891 letter (above), he had already made a firm decision to commit suicide in the Philippines in the form of a *martyrdom for assimlationism.*

Letter 176. Rizal, Hong Kong, 30 December 1891. The entire family reunited in Hong Kong.

"…On time I received your letter of the 15th November as well as another letter for my brother, who is presently here with my parents and sisters. My aged blind mother is also here to escape tyranny. From Manila, they sent her to Santa Cruz, Laguna Province, *through the mountain*, and from town to town, because she did not call herself *Realonda de Rizal* but simply *Teodora Alonso*. She has been, and always has been called *Teodora Alonso*! Imagine an old woman of 64 travelling through mountains and highways with her daughter under the custody of the Civil Guard! She asked to be allowed to travel by boat, offering to pay all the expenses, including the fare of the soldiers, but the 'noble Spanish gentleman' did not permit her! When I learned of this 'gallantry and nobility', I wrote to the 'noble man' telling him that his behavior towards women and girls is very noteworthy; the savages and the Chinese behave more nobly and humanely. When my mother and sister, after four days of travelling, arrived at Santa Cruz, the governor, deeply touched, released them.

"Now they are here and they thank God that they are in a free country! Life in the Philippines has become impossible—without morals, without virtue, without justice.

"For this reason, I believe that *La Solidaridad* is no longer our battlefield; *now it is a new struggle*.[81] I should like

---

[81] At first blush, Rizal was declaring Revolution here. What else could that "new struggle" be to supplant reform and assimilationist counter-revolution but revolution? And very quickly that was how every Philippine historian took it to mean. Accordingly, they interpreted the *Liga Filipina* which Rizal launched a few days after his arrival from Hong Kong (he disembarked on the 26th of June, toured the Central Luzon provinces, met with the Governor General, Despujol, twice, and on July 2 launched the *Liga*), as a legal front for the ultimately armed revolution, and

to please you, but I believe *all is in vain*; *the fight is no longer in Madrid*. All is time wasted." (423-24)

(25.)

Letter 178. Blumentritt, Leitmeritz, 30 January 1892. Blumentritt begs Rizal not to have anything to do with separatist-revolutionary plots:--proof that he knew Rizal to never have engaged in such activities before.

"...Above all, I *beg* you not to meddle in revolutionary agitations. Because one who initiates a revolution ought at least to have the probability of success, if he does not wish to burden his conscience with useless bloodshed.[82]

---

deduced that Bonifacio's KKK was born out of it, and that that was how Rizal intended it. But this interpretation is completely belied and wiped out by everything Rizal did and did not do from the time of his arrest, all throughout his Dapitan exile, to the vile, malignant and antihuman criminality of his Cuban international counter-revolutionary project, and, en route to that international crime, the series of betrayals of the revolution and the motherland on Manila Bay, repeated and shamelessly doubled during his trial, and his protestations of innocence in his last two letters written during his last afternoon on earth (to his brother Paciano and his friend Blumentritt), in which he finally, finally, finally rejected the revolution and refuted beforehand all those who later on suspected him to be secretly involved in it and concluded even that he it was who was the real founder of it.

[82] Was it true, as the liar and traitor ilustrado doctor Pio Valenzuela related, that Rizal gave this argument for his conditional rejection of the revolution? This is not certain, since Valenzuela was a demonstrated liar. Moreover, we cannot find anything like it in the many instances of Rizal's rejection of revolution. It would seem that—and this is

"It has always happened that when a people has risen against another that governs it—a colony against the metropolis—their revolution never has triumphed by their own forces. The American Union became free because France, Spain, and Holland aided her. The Spanish republics won their liberty because there was civil; war in the metropolis and because North America furnished them with money and arms. The Greeks became free because England, France, and Russia supported them. The Rumanians, Serbs, and Bulgars have become free with the help of Russia; Italy with that of France and Prussia, Belgium with that of England and France.

"Everywhere, the people who relied on their own strength have succumbed to the army of the *legitimate power*.[83] The Italians in 1830, 1848, and 1849; the Poles in

---

what his words on the matter would point to—Rizal rejected the revolution as a matter of principle—because it is wrong per se, immoral per se, and will bring suffering etc.

[83] Tyrants and apologists for tyrants, and here for the worst kind of tyranny, such as Blumentritt the Austrian – Spanish Roman Catholic crusader for Philippine assimilation, i.e., for the prevention of Philippine separation from Spain, for the pre-emption of Philippine revolution against Spanish tyranny, for the impossibilization of Philippine independence from Spain, and, with him whom he merely assists in this crusade and who is top Filipino crusader then against separation, revolution, and Philippine independence, Jose Rizal, must indeed, such as they are, manifest an altogether twisted, perverted, distorted and of course immoral, inhuman, evil, evil, evil sense of *legitimate power,* of *legitimate rule*, of *legitimacy*. Colonialism, the most direct denial of the humanity, the freedom, the transcendence, the dignity of an entire people, is, as we were saying, immoral per se, inhuman per se, evil per se; as such, it is unjust per se and therefore *illegitimate* per se. Here however, and in the circumstantial

1831, 1845, and 1863, the Hungarians in 1848 and 1849, the Irish in 1868.[84]

"If today a revolution should break out in the Philippines, it would end in tragedy, for her insular position indeed will make any revolution without a navy a failure. Moreover, the revolutionists will not have munitions to last for more than 5 weeks. Then, there are still many pro-friars among the Filipinos. A revolution will only lead many

---

entre nous of a personal letter of a crusader to his crusading associate, it is "the legitimate power". Such as it is, it is legitimate only in hell where damnation is the business on hand. Of course, and especially in the case of Spanish colonialism, it never fails to make hell of the colonized country. As such, and as the logic of hell goes, it never fails to *legitimize* itself. Whilst the *demonism*—the immorality, the inhumanity, the evil—of its defenders and apologists such as, in the Philippine case, this Blumentritt from Leitmeritz and his bosom friend from Calamba (evil name!) Dr. Jose Protacio Rizal Mercado y Alonso de Realonda, also never fails therewith to effectuate itself, to realize itself, according as its logic of hell goes, and here it did give rise to a retarded revolution, a revolution minus its predestined leaders and spearhead and funders, namely the colonial middle-class who were precisely Rizal and company, a revolution where at the beginning, there were only four or five ill-functioning guns to a battalion (!) so that at the beginning hordes of Katipuneros who only had buho spears and bolos plus indomitable courage were massacred by the enemy thanks to Rizal and Blumentritt and the *La Solidaridad* company

[84] Soon enough, the Cuban Katipuneros would make war with the metropolis; but this would have no effect on Rizal's decision not to join the Revolution here; instead, he was joining the Spanish soldiers in Cuba against the Cuban revolutionists!

educated Filipinos to certain death and intensify the oppression of tyranny. A revolution has no probability of success unless: first, a part of the army and the navy rebel; second, the metropolis is at war with another nation; third, there are money and munitions available; and fourth, some foreign country give its official or secret support to the revolution. None of these conditions exists in the Philippines.

"What I would like to see is the printing of little pamphlets in Philippine languages with the object of inculcating in the masses *human dignity* and imbuing them with enthusiasm for their own people, for *liberty*, for education. The illiterate ought to be attracted to the holy cause, to be convinced that they form part of a noble people and they need not pay homage to the *Kastilas*. The words of Schiller should be converted into reality: 'All men, born equal, are a noble race.'" (429-31)

(26.)

Letter 179. Rizal, Hong Kong, 31 January 1892.

"...My father is even more severe in his judgment and he does not want to go back anymore to the Philippines. He says, 'I want to die here, I don't want to return home; life there is unbearable for me.'... It is horrible to describe the dreadful happenings that my family has witnessed in Kalamba—sick persons thrown out of their houses; entire families had to pass the night outdoors; the Dominicans forbade the rest of the townspeople to give the unfortunates lodging and hospitality. Terrified, some saw how their houses were being destroyed and burned down by the government soldiers, some of whom refused to do it![85] Yes, I don't want to torment you more. Now I tell you: *I have lost my hope in Spain*! For that reason, I shall not write one more word for *La Solidaridad*. It seems to

---

[85] *There* is where you should see the premise for revolution, stupid!

me it is in vain. All of us are 'Voices crying in the desert where all is lost'".

(27.)

Letter 180. Rizal, Hong Kong 23 February 1892. Rizal acknowledges that he was responsible for the friar atrocities—the murders, the depredations, the exile and dispossessions suffered by his immediate family and the unfortunate people of Calamba, etc., for which reason he will not write for *La Solidaridad* anymore and will instead *colonize* North Borneo…And more—but not revolutionary more! For, as we shall see, he was *that early* and even earlier contemplating the possibility of ASSIMILATIONIST MARTYRDOM! This was that "other direction" he is talking about in mysterious tones in this letter…

"…Yes, the poor Filipinos feel so unfortunate under the present circumstances that they welcome any change.[86] My parents say: 'If they (the Germans) have so much pity on us, why don't they come to liberate us from the hands of the friars?'…

"I thank you for the novel you have written about Simoun. Even if all the newspapers, the whole world of literature, *clamor for our rights*[87] , it would be in vain, taking into

[86] Any change, even the most absurd, the most thoughtless, the most ridiculous and evil, like another colonialism, for instance, a German colonialism for instance, as in the next sentence Rizal will report that his parents suggested, which, based on the historical record of the unexampled inhumanity and barbarism of the people of Hegel, Nietzsche, Heidegger, Hitler, as of Blumentritt himself, could be worse…

[87] "To clamour for our rights…"—this all along, this dull and stupid thing, this farce, was what Rizal and his

assimilationist company was doing, and what Blumentritt was helping them do since their first exchange of letters which led to the Austrian armchair ethnologist's recruitment as journalistic crusader for "the cause". Enslaved natives clamoring for their "rights", pretending to be able to *effectively argue* for their rights, to, before, the colonial masters; which in the case of Rizal was already a martyr's mission and destiny. How would such a malaprop, a skewed and unplaceable thing like such "rights" look like? Derrida, that recently disremembered and effaced trace of an apostle of the neither this nor that which "is" neither neither this nor neither neither that nor neither neither neither either…, would have loved this thing, these "rights" being clamored for by the colonized natives before their colonial masters, as though in the regime of evil, of evil power which was/is colonialism, the essence of which—for there are essences, contrary to such as Derrida—was/is the denial of the very foundation of all rights which is freedom, one could at all unfarcically speak of the rights of the victims of that regime of evil...:--Derrida would have tremblingly embraced it and caressed it and polished it to pure negative metaphysical shiningness and theologicity and deposited it, after a hundred and 99 pages blazoning it through the imprint of editions seuil or gallimard or johns hopkins, in his fetish box labeled *undecidables* at the Bangko Sentral ng Pransiya… (But really; but really, and actually, one could, one should speak of the *rights* of the colonized within, under, and against that regime of evil that is colonialism, no matter that such rights must always partake of farcicality and absurdity and a besetting all-but-total effeteness; for as long as there remains a minimum of integrity to the being people of the colonized people and therefore a minimum of freedom to found those rights, the people would still be able somehow to exert enough democratic pressure on the colonizers to force the latter to respect some of their account the blindness of the government[88]. *I turn my eyes toward another direction[89].*"

---

basic rights; which is the same as saying, as long as there still remains a core of humanity in the colonized people as a people and not merely as individuals: for it is as a people no matter how degraded and ill-used that they alone could still matter and could still play their assigned role in the dialectic of sovereignty and legitimacy:--the evil, the inhumanity of colonialism is to be measured by how tenuous and well-nigh inexistent that freedom has become that constitutes the foundation of the rights of humanity, which in turn is the measure of what has become of the primordial sovereignty that belongs to the people. In a regime of freedom which as such can only be a regime of democracy, sovereignty, as Rousseau most perspicuously grasped and formulated it for the first time in history, belongs to the people.

[88]From the very start to the grim and farcical finish, this was the Rizalian refrain of a complaint—the evil of the friars who were pushing the Indios into that "greatest disaster that could befall us" (*The Philippines A Century* Hence), namely revolution, *and the blindness, the deafness, the muteness of the government.* The "government" here was of course the Madrid government with which the assimilationists had been trying vainly to "discuss", of the fruitlessness of which "discussion" or the actual impossibility of which Rizal here would be showing some signs of exasperation.

[89] As we shall exhibit elsewhere here in letters they wrote Rizal upon learning of the *Rape of Calamba* by the Dominicans with the able assistance of Gov. Gen. Valeriano Weyler's troops, artillery and gunboat (!), a number of ilustrado reformist friends of Rizal, notably Antonio Luna, Jose Alejandrino, Edilberto Evangelista, and even Mariano Ponce automatically thought that that

Separation at last! Independence at last! Revolution at last! Ahm, excuse me, but, no, it was not *that* that was meant by Rizal's "another direction" here. Farthest from it! Only North Borneo and a new colonialism, and this time by Rizal and Company, specifically, by Rizal and Family and other Calambenyos was meant. And so Rizal tells his good Austrian friend here that he is quitting writing for *La Solidaridad* and, instead, is colonizing North Borneo, his *Nueva Calamba*!

"What have we obtained from the campaigns of *La Solidaridad*, more than *Weyleradas*, Banditry Law and the drama of Kalamba? It seems to me that it is a waste of time to discuss with the government[90].

"another direction" would be, must be, separatism, revolution. In those letters, they declared their own leaps of faith telling Rizal to lead them for they were ready to die fighting, this time no longer merely for assimilationist rights but for *liberty*, for independence. Whilst, as we shall also display here, the assimilationist Austrian armchair ethnologist friend of his, Blumentritt, namely, was severely worried Rizal might indeed take that revolutionary turn and was all frenzy counseling him against it (he got a long and winding Manila street named after him for such heroic service to Spanish colonialism and against the Filipino people, heroically advising the greatest Filipino Spanish hero thus in defense of Spanish colonialism and against the Filipino people…

[90] As we have just pointed out, Antonio Luna, Edilberto Evangelista, Jose Alejandrino, Mariano Ponce (and who else?) automatically concluded that the *Rape of Calamba* by Weyler and the Dominicans must surely have pushed Rizal into revolution. Antonio Luna, as we shall in a moment show, even thought the Borneo colonization project to be Rizal's ingenious way of creating a foreign but nearby base of revolutionary operation. And almost all of the Filipino historians so-called followed suit. But they were all

"In Borneo, I shall not be a planter but a leader of the planters who are thinking of emigrating there with me. *I feel flattered by the thought that I can still serve my country with my pen. You know very well that always, at all times, I am ready to serve my country not only with the pen but also with my life whenever my country would demand of me this sacrifice*[91]. But

---

mistaken. Rizal never said anything like his North Borneo colony's being such a revolutionary base; nor did he do anything even merely slightly suggesting such intent. He felt so guilty having implicated his immediate family and townmates into so much perils and persecutions and all he wanted to do now was to be able to compensate them somehow for their lost lands and other possessions. And he said so, and went into the motions of doing nothing but that. The project was of course "aborted" because in the first place it was an absurd dream, an absolutely impracticable proposition: in real political terms, for Rizal and family and townmates to thus "colonize" North Borneo would be for them to run away from Spanish colonialism in order voluntarily to have themselves subjected to British colonialism. It was a muddled thing from the very start. Rizal showed himself utterly confused: *tuliro* si Rizal. The dawning upon him of the inherent farcicality of the project must have triggered his insistence that he also personally face the same dangers to life that his family and townmates were facing: he went home, launched the national coop, *La Liga Filipina*, and got his wish to be arrested—and exiled; to Dapitan, yes, to which instead, at least his own family and nearest relatives were able to temporarily live with him.

[91]This is the usual heroifical, martyristic, self-glorificatory pose exorbitant in Rizal but by no means absent in somewhat subdued form in the other assimilationist enemies of the Filipino people who, as they were doing everything to defend Spanish colonialism, forestalling revolution thus and preventing Philippine independence

as I see that I am getting old, my ideals and my dreams are vanishing. If it is *impossible* for me to give freedom to my country, at least I should like to give it to these *noble compatriots*[92] in other lands[93]. So I am thinking of emigrating

---

and succeeding greatly, as history ignominiously demonstrated a little later, incurring thereby in that great success of obstructing and delaying the revolution and thwarting independence (so that the Americans were able to intercept it), some 2 million murders (compliments of the same genocidal Yankees who annihilated the Indian race in North America) where the murdered were their own countrymen for loving whom they supposedly were bleeding in the heart with so much blood, were imagining themselves to be their country's redeemers who were always at the point nearest to the point of being almost ready to die for their country thus, when the truth was they were absolutely unpersecuted in the Spanish metropolis; whilst none of them would have been near to near to near to being somewhat somewhat in danger of being shot for anything had not Bonifacio's revolution overtaken them despite their luxurious Spanish-heroic *La Solidaridad* campaign to prevent it; whilst even Rizal would not have been shot had he not offered himself to be so shot or suffer persecution in lieu of, or at least alongside with, his immediate family whom he knew were being hounded and punished and by the by dispossessed by the friars, especially the super-voracious brethren, corporation, corpulentation of Santo Domingo de Guzman because of his attacks against them in his two novels and *La Solidaridad* articles…

[92]And suddenly now, his Kalambenyo compatriots are noble. And they must be, since Rizal is redeeming them.

[93] He says he's flattered to think that he can still write for his country. Again, the lying or dull (or both at once) historians immediately took this to mean that he intended

to Borneo. There are vast fields over there where we can found a *New Kalamba.* When the exiles and the persecuted have found an asylum in Borneo, *then I shall write in peace and shall be able to look towards the future, if not happy at least consoled*[94]

---

to go on fighting for the (assimilationist) rights of the Filipinos while (so they repeatedly imagined) waiting for the right time to launch and lead the revolution. But Rizal said nothing of that sort, and said instead a few words afterwards that he intended to remain stuck in his Borneo estate and there to write in peace and in consoled sadness. Consoled for what? Consoled that he shall somehow have compensated his absolutely beloved family and his Kalambenyo townmates for the sufferings and deprivations inflicted on them on his account. This already was his farewell to politics, as many times he repeated to many people, a withdrawal from the arena of reformist pleading and polemics which was for him finalized with his Dapitan exile; a resolve implemented by him with singleminded devotion and even treacherous tenacity when he denounced the political emissary of the KKK (who must not be mistaken for Pablo Mercado who supposedly was a friar-sent spy), and when he rejected not without acrimony Bonifacio's offer to have him join and even be the head of the KKK, and counselled Dr. Pio Valenzuela to abandon the KKK which the latter did.

[94]Translator Encarnacion Alzona writes in a footnote on page 436: "Rizal refers to Gov. Gen. Valeriano Weyler's intervention (October 1891) in the conflict between the citizens of Kalamba and the Dominican owners of the Kalamba Estate. Siding with the Dominicans, he made a show of force, sending the gunboat *Otalora*, loaded with arms and ammunition, and an expedition composed of 300 artillerymen, 100 infantrymen, and 200 cavalrymen. Terrified, the people fled to the neighboring towns where

(28.)

Letter 182. Rizal, Hong Kong, 20 April, 1892. Just arrived from North Borneo. Rizal will write again for *La Solidaridad.*

"...Estanislawa, with four small children... her whole body mangled for defending her house and the rice for her children... by the Dominicans...

"The translation of the *Noli* " (by Paciano) "continues, but I have already given up the idea of writing the third part in Tagalog, for it would not be appropriate to write a work in two languages as they would be like the sermons of the friars. So, I am writing it now in Spanish.

"...But my innermost desire, my most vehement desire, is to see myself relegated to second place by other Filipinos. When one day many Pilars and Letes emerge to eclipse Rizal completely, then I shall sleep in peace. The fate of my country will be assured, and I can go down to my grave smiling. My

---

they were denied shelter by order of the provincial governor. Compelled to return to Kalamba, they were forbidden to reoccupy their lots. Their houses had been burned down. Such inhumanity was the cause of despair that spread everywhere. As a result of this conflict, many prominent citizens of Kalamba were banished, among whom were Rizal's father and three sisters." All this because of Rizal, because Rizal had written his novels and articles attacking the friars. And he knew it. He knew Calamba was singled out for that kind of friar Spanish barbarity because Jose Rizal was from there. Hence, his genuine sense of guilt that he was all along far away in Europe and, unable to secure justice for them, at least suffer with them, and with them "face death", as we shall see him say in another of his letters here. Hence his severe reduction from a dream of Hispanity to a dream of Borneanity!

name, my little fame, my tranquility, everything, I would give for it. Oh, I am always waiting for the grand pleiad of young Filipinos.

"Now I am going to satisfy your desire. I shall write again for *La Solidaridad*, but not on politics. If ***after our long desire for assimilation and hispanization***[95] , they reply with

---

[95] Rizal's and Blumentritt's and the other social-climbing, race-climbing, white-ambitioning propagandists' **desire for assimilation and hispanization**—which he here circumstantially avows in his own words which his blind revolutionificators, who are almost without a single exception all the Philippine historians, and more recently miclat, quibuyen, and only yesterday a certain nery, are of course sightless, i.e., brainless, enough to fail to read!-- was long indeed! In despair, Rizal threatens to renounce that long and pertinacious desire, obsession, compulsion, mania. And did it even really end there for Rizal? From assimilationist counter-revolutionary, would he now begin to be a non-assimilationist, more or less passive anti-revolutionary as he manifestly and avowedly was in his four years in Dapitan (his anti-revolutionariness there being activated only four times in separate acts of national and international treason against the Filipino people and against humanity: 1.) when he reported a Katipunan emissary in late 1892 to the governor for, of course, the military to torture and murder him—a potential betrayal of the Revolution: the heroic man must have died with the secret for we know of no repercussions arising from a discovery of the KKK that early; 2.) when he applied for an *international counter-revolutionary* position as Spanish military doctor in Cuba in November 1895; and 3.) when he rejected the offer of leadership of the revolution by Bonifacio through Valenzuela on July 1, 1896, and was even successful in convincing the ilustrado—the same corrupt ilk-- Valenzuela to abandon the Revolution which he did by surrendering at once and

the destruction of Calamba, a serious man ought not to write one word more. For the ***same reason***, I cannot write on *separation*, at least in *La Solidaridad.* I have to content myself with writing on indifferent things. If I write in this manner, then the Filipinos will say that I am no longer interested in them, that I abandon politics asnd the Spaniards will believe it likewise. But my silence will give them much to think about. Well, for your sake, I will dare anything." (Including irrelevance.)

(29.)

Letter 184. Blumentritt, 4 July 1892. **Counsels Rizal against revolution....**

"...They were not Pilaristas but Rizalistas who have written me that Rizal ***should*** found a revolutionary newspaper or start a revolutionary movement[96]. I admonished them so that

---

asking forgiveness from the Spaniards, and, of course making a number of betrayals; and 4.) when on a number of occasions he refused to escape or be rescued from Dapitan—a refusal which should be taken directly as a rejection of the Revolution)? The answer is *no.* For he would yet try to stage a melodramatic *assimilationist finale* by coming home to the wrath of the friars to provoke them to martyr him for assimilationism, thinking to "put the finishing touches" on his lifework thus, thinking of "meeting my destiny" there thus, imagining that his martyrdom w2ould trigger an international outrage culminating in the expulsion of the friars and the assimilation of the Philippines!

[96] These must be Antonio Luna, Edilberto Evangelista, Jose Alejandrino, Jaena, the Barcelona colony, who as we shall see had been radicalized into separatism by that which however failed to make a separatist of the one most responsible and most damaged by it, *the Rape of Calamba*...

they would not advise you to do such a thing, and so I wrote you at once.

"I cannot agree with your opinion about *La Solidaridad*, inasmuch as its very enemies have recognized its importance and founded a forthnightly whose objective is to fight it. We should not expect miracles from *La Solidaridad*. We cannot achieve in four years what it took other peoples four decades…

"I repeat: a political party needs an organ, a newspaper, and the Filipinos have it and they should not despise it as it defends the honor of the country and their people. Through force the Filipinos cannot obtain absolutely anything at this time. Therefore, only with the pen can we fight[97].

(30.)

Letter 193. Rizal, Dapitan, 19 December 1893. The coming of Pablo Mercado…

"…A man came to me here sent by persons who are considered respectable by many, with the object of wresting from me some papers and books. I do not wish to do anything against him, but I found out **later** that he was posing as my relative, etc. etc., and so I reported him to the commander who immediately seized him and sent him to Manila. And he himself declared that he was sent by the friars from whom he received 70 pesos…

(31.)

Letter 202. Rizal, Dapitan, 9 May 1895. Rizal thinks he has reached the highest intellectual development he could reach…

---

[97] For *masked racists* like Blumentritt and his friend Rizal, the proper time for revolution can never come; the masking consists in repeatedly saying "It's not yet time" ad infinitum ad nauseam.

"...Your mind, ever more tolerant than mine, if possible, alone can follow without conflict my way of thinking. It matters little to me what the Madrid newspapers may say about me[98]; it matters little to me that they wish to lock me up in Santiago or in Santo Domingo. My spirit will always be free. As regards my physical liberty, I believe that instead of serving me much, it can hurt me more. *I have reached the highest point I can attain and I am afraid that if they will let me walk further, I may descend more rapidly than I have climbed up.* It is God's providence that the government has eliminated me: it makes my name famous..." (p.508)

(32.)

Letter 204. Rizal, Dapitan, 20 November 1895. **Blumentritt's advice for Rizal to go to Cuba—"most excellent..."**

"...Concerning your advice on going to Cuba as physician, it seems to me most excellent, and right now I am going to write to the Governor General...

(33.)

Letter 210. Rizal, en route to Spain, 28 September 1896. Rizal's upsurgent megalomania cum paranoia...

SS Isla de Panay, Mediterranean Sea

28 September 1896

My very dear Friend,

98 How humble of you naman! And why should they even take notice of you, who are you ba, ha?

A passenger on board had just told me news that I can hardly believe and should it be true, would bring to an end the prestige of Philippine authorities[99].

You will remember that last year you notified me that physiucians were lacking in Cuba, that many soldiers were dying without medical assistance. Instantly I presented myself to the authorities applying for the post of temporary physician for the duration of the campaign. Months and months elapsed and in view of the fact that I did not receive any reply, I started to build a wooden housed and a hospital and thus earn my livelihood in Dapitan. On 30 July I received a letter from the gtovernor general of the following tenor:

---

[99] Oh, really, but why? How come? Who are you, just who are you nga ba, Jose, ha, that having you arrested thus and thrown in jail by the Governor General and others who call the shots in the colony called *Felipinas*, could ruin, destroy, erase, eradicate, bring down and kill, "the ***prestige*** of Philippine authorities"? When you come to the passage below in a letter to Dr. Lorenzo Marquez sometime in 1895 concerning his reasons why he refusded to escape or be rescued from Dapitan, this episode will be recalled to your mind by the manner in which he allowed himself the pure megalomaniacal pleasure of remarking that the longer he was held prisoner there in Dapitan the worse it was for the prestige of the Government!

Chapter 14

REPLIES TO E. SAN JUAN, JR., OR WHY AND HOW ANDRES BONIFACIO INVENTED THE PATRIOT AND HERO JOSE RIZAL

{i}

"THE E.SAN JUAN INTERVIEW

On the Legacy of Noli Me Tangere and El Filibusterismo
By J.V. Ayson - Dec 30, 2016

"A high school kid, on one's own, may pass on the Noli and the Fili for the new Wattpad story. But what tragedy, as in those two novels, to not experience world-class, historical, enduring literary works. The two should have well served as our appetizer to prose, Filipino or international.

"Schools have required the full reading of Jose Rizal's Noli Me Tangere and El Filibusterismo in high school. Upon many changes in the curriculum (subsuming Filipino and Social Studies in Makabayan, making History only among choices in General Education subjects, attempts to remove Filipino in tertiary education, etc.) and the ever-present dilemma of raising the quality of education (especially, public education), such practice may now be deemed a lucky turn or vestigial tradition.

"Many consider the two as his most notable socio-political works and as catalysts for inculcating social realism in the people's consciousness and mindset. This interview with Prof. Epifanio San Juan should remind us why.

"What did 'Noli' and 'Fili' suggest about the grim conditions of the Filipino masses and the chronic ills of Philippine society?

“Prof. San Juan: Practically all the Propagandistas and those who joined Rizal’s Liga, like Bonifacio, Mabini, and others, confessed their debt to Rizal’s writings, in particular the two novels. They conform to the realist convention in drawing typical/exemplary situations and characters that compress the urgent problems of the time. In doing so, they incited and agitated readers. They rendered lived experience in its stark ferocity—feudal exploitation, abuse of power, etc., but they also comically distanced it so that people can act to alter and change them. They performed the function of conveying truth but also of how to transform life in accord with libertarian principles and democratic ideals. The generation of 1896 was a product of Rizal’s agitprop intelligence.

“Prof. San Juan: The story of Cabesang Tales demonstrates the limits of stoic patience. When

families are destroyed, and children tortured, the colonial authorities have lost their legitimacy. Religious habits cannot suppress human affections and feelings of sympathy for others. Reforms were tried (by Ibarra and others), but the reactionary theocratic state refused to change, hence others were forced to become rebels, then called outlaws or “tulisan.” Rizal recognized the need for armed revolution when a critical mass has emerged. When in prison he was forced to sign a statement disavowing the Katipunan uprising, it was hedged with qualifications—the Spanish government did not publish it because Rizal rejected only a riotous demonstration, not revolution in principle. Many think Rizal was against the Katipunan, but Bonifacio himself and the whole Katipunan idolized Rizal and used his name as a slogan.

“Did the twin novels reveal anything about Rizal’s real stance regarding the armed revolution? Is Rizal really against the armed revolution, as many stories are wont to differentiate this tidbit about him with the ‘great plebeian’ revolutionary Andres Bonifacio?

"Prof. San Juan: As I said, under great pressure, Rizal wrote that last pronouncement which did not reject, in principle, armed revolution. It is a question of what in totality you regard as Rizal's contribution to mobilizing the ilustrados, and with them the plebeian masses of workers and peasants. Rizal's novels presented a dialectical, materialist analysis of the various classes and sectors locked in struggle, from the top of the hierarchy down to the proletariat, so his enduring contribution is this vision of a whole society in the process of radical, inexorable change. That is something no Filipino in his generation was able to do. Only the great Tagalog novelists Lope K Santos, Faustino Aguilar and Amado Hernandez were able to capture in totality that dynamic processes of change in a class-divided society dominated by US imperialism.

"Did the twin novels became the final straw for Rizal's martyrdom in the course of the 1896 Philippine Revolution?

"Prof. San Juan: Due to censorship and autocratic control of the media, and means of communication, only a few copies of the novels circulated. But once the ilustrados read them, their ideas were disseminated throughout the population. It was not the final straw. Actually, the Church, especially the Dominicans and Jesuits, conspired to kill him not primarily because they were caricatured in the novels. There were Rizal's other works, the satirical essays, that the friars could not forgive. Rizal was our Voltaire in crying for the destruction of obscurantism, religious hypocrisy, and blind obedience to authority— the main core of all progressive and liberal ideals propagated by Rousseau, Kant, and the whole European Enlightenment.

"How do you explain the role of Rizal's twin novels in the continuing mass nationalist awakening?

"Prof. San Juan: Reactionary educational administrators have tried to suppress courses in history, in particular courses on Rizal. When I was a UP undergraduate, I watched the debates in the Congress between Senator Claro Mayo Recto and those who spoke for the Church. Our generation witnessed the conflict between Fr. Delaney in UP who denounced Dr. Ricardo Pascual, Prof. Leopoldo Yabes and other liberals who followed Recto's nationalism. The struggle between these two camps is continuing, so If Rizal is still read and discussed, this can be explained by the fact that religious bigotry, dogmatism, authoritarianism, in a world of obscurantism, still prevails among the middle stratum, drugged by consumerism, US mass culture, spectacles of Hollywood stars and celebrities. But Rizal's function is being performed by other artists and thinkers—indie media films on General Antonio Luna, for example, and by street guerilla theater. There are many Rizals in the making among the young generation, the millenials.

"How do you assess the influence of the twin novels on the Filipino people's consciousness?
"Prof. San Juan: Rizal's novels were the inspiration of Amado Hernandez's cinemascopic MGA IBONG MANDARAGIT. Unfortunately that long novel, like Santos' Banaag at Sikat, has not yet been widely discussed. But characters in the novels, like Capitan Tiago, Dona Victorina, Ibarra, Simoun, Maria Clara, Sisa—these character types (in Engels' sense) have been absorbed in our culture, so you encounter them everywhere in the media, conversations among workers and peasants, even among the vulgar elite. Rizal's horror-museum is well-known among the satirists and comedians of our society. Even the figure of Pilosopong Tasyo can be found in the corridors of U.P., Ateneo, La Salle, UST and other sacred halls.

"Do you believe that Rizal's ideas, principles, and warnings, especially through the characters in his twin novels, are still applicable in the present period when an apparently chronic social and political crisis in this nation is possible?

"Prof. San Juan: Ideas concerning democratic participation, individual autonomy, and respect for the integrity of communities are now found in all struggles against colonialism and imperialism. They are even articulated in the UN charter, especially, the right of peoples to self-determination. Those Enlightenment principles were given a historical-materialist foundation by Marx, Engels, Lenin and the formidable thinkers of the Marxist tradition—Gramsci, Fanon, Amilcar Cabral, Ho Chi Minh, Mao Zedong, Che Guevarra—and in our country by Isabelo de los Reyes, Teodoro Agoncillo, Renato Constantino, Benigno Ramos, Amado Hernandez, Jose Maria Sison, the exiled

Carlos Bulosan, Edberto Villegas, among others too many to list here. Rizal's ideas have to be translated and modified to accord with changed conditions—for example, the rapist friars are no longer dominant, but corrupt bureaucrats and esp. the barbaric police and military, are still around, as well of course subtle and covert U.S. intervention in all sectors of our society—and also with the changing level of political consciousness and mobilization of the people. Concrete analysis of concrete conditions (concrete means multi-dimensional)—that's the key, the momentous legacy of Rizal.

"What is the main significance of Rizal's twin novels in arousing the Filipino people's consciousness and enlightenment in their continuing struggle for national liberation and social emancipation?

"Prof. San Juan: The significance depends on how our mass leaders/guides translate Rizal's analytic mind and critical sensibility to the needs and demands of every situation they are facing. Do the Moros and the Lumad need Rizal? Maybe not, because they have their own cultural sources of inspiration and enlightenment. But they need Rizal's pathos, to help mourn and celebrate the sacrifices of our Maria Lorena Barros, Cherith Dayrit, all the martyrs of the Marcos dictatorship. But above all, they need Rizal's cunning and humor—without humor, how can you dance to the victories of the revolution?

"(Prof. Epifanio San Juan Jr. is an essayist, editor, critic, and poet whose works have been translated into German, Russian, French, Italian, and Chinese. He is a professorial lecturer at the Polytechnic University of the Philippines (PUP) in Manila. He authored countless books on race and cultural studies for which he has been described as a "major influence on the academic world", such as US Imperialism and Revolution in the Philippines, In the Wake of Terror, Between Empire and Insurgency, and Working through the Contradictions. He received the Centennial Award for Achievement in Literature from the Cultural Center of the Philippines (CCP) in 1999 for his outstanding contributions to Filipino and Filipino-American studies.)

{ii}

JV AYSON: “What did ‘Noli’ and ‘Fili’ suggest about the grim conditions of the Filipino masses and the chronic ills of Philippine society?”

PROF. SAN JUAN: “Practically all the Propagandistas and those who joined Rizal’s Liga, like Bonifacio, Mabini, and others, confessed their debt to Rizal’s writings, in particular the two novels. They conform to the realist convention in drawing typical/exemplary situations and characters that compress the urgent problems of the time. In doing so, they incited and agitated readers. They rendered lived experience in its stark ferocity—feudal exploitation, abuse of power, etc., but they also comically distanced it so that people can act to alter and change them. They performed the function of conveying truth but also of how to transform life in accord with libertarian principles and democratic ideals. The generation of 1896 was a product of Rizal’s agitprop intelligence.”

E. SAN JUAN: “Practically all the Propagandistas and those who joined Rizal’s Liga, like Bonifacio, Mabini, and others, confessed their debt to Rizal’s writings, in particular the two novels…”

1.0.) What Rizal really said/wrote bore, and should bear, no ambiguity at all. Everything he wrote that pertained to revolution was anti-revolution and counter-revolutionary: and here I repeat the challenge I have many times made to my readers and audiences to try to find at least a sentence in which he directly or indirectly endorsed revolution or the Revolution, or one in which he mentioned revolution or the Revolution without cursing, condemning, abusing, vituperating, criminalizing, even demonizing it. Everything he said, everything he said he said, or reported he said about revolution or the Revolution rejected, cursed, condemned, excoriated it in the most forthright terms, in among others the following places: 1.) in his extensive correspondence, most importantly his letters to Marcelo del Pilar on the NOLI and FILI which we intend to cite here, but also in his letters to his dearly beloved Austrian-Spanish friend and most intense partner in preaching and agitating for that most intense and utterly effective anti and counter revolutionary doctrine and program called assimilationism--"the Philippines as a province of Spain, representation to the Spanish Cortes, expulsion of the friars, return of the friar lands (thieved by the friars) to their former owners", namely Rizal and the other rich colonial middleclass natives, etc.,{kaagawan nina Rizal at ka-cofradia niyang ilustrado propagandists ang mga masisibang prayleng ito sa mga lupain at kayamanang kapwa naman nila dinambong at dinarambong, syempre, sa 97 porsyento ng mga kapwa nila, nina Rizal at mga prayle, inaalipin, inaabuso, pinagsasamantalahan at ninanakawan at ginagahasang mga Pilipinong magsasaka, mangingisda, karpintero, atsero, piyon, manggagawa…, na kaya naman galit na galit sina Rizal at mga lintang mayayamang ilustradong propagandistang ito sa mga prayle, na bukod dito, ayon sa walang sawa nilang idinidiga sa mga Kastila sa gobyerno ng Madrid, ay ibinubulid ang Pilipinas sa impyerno ng Rebolusyon dahil daw sa labis na pagabuso ng mga ito sa mga Pilipinong mahihirap na iyon, na kaya naman daw dapat lang na patalsikin kaagad upang huwag mangyari dito ang pinakakinatatakutan at kinamumuhian ni Rizal at mga asimilasyonista niyang ka-propagandang mga ilustrado, na ang Rebolusyon nga}; and yes 2.) in his introduction to Blumentritt's review of the Noli Me Tangere, published in La Solidaridad; 3.) but most damningly and most damnably and unspeakably shamelessly, in his Letter of Absolute Sacrifice In Order to Suppress the Revolution addressed to Gov. Gen. Ramon Blanco y Erenas written on board the Spanish warship Castilla where he was an honoured guest waiting for the next boat to Spain which he expected would ultimately take him to the site of his international counter-revolutionary mission of helping the Spanish Army there kill the Cuban Katipuneros and "SUPPRESS the {Cuban} Revolution" (and why indeed should you or anyone be surprised that in that letter he was making the same offer of his life and his everything in order to suppress another revolution, namely the Bonifacio Katipunan Revolution here?—and this E. San Juan has the wanton moronic stupidity and the only-in-the-Philippines intellectual dishonesty to repeat all the textbooks in saying that Rizal did not reject revolution/the Revolution "in principle," tanginang doble-karang apologist ng ruling class at kultura NILA ng corruption yan na pumapatay ng dalawa hanggang tatlong libong sanggol at mga bata dito sa Pilipinas araw araw dahil sa paghihikahos na dulot ng descendants nina Jose Rizal na ruling class na ito at mga gobyerno nila!); 4.) in the trial documents which he himself wrote, namely, a.) the December 15, 1896 Fort Santiago Manifesto, b.) the December 12, 1896 Data for my Defense, and c.) the December 26 Additional Data for my Defense; 5.) in the eurekically revealing final letters to 1.) his brother Paciano, and 2.) his friend Blumentritt written in the afternoon of December 29, 1896; 6.) in the long essay The Philippines A Century Hence, etc…

1.1.) Since it is brutally clear that there was no revolution being endorsed in the two novels but rather the direct and forthright opposite, namely, revolution being denounced and condemned there as "the worst disaster that could befall us", as he put it in The Philippines A century Hence—where "us" in Rizal's assimilationist counterrevolutionary lexicon refers to the rich, collaborationist, colonial middleclass represented in the assimilationist counterrevolutionary Propaganda Movement by Rizal and his ilustrado band on one hand, and the Spanish ruling class, the Spanish politicians, the Spanish authorities in the Madrid Government who were being prayed to by Rizal and company to grant assimilation status to the Philippines on the other hand—it is brutally clear that in Epifanio E. San Juan, Jr of the University of Connecticut, we have another petty bourgeois liberal victim-upholder-continuator of a hundred and more years of historiographic brainwashing whose egregious motive was, is, to convert the treasonous, cowardly pigly, opportunist class-ancestors of the present ruling class, namely Jose Rizal and the ilustrados, Aguinaldo and the caciques, into this country's solely true and greatest heroes…

{iii}

E. SAN JUAN, JR., DEFENDS RIZAL AND BRANDISHES DEEP, VERY DEEP IGNORANCE, A CREEPING INABILITY TO READ AND USE HISTORICAL DOCUMENTS, FAULTY REASONING, A SOPHOMORE'S GULLIBILITY, INTELLECTUAL IRRESPONSIBILITY AND FLABBINESS, AND SHEER LAZINESS TO THINK…

MON RAMIREZ quoted and posted a few hours ago a section of JV Ayson's interview of E. San Juan, Jr. titled, ON THE LEGACY OF NOLI METANGERE AND EL FILIBUSTERISMO. We are reproducing this excerpt here plus the reactions of some of E. San Juan's friends. Before sighting this Mon Ramirez excerpt, I had actually shared/reposted on my timeline his posting of the abovementioned interview which however I could not open because I have been on free fb for months now; I there requested my friends to please copy paste and send the thing to me, and Ka Ruel Pepa did. When I saw Mon Ramirez' excerpt then I have already read the whole interview. Although I am focusing my critical eye on this excerpt then I have already formed some overall critical evaluation of E San Juan's thinking here and this shows in the following critical commentary. Here then is the except with reactions from E San Juan's friends followed by my critical commentary:

EXCERPT FROM INTERVIEW:
"JV AYSON; What do you say about Rizal's views on the prospects of domestic socio-political crisis, reform, reaction, and armed revolution as he had pointed out in "Noli" and "Fili"?

"PROF. SAN JUAN: The story of Cabesang Tales demonstrates the limits of stoic patience. When families are destroyed, and children tortured, the colonial authorities have lost their legitimacy. Religious habits cannot suppress human affections and feelings of sympathy for others. Reforms were tried (by Ibarra and others), but the reactionary theocratic state refused to change, hence others were forced to become rebels, then called outlaws or "tulisan." Rizal recognized the need for armed revolution when a critical mass has emerged. When in prison he was forced to sign a statement disavowing the Katipunan uprising, it was hedged with qualifications—the Spanish government did not publish it because Rizal rejected only a riotous demonstration, not revolution in principle. Many think Rizal was against the Katipunan, but Bonifacio himself and the whole Katipunan idolized Rizal and used his name as a slogan."

COMMENTS BY E SAN JUAN'S FRIENDS

Elpedio Supremo Caterbas: Rizal's contributions to the Philippines Revolution was his inspiration to Andres Bonifacio and to the formations of the Katipunan. Adelbert Batica His views on armed revolution are hidden in prose and poetry. In "Mi Ultimo Adios", he writes "En campos de batalla, luchando con delirio, otros te dan sus vidas sin dudas, sin pesar; EL SITIO NADA IMPORTA - CIPRES, LAUREL O LIRIO, CADALSO O CAMPO ABIERTO. LO MISMO ES SI LO PIDEN, LA PATRIA Y EL HOGAR! (Caps mine). in "Fili", in the chapter entitled "La Ultima Razon" ("The Final Argument (for revolution), he writes: "Es menester renovar la raza! Padres esclavos solo engendraran hijos esclavos y no vale la pena destruir solo para volver a edificar con materiales podridos. HAY QUE MATAR EL DRAGON Y BAñAR EN SU SANGRE UN PUEBLO NUEVO PARA HACERLO FUERTE E INVULNERABLE. (Caps mine) "We must slay the dragon and bathe in its blood a new people, to make them strong and invulnerable. (Images from "Siegfried")

MY FIRST CRITICAL COMMENTARY:

"Rizal recognized the need for armed revolution when a critical mass has emerged. When in prison he was forced to sign a statement disavowing the Katipunan uprising, it was hedged with qualifications—the Spanish government did not publish it because Rizal rejected only a riotous demonstration, not revolution in principle. Many think Rizal was against the Katipunan, but Bonifacio himself and the whole Katipunan idolized Rizal and used his name as a slogan."

1.0.) "Rizal recognized the need for armed revolution when a critical mass has emerged." This statement is vague and intellectually irresponsible. Is E. San Juan referring here to the Cabesang Tales episode or storyline as Rizal's recognition of the need for "armed REVOLUTION"? But there is no revolution in this story; in fact just like the main storyline, that of the personal vindictive terrorist Ibarra/Simoun, what Rizal ignorantly and pitifully shows up here is the utter foolishness and withering futility of armed struggle against the colonial power.

2. 0.) "When in prison he was forced to sign a statement disavowing the Katipunan uprising, it was hedged with qualifications—the Spanish government did not publish it because Rizal rejected only a riotous demonstration, not revolution in principle." This is stupid, and so perfectly stupid that it must of necessity belong also to Floro Quibuyen which, to further perfect his own stupidity, he did appropriate in a number of places in that unclassifiably incoherent and totally fallacious book of his, *A Nation Aborted* in which Quibuyen is supposed by himself to argue for the existence of a superwonderful concept of "the nation" in Rizal's writings, and lament the abortion of the same by the invading Martians; he who as charismatic leader of the insane Assimilationist counterrevolutionary, anti-revolutionary, anti-separatist, anti-independence, anti-nation, anti-Filipino nation, anti-nationalist 'the Philippines As A Province of Spain" Propaganda Movement, never wanted to have a nation of his own, let alone a free and independent one, for, just like his ilustrado cohorts, all he ever really wanted was to become a brown, even if merely an overseas provincial, Spaniard...E. San Juan is of course unspeakably ignorantly referring here to the notorious *December 15, 1896 Fort Santiago Manifesto*, and I am sorely tempted to reproduce the whole brief thing here the more handily to enable me to slap E. San Juan with it with a husband and wife double slap so as to catch his two eyes with its perfidiously spiked supertraitor's venom before he is

able to shut them...But really this San Juanian stupidity is infuriating...Here then is the *Manifesto*:

"Countrymen: On my return from Spain, I learned that my name had been in use among some who were in arms as a war cry. The news came as a painful surprise, but, believing it already closed, I kept silent about an incident which I considered irremediable. Now I notice indications of the disturbances continuing, and if any still, in good or bad faith, are availing themselves of my name, to stop this abuse and undeceive the unwary, I hasten to address you these lines that the truth may be known.

"From the very beginning, when I first learned of what was being planned, I opposed it, fought it, and demonstrated its absolute impossibility. This is the fact and witnesses to my words are now living. I was convinced that the scheme was utterly absurd and, what was worse, would bring great sufferings. I DID EVEN MORE. When, against my advice, the movement materialized, OF MY OWN ACCORD, I OFFERED NOT ALONE MY GOOD OFFICES BUT MY VERY LIFE, AND EVEN MY NAME, TO BE USED IN WHATEVER WAY THEY MIGHT DEEM BEST TOWARDS STIFLING THE REBELLION; for, convinced of the ills which it would bring, I would have considered myself fortunate if, at any sacrifice, I could prevent such useless misfortunes. This, equally, is of record.

"My Countrymen, I have given proofs that I am one most anxious for the LIBERTIES of our country, and I am still desirous of them. But I place as a prior condition the education of the people, that by means of instruction and industry, our country may have an individuality of its own, and make itself worthy of LIBERTIES. I have recommended in my writings STUDY AND CIVIC VIRTUES WITHOUT WHICH THERE IS NO REDEMPTION. I have written likewise (and I repeat my words) that reforms, to be beneficial, MUST COME FROM ABOVE, for those that come from below are irregular and insecure. Holding these ideas, I cannot do less than condemn, and I do condemn, this savage and absurd uprising plotted behind my back, which dishonours us Filipinos, and discredits those who would plead OUR CAUSE. I abhor its criminal methods and disclaim any part in it, pitying from the bottom of my heart the unwary who have been deceived.

"Return then to your homes, and may God pardon those who have worked in bad faith.!
"Signed: JOSE RIZAL, Fort Santiago, December 15, 1896."

"Rizal recognized the need for armed revolution when a critical mass has emerged. When in prison he was forced to sign a statement disavowing the Katipunan uprising, it was hedged with qualifications—the Spanish government did not publish it because Rizal rejected only a riotous demonstration, not revolution in principle. Many think Rizal was against the Katipunan, but Bonifacio himself and the whole Katipunan idolized Rizal and used his name as a slogan."

Rizal, E San Juan says, "was forced to sign" this "statement". Who forced him? And how did he know there was such a forcing? Was a gun shoved against his temple to make him sign it? Was the Manifesto written by someone else then and was handed to Rizal ready-made for him to sign at gunpoint? Or was it dictated to him? But for what? The Spaniards were intent on formally convicting him. If there was such a forcing, it must be because they intended to use the document to inculpate him. It must thus contain highly incriminating expressions of his supposed revolutionariness which was the crime for which he was charged. In fact, the Judge Advocate General, Nicolas dela Pena in a written opinion was the one who ruled that Rizal's request to have it published and distributed to the Katipuneros be denied, and it was him in the same opinion who said that Rizal's rejection of the Revolution was rather lame, that, as E San Juan puts it here, "it was hedged with qualifications", and that Rizal did not there reject "revolution in principle." And he went even further saying that, distributed to the Katipuneros, the Manifesto would only serve to inflame them and confirm them in their revolutionary resolve! (I am writing this away from my library and cannot thus reproduce here dela Pena's words, but I promise to do so asap.) Faced with these fantastic claims, a reasonable scholar's instinctive resort is to get hold of the Manifesto and verify or impugn them by the simple act of *reading* the document. Did E. San Juan do so? Is E. San Juan at the very least a reasonable rather than an unreasonable scholar? And here, dear reader, having yourself read the document, you know at once that E. San Juan did *not* do so. He did not read the document! E. San Juan is an unreasonable scholar. He is a sloppy scholar. He is an irresponsible scholar. He does not read, he does not make use of, documents! He is a tsismoso, he propagates rumours, he is not, perhaps, a scholar at all? Moreover, he is exceedingly gullible. He got wind of what Dela Pena said of the Manifesto and, because it suited perfectly what his own brainwashing victimization by the perverted textbook tradition must make him want to believe, he believed it at once, like a frog jumpingly biting the still wriggling skewered worm of a bait. For—and let us be redundant because the public is large--what, reading the document, does the document say? It absolutely belies everything Dela Pena, and here, aping him, E.San Juan, said of it. Which must then prompt us to ask why Dela Pena so perversely lyingly said what he said of it, and refused thenceforth not only to have it published and distributed to the Katipuneros but to make use of it in the trial. Why, when such a powerfully worded and composed counterrevolutionary tract made even more powerful by the fact that it came from the great idol whose name the Katipuneros were ritualistically taught by Bonifacio to solemnly invoke and whose picture Bonifacio also taught them to venerate (making use of him thus in the increasingly vain effort through such misrepresentation to recruit the native rich, since he three times adamantly and even angrily refused to join them and do the recruiting himself:--yes indeed, it was Bonifacio himself who invented, who fabricated the patriot and hero and inspirational revolutionary Jose Rizal as against the true and real genocidally deadly counterrevolutionary Rizal—more on this Bonifacian stratagem below…) could indeed make many Katipuneros waver and eventually heed Rizal's injunction for them to abandon the Revolution and "return to {their} homes"? Two things:--one, the Court's foregone resolve to convict and execute Rizal no matter what, was immovable, and two, there is something in the Manifesto that must not be taken up and must thus be deleted from the reckoning of the

Court and must never be espied by the metropolitan media. And this because to allow it to come out would mean Rizal's exculpation and worse, his blazoning as a great brown Spanish hero! And what else indeed was this absolutely delicate something but Rizal's "unconditional offer" of his life, his name, of everything he was capable of doing, of his all in all, in order to "stifle" or "suppress" (Zaide's translation has the latter word) the revolution? About which Rizal could not possibly have been lying, for it was very easy to check the thing out with the letter's addressee, no less than Gov. Gen. Ramon Blanco, and its signed witness, the Spanish naval commander, Col.Santalo who, being Rizal's close friend must have been attending the sessions of the trial. Whilst it should be obvious to normal observers or readers that as a matter of life and death urgency, Rizal wrote the Manifesto in order to centrally, focusedly, spotlightedly mention that supergreat act of brown Spanish heroism of his offering to die, and for them to make use of his great and megalomaniacal name to fool the revolutionists, and to do absolutely anything (like kill Andres Bonifacio for instance, and with him so many of the Katipuneros) "in order to suppress the revolution" (—for how else do you supress such a thing?)...In short, he wrote that Manifesto and presented it in Court because he wanted to force the Court to subpoena Blanco and Santalo to stand witness, with Blanco of course brandishing the letter and Santalo authenticating his signature there...

That! And you, you wrote this ultimate insult to the memory of Maria Lorena Barros and Cherith Dayrit, this, this braggartly shining efflorescence of your farcical stupidity:--"But they need Rizal's pathos, to help mourn and celebrate the sacrifices of our Maria Lorena Barros, Cherith Dayrit, all the martyrs of the Marcos dictatorship. But above all, they need Rizal's cunning and humor—without humor, how can you dance to the victories of the revolution?"--Hitler murdered Rosa Luxembourg and decimated the German Left and you invoke his coprophiliac tenderness to mourn and celebrate their heroic death. And this utterly painful vulgarity of a Nietzscheism like a chainsaw whirring against the brain, about "Rizal's cunning and humor"--this huge dancingly traitorous tumor from Calamba cavorting over the massgraves of the two million Filipinos genocided by the Americans who would never have been able to materialize thus on these Philipppine shores had not Rizal's Counterrevolution injured so much and delayed for a decade the Philippine Revolution...--the genocidal conning of the native colonial middleclass by this treacherous tumor of an indoctorated anti-Filipino counterrevolutionary brown Spanish mental colony...

{iv}

1.) NAKAKAPAGOD NA ITO at para mo nang pilit kinakagat ang siko mo dito, pero walang magagawa, kailangang maging mapasensiya at matiyaga; at saka, ako lang din naman ang nagpasiya para sa sarili ko na akuin ang nakamamatay sa kunsumisyong trabahong ito ng isang manunulat na huwag sumuko sa mahigit isang dantaong higanteng puwersa ng katangahan, korupsyong intelektwal, panggagago at madugong kadayaan ng naghaharing uri at mga GOBYERNO nito (na liban sa Gobyerno ni Andres Bonifacio ay sa naghaharing uri nang ito nagsisilbi, at nageksist at nageeksist hanggang ngayon upang isulong ang interes ng naghaharing uring kumukontrol sa bawat isa dito, mula sa Gobyerno ni Aguinaldo hanggang sa kay Marcos at sa kay Aquino; at ngayon, kay Duterte ay EWAN nga ba) at mga direkta o indirektang bayarang matatapang ang hiyang historians daw at manunulat daw...

2.) We have demonstrated in full documentation a hundred times and more that you will not find in Rizal's writings including his correspondence a single forthright endorsement of revolution; but also never a single mention of revolution that did not execrate, curse, condemn it as "the worst disaster that could befall us" (in The Philippines A Century Hence), as "absurd", "criminal", "savage", "shameful", "discreditable", "the work of bad faith", "absolutely impossible" (The December 15, 1896 MANIFESTO, and elsewhere, everywhere). And I have issued it time and again as a challenge to those who refuse to read these documents and analyses and demonstrations, and therefore refuse to really read Rizal, and who must thus have never really read him, to find and present a single sentence of the one or the other or both species. As for the novels and poems, there cannot of course be found in them any such forthright endorsements of revolution too, or even relative noncondemnations; and that is because these are literary forms and, just like Biblical literature, you can, if you are paid enough or simply perverse enough, or like Batica here illiterate enough, to read absolutely anything into them. And that is why it is illiterate to pick at random necessarily mangled and/because decontextualized passages from those novels and those poems--as a certain Batica does here, and of course of course of course an Epifanio San Juan Jr citing Cabesang Tales etc... Mountainous literary-historical and social-historical conjunctural contextualizations of such passages and indeed of such entire works are here absolutely necessary.

3.) I am all set to write a huge configuration of EPICHEIREMATA (as in my ongoing, now 600 pages of ATTACKS against Nietzsche and the Nietzscheites, many of whom French poststructuralists whom E. San Juan Jr had allowed himself to be influenced by toward a liberal-tending watering down of Marxism, triggered by JV Ayson's interview of E. San Juan, Jr.--a confrontation that, as I put it in a message of thanks to Ka @Ruel Pepa for copy-pasting-sending the interview transcript to me (which I could not open with my wifi because I have no money to load it: I'm on free fb for months now), has been "long in coming". But I just cannot let this taunting quoting of this passage from that interview by Ka @Mon Ramirez here (which does not offend but rather merely excite, incite, me, and I have to thank him for it) and I have somehow to make a response. This to which I will have to limit myself. Aside from the challenge to find in all of Rizal's works and correspondence a single sentence of endorsement of revolution, or a single sentence mentioning revolution without vituperating it, will E. San Juan, Jr., please take, in writing, a clear and honest position concerning Rizal's letter to Gov. Gen. Blanco "OFFERING

UNCONDITIONALLY NOT ALONE MY LIFE, BUT EVEN MY NAME, AND EVERYTHING I AM CAPABLE OF DOING, TO BE USED" (BY THE SPANIARDS) "IN WHATEVER WAY THEY MIGHT DEEM MOST FIT IN ORDER TO SUPPRESS THE REBELLION" (Rizal's own words)? Correlatively, his position on that prior crime against revolution, against the Revolution, against humanity, that was his international counter-revolutionary project of joining the Spanish colonial Army in Cuba as a Spanish military doctor to, of course, help the Spaniards kill as many Cuban Katipuneros as possible and thus "SUPPRESS the revolution" there? A suicidal-martyrical mission in defense of Spanish colonialism which, before he could do it in Cuba, and a few days before his departure for Spain en route to that fantasized scene of his international counterrevolutionary criminality, he proposed in THAT LETTER to perpetrate here against his own countrywo/men and their Revolution... And please do tell us how you propose to read all these alongside your unbelievable "revolutionization" of Rizal's literary “practice” and its ideologico-political-cultural effects. I have posted more than a hundred pages of analyses and documentation directly bearing upon these twin *counterrevolutionary treasons* here on Facebook and published the same number of pages in my four books on *The New History of the Philippine Revolution and of the Filipino People*. Please read me there so we don't waste time asking and replying to pre-answered questions.

{v}

ANO KAMO, EPIFANITO?--RIZAL’S ANALYTIC MIND AND CRITICAL SENSIBILITY?

“JV AYSON: What is the main significance of Rizal’s twin novels in arousing the Filipino people’s consciousness and enlightenment in their continuing struggle for national liberation and social emancipation?

Domingo DC De Guzman

"PROF. SAN JUAN: The significance depends on how our mass leaders/guides translate Rizal's analytic mind and critical sensibility to the needs and demands of every situation they are facing. Do the Moros and the Lumad need Rizal? Maybe not, because they have their own cultural sources of inspiration and enlightenment. But they need Rizal's pathos, to help mourn and celebrate the sacrifices of our Maria Lorena Barros, Cherith Dayrit, all the martyrs of the Marcos dictatorship. But above all, they need Rizal's cunning and humor—without humor, how can you dance to the victories of the revolution?"

COMMENTS

1.) We have already exhaustively and exhaustingly shown in our 6 preceding replies to E SAN JUAN posted on this page, that the two novels were powerfully anti- and counter-revolutionary in being the pernicious vehicles of colonial-conservationist assimilationist, anti-separatist, anti-independence *ideology*:--and that *that* exactly was what Rizal intended them to be, to do. The twin novels were made up of so many literarily couched brainwashing, fallacious arguments against revolution, against separation from his dearly beloved Mother Spain, against independence from his dearly beloved Mother Spain, against the colonized natives' founding, precisely through the Revolution, a free and independent Filipino nation—and thus against his own countrymen's freeing, liberating, precisely through that Revolution, their, his, own native land! What can be read in all of Rizal's other writings including his massive correspondence, which precisely are those assimilationist counterrevolutionary brainwashing and fallacious arguments, Rizal merely translated into novelistically cobbled assimilationist counter-revolutionary brainwashing and fallacious arguments. Little wonder that *all* those natives who were able to read them, who were mostly his own ilustrado and other colonial middleclass assimilationist counterrevolutionary disciples, became such staunch counterrevolutionaries and deadly national traitors. Whilst it has never been proved that a single reader of them—and a reader therefore of such literarily toxined and laced anti-revolutionary, anti-separatist, anti-independence, colonial conservationist, anti-Filipino-nation arguments--became a revolutionary because of it. The singular case of Andres Bonifacio which the entire utterly dishonest textbook-historiographic tradition regularly adduces proves the exact opposite, as we have in the 6 posts above demonstrated:--Bonifacio became a revolutionary *despite* it, *against* it… Meanwhile, the sometimes also cited case of Apolinario Mabini is simply a blatant lie and proves rather the exact contrary:--Mabini who was able to read the two novels was already a leading local ilustrado assimilationist propagandist stalwart counterrevolutionary when Andres Bonifacio and company tried many times and mightily to recruit him to the Revolution—and failed. In fact, as we have shown in one of those six posts here and elsewhere in this now two-year-old facebook historiographic column, prior to those persistent and mighty efforts at recruitment by Bonifacio and his Katipunan comrades, Mabini was even, with Deodato Arellano and Domingo Franco, the chief prosecutor in the denunciation and expulsion of Bonifacio and his Katipunan comrades from the revived *Liga Filipina* for the crime of engaging in separatist-revolutionary recruitment and fundraising activities instead of recruiting and fundraising for the support of the assimilationist counterrevolutionary *La Solidaridad* of the assimilationist counterrevolutionary supertraitor Marcelo del Pilar for which supertraitor purpose Marcelo del Pilar instigated, through his brother in law Deodato Arellano (who, thus, was *never* a Katipunan member let alone its first president!!!), the *Liga's* revival (see Mabini's confessional LIGA FILIPINA chapter on this in his *History of the Philippine Revolution* which of course E. San Juan Jr., *must not have read…*). Whilst, when finally Mabini joined the Revolution on June 12, 1898, it was not so much the Revolution that he joined but the perversion of it by the Aguinaldo cacique group into the Aguinaldo Counterrevolution from inside the Revolution and its merger with the Rizalist ilustrado Counterrevolution from outside the Revolution (which merger we may now call the Colonial Middleclass Counterrevolution):--the two super-scandalous acts of this merger, of this Colonial Middleclass

Counterrevolution, were of course the sale of the Revolution for 800,000 pesos at Biyak na Bato in November-December 1897, and the murder of Antonio Luna in Cabanatuan because Luna discovered the new plot by Aguinaldo and the Rizal-Counterrevolutionary group to once more sell the Revolution, this time to the Americans…

2.) "The significance depends on how our mass leaders/guides translate Rizal's analytical mind and critical sensibility to the needs and demands of every situation they are facing". E bakit ba naman kasi ipinaguukilkilan mo yang over-demonstrated at over-documented national and even (in view of his Cuban counterrevolutionary doctoral project) international traitor na yan, yang hinayupak na enemy of humanity na yan, na basahin at gamitin sa *Rebolusyon* dito, ha USLOG? Bakit ba miriting-miriti kang ma-counterrevolution ang revolution dito ngayon? Kopyang-kopya mo si Rizal sa pagkahunyango ah! "Rizal's analytical mind and critical sensibility" ba eka mo? Na nanganak ng super-effective na brainwashing counterrevolutionary novels and mental-colonial assimilation-begging, gawin-mo-kaming-Kastila-para-mo-nang-awa importuning counterrevolutionary, anti-independence journalism tangina ka! Which, through the treasons, the perfidies, the mass-murders, the series of delays they, he, caused, were decisive in ensuring the genocidal extermination of 2 million Filipinos by the Americans during the Philippine-American War…For which genocide then he must be held responsible… The "analytical mind and critical sensibility" ba eka mo ng walang katulad sa kasaysayan ng mundong mental colony na basag na kalambang itong nakayang ihandog nang walang ano mang kundisyon ang buhay niya, ang pangalan niya, at lahat nang kaya niyang gawin "na gamitin ng mga Kastila sa anumang pamamaraang sa palagay nila ay pinakamainam UPANG SUGPUIN ANG REBOLUSYON"?

3.) I wonder… Is it possible to explain anything to such as E San Juan Jr.? Is it still possible to communicate anything to so uncomprehending a being, to dialogue with him who cannot seem to think at all? For does he think at all who can at this late hour of his life go on believing in Rizal's "analytical mind and critical sensibility"? He who has not even read him? He who shamelessly repeats like sacred formulae everything the textbook tradition says about this most despicable national traitor in world history and absolutely does not know anything about his being the most despicable national traitor in world history...

{vi}

THE FILI WAS ANTI-REVOLUTION--RIZAL.
REPLY TO E SAN JUAN

In this fifth of a series response to JV Ayson's E SAN JUAN INTERVIEW, we cite a number of letters in which forthrightly and more compellingly because circumstantially, Rizal himself declared that the FILI was written by him in furtherance of the assimilationist counterrevolutionary goals of "their", Rizal's and del Pilar's Propaganda Movement.

Here is Letter 313 from *Rizal's Correspondence With Fellow Reformists* (pp 680 et seq.) in which he wrote: "That was my purpose in making Simoun a dark figure--in order to show that those of La Solidaridad are *not* filibusteros..."

"Hong Kong, 23 May 1892
Mr. Marcelo Del Pilar

Friend Pilar,

"I have just written a letter to Naning and I am not satisfied unless I write you too. I have read Lete's article against me. I have reflected much on the purpose you might have in attacking me and in truth I am lost in conjectures. There are moments when I believe that you act following a most profound policy which is useless to explain, and there are moments when it seems to me that you operate with earnestness and on your own account. I screw my wits uselessly ....and I do not know what to think. Had I not told you before leaving Europe that I would never undertake anything against you? What animal has bitten you that you attack me when here I do not meddle at all in politics and I work only to prepare a free place for refuge for the Filipinos, devoting the rest of my time to writing some books? Have I not told you that I was leaving you in politics so that you may earn much prestige? Do you need to attack me for that? I cannot explain myself. So that I say to myself: If you have acted for political reasons, I applaud you and I should like you to continue, for it seems to me that you are on the right road. THAT WAS MY PURPOSE IN MAKING SIMOUN A DARK FIGURE--IN ORDER TO SHOW THAT THOSE OF LA SOLIDARIDAD ARE NOT FILIBUSTEROS. I thought you had understood my ideas, only that in executing it you have played your role with such naturalness that you strike even me. But then, why do you not name me at once so that the Spaniards who are not well informed about our affairs and may not know how to read the allusions may have no doubt that you are attacking me? Why do you do it under so much cover? Are the Filipinos going to say that there is hatred in the attack, real hatred, only that the author does not want to do it face to face? If the attack has a political purpose, I confess that it is rash and imprudent, and I fear that La Solidaridad has staked in it its last cent. May God grant that that attack may be understood by my friends in the Philippines so that differences may be not be exacerbated. If I were sure that you did it for political reasons, i would now write to Manila to tell them not to take it ill. But I am afraid to commit a mistake, for as I have said, I doubt and doubt.

"Blumentritt writes me that you fear that La Solidaridad may die, and this also makes me believe that you might have written the article in a moment of ill-humor. I do not know yet the consequences that the article may produce, but as it has been a long time that I do not pay attention to politics, nor do I know the state of things in Manila, I cannot prejudge anything. Let the responsibility fall on those who have premeditated it without warning me. If I were sure that it is a political trick, I would write now to Manila telling them not to take it ill, that only a personal question is involved in it, and that politics has nothing to do with it.

“Nevertheless, I will write my friends and those who are not my friends that I have written you and not to adopt any resolution until you answer me.

“This is not to say that I ask you for an explanation of the article; neither is it to say to you that I despise it; on the contrary it attracts my attention very greatly and I esteem the courage of Lete in attacking me with so much fierceness and courage and above all with so much confidence. I like determined men. Give me an explanation if you wish; I warn you only that the step taken is most delicate and of great importance. I wash my hands.

“I had already prepared an article for La Solidaridad, telling about Borneo and its colonization, and now I abstain from sending it. The Governor of Borneo grants us 100,000 acres, port, government, and the like, all free for a period of 999 years.

“I am anxious to receive satisfactory explanations for it seems to me that we are now entering a crisis. To my regret, you are making me enter politics again, and I shall have to write again letters these days to Manila and to other places in order to prevent the schism. More and more, I am getting convinced that in writing that article Lete has been too precipitate and you have already allowed yourself to be dragged along. Friend or enemy, if the article could hurt me, it will hurt more the interests of the Philippines. Who knows, however, if, after all, it is a blessing? It awakens me and after a long silence, I enter the campaign again and assure you: I enter the campaign but I will not attack you or any other Filipino. I WILL REACTIVATE THE [ASSIMILATIONIST] CAMPAIGN AND SRENGTHEN THE LIGA.

"You can read this letter to Lete and you will tell him that, at worse, I will consider his article an unbosoming in his moments of ill-humor.

Yours,
Rizal.

1.0.) Here it is then, from the horse's mouth. Ibarra-Simoun was himself sacrificed at the altar of assimilationism, i.e., of anti-and-counter-revolution, of anti-independence and anti-separation from *their* ultra-beloved *Mother Spain*, of eternal Spanish colonialism for the Filipinos, of erasure of the Filipinos as a prospective independent nation. Rizal wanted to dramatize to the Metropolitan Spanish reading public and most particularly to the Spanish political authorities who were going to decide whether to grant or deny what to Rizal and company was heaven itself, namely assimilation to the Philippines as overseas province of Spain, *how and what they, the native Filipino assimilationist propagandists really think of filibusterismo, of separatismo, of revolution*. Ibarra-Simoun was to be its personification: cynically evil, brutal, savage, criminal, treacherous, and, most importantly, bound only to most miserably fail—exactly as he in his December 15, 1896 Fort Santiago Manifesto excoriated and cursed the Katipuneros and their Revolution. It was a poor, squinted, even stupid picture, betraying therewith Rizal's profound ignorance of what revolution was all about.

But let us first clarify the tangled and shameful background of this letter.

2.0.) There was, prior to this letter, a bitter quarrel between Rizal and MH Del Pilar over *La Solidaridad* policy in particular and the Propaganda Movement policy in general. Rizal realized that, although the propaganda money and disseminative efforts and mortal risks were actually contributions from and by wealthy members of the native colonial middleclass in the Philippines whom Rizal had thus cathechized to hate and fear revolution and love to death their Mother Spain and thus part with their cash to support their movement clamoring for assimilation *in order to forestall revolution at all costs* ("the Philippines as a province of Spain", etc.,), and to achieve thus eternal Spanish colonialism for the Filipinos, Marcelo H. Del Pilar considered *La Solidaridad* his own "private enterprise" (as Rizal put it in a letter to Baldomero Roxas—Letter 312. Rizal, Hong Kong, 17 May 1892, pp. 678-679 of *Rizal's Correspondence with Fellow Reformists*) in which therefore he, Del Pilar, deemed himself responsible for his actions and policies only to himself, and *thus, concerning money-matters, accountable only to himself* (in fact, a later audit showed that Marcelo the great—UP Masscom's journalism center is named after him to ensure mass-production of his clones—had made away with 700 golden pesos!). Rizal wanted to make the thing a purely, and so to speak, a formally, public affair, actually a class-political affair, a colonial middleclass political affair:--one would want to be able to refer to it as a "national" affair or undertaking except that, *as we all know*, it was dedicated to the assimilation of the Philippines, i.e., the swallowing and digestion of the Philippines by Spain as an overseas province of Spain, and thus the total erasure of what would be a distinct Filipino nation (kaya nga isang kaululan at kabaliwan na ituring na "nationalist" si Rizal at ang sino man sa sindikatong ito ng mga anti-Filipino, anti-Filipino nation, anti-nationalist traitors—baligtad ang history sa lahat ng history textbooks at sa lahat ng libro ng lahat ng historians dito!). There was a general assembly and in the first voting it was a tie between Rizal and Del Pilar. In the second voting Rizal won by a margin of one. He did not like it that amongst the Filipino anti-Filipinos and anti-independence and anti-revolution traitors there he was preeminent by only one vote, namely, his own. He strode mightily out in unappeasable tantrum and swore never again to involve himself in what he called "politics":--he would thenceforth do his assimilationist anti-revolution thing alone or as sole dictator. He had actually, even then, decided to go home to the Philippines to die at the hands of the friars in the wake of the horrendous *Calamba Massacre*. The Dominicans claimed two years ago that Calamba was a part of the Hacienda of the Diocese of Binan and arrogated therewith the right to treat the Calambenos as taxable tenants. There was a legal tussle in which of course Rizal led his townmates. The case had been dragging on for two years already as it even reached the Madrid Court. The Dominicans lost patience and, with the help of the new Governor General, Valeriano Weyler, through the insidious representation of his Imeldific wife who became extra-intimate with the Dominican friars, had had Calamba invaded by four hundred heavily armed soldiers ferried by a boat across the lake, and one hundred bigoted cavalrymen (it was the height of the Dark Ages there then). At the head of the invasion were, of course the ravenous and lustful bloodquaffing Dominican friars who, as Rizal himself was wont to portray them in his pornographic imaginings (yes, those novels were world-class pornographic material, especially Salvi and Maria Clara and Juli and Camorra, and of course Pia and Damaso…) went on a rampage of rape and rapine all over Calamba, waylaying every female of the species and indeed of the animal kingdom—nor did they spare the dumalagas and matsoras, which explains how even to this day there are way too many white carabaos ungaing there…The rich, and especially the entire Rizal family, were all arrested and later deported; the poor were driven out of the town and their hovels burned to the ground. Those who resisted were killed, the girls and women after ravishing them of course. Rizal blamed himself for this wholesale atrocity, and, unable to sleep any longer for the heartbreak of thinking his beloved Mama Teodora distracted and bereft and weeping weeping in some strange land, resolved at last to go home and deliver himself wriggling and naked like early worm to the bladed talons of those behooded and becowled aves de rapina, thinking that (and telling them so in a letter) his death could ransom the freedom of his family and collaterally of the other Calambenos and move the disciples of Santo Domingo de Guzman to allow all of them to be restored to their homes. And that primarily was why he was in Hong Kong at this exact time, whilst in exactly one month afterwards he would be sailing for Manila to meet his destiny and seek his pre-announced assimilationist martyrdom…All this coincided with the publication of the *Fili*, which he must have thought was construed by Del Pilar to be a separatist-revolutionary work! Hence, the satirical attack.

Here Marcelo Del Pilar and his *La Solidaridad* staff writer Eduardo de Lete were, according as Rizal read the satirical piece (Del Pilar and Lete denied his reading), accusing Rizal of plotting revolution and ridiculing him for it. Rizal was furious. He was beside himself. He protested against the, to him, mis-informed and malicious accusation. He pleaded not guilty. And he showed proof that he was not a filibustero, that he was not a separatist, that he was as against revolution and Philippine independence from Spain as he ever was, and the ultimate proof of it, for him, which he here put forward was this—that he actually wrote the *Fili* to help in such a major way in the Propaganda Movement's ongoing campaign to convince the Spanish authorities in Madrid to finally assimilate the Philippines as a province of Spain, and this by showing through juxtapositional contrast how utterly refined, peaceful, benign, and devoutly devoted to the conservation of the colonial oneness of the Philippines with their Mother Spain the Madrid Propagandists were,--yes, how "white" those monkeys were!,--and this by making Simoun (who apparently was to him the very personification of revolution--and this shows how ignorant Rizal was of what constitutes revolution!) such a dark, evil, desperate, terroristically destructive and utterly futile figure…

3.0.) "May God grant that that attack may be understood by my friends in the Philippines so that differences may be not be exacerbated." But suppose Del Pilar and Lete attacked him so because they, like Antonio Luna, Ponce, Evangelista, Alejandrino, (and who else?, perhaps almost everyone?) must have thought that the Rape of Calamba in response to which Rizal suddenly left Europe for Hong Kong (and eventually, the Philippines to suffer persecution and death here with his family and townmates who were being hounded by the Dominicans and Weyler because of him), must already have precipitated Rizal into separatism and revolution; whilst they like the fanatical assimilationists that, like Rizal himself, they were, must of course have thought that such quixoticism deserved nothing but a lousy failure and noisy ridicule, and meanwhile, they must at all cost dissociate themselves from any such separatist caper because it would of course endanger the assimilationist cause. Hence the attack.

What all this attests to was the enormous reformist-assimilationist clout Rizal had had in steering the course of Philippine history against separatism, against revolution and ultimately into the genocidal arms of the Americans who were able to intercept the Revolution because of Rizal's perverting and corrupting influence that lined up the upper middle class and the main bulk of the colonial middle class against the Revolution. Hence Rizal's massive responsibility for the American genocide of 2 million Filipinos.

4.0.) "Friend or enemy, if the article could hurt me, it will hurt more the interests of the Philippines." This is true if the interests of the Philippines lie in assimilation, i.e., eternal colonialism (as Rizal himself has put it in an article titled "THE PHILIPPINES AS A SPANISH COLONY—FOREVER"—see Rizal's Political and Historical Writings, NHI, 2007, pp. 355-358). And here then, the megalomania. Which was more megalomanic because utterly false. This concerns the identification of the interests of the Philippines with the person of Jose Rizal. In fact, if true, it would simply have been a statement of brute fact. Andres Bonifacio could have said it of himself matter-of-factly, without necessarily falling into insanity. But he did not, and we could admire him more for it, for not saying it. Utterly, even massmurderously false was this self-identification because he was an assimilationist—the exact and bloody opposite of that which especially during those revolutionary times represented the truest interests of the Philippines, namely, of course, revolution, independence—which of course was the singular, abiding, interest and political goal of the people's existence, from the very beginning of that state of war that was the (of course) forcible conquest and colonization of the Philippines, the first condition of which being the destruction of the native people's independence and the forcible denial of their right of sovereignty.

5.0.) LETTER TO MARIANO PONCE...THE FILI IS ANTI-REVOLUTIONARY—RIZAL...
Reply to the E. SAN JUAN INTERVIEW ON THE NOLI AND THE FILI

Letter 314. Rizal, Hong Kong, 23 May 1892, To Mariano Ponce: "In making my enraged Simoun speak, I had wanted to pursue the same end, setting a darker background so that the Filipinos in Madrid may appear white..."

"MY DEAR FRIEND PONCE,
"Today, I have received an issue of La Solidaridad of 15 April and I have read its articles, including that of Lete attacking me. I cannot express either contempt or indifference upon reading such an article, for after all, he is a Filipino and among the good ones, inasmuch as he has been awarded the prize of patriotism. Neither can I show indignation nor dismay, for, as I have not told anyone for sometime what I am doing or what my political thoughts are, it is possible that Lete may not know what I am doing. Moreover I take into account the state of your minds there and of the Madrid atmosphere. Judging by what Blumentritt writes me, it seems that some believe that I am the cause why Solidaridad lacks funds or is about to die. There is nothing in this, for I always bear in mind that I have promised Pilar that never will I join any conspiracy against him or against the publication and until now I have fulfilled and will fulfil my promise. I am very sorry that Pilar has allowed the article to be published, for this will make many believe that there is a schism among us. I believe that we can well have little displeasures and personal differences among us without the necessity of making them extend to the party. We should keep them to ourselves and respect one another. This is what I believe, but Pilar and Lete can believe otherwise, and I admit that there is liberty for all. I do not know the effect of this article on the Filipinos in the Philippines. I on my part will not consider myself offended so that matters will not become worse, and I will not write a single word as I have not done for a long time. I do not write either Pilar or Lete for reasons you can understand, as they are

persons directly interested in the matter and because a letter of mine can protest against this procedure, and then they have to give me explanations, or it can advise and then I would appear as a counselor or a semi-protector. Tell them only that I am very sorry, but neither do I despise it nor am I indignant at it. What fault have they if they have not understood me better? Perhaps I am to blame for having supposed that they would understand my purposes without the necessity of explaining them. However, for the ends I am pursuing, I prefer not to give explanations. PERHAPS THEY ARE ALSO PURSUING A MORE PROFOUND POLICY, AND THEY ARE PRETENDING TO GO AGAINST ME AND ATTACK ME FURIOUSLY IN ORDER TO PLAY BETTER THE ROLE OF PRO-ASSIMILATION PARTISANS. IN THIS REGARD I PRAISE THEM, but in that case, I believe they ought to attack me strongly, mentioning my name, because many Spaniards who are not well informed about our inside affairs do not understand Lete's allusions and the article does not achieve its purpose. I only warn them that the idea is somewhat risky, but if it were thus, they may believe that I sincerely applaud them and they can increase the attack with my secret congratulations. Only I observe that in following that policy, Lete sells himself and sells us. ON MAKING MY ENRAGED SIMOUN SPEAK, I HAVE WANTED TO PURSUE THE SAME END, SETTING A DARKER BACKGROUND SO THAT THE FILIPINOS OF MADRID MAY APPEAR WHITE, BUT IN DOING SO, I DID NOT SELL ANY SECRET. In short, you may say whether my conjectures are false or true. Whether true or not, I will pursue my policy and will try to guess the purpose of your movements IN ORDER TO ADJUST MY STEP TO THAT OF YOURS AND ACHIEVE THE BEST END... As I have heard that you and Selong are thinking of withdrawing, I do not understand that policy...

"Against wind and tide I will always be the same with regard to the friars affair of the Philippines. The interests of the Philippines are above me...."

5.1.) "I do not know the effect of this article on the Filipinos in the Philippines".-- That is to say, on the rich Filipinos in the Philippines who were supporters of the Assimilationist campaign: the funds for the publication of La Solidaridad and for other campaign activities all came from the Manila Committee which was in charge of collecting them from the rich Filipino colonial middle class: think of what could have been sooner and more powerfully, more decisively achieved thus for revolution and independence if the same money and effort from this class led and deluded by Rizal and company were used and devoted to revolution and independence instead!

5.2.)"Against wind and tide I will always be the same with regard to the friars affair of the Philippines"...Yes indeed, assimilation and expulsion of the friars...The friars who should be expelled soonest time possible because, according to Rizal in everything he wrote on the matter, it was the friars through their abuses who were pushing the natives to the brink of "that worst disaster that could befall us", namely, "revolution", as he put it in THE PHILIPPINES A CENTURY HENCE, for instance. Revolution, separation, independence were out of the question for Rizal—only the friars, assimilation and the friars...

5.3.) "...in order to adjust my step to that of yours and achieve the best end..."—their common best end, which was to prevent revolution from happening through the removal of its main, and to Rizal, sole cause, namely the friars, and achieve eternal colonialism for the Philippines through assimilation....

5.4.) "PERHAPS THEY ARE ALSO PURSUING A MORE PROFOUND POLICY, AND THEY ARE PRETENDING TO GO AGAINST ME AND ATTACK ME FURIOUSLY IN ORDER TO PLAY BETTER THE ROLE OF PRO-ASSIMILATION PARTISANS. IN THIS REGARD I PRAISE THEM..." This is a crazy surmise and one feels absurd having to confront it here. Was Rizal in earnest saying this? In effect, without naming him, Del Pilar and De Lete were here denouncing him to the Spanish authorities as a separatist, a filibustero, a revolutionary. Rizal was here suggesting that they were doing this denunciation and attack to more effectively dissociate themselves from the suspicion of being separatists; thus they would be able "to play better the role of pro-assimilationist partisans…" In any case, in that Rizal, they knew, was on his way to the Philippines, the article was among other things a malevolent denunciation of the mental colonial Calambeno doctor as a separatist filibustero to the Spanish authorities in Manila and a recommendation for them, especially to the friars who were in great thirst to open him up in several places and quaff his blood, to seize him and execute him. National, even international, traitors and cowardly counterrevolutionaries (traitors are necessarily cowards—the logic of essence necessitates it!), these illustrious mental-colonial morons were the perfecters of the art and tradition of fraternal backstabbing which in these ilustrado scions of the super-traitorous marrows-deep mental-colonial native colonial middleclass was the soul-distorting legacy of 350 years of collaborating with the massmurdering thieves, trampling oppressors and rapist alien colonizers against their own countrywo/men…

{vii}

THE PROBLEM WITH RIZAL IS THAT HE WAS THEORETICALLY OBTUSE, POLITICALLY REACTIONARY, AND MORALLY INCOMPETENT…

"JV AYSON:--What did 'Noli' and 'Fili' suggest about the grim conditions of the Filipino masses and the chronic ills of Philippine society?

"PROF. SAN JUAN:- Practically all the Propagandistas and those who joined Rizal's Liga, like Bonifacio, Mabini, and others, confessed their debt to Rizal's writings, in particular the two novels. They conform to the realist convention in drawing typical/exemplary situations and characters that compress the urgent problems of the time. In doing so, they incited and agitated readers. They rendered lived experience in its stark ferocity—feudal exploitation, abuse of power, etc., but they also comically distanced it so that people can act to alter and change them. They performed the function of conveying truth but also of how to transform life in accord with libertarian principles and democratic ideals. The generation of 1896 was a product of Rizal's agitprop intelligence."

1.0.) "Practically all the Propagandistas and those who joined Rizal's Liga, like Bonifacio and Mabini, and others, confessed their debt to Rizal's writings, in particular the two novels."

We have already exposed in a previous reply the stupidity that produced this sentence. And it is the stupidity or the simple inability to think and to be intellectually honest, the same as that syndrome which is responsible for the entire output of the textbook tradition, for all the historians who ever wrote anything on this subject belong to this textbook tradition and all of them have said and repeated this same sentence. This also is thus E. San Juan's stupidity. They all assume, as E San Juan does in this sentence, some or all of the following: that in his writings and other political activities and actuations 1.) Rizal was NOT a counterrevolutionary traitor, or 2.) that he was in fact a secret revolutionary, or 3) a reluctant revolutionary, or 4.) a revolutionary waiting for the proper time, or that 5.) the objective effect of his writings, especially the novels, was to recruit all the Filipinos who read them into the Revolution.

1.1.) Practically all the Propagandistas became Propagandistas or were affirmed and fortified in their being Propagandistas because they read Rizal (and we may add, Del Pilar, Jaena,

Blumentritt, Antonio Luna...). And they did acknowledge zealously and repeatedly this indebtedness of theirs to him. The only problem is, those Propagandistas were by definition and actuation and effect, rabid anti-and-counter-revolutionaries and were made so precisely by their reading of Rizal's actually purely anti-and-counter-revolutionary works—and especially the NOLI and FILI. And how else indeed when what they were, with Rizal as their acknowledged leader, propagandizing for was ASSIMILATIONISM:--the Philippines as a province of Spain, representation to the Spanish Cortes, expulsion of the friars, the erasure and dissolution of what there was of a Filipino nation by having it gobbled-up and assimilated by Spain, and hence the pre-emption of the very possibility of a free and independent Filipino nation by preventing its only true foundation from happening, namely the Revolution. And that is why it is not merely stupid but insane, yes insanely stupid but also massmurderously so, to call Rizal and those ilustrado propagandistas nationalists, let alone revolutionaries.

1.2. As it turned out, ASSIMILATIONISM as counterrevolutionary ideology was so effective that, and thanks largely to the charismatic leadership of Jose Rizal, the brown Spanish counterrevolutionary hero and defender of Spanish colonialism (he deserved for the life-and-death effort a huge monument in Madrid!), Rizal was able through it to convince practically the whole native colonial middleclass to fear, hate, oppose and betray the Revolution. We don't even have to prove this. For when the Revolution after four years of underground recruitment and organizing and at a point when it was already archipelagic in scope, was exposed on August 19, 1896 by Fr. Mariano Gil, and the Katipuneros were forced to fight to defend themselves, they were practically without guns and bullets; they faced the cannons, remingtons, and mausers of the enemy with bows and arrows, buho spears, boloes, and as few as four or five guns to a battalion... And the only reason for this was this: thanks to Rizal's counterrevolutionary assimilationist campaigning, the native rich from whom alone the money to buy arms could have come, boycotted the Revolution. Andres Bonifacio understood this very well, and that was why, although angrily refused many times by Rizal, he persisted to the very end to recruit Rizal, even offering him the Katipunan leadership:--for he knew that if anyone could recruit into the Revolution the colonial middleclass he so solidly because assimilationistically alienated from it, it was their stupendous idol Dr. Jose P. Rizal himself. Snubbed by Rizal thus, Bonifacio had had to resort to the trick of using Rizal's name and picture in the Katipunan initiation rites coupled with tall stories of his patriotism to make it appear that he was the Revolution's true if secret leader. Thus did Bonifacio invent the Filipino hero called Jose Rizal. And thus did it happen that the Katipuneros themselves whom he offered to genocidally massacre "in order to suppress the Revolution" in his infamous and unique in the entire history of the world letter of betrayal to Governor General Blanco, had come to heartrendingly believe THAT BIG FAT WORM OF A LIE. And thus did it happen too that right after Rizal's death, and with the same purpose in view, Bonifacio translated Rizal's final act of dishonesty and opportunism, his MI ULTIMO ADIOS, into Tagalog in which he attempted in the second stanza to sneak a ride on the chariot of history by insinuating an unspeakably shameless last ditch approval of the Revolution, offering his rancid blood even to, by daubing them with it, make the rays of his country's redemption daw, shinier...Nang wala na siyang maaaring gawin kundi bumulagtang isang matapat at kailanma'y hindi nagtaksil sa tangina niyang Inang Espanya nya ay bigla na lang niyang ihahandog sa bayan daw niya (na alin? aling bayan?) ang bulok niya at malansang dugong kahit dengueng lamok ay tatanggihang simsimin... At si E San Juan ay parang miriting miriting halos magkandataeng unggoy na nagtatatalon, at siyang nagsabi naang kra kra kra, kra kra kra, at siyang nagsabi naang kra kra kra, kra kra kra...

1.2.1. In that unique in all the history of the world letter of betrayal which E. San Juan did not even seem to know anything about, ah the poor detrimental idiot!, Rizal "unconditionally offered not alone my life, BUT EVEN MY NAME, and everything I can do, for them to use in the manner they deem best in order to suppress the revolution". Bonifacio and company without his permission, and indeed against his execrating refusal, used that same NAME of his "as a battlecry", and Rizal upon learning of it cursed them as savages and criminals and absurd and uncouth semi-humans unfit to govern themselves and therefore unfit to be free and therefore unfit to be human and therefore not yet human...Tanginang basag na cultural racist na kalambang yan!

2.0.—"They", the novels, "conform to the realist convention in drawing typical/exemplary situations and characters that compress the urgent problems of the time. In doing so, they incited and agitated the readers." That may be so; however, the problem with Rizal was his theoretical intelligence itself, his social-historical-political-moral grasp of the colonial conjuncture, specifically of the critical life and death issues and imminent confrontations which defined his and Bonifacio's present as a revolutionary situation. The problem with Rizal was that he was theoretically stupid, politically reactionary and morally obtuse; the problem with Rizal was that he was a sonovabitch mental colony who mindlessly, bluntly, crudely, and truculently equated patriotism with the erasure of his native patria in its assimilation into the Spanish political body as an overseas province of Spain...

Chapter 15

EXCHANGES WITH FLORO QUIBUYEN'S PUPILS TRIGGERED BY MY ARTICLE

"RIZAL'S MISSION TO KILL ANDRES BONIFACIO AND PUT DOWN THE REVOLUTION'

TO MY FB FRIENDS: Please read/reread the abovenamed article which I posted here 2 days ago, for a fuller appreciation and more bountiful enjoyment of the following exchanges. Mr. Dencio Yuson is a faithful replica of the latest congelation of pigly reasoning and idiot logic assembled in the book A NATION ABORTED by Floro Quibuyen. To clarify and defend my argument, I have interspersed explicatory remarks here and there.

Here first of all is the infamous *DECEMBER 15, 1896 FORT SANTIAGO MANIFESTO*

"Countrymen: On my return from Spain, I learned that my name had been in use among some who were in arms, as a war cry. The news came as a painful surprise, but, believing it already closed, I kept silent about an incident which I considered irremediable. Now I notice indications of the disturbances continuing, and if any still, in good or bad faith, are availing themselves of my name, to stop this abuse and undeceive the unwary, I hasten to address you these lines that the truth may be known.

"From the very beginning, when I first learned of what was being planned, I opposed it, fought it, and demonstrated its absolute impossibility. This is the fact and witnesses to my words are now living. I was convinced that the scheme was utterly absurd and, what was worse, would bring great sufferings. I did even more. When, later, against my advice, the movement materialized, of my own accord, I offered, not alone my good offices but my very life, and even my name, to be used in whatever way they might deem best towards stifling the rebellion; for, convinced of the ills which it would bring, I would have considered myself fortunate if, at any sacrifice, I could prevent such useless misfortunes. This, equally, is of record.

"My countrymen, I have given proofs that I am one most anxious for the liberties of our country, and I am still desirous of them. But I place as a prior condition the education of the people, that by means of instruction and industry, our country may have an individuality of its own, and make itself worthy of liberties. I have recommended in my writings study and civic virtues, without which there is no redemption. I have written likewise (and I repeat my words) that reforms, to be beneficial, must come from above, for those that come from below are irregular and insecure. Holding these ideas, I cannot do less than condemn, and I do condemn, this savage and absurd uprising plotted behind my back, which dishonours us Filipinos, and discredits those who would plead our cause. I abhor its criminal methods and disclaim any part in it, pitying from the bottom of my heart the unwary who have been deceived.

"Return then to your homes, and may God pardon those who have worked in bad faith!

Signed: Jose Rizal

Fort Santiago, December 15, 1896"

COMMENTS

Dencio Yuson:-- The mere fact that the Spaniards did not see fit to publish Rizal's manifesto denouncing the Revolution is proof enough that to the eyes of the Spaniards such manifesto is worthless.

Domingo C. de Guzman: What kind of logic are you using, Mr. Dencio Yuson?

Dencio Yuson:-- The 'common sense' kind. I just placed Rizal's manifesto in the context of the time and place it was written and the fact that the Spaniards found it worthless... The Judge Advocate General refused to publish the Manifesto, which would surely have been read by the revolutionaries, because Rizal (and here Dencio Yuson quotes Judge Advocate General Nicolas dela Pena himself in his argument recommending to the Court, but actually to the Gov. Gen. Polavieja who was deciding everything and had already decided, even before the trial, to convict Rizal) "limits himself to condemning the present rebellious movement as premature and because he considers its success impossible at this time, but suggesting between the lines that the independence dreamed of can be achieved ... For Rizal it is a question of opportunity, not of principles or objectives. His manifesto can be condensed into these words: 'Faced with the proofs of defeat, lay down your arms, my countrymen; I shall lead you to the Promised Land on a later day'." (Guerrero's translation)

REMARK 1: This is exactly Floro Quibuyen's argument, and as dishonestly quoted thus by Mr. Dencio Yuson here, it, among other things, has succeeded to confuse Hill Roberts who in the comments section later declares that she no longer knows what to think of the whole thing. The Judge Advocate General said so; *does that then mean that that was so or that that must be so*? This strange argument and looseminded reasoning should first of all be referred to the document itself, the December 15 Manifesto which is actually a mere half-page in length: *read, reread*, the Manifesto to find out if what the Judge Advocate General was saying was true, and with the latter, all those other things Quibuyen, and here Mr. Dencio Yuson, assert of it, namely that 1.) Rizal did not categorically and in principle reject the Revolution there; 2.) that the Manifesto was even insidiously agitating for revolution so that it would have been dangerous for the Spaniards if they allowed the Katipuneros to read it; 3.) that there was any such thing there as subtle suggestions between the lines that "the independence dreamed of can be achieved", rather than the exact contrary, namely, that it was, as Rizal himself brutally declared it there, "impossible", "savage", "criminal", and "absurd"; 4.) that, as implied in the latter phrase, Rizal ever dreamed of an independent Philippines at all, instead of his assimilationist counterrevolutionary "the Philippines as a province of Spain", and, as in his *The Philippines as a Spanish Colony* (in *Rizal's Political and Historical Writings*, NHI 2007, pp 355 et seq.), "the Philippines as a Spanish colony"—"*forever*". Now then we say in the face of the document itself that all the foregoing four points are false, nay, blatantly so—a thing which any reader of average intelligence will without fail be compelled by logic and direct evidence to realize and acknowledge. This means that, in the face of the Manifesto, the Judge Advocate General *was blatantly lying* and, in the face of the Manifesto, that Quibuyen—and here Yuson—are blatant, conscienceless liars. And this *must be* the reason why in his discussion of this wrangle about what he claims to be the revolutionariness of the Manifesto as against Constantino's claim that Rizal rejected the Revolution there, Quibuyen very conveniently *failed* to quote, let alone cite in toto, the Manifesto! For, with the Manifesto there, it would be simply impossible for any reader of average intelligence not to see at once that all the sentences of the Manifesto taken singly and in combination as the entire Manifesto directly and brutally contradict all of the above claims made of it by Quibuyen and the Judge Advocate General. That the latter did lie about the reasons why the Court Martial decided not to publish the Manifesto and have the Katipuneros read it could seem strange at first, but this seeming strangeness is not a reason why those reasons must be true. The honest and reasonably intelligent researcher, let alone historian, should instead ask in the face of this seemingly strange thing, why the Judge Advocate General should be prompted to propound so blatant a lie. As for Quibuyen, well, my hunch is that he is very probably a congenital liar…

Domingo C. de Guzman:-- Dencio Yuson At naniwala ka naman sa kinowt mong Kastila? Bakit di mo basahin yung Manifesto at magpasiya ka nang buong katapatan kung ano ang talagang nakalagay doon? Pero, bago yan, ang dapat mong urirating mabuti at sagutin ay hindi ang Manifesto kundi yung sulat ni Rizal ng "unconditional" na paghahandog ng buhay niya, ng pangalan niya, ng lahat ng kaya niyang gawin, 'UPANG SUGPUIN ANG REBOLUSYON". Bakit nilihisan mo ang usapin tungkol sa dokumentong ito? Dahil walang sagot sa katotohanan ng katraidurang walang katulad ni Rizal, na ang PRIMA FACIE evidence ay ang sulat na ito. In other words, dishonest ka at burak din ang intellectual conscience mo, kung meron man. Sa harap ng katotohanan ng sulat ng "unconditional" na pagtatraidor na ito, ay walang magagawa ang sino mang magtatangka pang ipagtanggol ang malababoy na taong itong Jose Rizal ang pangalan kundi kwestiyunin ang authenticity at reality ng sulat na ito. Kasi, kung totoo ang sulat na ito ay wala nang dapat pang pagusapan sa walang katulad na kriminalidad at EVIL ni Rizal. At walang dudang kaya mo iniwasang magbanggit ng kahit ano tungkol dito ay dahil alam mong wala ngang sagot ng pagtatanggol kay Rizal sa harap ng dokumentong ito. Burak ang intellectual conscience mo kung meron man, kaya iniwasan mong harapin, at sagutin, ang dokumentong ito. Ito rin syempre ang dahilan kung bakit ang amo mong si Floro Quibuyen, ay ni hindi napansing hindi niya pala napansin ang tungkol sa sulat na ito, at tulad ng ibinibintang mo sa akin na kinopyahan ko kamo na si Constantino, ay nag-concentrate lamang sa Manifesto na ni hindi niya *nakayanang* iprisinta ang mga letra sa dapat at matapat na lugar sa libro niya!. At magiging comprehensively annihilative ang epekto ng sulat na ito kapag nakita na at natanggap na ang katotohanang lahat ng sinulat ni Rizal at lahat ng ginawa ni Rizal ay punong-puno ng pagkatakot, pagkamuhi, pagkondena at pagalimura sa rebolusyon at kung gayon ay sa sambayanang Pilipino; na sa liwanag nito ay makikita agad na wala naman palang dapat na ibang asahang gagawin si Rizal sa gayong pagkakataon (noong Agosto 19 hanggang 24, 1892, nang magdiskubre ni Fr. Mariano Gil ang Katipunan) kundi *ang paghahandog ng ganoong handog ng buhay, pangalan, at lahat lahat niya upang sugpuin ang Rebolusyon.*

Tungkol naman sa Manifesto kung saan buong katapangan ng hiya o kawalan ng hiya na ipinagmagaling pa niya sa buong mundo ang walang katulad sa kasaysayan ng buong mundong katraidurang ito. Balbal ang pangangatwirang namana mo kay Quibuyen na *dahil hindi ipinublish ng Court Martial ang Manifesto* ay *therefore* pagpapatunay ito na hindi ito kontrarebolusyon at kung gayon ay "worthless" bilang ebidensiya ng pagpanig ni Rizal sa Inang Espanya niya at ng katraiduran sa Inang Bayan niyang Pilipinas. In fact, napakatindi at garapal ang pagka-kontrarebolusyon ng Manifesto at mamaya lang ay uulitin natin ang nasabi na natin sa itaas tungkol dito. Na kaya naman ang sino mang may nalalabi pang isip ay hindi makakapaniwala sa sinabi ng Judge Advocate General na Kastila na dahilan kung bakit hindi na ito dapat pang mapublish at maipamahagi sa mga Pilipino.

Sapagkat talamak nga ang pagkakontrebolusyon ng Manifesto, natural lang na magustuhang ipublish at ipakalat ito ng mga Kastila, at nakakaintriga naman talaga na hindi nila ito ginawa. Pero dahil gunggong lang at sinungaling ang magsasabing hindi ito talamak na kontrarebolusyon, hindi maaaring ang motibo ng mga Kastila sa hindi nila pagpapapublish at pagbalewala nila sa Manifesto ay *dahil hindi ito kontrarebolusyon at bagkus ay pro-rebolusyon pa*: hindi naman siguro sagad na illiterate at marahil ay semi-illiterate lang si Mr.Dencio Yuson, kaya imposible niyang mabasa ang sinasabi ng Kastilang Judge Advocate General na kinowt niya sa Manifesto. Ang kalaykay ay kalaykay at ang kabayo ay kabayo, at tangina ka, wag mo kaming gaguhing pilit paniwalaing pala ito o kambing. Eh ano kung ganon ang totoong dahilan, motibo, kung bakit ayaw itong ipublish ng mga Kastila? *Obvious dapat ito sa sinomang matapat na nagimbestiga at nakakita sa katotohanan ng sulat ng "unconditional" na paghahandog na naturan*:--kaya nagkukumahog si Rizal na sulatin ang Manifesto at ibulgar dito ang tungkol sa pagkasulat niya kay Blanco ng sulat na iyon ng *unconditional* offering, at kasama ang nauna nang December 12, Data For My Defense, ay dahil gusto niyang ipatawag ng Korte si Gov. Gen. Blanco na tumestigo *dala ang naturang sulat*!!! Na kung nangyari iyon ay *tiyak, abswelto si Rizal at tatanghalin pang bayaning Kastila kahit medyo sunog at kamukha ni Manny Pacquiao*!!! Kung ipinublish nila ang Manifesto, tiyak makakarating ito sa mga dyaryo sa Madrid at mag-gegenerate ito ng political pressure na sapilitang patestiguhin si Blanco *dala ang sulat*. At maaabswelto si Rizal—at ito ang ayaw na ayaw mangyari ng Korte, *na maabswelto si Rizal*!!! And so, sa kasamaang palad, hindi na nga nakatestigo si Blanco, una dahil *ayaw nga siyang patestiguhin ng korte*; idagdag pa rito na noong December 13 ay biglang dumating na sa Maynila si Polavieja na sa utos ng Madrid government ay papalit agad-agad kay Blanco. Samantala, nagmamadali na si Polavieja na mabitay si Rizal kaya *kahit napakalakas ng ebidensiyang hindi lang walang kakasakasalanan si Rizal sa ibinibintang na rebelyon, kundi prima facie at absolute ang lakas ng mga ebidensiyang ginawa ni Rizal ang lahat, at nakahanda siyang magpakamatay upang sugpuin ang rebolusyon at tanghalin siyang national hero ng Inang Espanya niya,* ay agad nang pinirmahan ang death sentence. Gusto niyang sampulan ang isang ito. Anyway, basahin mo yung huling sulat ni Rizal kina Paciano at

Blumentritt (both of them written in the afternoon of Dec 29) para makita mong hinding hindi kayang tanggapin ni Rizal na siya ay isang rebelde at nagtaksil sa p.....INA niyang Espanya.
Like · Reply · 11 hrs

Dencio Yuson:-- One must take in consideration the Spaniards view for the reason that the Revolution was against them. That they did not publish it to stop the Revolution given Rizal's so-called influence, that its publication can stop the Revolution already speaks volumes to the worth of this document as in worthless. Now again that is a historical fact and documented. With regards to Rizal's letter to Blumentritt and Paciano of course he was telling the truth that he is not guilty of that particular rebellion but no were in that private letters will you read his condemning the Revolution like in manifesto. Significant also that Josephine Bracken and Paciano Rizal joined the Revolution after his execution. Let us refrain from cursing. (*sic*)

Domingo C. de Guzman:-- Rizal wrote it and sought avidly to have it published and distributed to the Katipuneros and the people in general. What does the writing of it say about your hero, then? Whether it was published or burned at once by the Spaniards is irrelevant to the question at hand. Anyway, what you just said has been hundreds of times said by desperate Rizalists like you who must not be able to think logically in order to save this rotten human being, Rizal. Moreover, it is not the Manifesto that is really spotlighted here but *the letter of unconditional offer of Rizal's life, name, and everything he could do for the Spaniards to use them "in the manner they deem most fit to suppress the rebellion"*...Rizal was merely reporting this unspeakable treason to the whole world in the Manifesto. Direct your response to this document if you are honest enough.

Dencio Yuson:-- And again the Spaniards rejected it, plain and simple, to their eyes it is a worthless document. What ever your modern interpretation of this document, historical fact is the Spaniards find it worthless, unfit for publication.

Domingo C. de Guzman:--You mean *the Letter of Unconditional Offer*? You mean to say, Dencio Yuson, that

Gov. Gen. Ramon Blanco to whom he made the *offer* to die to suppress the revolution, did not accept it and thought it better instead to go on sending this *idiot pig Rizal* to Cuba to help the Spanish Army there *kill as many Cuban Katipuneros as possible* and suppress the revolution there? That is to say, Blanco decided that Rizal would be more useful as a *Spanish international counterrevolutionary in Cuba* than a counterrevolutionary agent here in the Philippines? And that Blanco decided that way cancelled the *treason, the infamy, the only in the Philippines and only by this Filipino "national hero" criminality of the letter, of the act of absolute betrayal*?

Dencio Yuson:-- Rizal went to Cuba as a Doctor and as a Doctor Rizal will treat both Spaniards and Cubans because of his oath as physician. Please keep this polite as much as possible.

Domingo C. de Guzman:-- Dencio Yuson are you really that simpleminded? Ano yan, teleserye? And even your simplemindedness or downright mindlessness is *beside* the point.

Dencio Yuson:-- Well it is historical fact that Rizal went to Cuba as a Doctor, as a healer. Not as a soldier for Spain. Doctors by their oath treats and heals every one. You can deal with this historical fact is up to you. Again let us keep this polite, civil and avoid Ad Hominems.

Domingo C. de Guzman:-- Dencio Yuson You are misinformed, Rizal never went to Cuba. Ganyan ka katanga. At tigilan mu yang kapupuna ng ad hominem, ikaw mismo ay isang ad hominem--you are an argument against humanity. Kung makikialam ka, siguruhin mong meron kang alam. Tandaan mo lang na lahat ng pinagsasasabi mo rito ay pag-ulit lang sa 120 years nang inuulit-ulit ng textbook tradition, kaya wag kang mayabang. Basahin mo yung mga dokumentong ipiniprinsinta ko, at wag kang magsisinungaling sa sinasabi ng mga ito sa commonsense mo--oo, commonsense lang. Kailangan lang honest ka, at may commonsense. At tatandaan mo, tayong lahat ay na-brainwashed nang mahigit isang siglo tungkol dito. Na kaya nga kinakailangan ang pagharap ng mga dokumento ngayon at honest commonsense na pagbasa sa mga ito at kaakibat nito, ng mga pangyayari. Halimbawa: Bakit after four years wala pang baril at bala ang Katipunan? Sagot: Kasi, hindi sumama ang mayayamang Pilipinong tulad nina Rizal, Del Pilar, Jaena, sa Rebolusyon, kaya hayun, walang pondo para sa baril at bala. *Sino ang may kagagawan nito*? Si Rizal at iba pa niyang kasamahan sa Propaganda Movement na humimok sa mga mayayamang Pilipino na huwag sumama at bagkus ipagkanulo pa ang Rebolusyon *tulad ng aktibong ginawa ni Rizal mismo sa paghahandog niya ng buhay niya, pangalan niya, at lahat lahat upang sugpuin ang rebolusyon*, etc. Sinasabi mong hindi guilty si Rizal ng treason dahil hindi naman tinanggap ni Blanco ang paghahandog niya ng buhay, pangalan at lahat ng kaya niyang gawin upang sugpuin ang Rebolusyon? *NAPAKAGAGO MO NAMAN YATA*? Gago, kasi dishonest, kasi, hindi ako naniniwalang naniniwala kang dahil diyan ay hindi nga guilty ng walang kasing karumaldumal na krimen si Rizal na pagtatraidor sa Bayan at sa Rebolusyon, tangina mu.

Dencio Yuson:-- We have a saying that, "The water is sweetest at it's source." The Katipuneros, those who actually fought during the Revolution against both the Spaniards and Americans revere the memory of Rizal that too is historical fact. And what did they think of Rizal? We can have our choice of testimonies from Katipuneros and revolutionists. Here is one from someone who was proudly both. Writing in 1899, the Katipunero known as Matatag (Antonio Guevara) recalled a day at the Luneta in January 1898, when the people were celebrating the phony peace of Biak-na-bato. “At that time, while seated on one of the granite benches along the promenade at the Luneta, I pointed out the spot where our distinguished countryman, the hero and unfortunate Dr. Jose Rizal, was executed by the firing squad. I told Pedro Guevara, Teodoro Arquiza, and others from the town of Magdalena, who were with me: ‘There, my friends, is the place where our hero fell, irrigating that soil with his precious blood in defense of our beloved fatherland. May his life serve as a model for us. Let us pray for his eternal rest, and let us beseech God to give us many doctors such as Sr. Jose Rizal whenever we find ourselves wanting, in order that we shall gain our coveted independence.’” (from the Corpuz translation)

Domingo C. de Guzman:-- *AH, BUT I HAVE PROMISED MYSELF TO BE REALLY REALLY PATIENT*...If it is true, as we have documented and demonstrated that Rizal was the supertraitor that he was in all his writings and in all his deeds, then this testimony *must either be spurious or wrong or a lie*. Supposing this testimony to be unspurious, does it erase the fact that Rizal was the charismatic leader of the counterrevolutionary Assimilationist Propaganda Movement that convinced the entire colonial middleclass to boycott and actively betray--as Rizal himself most heinously did--the Revolution? But I have already demonstrated the genocidal repercussions of this counterrevolutionary movement here and elsewhere:--the fact that already archipelagic after four years of recruitment, the Revolution was still without guns and bullets when they were forced to face the enemy on August 29, 1896 *(and they had to pit their buho spears, bows and arrows, bolos, against the cannons, the remingtons and mausers of the enemy, and they died like chicken in the initial battles)*, because, of course, the rich Filipinos were not there to contribute the money to buy arms, thanks to Rizal and his counterrevolutionary propagandizing...etc., including all the betrayals and the delays which made possible the sale of the Revolution at Biyak na Bato by Aguinaldo, and the American invasion (which would never have happened had we been able to liberate ourselves from Spain ten or seven or five years earlier, before the Spanish-American War flared up) which enabled the Americans to murder some two million Filipinos (Si Rizal din ang may pinakamalaking responsibilidad sa pagpatay ng 2 milyong Pilipinong iyan!!!), and the escalation of the culture of corruption whose multicenturial bearers were precisely Rizal and the ilustrados and generally the colonial middleclass colonial collaborators who were marrows-deep corrupt precisely because they were colonial collaborators), whilst that culture of corruption could have been arrested right in the souls of its very bearers, Rizal and company, had they theorized and organized and led the Revolution *instead of rejecting and betraying it*, which rejection and betrayal served directly to geometrically escalate, again in their very souls this culture of corruption, for this first betrayal led automatically to the second where the same rich native counterrevolutionaries who were all Rizal's disciples betrayed it to the Americans, and then the third, where the same Rizalistas betrayed it to the Japanese; just as they would have been ennobled and made truly great human beings and heroes had they done the former:--think of Rizal's and the local ilustrados' counterparts in America, Simon Bolivar and company, who *did exactly the opposite*, founding their Revolution and liberating their countries in 6 years from 1820 to 26.... In a word, we have directly to trace the fount and origin of this world famous culture of corruption to Rizal too and his powerful leadership of the ilustrado counterrevolutionary movement. Because after all the foreigners were out, this Rizalian-Counterrevolutionary class once more became this country's ruling class in 1946; which is to say that *we are the most corrupt country in the world because we have the most corrupt ruling class in the world--thanks mightily to Jose Rizal.* But I have fleshed out these demonstrations complete with documents in my four books and in my columns in my timeline here, and right here in this article, if only such readers like you could have the patience and the honesty to read--for it does not require any above-average intelligence to grasp the thing in this fully scientific and logical-analytical demonstration....

These then were the facts, fully documented for the first time, of Rizal's and the ilustrados' betrayal of the Revolution and the genocidal repercussions of this betrayal. And in the light of these, instead of insisting on the textbook tradition's stock lies, you have to explain how there can be scattered testimonies and wild stories like those you cited, and explain them therefore as lies and fabrications, for they contradict the facts and *all* the documents. In short, what has to be explained is why a few Filipinos of the time could write such testimonies and make such lying claims:--for, in the light of the documents, those contemporaries of the Revolution who made such pronouncements were indeed *few--very few*!!! Now, in my four books and in this FB column, and even here, in this article, I have already shown that it was in fact Bonifacio who was mainly responsible for the *MYTH* of Rizal's being a revolutionary, a patriot, a hero; and he did it despite his better knowledge, for he was rejected at least thrice in his offers to Rizal to join and lead the Revolution, and would thus know best that indeed Rizal was absolutely adamantly set against it. And the explanation is this: Andres Bonifacio knew from the very start that the Revolution mortally needed not only the support but the active leadership of the colonial middleclass; and he knew also that the Propaganda Movement was--*of course*!, how else?--*counterrevolutionary* (otherwise, he would simply have JOINED it if he wanted revolution!!!). Knowing that Rizal was its charismatic leader, he first gambled on the delusion of being able to convince him to join the Revolution and even lead it--hence the three offers, and the three rejections (we have demonstrated right here that Bonifacio first presented the Revolution to Rizal between June 26 and July 2, 1892, but that Rizal, as he put it, "rejected it, fought it, and demonstrated its absolute impossibility" etc...). Rebuffed thus, Bonifacio, wanting no doubt to entice the other native rich Filipinos to join him, then decided to use Rizal's name in recruiting, and even went so far as to trick the counterrevolutionary Mabini, Franco, and the other ilustrado leaders and members of the defunct LIGA in in joining the move to revive it: Mabini and company later on discovered the trick and expelled Bonifacio and his Katipunan comrades. When Bonifacio sent the *liar extraordinaire* Pio Valenzuela to Dapitan to convince Rizal to join the KKK and even lead it, one of the things he instructed him to do was to tell him that the KKK had been using his name, and to alert him therefore that should it be discovered, he, Rizal would surely be implicated. Again, of course, Rizal rejected the offer and was able instead to convince Valenzuela to abandon and betray the Revolution (see above). Later on, in the Manifesto, Rizal who offered "not alone my life, but even my very *name*, and everything I could do, for them to use in the manner they deem fit to suppress the rebellion", would excoriate and curse and declare as backstabbing criminals Andres Bonifacio and company for *using that name of his without his permission*!!! And that then was how the *legend* originated and got cultivated about the great revolutionariness and heroism of this pig. It was also for the same purpose and with the same intent that Bonifacio translated the Ultimo Adios into Tagalog--for use in the possible recruitment of the rich natives...Meanwhile, *si Rizal mismo, sa lahat ng kanyang sinulat, sinabi, ginawa at hindi ginawa, ang testigo na ang sinasabi ng mga tanga at dishonest na historians na tulad ng salahulang si Quibuyen, ng ututing si Corpuz, etc. ay mitolohiya nga, na pinalobo ng mga walang konsiyensiya at tangang mga historians daw na ito.* Biktima ka nila Dencio Yuson, kawawa ka naman...

Dencio Yuson:-- It simply means to the Katipuneros and Revolutionaries like those mentioned above and to include

Artemio Ricarte, Santiago Alvarez and one can also add Herminigildo Cruz the labor leader who wrote 'Kartilyang Makabayan' have a very different opinion of Rizal than you . I prefer the views of the Katipuneros themselves, after all they are the actual ones who fought in the Revolution.

Pilosopo Tasyo:-- Dencio Yuson thank you po sir,...im learning from you,.. at the end of the day its better like what Dr. Floro Quibuyen in his book A Nation Aborted mentioned and i will paraphrase we should see the Revolution and the events of their times using their lenses and not based solely on our interpretation,.. and reading your exchanged of opinions its inspiring how you stayed cool,.. cooler minds prevails indeed,...

Dencio Yuson:-- Pilosopo thank you. I also read Quibuyens 'A Nation Aborted, Rizal and the American hegemony.'

Dencio Yuson:-- Thank you for your patience. But at the end of the day what you have is still a historical interpretation and sad to say not new. Renato Constantino did it first. Another historical fact is the Katipuneros and Revolutionaries did not subscribe to this Marxists historical framework you are propagating. What is most interesting is Rizal was also influential in Asian and Burmese Nationalism. Are the Indonesian, Malaysian and Burmese Nationalists also guilty of 'Venerating Rizal without understanding?" like the Katipuneros pictured below, bringing the 'alleged' bones of Bonifacio to the Rizal monument for equal veneration:

Domingo C. de Guzman:-- Dencio Yuson Well. I have done my bit with recalcitrant- repeater-of-120- years-of-lies you, and I have to stop here. But please do not again accuse me of copying from Constantino or anyone else. You don't know what you're saying...About being cool, polite, no one can be more than that than a taong grasa who as such does not care about absolutely anything. You don't care at all *because you don't know* and are so stupid to (at this moment) *be able to know*: kailangan kang iuntog ng 120 times sa pader. Kalmante ka dahil ang kakampi mo at ipinagtatanggol ay ang estado, ang establishment, ang status quo, ang gobyerno, ang ruling class, na sa pamamagitan ng kultura ng korupsyong dala-dala nina Rizal at mga katulad niya ngayon sa ruling class ay pumapatay ng mga 2 hanggang tatlong libong bata sa Pilipinas araw araw sa pamamagitan ng paghihikahos na syempre likha nila, ninyo nina Rizal, Quibuyen, Corpuz, at ruling class...

Dencio Yuson:-- Thank Sir for this interesting exchange. And I am sorry if I gave the impression that you are copying from Constantino.

Domingo C. de Guzman:-- You're a liar, a tergiversant one: you said I copied, you did not merely give that impression!...

Domingo C. de Guzman:-- Dencio Yuson As for Quibuyen, read my complete, annihilative refutation of this charlatan's book, A NATION ABORTED, in my 2013 book, ANDRES BONIFACIO/Matakot sa Kasaysayan, Preface.

Domingo C. de Guzman:-- Tungkol sa impluwensiya diumano ni Rizal sa mga Asian nationalists—tsismis yan and beside the point. If it shows anything, they were also fooled by this lying historiography.

Dencio Yuson:-- Hindi ko na kasalanan kung hindi mo maintidihan ang sinabi ko. Or ayaw mo lamang intindihin. Just deal with the fact that Rizal was revered by the Katipuneros and fellow Asian after all that is already a matter of historical record. As for Sukarno and the rest for bring tsismoso, it says a lot about your state of mind. And it relevant because this counter revolutionary Rizal was influential to Asians Nationalists.

Domingo C. de Guzman:-- May mga Katipunerong *nabrainwash* din incidentally ni Andres Bonifacio na "i-revere" si Rizal. Pinalobo ito ng mga historians. Hanggang sa lahat na ng Pilipino halos ay ni"revere" na siya. Yan lang ang pwedeng maging conclusion diyan, dahil ang kadakilaan ni Rizal ay hindi totoo ayon mismo kay Rizal, sa lahat ng kanyang sinulat na puro kontrarebolusyon, at sa lahat ng kanyang ginawa na puro kontrarebolusyon. Ginawa ko na nang paulit-ulit ang hamon na ito: Humanap lang kayo ng kahit isang sentence na sinabi ni Rizal tungkol sa rebolusyon na pabor siya sa rebolusyon; humanap lang kayo ng kahit isang sentence na

sinabi ni Rizal tungkol sa rebolusyon na hindi pagalimura at pagsumpa at pagmumura sa rebolusyon--at iharap ninyo dito, sa publiko. Lahat ng Aleman ay naniwalang si Hitler ay manunubos na patriota, at, tulad ni Rizal dito, ay halos diyos na sa kadakilaan at kagalingan. Pero, syempre, gago ka pag kinonclude mo na therefore totoong dakilang manunubos etc. si Hitler. Ang ilusyon ng iba na si Rizal ay dakila at hindi karumaldumal na baboy na traidor ay hindi pruwebang dakila nga siya at hindi baboy na karumaldumal na traidor. Sasabihin mo--at sinabi mo na nga--na opinyon ko lang na traidor siya. Gago ka. Basahin mo muna ang mga dokumento kong ihinarap at ang mga demonstrasyon ko, tulad dito: pag dito sa mga dokumentong ito dito at demonstrasyon ko dito sa artikulo kong mismong ito ay sinabi mo pang opinyon ko lang ang sinasabi ko, at interpretasyon lang na kung gayon ay katimbang ng mga sinasabi ng mga sinasabi mong :"Katipunero" "Asyanong nationalists", etc., na nag-"rerevere" kay Rizal, ay gago ka nga, sinungaling, at tanga. At kung gayon ay hindi na dapat kausapin. HULI SA AKTO SI RIZAL SA MGA DOKUMENTONG ITO.
Like · Reply · 15 mins · Edited

Chapter 16

F. SIONIL JOSE & MARNE KILATES ASK WHY WE ARE SHALLOW?

OR WHY RIZAL'S "MI RETIRO" IS A BAD, A VERY BAD, POEM

OR WHY THE GENERAL SHALLOWNESS OF FILIPINO WRITERS/ INTELLECTUALS HAS TO BE TRACED BACK TO THE INFLUENCE

OF THE FAKE MODEL JOSE RIZAL…

and oh how these idiots who are top honchos in whatever sordid thing they're at have never neglected to make much, in fact infinitely too much, of how the gargoyle from calamba did swivel around at the point of death like a barber's chair to embossom the bullets without their once being caused to pause as by a point of intelligence and wonder how the gargoyle pivoting thus upon the abyss of death like pixilated barber's chair could possibly on the other hand be loyal to his native land and to the revolution or how indeed he could evade being such a vomit of a traitor to his own native land and to the revolution in swivelling so like pixilated barber's chair to embosom the blazing tokens of his undying loyalty to his mother spain and his deathless devotion to the cause of spanish colonialism…ugh ugh ugh gwark gwark puke puke

oh what a puke

{i} This is an off the wall facebook essay…I have referred to this unfinished essay in a mis-repost as a kind of litmus test. Filipino intellectuals in general--measure too of their general smallness and shallowness and banal perversity--are perseverating equivocators, i.e., LIARS. And for this they have to thank Rizal first of all, the arch-liar who kept orating and declaiming his endless love for his native land and people whilst doing everything to preempt and prevent and BETRAY the Revolution (he offered Blanco unconditionally his very life, his name, everything he could do, to be used by the Spaniards "to suppress the rebellion", the pig!), i.e., their liberation from multicenturial colonial enslavement, loving them heartrendingly so as he precipitated them into genocide:--this murky man from Calamba is also the great model of all Filipino politicians. Even McKinley appears to have copied from him in his BENEVOLENT ASSIMILATION PROCLAMATION:--and what better proof do you want of Rizal's and the ilustrados' ASSIMILATIONIST Propaganda Movement's counterrevolutionariness, ha, Schumacher?, ha, Quibuyen? ha Kilates? ha Almario? They are OPPORTUNISTS, invoking opportune friendship and gainful timidity against principles. i.e., in this particular case, against taking a principled position. Their silence will thus condemn them to suffer being themselves--small small small, shallow to protrusion, narrow to rizality, substanceless to the point of inexistence, tenuous they can't even cast a timorous shadow… Is it true that the two poems by Rizal, MI RETIRO and MI ULTIMO ADIOS, translated and holified by Marne Kilates and forming as it were the centerpiece of his recent National Book Award winning volume LYRICAL OBJECTS are great poems? Are they even passable poems? Must they not be very bad because, first of all, lying and opportunist and even macabre, genocide-masking poems? I invite the "critics" who gave Kilates that award to justify their stupid position. And those friends of Kilates who opportunistically take his side, Almario's side, Rizal's side, the Counterrevolution's genocidal side, by being silent...This too is going to be a radical question of poetics...As for Kilates, he knew as early as December 30, 2014 that this confrontation is bound to happen; that fatal day he first posted his translation of MI RETIRO on FB and announced in the intro his translation of MI ULTIMO ADIOS (that other poem of unwordably shameless blood-donating opportunism) too and their imminent publication in the abovementioned volume as exemplars of what he calls LYRICAL OBJECTS. I very naturally considered right then and there his act of translating and publishing those fake poems as extreme provocations aimed directly against me--against my now multivolume project of among other things exposing Rizal and his Counterrevolution and laying therewith the foundations of a genuine, honest-to-goodness, philosophically grounded, critically educated intellectual--literary-philosophical--tradition... I cannot do less than denounce him...

{ii} What was Rizal doing all his 3 years and 3 and a half months in Dapitan when towards the end of that period he wrote this hypocritical, dishonest and mediocre poem called MI RETIRO? And, but, how come Filipino writers like Marne Kilates, Virgilio Almario, a certain Manuud, could at all like it, nay, consider it a great, even a very great, poem?

{iii} Lesson number one: of a poem, a novel, any written work, but most especially a poem, EXISTENTIAL STANCE/SITUATEDNESS IS ALL; Hitler or his queasily rumoured father could be a wizard in stringing words like bright gewgaw, but because his very existence was wrong, anything by him on himself which was not a direct self-condemnation and therefore a disavowal of his wrong existence, can only be a wrong work, a lying, fake work; for exactly the same reason, to praise Hitler or his queasily rumoured father in a poem/novel, is impossible—the purported poem's/novel's existential stance will block the very possibility of the poem/novel...; you cannot celebrate inhumanity, hypocrisy, dishonesty, opportunism, and sheer stupidity, let alone genocidal murder such as Rizal must be held responsible for, in a poem, without destroying the poem...}

{iv} To more clearly grasp what kind of human being, writer, poet, Rizal was when he wrote this poem and which this poem when read in its real existential and historical context exhibits him to be, we have to construct a calendar of events which will reveal to us better than what he said who he was what and who he really was—for Rizal's dishonesty and hypocrisy was so dense as to be wellnigh unconscious. He was a liar (chiefly concerning his heaven hounding avowals of his love for his country and people whom he precipitated into genocide instead, and upon whom he inflicted this hellish culture of corruption which diminishes the humanity of the Filipinos so, apart from murdering through the mass-poverty and criminality it effectuates and perpetuates, some three thousand children everyday) who seemed to have been able to believe his own lie. Nay, he was a lie, a grave one and malevolent, who seemed to have been able in all solemnity to believe himself. Hence this poem, this dishonest, this hypocritical, this fake poem.

Here then is Marne Kilates' translation of Rizal's "Mi Retiro":

(Kilates' prefatory remark) "December 30, 2014 at 7:10 am "Mi Retiro, Rizal's pastoral paean to his place of internal exile, Dapitan, was written in response to his mother's request for him to resume writing poetry. Critics often describe Mi Retiro as superior to, and possibly more significant than, the Valedictory (Ultimo Adios) since it shows Rizal at the height of his literary powers. Antonio G. Manuud (1967), cited by Virgilio S. Almario in his landmark examination of Rizal's poetry, Rizal: Makata (Rizal: Poet; Anvil, 2011), remarks the arrangement of the poem as a 'temporal barcarole', with its "undulatory motion" from past to present to the future and back. While stating early in his essay that Mi Retiro does not make Rizal a Modernist (it is in fact very much Symbolist in the tradition of Baudelaire and Verlaine, as Manuud himself says), Almario characterizes it as a superbly refined Romanticist poem in the best sense of the word. Almario concludes that instead of simply saying that Mi Retiro is "superior to" or "more important than" Ultimo Adios, it must be studied in "tandem with it, to mark two very significant reference points in both the poetry and biography of the

Filipino intellectual and martyr. It is for the same reasons I chose to feature and repost it here on the anniversary of his martyrdom (although I also have my own translation of the Valedictory poem, also in my upcoming book, Lyrical Objects)."

"MY RETREAT
"(to my mother)

{v} How can anyone fail to be shallow and narrow and small small small who, thanks to some one hundred and twenty years of brainwashing and, in Marne Kilates' case,-- wanting in all sincerity to be kind to him here--, against some possible huger and deeper stirrings in himself, one falls into exalting this necessarily mediocre lengthily boring romantical tergiversation?

"By the sweep of beach, of soft, fine sand,
At the foot of mountain wrapped in green,
I planted my humble hut in the shady wood,
Seeking among the boughs a quietude,
The mind's respite, a silence for my pain.

{vi} Not a bad start… October 22, 1895. And at the end of the 14th month the friars would have him shot...The poet is in pain and here silence is his balm; there is some kind of inquietude in him, a remaining turmoil of the mind despite the great distance of space and time imposed now by this exile between him and the scenes of raucous wranglings, petitions, argumentations that was his life as the powerfully convincing leader of the ilustrado counterrevolutionary assimilationist Propaganda Movement which with great success was able to scare the entire native, mestizo and creole colonial middleclass away from the impending Revolution and set them against it, making them boycott and betray it later on, and murder some

2 million Filipinos therewith. The delays (for had Rizal been a better human being, had he been less of a class-interest-determined opportunist, had he been more intelligent, had he been less of a mental colony, had he been a true human being, had he been less obtuse, had he been less stupid, had he been less small, less shallow, less narrow, less pigly, he could have founded the Revolution in the mid- 1880s and could thus have obviated a genocide:--the betrayals, the sell-outs all made well-nigh imperative by his great counterrevolutionary leadership, culminated in the murder of some 2 million Filipinos by the Americans and the complete military and political destruction of the Revolution:--Jose Rizal was chiefly responsible for this genocide, but also for the galloping culture of corruption his successful counterrevolution gave birth to.

{vii} That is to say, these are passable lines until it occurs to you that the quietude he was seeking was 1) a scoundrelly political position in which, as he himself put it in his December 15, 1896 Fort Santiago Manifesto, he, upon first learning from Bonifacio himself about the plan to revolt (this happened between June 26 and July 6, 1892), "rejected it" (for he was asked by Bonifacio to join it), he "fought it", and he "demonstrated its absolute impossibility"; 2.) Rizal had just had a bitter quarrel with Marcelo del Pilar over the financial management of La Solidaridad (Del Pilar was using the Propaganda money--which was of course being contributed by the colonial middleclass which they had thus indoctrinated against the Revolution and into Assimilationist Colonial Conservation—like the Soli was his own "private enterprise" (Rizal's own description of it): Rizal wanted to "nationalize" it—:nationalize what?, why of course the COUNTERREVOLUTION that was the Propaganda Movement; this quarrel escalated into shameful scandal when, mistakenly imagining that Rizal might be going home to found the Revolution, Del Pilar and his hatchetman Eduardo de Lete spoofed him in an article titled ILUSO, which came out in the April 15, 1892 issue of La Solidaridad (the dishonest, stupid, small, shallow shallow shallow government editors of the NHI bilingual edition of La Solidaridad would later on delete the article from both the original Spanish and the English versions); Rizal was furious and he wrote all his ilustrado friends denouncing Del Pilar: he wanted to seek quietude "among the boughs" too and away from that unseemly fracas.

While Rome was burning, Nero was fiddling as deliriously he watched. Infinitely kinder in comparison, infinitely less insane, infinitely less evil must Nero be pronounced! I must have written more than 150 pages on this wretched "patriot's" counterrevolutionary rejection, vituperation, knifing in the back, and abandonment of, and fleeing from the Revolution, and how he three times angrily refused to escape from Dapitan to the possibility of joining the by then already almost four-year-old Revolution-in-the-making, and how with unspeakable shamelessness and evil stupidity he would persist in it to the death as an international counterrevolutionary Spanish colonial doctoral agent in Cuba:—and his last split-second denial of it when, to valedictorily affirm his pure and absolute loyalty to his Mother Spain this gargoyle of dwarfish humanity mightily turned around to face the bullets, for as he himself put it as he pleaded to the Spanish officer of the death squad, only traitors to Mother Spain were shot from behind...(and here we still have to add, because Filipino intellectuals like Kilates and Almario are indeed small small small to the point of nullity and shallow shallow shallow to the point of depthlessness, of superficiality, of near-protrusion:--FOR HOW CAN ONE BE FOR THE REVOLUTION WITHOUT BEING A TRAITOR TO "MOTHER SPAIN"?).

{viii} And oh how these id..ts who are top honchos in whatever sordid thing they're at have never neglected to make much, in fact infinitely much, of how the gargoyle from Calamba did swivel around at the point of death like a barber's chair to embosom the bullets...without their once being caused to pause as by a point of intelligence and wonder how the gargoyle pivoting thus upon the abyss of death like a pixilated barber's chair could possibly on the other hand be loyal to his own native land and to the Revolution, or how indeed he could evade being such a vomit of a traitor to his own native land and to the Revolution, in swiveling so like a barber's chair to embosom the blazing tokens of his undying loyalty to Mother Spain and his deathless devotion to the cause of Spanish Colonialism...ugh ugh ugh gwark gwark puke puke...Oh what the puke!!!

{ix} As for the poet's "pain" for which he pruriently vulgarized and insulted the silence of the injured boughs en-balming it with it, he richly deserved it in the evil of his and his ilustrado confraternity's quarrel with the of course evil friars over the multicenturial colonial loot which these evil pens of pigs dispute. Again, and for the nth time:--Rizal and his ilustrado confraternity were even more reactionary and counterrevolutionary than the friars they had been gleefully and safely attacking through La Solidaridad in the European metropolis and in the two novels, Noli and Fili. If you do not know yet—despite my four volumes and a thousand columns of historiography—that Rizal (and his counterrevolutionary "Indios Bravos") attacked the friars in his two novels and in all his La Solidaridad journalism in order to defend Spanish colonialism against them who were voraciously exposing it to the (to Rizal) horrific danger and horrendous evil of revolution, then of course you haven't read me nor Rizal and are indeed small small small and shallow shallow shallow. And dishonest and opportunist in helping yourself to the shitty fruits of your own brainwashing by admiring and exalting this pigly intellectual from Calamba to the point of holifyingly translating him and making a lying career out of his poetic lies. And some money by the side too. It is never too late, though, as Rilke put it in the ultimate line of his poem THE TORSO OF APOLLO...:--"you must change your life"...And your poetics...

"Its roof is flimsy thatch; its floor, fragile bamboo;
The beams and posts are rough-hewn wood:
Of no great worth, surely, is my rustic shelter;
But upon the eternal mountain's lap it slumbers,
And nights and days are lulled by the crooning sea.

{x} And was he worthy of nature's lullaby thus? Did he not pollute such beauty with his genocidal traitor's obscene presence there? Imagine Hitler in his "father's" stead there. Or even Aguinaldo, such as we now know him to be. Or Marcos, or Gloria Macapagal Arroyo of HELL-O-GARCI infamy…Must not nature itself turn sinister at the presence of such massmurderously evil evil evil evil beings? Whilst in this list, only Hitler his "son" surpasses him in THAT. Yes indeed, for even the pigly massmurderousness of Emilio Aguinaldo was greatly indebted to his counterrevolutionary influence. The great delay of at least ten years he inflicted upon the Revolution made possible Aguinaldo's having anything to do with it at all; for had it commenced ten or 8 or even 7 years earlier Aguinaldo would still have been 12 or thirteen years old, entirely too young to do any harm. Whilst in his MALABAR MANIFESTO (otherwise titled, TO THE BRAVE SONS OF THE PHILIPPINES which the pig Agoncillo cited in his textbook as such, but which, after I have pointed out that it was treason no less, he withdrew in the next editions) Aguinaldo already enumerated Rizal's and the assimilationist counterrevolutionary Propaganda Movement's demands as the remaining and true reasons for his "revolt", such as: 1.) The Philippines as a province of Spain, 2.) representation to the Spanish Cortes, 3.) expulsion of the friars and return of the friar lands expropriated from the rich Filipinos like the Rizal family to their former owners, etc…This was before the final sell-out in November-December 1897 at Biyak na Bato: together with his release of the Spanish soldiers captured in the successful battle of Puray a little later (a battle in which he of course did not participate because it was a real battle and not a tall tale), this manifesto was his shrewd way of communicating to the Spaniards to come to negotiate for the surrender for pay which as we know did materialize in the sell-out called the Pact of Biyak na Bato in which Aguinaldo was paid 800,000 pesos and two pesos per rifle surrendered (they surrendered, according to Aguinaldo himself, "thousands", despite the fact that the "pact" stipulated only a minimum of 700:--thousands, then, and that was for the money of course, but more significantly because they never intended to return to their native land to resume the revolution:--the Americans baited Aguinaldo with, of course, another chance to make trunks of dollars by selling himself another time). And of course, had not Rizal been so successful in preventing the colonial middleclass from joining the Revolution, the ilustrados themselves—with Rizal at their head—would have been, with Bonifacio and Jacinto with them, the founders and leaders of the Revolution so that the semi-illiterate Aguinaldo, apart from being too young, would never have been able to gather enough bravery to insinuate himself into the revolutionary leadership.

"The brimming brook, that in the sylvan shade
Descends among the stones, gently washes it,
Streaming through makeshift pipes of bamboo;
It is the silent night's song and melody,
And crystal nectar to soothe the noonday heat.

{xi) "Sylvan shade"—why not just "forest shade"?

{xii} Nectar—arnibal yan...hooo lagkit...

If the sky is tranquil, the spring flows meekly,
Strumming without cease its unseen zither to me;
But when the rains come, their impetuous torrent
Spills over stones and gullies—raucous, frothing, roiling—
Heaving with a frenetic roar into the sea.

"A dog barking, birds twittering,
And the hoarse calls of the hornbill are all I hear;
No boastful man nor importuning neighbor
Intrude into my mind or disturb my passage;
Just the forest and the sea are all I have near.

{xiii} Again these are passable lines, not so extraordinary, not very commonplace, but commonplace, in some places stickily so—as were the pampered petty-bourgeois social-climbing sentiments of enforced rustication that went with them. I don't remember having comminated such somewhat predictable lines ever. And the petty-bourgeois social climbing sentiments when his country, his LUPANG TINUBUAN, was in the grip of a revolutionary convulsion and his countrymen were preparing to die for the country's freedom?

{xiv) Quite alright then nonetheless, and still quite excusable, although the lines themselves look academic: remember that this was the last decade of that century of anticolonial revolutions that was the 19th century, and he should instead be writing poems like Bonifacio's PAGIBIG SA TINUBUANG LUPA if he were not the pampered petty-bourgeois social climbing opportunist he in his inconquerable greed and invincible obtuseness was...

{xv} Quite alright until by brute force he rather misanthropically boasted of how "no boastful man nor importuning neighbor intrude into (his) mind or disturb (his) passage". Read this with Andres Bonifacio, Emilio Jacinto, Gregoria de Jesus, in mind, across the deadly dangers of the last four years of the underground propagation of the Revolution:--joyful and glorious in being able to seek out as many Filipinos as they could...

"The sea, the sea is all! Its sovereign reach
Brings me atoms from worlds beyond;
Its smile enlivens my limpid mornings;
And when late in the day my faith falters,
Waves of sorrow spill inside my heart.

{xvi} What "faith" is this historical laggard and heinous supertraitor talking about here? Romancing the sea thus, what the puke! "The sea...is all?" He should instead be shouting, "The Revolution is all", "Freedom is all"... The sea is only the sea in the face of the revolutionary situation where to awaken the people is all and to brave death doing so is the only honourable thing to do. And of course it is simply false that the sea has a sovereign reach, it reaches only as far as it reaches. "Brings me atoms from worlds beyond"—he must mean Europe, the colonial pervert! A counterrevolutionary and a bloody traitor's "limpid mornings"—what aesthetic dishonesty this is! And he pretends the sea could smile at him so! As for the "waves of sorrow," can so shallow a man with a conscience so murky be available for any true sorrow?:--remember that this same man would a few months afterwards write a letter to Gov. Gen. Blanco offering him without conditions his life, his name and everything he could do for the Spaniards to use "to suppress the rebellion", and he did it not to save his own neck as narrow and shallow and little little little small small tiny tiny Filipino intellectuals like Randy David and Walden Bello once suggested, for he was then not a prisoner but an honoured guest on board the Spanish warship CASTILLA docked in Manila Bay where he was hiding from the Revolution incommunicado whilst waiting for the next boat to Spain en route to his scandalously evil assignment as a Spanish military doctor and international counterrevolutionary agent in Cuba against the Cuban Katipuneros…And this atrocious emotional masturbator speaks here of waves of such spilling inside his pigly heart, what the puke!...Pukes of sorrow, yes…Or sorrowful pukes…inside his heart.

"At night, what mystery!…Its diaphanous stretch
Sparkling with thousand points of light;
The breeze drifting cool, the firmament brilliant,
The waves whisper to the wind—all ears—
Histories lost in time's dark cloak.

"So it is said of the first morning on earth,
When the sun first set her afire with a kiss:
Creation's multitude emerged from the Nothing,
To populate the deepest chasms and highest peaks
And everywhere the trembling kiss was pressed.

{xvi} And he believes in "Creation!" Whilst Darwin set forth on The Beagle 65 years ago to document its falsity. Such stupidity is never innocent.

"But when the winds rage in the dark of night,
And the waves in their disquiet begin to heave,
Across the air fly such terrifying shrieks,
A chorus of piteous prayers and laments
From those who, long ago, drowned in the depths.

{xvii} Ha ha ha! Nagdadaingang multo. This is childish and miserable.

"Then high above the mountains vibrate,
Trees sway this way and that as if in a fit;
Beasts moan, their cries resound in the forest;
Their spirits say they're on their way to the plains,
Summoned by the dead to a funereal feast.

{xviii} Zombies naman! A necrophagous imagination...

Enough. Such as they are, abstracted from the poet's existential-historical situation which happened to be that of the Revolution, and forgetting that in counterrevolutionarily rallying his fellow native rich he had in fact inflicted as severe a damage on the Revolution as that other chief counterrevolutionary and vendor of the Revolution and the Motherland Emilio Aguinaldo y Famy did, and perhaps even more, these lines are mostly ordinary, in many parts ludicrous, incongruous, even stupid...But of course, the real and worst crime which this poet through this poem perpetrates is the moral and aesthetic coarseness and vulgarity and perfidy of poetically masturbating in full view of the life and death birthing of the Revolution by Andres Bonifacio and his Katipunan comrades—and this obscene performance after he maniacally angrily rejected Bonifacio's offer and entreaty for him to join and even lead it

Chapter 17

THE BAGUIO INTERVIEW--A SUMMARY OF ARGUMENTS

{The interviewer was the author's philosophical friend who for personal reasons wished to postpone revealing his true identity until after some people are dead. He wants us to just call him Joe Blue here. Ingoo is of course the author himself who thus expresses his of course futile wish to anaclitically reciprocate postponing the making known of his true identity through the capital mask of an ontological cipher transposing the inexistence of a letter into its zero materiality. The interview was held across three days in the author's rustic residence in Baguio City sometime during the last week of February 2011.}

Joe Blue: In the open forum of a lecture by Dr. Floro Quibuyen on February 20, 2011 at the University Hotel in UP Diliman, Dr. Antonio Nepomuceno Pangilinan defended both Quibuyen and Rizal against your published attacks on them by finding you guilty of what he, Pangilinan, calls a *retrospective fallacy*. I was there and I electronically recorded everything in my cellphone. This is what Dr. Pangilinan said: "We must place things in proper perspective. Gene (Dr. Eugenio Demigilio, formerly professor, Philosophy Department, UP Diliman) was raising a question, and the other points related to it, *with the full knowledge and certainty of things that happened a hundred years ago.* We now have definite information about the revolution, about Rizal and about the war against Spain. But at that time, Rizal's ideas about assimilationism *were the most progressive that the liberals could advocate*[100], and

---

[100] Quibuyen's disciple's officious ignorance here is thick indeed. The entire 19th century was a century of anticolonial revolutions. Everywhere in the colonial world, conditions were ripe, even overripe (in the case of the Philippines) for revolution. In the 1820s in Latin America, in a continental wave of revolutions theorized, organized, and led by the colonial middle-class intellectuals (Bolivar

and company) who were the counterparts of the Philippine colonial middle class led by Rizal and Del Pilar (the so-called--self-called, self-inflated--*ilustrados*), all of Latin America, with but Cuba and Puerto Rico as exceptions, was liberated. While the in fact also very belated ardour of the Cuban intellectuals in Spain had prompted them to organize themselves into fiery *separatistas* and spearhead the Cuban Revolution (which Rizal between November 1895 and September 28, 1896 most assiduously offered his life to help the Spaniards suppress, making himself thereby an *international counterrevolutionary*—and if you are tolerably human and not intolerably because meddlingly cantankerously stupid, should you not at once, in fairness to the Cuban people, to Jose Marti and Camilo Cienfuegos and to the humanity you share with them and with yourself, put yourself in the shoes or shoelessness of the Cuban Katipuneros whom Rizal proposed and projected thus to help murder more effectively, and, earning your right to be called a human being thereby, normally sane, normally fair and just, view Rizal's and his Austrian-Spanish assimilationist and therefore execrable friend Blumentritt's Cuban project from *there*, from that Cuban people position, from that Cuban Katipunero human-historical-existential position?,;and, seeing Rizal from *there* thus, you being at the same time a Filipino, must you not at once die of shame sharing ineradicably with that *international counterrevolutionary* your nationality?), Rizal and company had organized themselves into the exact opposite, into advocates of eternal colonialism, i.e., into assimilationists! And this Quibuyenista of a Rizalist says assimilationism was the most progressive that the Philippine colonial middle class in their supposed liberalism could advocate then! The *fin de siecle* intellectual and political atmosphere in Spain was actually strongly liberal; and the Spanish liberals Rizal and company were addressing their pleadings to were of course liberals, and it was indeed their being liberals that instigated in Rizal and company the delusive and stupid and inhuman and utterly cruel—to the Filipino masses--hope that assimilation was a feasible project; nor is there any doubt that Rizal and company were identifying with and emulating those Spanish liberals (Rizal was without a doubt idolizing them when he oratorically wrote in an article--the infamous *The Philippines A Century Hence*, in *Rizal's Political and Historical Writings*; NHI 2007; p147-- pleading for the nth time for Philippine representation to the Cortes, that those Spanish statesmen were masters of the word who were invincible in oratory and debate:--deeper minds, writers with more than a touch of philosophy in them, let alone real philosophers would not be so vulnerable to ciceronical declaimers and thickly pomaded stage actors who happened not to be on a real stage where to the contrary it is of course possible to be great as an actor); and it was of course because of such stylistic identification that they were able to fancy themselves as likewise liberals; but in that their main preoccupation and consuming advocacy was eternal colonialism at the turn of that revolutionary century, they were in actual fact the opposite of liberal and were certainly in being such assimilationists exceedingly illiberal. As the historical-political philology of these polar terms go, liberal was at that time the antipode of conservative; to oppose revolution when revolution is there is semantically quite simply, anywhere anytime, conservative, and, in light of this polar opposition, illiberal; Edmund Burke, famously opposing the French Revolution and excoriating therewith Rousseau and Robespierre, was in doing so, conservative, in fact, in view of the world-historical disemboguements of that earth-shaking, king-caputing and even queen-depilating (but, unluckily for Marie, together with the neck) event, ultra-conservative; and when the revolution one opposes thus is, as in Rizal's and Blumentritt's and indeed the entire Filipino ilustrado's therefore looked radical rather than reformist from that vantage point. Of course, today, those ideas may sound not revolutionary enough, that's true. Rizal did not have enough information[101] at that time that could have led him to the

---

evil and truly mass-murderous case, the most righteous one for being against the most unrighteous one, for being against the *evilest* one, the foreign invader and alien parasite, the Calamba (Dominican) rapist, the colonizer? Ultra-ultra-ultra conservative! Whilst this assimilationist, ultra-ultra-ultra-conservative opposition culminated in the murder of more than 2 million Filipinos by the Americans during the American conquest and pacification of the Philippines which Rizal and company made possible and facilitated first of all by literally pulling away the entire colonial middle class, *whom they were*, from the revolution almost to a man, the upper middle class literally completely, to a man, so that literally again, Bonifacio was able belatedly to launch only half a revolution for the main bulk of the middle class which should have constituted its spearhead as it did in Bolivar's Latin America for instance, was effectively pre-withdrawn from it, pre-judiced and pre-disposed against it by Rizal and company's effective assimilationist derailment campaign:--bloody, genocidally bloody, for it led directly to the murder of more than 2 million Filipinos whom Rizal "loved" so heart-bleedingly much.

[101] Before we forget the urgent point, let us inscribe it here: that revolutions can and do ripen means that there are historical, social-existential forces that push and impel enslaved, oppressed peoples to do something to regain their lost freedom, and these can only be forces of freedom themselves, forces which derive from the fact that human beings are, as Rousseau puts it in the opening sentence proper of the *Social Contract*, "born free", and society is an association of beings who are free, that is to say, of human beings and not of mere brutes, and that

realization that the Katipunan would be as potent as we now know it to be; so he could not have made so easy a decision to join the Katipunan. This lack of enough information on his part should caution us and restrain us from cursing him for not joining it in the end. To curse him so for it (as Ingoo did) would be to commit a *restrospective fallacy.*"

Ingoo:--Before I proceed to demonstrate to you the invidious fallacy of this "retrospective fallacy" invented by Dr. Antonio Pangilinan, I would like to announce here that in my latest book on the matter, *Rizal Against Humanity, Rizal Against the Revolution, Rizal Against the Filipino People—The*

---

beings who are free are contradicted in their very nature, in their very essence which is freedom/transcendence, by colonialism, by oppression, by regimes of unfreedom and base immanence, and this cannot go on forever (which is why every society *must* be founded on a *core or bedrock democracy* which we call *primordial democracy*, a necessity which does not obtain in mere animal colonies or herds: primordial democracy is *the minimum, the bare, social substructure of freedom* which must obtain in a permanent association of *free* beings, i.e., of *human* beings and which is itself demanded and necessitated by the fact that those who contract such an association are free beings and not brutes). That human beings, being in their very nature and essence free beings, must desire freedom, must want constantly to be free, means that the demand for such freedom under conditions of oppression such as colonialism must mount with time; this mounting like everything else has a limit point; that limit point is the point of ripeness of the revolution...Let us also add here the important point that it is precisely this primordial democracy that constitutes the political foundation of the being people of the people. This primordial democracy is at the same time the primordiality of the sovereignty of the people, and of course the primordiality of the political itself.

Documentary Evidence, a decisive breakthrough has been made towards definitively settling and giving a once and for all closure to this bitter question of whether Rizal died an assimilationist or a disguised revolutionary, and this momentous breakthrough happened in the new reading I have uncovered and instituted of the two letters Rizal wrote on the eve of his June 22 or 23 1892 departure from Hong Kong to the Philippines to save his family or in any case suffer with them and even, as he himself put it, die for them, in the ravaging greed and sadism of the Dominicans in the wake of the *Calamba Question, Invasion, Massacre, Rape*. I am referring to the twin letters which in the anthology *Rizal's Political and Historical Writings* (2007 NHI edition, pp 331-333) bear the collective title *To the Filipinos*. Equally decisive though documentarily less forthright is our reading in this same book of the meaning, personal and political, of what Rizal did not do and did do in the four years of his exile in Dapitan. Definitive closure has also been given in this book to the, for us Filipinos, twistingly shameful question of whether Rizal was going to Cuba to study firsthand the revolution there so that he could do it better here "when the proper time comes" (the vulgar stupidity of the claim that he did so with this "motive" and "intention", let alone the unanimous and hot credence accorded it by Filipino historians so-called and journalists and media(eval)(wo)men like the unthinkingly retrogressive Howie Severino of *Rizal is my Hero* infamy, is possible only in the Philippines, in the blankminded and blinky-eyed and venal venal venal opportunist opportunist opportunist intellectual-academic-media culture of the Philippines...).

Joe Blue: Oh, but I mean to inquire of you about those things here too. In fact, I was thinking that this thing about Dr. Antonio Pangilinan's *retrospective fallacy* should merely serve as some kind of theoretical opening into the real heart of the matter which is precisely the question which you say you have just decisively settled in your new book...Could you please sum up these breakthroughs before we proceed to the question at hand on the fallacies?

Ingoo: Yes, I will do that. But first, I'd like to put definitively to rest a certain question, or rather, I'd like to once and for all silence the stupid, the unqualifiedly stupid historians and the equally stupid, unqualifiably stupid professors of history and those others, mainly declaimers and speechifiers who, whenever the question of Rizal's rejection of revolution crops up cannot wait a second to blurt out that saying of Rizal's to the effect that he did not want revolution and thus independence for the Filipinos *as yet*, because they still lacked all those qualifications which would entitle them to be free, so that, if they by rising in arms should win independence today, then, those unqualified human beings who were our ancestors would merely be today's slaves who will then become the tyrants of tomorrow. As I was passing by the *Oblation* on my way home thinking of Rodin and Michelangelo, the answer which will be the final nail on the coffin of their dull and shabby silence occurred to me, and I must not waste the first opportunity to permanently record it or I could forget all about it and lose the precious thrust and explosion altogether.

Joe Blue: That will be great. I too have long sensed that there must be something profoundly wrong with that Rizalian piece of rhetoric, but I cannot tell exactly what... And that also because if you look at what the same history has come up with, which presumably has something to do with that revolution Rizal rejected, he seems to be mainly right: The tyrants of today were indeed yesterday's slaves of Spanish colonialism.

Ingoo: We shall deal with that seeming confirmation of that bad piece of Rizalian oratory in more detail later, but for now, and at once, I say it is not true at all that the tyrants of today who are exclusively responsible for this culture of corruption which has made us number one in the list of the world's most corrupt countries, and this mass poverty that goes with it and which they also inflict upon the people, were the slaves of Spanish colonialism, no! Today's tyrants were the colonial middle class who were the privileged collaborators of Spanish colonialism and yes of American and Japanese imperialism as well, the class to which Rizal and Aguinaldo and all the assimilationist betrayers of the native land and of the revolution belonged; they were the middling but more numerous tyrants of yesterday who today and since 1946 are now the big, full-fledged tyrants; whilst their slaves, the peasants, the workers, are still the same kind of people whom they were helping the Spanish masters (and yes the American and Japanese) tyrannize yesterday.

Joe Blue: Yes, that's true, yes! Now that you say it…I know it already. You have demonstrated that in your last two books!

Ingoo: That will do for now. Let us now dismantle that piece of bad Rizalian oratory. He always had such set orotund words in readiness for insertion here and there and that really makes for so much of the bad in his truly bad writing….

Joe Blue: Hmmm… You've also seen that—that Rizal's writing, outside of the two novels[102] is bad?

---

[102]Novels are not eternal essences and novelists are not God/s. However, in any passable novel, as indeed in any passable work of art, there is always a making present of the truth of (of course) the human condition, seen, of course, from the peculiar angle of the artist's vision. It is the marriage between this peculiarity which is always irreducible (it is sometimes called style) with the universality (to be exact, the universalizability) of (the truth of) what is thus made present (or present-able, appropriable) there that constitutes the *truth of the novel*, which as such is always a peculiar way, then, of grasping and presenting the *essence of the human*, which is always a *becoming essence*, conflicted always and struggling towards itself. There is always thus in a work of art as in a society a living, conflicted, struggling, *becoming essence* against which it can be measured—the very principle then of its own critique (this also is how I propose to solve the problem of *critical social theory*). There is a fundamental reflexivity that belongs to art in general. A reconstruction and description

of this fundamental reflexivity has not been attempted yet, whilst of course, the novel, as can be expected, has its own peculiar reflexivity. This of course has also not been sufficiently grasped yet. Reflexivity implicates truth and every question of reflexivity is a question first of all of truth. The first difficulty concerns the nature, the essence, of truth. Elsewhere in this work we propose a notion of truth which will be its own criterion of internal critique: the *truth of essence*. We hold—and attempt to show—that this is the kind of truth that pertains to 1.) all living things, and 2.) all things of freedom and transcendence (including, and first of all society, and yes of course, the individual human *ex-istent*). There is first the truth of essence that belongs to the society of its time and place: this is the essence of the living, conflicted, struggling, truth. This struggle for truth, by the forces of truth, and thus in this sense *of* truth itself, and which as such defines the essence of society is always for society, for the people that constitute the *body-social and the body-politic*, a struggle to realize itself, i.e., to realize its own essence, i.e., to realize its own truth. It is always a conflicted truth and there is always a struggle for it, because the way things are, there are always forces of untruth that deny and oppose and repress and seek to destroy it; and it, as the truth it is, always happens as this struggle and should be grasped and presented as such—and that indeed is why this truth is always grasped critically and presented thus critically. The inexhaustible impetus behind this struggle is rooted in transcendence itself, in freedom itself which "naturally" enough desires itself and powers itself, forces its way towards such realization. (Is this a Hegelianism without the Absolute Spirit, without the One, without God? And therefore without metaphysics, without theology? Perhaps it is. In a manner of speaking, it is. Although it is certainly difficult to see what of Hegel remains without the metaphysics, indeed the theology, of the necessary dialectical progression towards the comic return of the Absolute Spirit, the self-estranged One, the self-sundered God to itself—which of course is but another version of Christian redemptionism, or, as in Marx's "inversion" of *it*, another enlightenmentism.) It is this *truth of essence* of the society of its time and place that the novel, the work of art, attempts to present, from its own irreducible angle of vision, as truthfully, and therefore as deeply and as comprehensively and as *richly* as possible (the richness belongs to the style). Hence it is that, the presentation of what it seeks to make present being first of all a question of grasping the truth of the society of its time and place—a truth of essence which, we repeat, is necessarily conflicted and thus can only be grasped critically—writing a novel is first of all a matter, a question, of intelligence, of, shall we say, wisdom which comprehends the intelligence of the heart, a largeness and profundity of humanity. Now there is a most treacherous falsehood and a deviously ensconced littleness and narrowness of humanity, indeed a most alluringly masked, a powerfully duplicitous, a most insidious inhumanity and cruelty in Rizal's grasp and version of the truth of the society of his time and place, a treachery, a falsehood, an inhumanity, a cruelty, a deviousness summed up in the word *assimilationism*. It is this falsehood, this lie, this evil, a most bloody, a genocidal evil as we have demonstrated and computed, that vitiated and continues to vitiate from deepest within whatever truth belongs to Rizal's novels. You cannot write a less than utterly bad novel praising Hitler and approving the Holocaust. Or one that does the same to Stalin and approving his "Marxism", just as it is certainly impossible to write a less than unspeakably bad novel extolling or affirming capitalism, which needs no refutation and which is well on its way to refuting history itself and with it all of humanity, and with it, all of us. Of course, it does not necessarily follow that because Rizal was an assimilationist,

Ingoo: Stupid is bad, Joblo, in anything the first requirement of the being good of which is intelligence, and where then there is no such thing as good or beautiful stupidity… Rizal's writing was bad because they were assimilationist—assimilationist, Joblo, and than *that* you cannot be more stupid. Or more cruel, or more wicked, or, bloodier—or more evil!... But before I forget it in these meanderings and divagations, let me say *it* now, at once, this insight about the utter wrongness, indeed the bloody, the evil wrongness of this "the slaves of today will be the tyrants of tomorrow"—if before setting them free, or before allowing them to free themselves by way of revolution, they are not educated first and inoculated with "civic virtues"!… The first and the most fundamental of human rights is freedom, the right to be free; for freedom is that singular thing without which one is not yet human but a brute, a mere animal. To postpone the freedom of any human being is to postpone his humanity and thus to deny it. And no one has the right to do that; no one has the right to deny the humanity of another. This is even truer of a people, and here, a colonized people. Indeed it is clearer in the case of an enslaved people. The first and most imperative thing, the most right and most just thing

---

an international counter-revolutionary and traitor against his own people and against humanity, his novels were as thoroughly assimilationist and counter-revolutionary, and anti-humanity as his politics. Talent, let alone genius, happening in the acts of writing could at times get the better of such unfortunate contingencies as the author's politics. And Rizal, who was most definitely *not* a genius, had talent, although it was not a very strong one. And especially in the *Noli*, in many places, talent does triumph over assimilationist evil and stupidity. Whilst it is in those junctures where he had to make significant and give expression to the intended general assimilationist-enlightenmentist and therefore anti-revolutionary, anti-independence direction of the novel that it begins to smell really bad…

that can happen to an enslaved people is for them to be set free, for them to regain their lost freedom. No premise whatsoever can be valid on whose basis such setting-free, such liberation, such regaining of their lost freedom and humanity is delayed or postponed. What this means is of course that the worst thing that can happen to a person and even more so to a people, is to be enslaved, to lose freedom, to be colonized. Which is why there absolutely cannot be any valid justification for a people to colonize another. Colonialism is evil, period! And nothing whatsoever can justify it. Which is why nothing, absolutely nothing, can justify any postponement of its termination anytime. Anyone who, like Rizal, argues for such a delay is a fascist. In the first place, the colonized people were free before they were colonized. How, without damning colonialism itself by owning that it had so brutalized and corrupted them to the point of destroying their very humanity and turning them thus into beings who no longer deserve to be free, beings who are no longer fit to be human beings because no longer fit to be set free or do something (as in revolution) to set themselves free, could one argue for postponing their freedom thus? Whilst at the same time, such argument in the case of Rizal as in that of the most rabid friar (redundant) of his time, and in that of McKinley's Benevolent Assimilation Proclamation which but summed up Rizal's and Western-Christian capitalist global colonialism's "white man's burden" Enlightenmentist metaphysical and-- because Christianity was there too-- theological ideology and lie, had its fundamental premise in the necessarily fascistic fetishization and metaphysical absolutization of so-called "enlightenment", which Rizal in true European colonialist fashion phrased as "education and civic virtues" and in the two novels and the *Liga Filipina* as "industry and progress". The colonialist, the friar for instance whom Rizal hated so, is a fascist. And fascistic results necessarily come out of this Rizalian maxim: If lack of education or of some kind of virtue, which moreover, in Rizal's and Western-European colonialism's case was Western-Christian-Capitalist education and civic virtue or culture, is a valid justification for postponing the liberty of a colonized people, then it must follow that the Westerner or the Westernized

Christian-Capitalist has an inherent right to colonize and enslave non-Westerners or non-Westernized peoples—*to enlighten them, to civilize them, to redeem them, to save them from their pre-human, non-human selves, to progressify them, to teach them the lightning rod and good manners and right conduct ha ha ha*. Hence the *white man's burden* bluff which is shit, plain evil shit. And this indeed is how stupid and fascistic—fascists are always exceptionally stupid—this Rizalian argument is and Rizal with it. In fact, of course, as I already pointed out, it was not original to Rizal; it was a standard Enlightenmentist argument, Enlightenmentism being the chief ideology of Western-Christian-Capitalist global colonialism. Rizal's genocidal project which he masterminded with that half or one-fourth Spanish Roman Catholic Austrian journalist Ferdinand Blumentritt, and in which of course he was greatly aided by the moustachioed scribbler from Bulacan, Marcelo H. del Pilar—resulting in the murder of more than two million Filipinos—was *Assimilationism*, and its religio-metaphysical Absolute was of course the same Western-Christian-Capitalist Global Colonialist Absolute, namely *Enlightenment/Progress*... McKinley was a Rizalist in his *Benevolent Assimilation* genocidal project, just as Rizal was McKinleyist in his "*Education and civic virtues first before freedom, before liberty, before independence (and thus before revolution forever postponed thus, before the humanity of the Filipinos forever postponed thus*...)" project. And again, before I forget, that flash of light by the Louvre had a twin, just as, in Rizal's enlightenmentist oratory the "slaves of today...tyrants of tomorrow" bombast has a twin, namely, "The pen is mightier than the sword", and the former's twin is of course the flash of light on this latter one's twin. Invocation of it, starting with Rizal himself, by the brainwashed pedants, mostly half-illiterate university professors and enterprising always-already-bought journalists like that one from UP who contrived that shameful and execrable *Rizal is my Hero* thing (I forgot the irrelevant name, what's that na nga?), is routinely perpetrated in like attempts to justify and heroify Rizal's rejection of the Revolution. Hence the maliciously ignorant juxtaposition: Rizal's "mighty pen" versus the "puny sword" (gulok) of Bonifacio! "The pen is mightier than the sword"—to which I say: pen and sword together are mightier. And we must not be made to choose between the one and the other because we are talking about revolution and to the success of such an epochal collective action both are indispensable. In other words, they are once more the same half-illiterate pack (they hardly have any *literate-ure* in their lives) who, misled by Rizal the great tergiversator and prestidigitator himself, are misleading the people, are misleading the youth, away from the real question which is that of the Revolution by unconsciously posing that question in that trivialized form of choosing between Rizal's pen and Bonifacio's sword, whereas the real question is why, and how, did it happen that despite the fact that the time not only was ripe but already overripe—no longer disputable nowadays in view among other things of what Bonifacio was *forced by the over-ripeness of the time and of circumstances to launch despite the utterly banefully successful pulling away from it and against it of the key element of the colonial middle class, especially the ilustrado, and the upper crust of that multicenturially criminal-collaborationist colonial middle class which thanks mainly to Rizal remained multicenturially collaborationist and criminal because counter- and- anti-revolutionary thus*—Rizal's and the ilustrados' pens (and *funds*, and other material resources!) were not there with Bonifacio's sword to make the revolution... Let us go now to the deferred questions...

Joe Blue: First , the invidious, odious--I should add, and stinking too--fallacies of the "retrospective fallacy" invented for your denigration and downfall and Quibuyen's and Rizal's exoneration and exaltation by Quibuyen disciple and amanuensis, Dr. Antonio Pangilinan[103], and then the urgent

---

103 There is more than the smell of prostitution here. Which is not surprising. For what else was Rizal and company doing pushing the colonial ideological dope, the lulling lie and venomous, fatal stupidity of *assimilationism*, leading away, derailing, the colonial middle-class most banefully powerfully thus, and very, very, decisively, from their very own historical destiny which was to theorize,

manifestation of the breakthroughs you have promised concerning the reading of the two letters Rizal wrote in Hong Kong in June 1892 just before his second, *prelude to Dapitan*, return to his native land, and left to the care of his friend and collaborator Jose Ma. Basa for dissemination later…

Ingoo: Yes, of course… On the two letters first. In these two letters, he was telling the Filipinos in general and his parents and relatives and Calamba townmates in particular that he was going home to surrender himself to the wrath of the Dominicans whom he perceived to be persecuting them on his account—chiefly because he wrote the two novels attacking the friars; he was saying that he believed he would be able to free those loved ones of his from such persecutions and restore them to their homes and property by thus suffering in their stead and even dying for them. At the same time however, he kept insinuating and even at some points directly claiming that dying thus for his relatives would also be dying for his native land! The contradiction should be obvious: for him to die for his relatives would be for him to abandon his country and people. This apparent contradiction is what must puzzle and confuse the reader of those letters, especially those Filipinos who automatically presume that Rizal was a hidden revolutionary and was thus going home to start the revolution or to do something towards starting it instead of rejecting it by dying for his relatives. This apparent contradiction and the puzzlement and confusion it generates dissolve instantly once we give up on Rizal's being a hidden revolutionary and take him for his word in the same letters when he there reaffirmed his assimilationism, saying that he was going home to die an assimilationist[104]. To Rizal then, dying thus for his family's

---

organize, lead, spearhead, the revolution--what else was all *that*, what else was *La Solidaridad*, the *Noli*, the *Fili*, but original and rampant intellectual prostitution?

104 Did he really say he was going home to die *an assimilationist*? Writes Rizal in the first letter: "TO MY BELOVED PARENTS, BROTHERS AND FRIENDS:…I know that I have made you suffer much,

but I do not repent for what I have done, and if I should start all over again, I shall do the same things that I did, because it is my duty… I leave (from Hong Kong to the Philippines--oingoo) willing to expose myself to danger, not in expiation of my faults (***which up to this point, I believe having committed none***) but *to put a finishing touch to my work* and to witness by my example what I have always preached" (ibidem, p.331). All his writing and propagandizing lifelong, he was, according to him himself faultlessly, errorlessly doing *one and the same thing* to which he wanted now by suffering and very likely dying "to put a finishing touch"; he wrote the two novels for *that one and the same thing*, and the historical and political essays, works which, being uncompromisingly anti-friar had motivated the ever-evil friars to avenge themselves on his parents, brother, sisters, and even town-mates (the *Rape of Calamba*: the greed of the friars and their insurpassable malevolence of course predated Jose Rizal himself, but it could indeed be true that his attacks on them had exacerbated their greed and their malevolence against Rizal's relatives); but despite the suffering he had collaterally inflicted on them by writing those works and doing those propagandizings, he was not regretting anything and would do all of them all over again should he be made to repeat his life. And that *one thing, that one and the same thing* to which he wanted now *to put a finishing touch* cannot be anything but *assimilationism.* He was going home to suffer and die and through that act of—of course, what else?—martyrdom, "put a finishing touch" to all of it. Now anyone who still has doubts that he was referring here to *assimilationism* as his lifework for which he was about to die and in dying consummate in a finishing touch, should read in particular the voluminous correspondence between Rizal and his fellow assimilationist Austrian-Spanish friend, Blumentritt across which they were for ten years and to the very end constant and solicitous in reaffirming to each other their common sake was at the same time dying for assimilationism, and dying for assimilationism was (for him) dying for the redemption of his country and people. We get puzzled and confused because we automatically equate dying for the country and the people with, *of course* (for us, but not, antipodally not, for such loving traitors and bleeding-in-the-heart *mental colonial* patriots like Rizal, Del Pilar, De Lete, etc.), revolution; whilst, of course, of course, for Rizal to die for his family just like that would be for him to turn his back on revolution and on his country and people. But would not dying for his relatives be also an abandonment of assimilationism? It would be so if such death would not at the same time be a huge and powerful thing capable of catapulting assimilationism to triumphant realization. And here then is the ultimate key: Rizal, with his usual megalomania, was convinced that his death, i.e., his *murder* by the friars, would cause such political upheaval in Madrid and prompt the Madrid government to assimilate the Philippines and punish, perhaps even expel (sweet revenge, O O!) the friars from the Philippines! Here is the crucial passage: "I leave willing to expose myself to danger, not in expiation for my faults (which up to this point, I believe having committed none)*but to put a finishing touch to my work* and to witness by my example what I have always preached" (ibid., p 331).There. He is not aware of any faults and is confessing to none. In his work, pure assimilationist work, he has not committed any errors, crimes, sins. This act of possible ultimate sacrifice (he could die doing it, O ass...O ass...O ass...i...m...i...lationist martyrdom O ASS!)is for burning love of country, of people, of—family, too. And here another illumination, insight, revelation is emergent for us: the *Liga*, otherwise so senseless and, viewed

---

assimilationism. Read also s/he should Blumentritt's review of the *Noli*, and the final letter Rizal wrote Blumentritt on the afternoon of the day before he was shot in which—as he did to his brother Paciano in the same kind of final letter of the same afternoon—he reaffirmed his assimilationist innocence by declaring that "I will die innocent of the crime of rebellion…etc"

in relation to possibilities of revolution, separation, independence, criminally idiotic and insane, was a not altogether unbright premeditated *assimilationist, emphatically not revolutionary,* strategy to bait the friars to have him arrested for the megalomaniacally hallucinated Madrid liberal furor, and, should such furor not be enough to propel the liberal Madrid government to legislate assimilation at once (and save his life), perhaps executed for the *consummatum est*!!! Such an organization too would be needed by the (would be) *assimilated Filipinos* in their of course continuing struggle to more fully secure and make concrete their newfound rights and privileges as brand-new Spanish citizens. Collateral damage was of course also contracted thereby since of course the fantastic (megalomaniacal) idea could only fail: the list of *Liga* attendees and members inevitably fell into the hands of the paranoid and hysterical authorities during the first days of the outbreak of hostilities and the ensuing reign of terror; they were arrested, tortured and many were executed. This was later blamed on Andres Bonifacio who supposedly planted lists of rich Filipinos tagged thus as supporters of the Katipunan. That, aside from being entirely out of character for Bonifacio, was of course pure hearsay and confabulation; there is no existing document to prove it[105]. Of the fact

---

[105] As for the traitor and notorious confabulator Pio Valenzuela's supposed testimony to that effect, *that* is exactly what we mean by pure hearsay and from a most impure, utterly polluted, severally perjured mouth. Valenzuela gave on different occasions as many as five *contradictory* testimonies on this and other matters pertinent to the revolution, to Rizal, Bonifacio, etc. Of him, Rizal himself testified in writing In his *Additional Data For My Defense* (see page 350 of the 2007 NHI edition of *Rizal's Political and Historical Writings*) and in court during his trial, thus: "With respect to the rebellion: Since 6 July, 1892 I have absolutely not taken up politics until 1 July of this year when, informed by Mr. Pio Valenzuela that an uprising was planned, I advised the opposite, trying to convince him with reasons. Mr. Pio Valenzuela separated

from me seemingly convinced, *so that instead of taking part later in the rebellion, he presented himself to the authorities* ***for forgiveness.***" Another ilustrado and *therefore* another traitor!—and see how weak in mind and character and double-headed and unspeakably treacherous and perfidious (he was Andres Bonifacio's kumpadre!) this doctor, this *ilustrado*, this *illustrious* doctor, was! And, but, was not Rizal's testimony against him thus (which actually Rizal thought and intended to be testimony to his, Valenzuela's, *good manners and right conduct*) not also mere hearsay? No, of course not! For if it was true—as it was bound to be true, as we shall in a moment see—that Valenzuela did not "take part later in the rebellion" and instead had "presented himself to the authorities" and asked their "forgiveness", then it must have been to those very same military officers sitting there as his, Rizal's, judges that he, Valenzuela, had presented himself to ask to be by them forgiven for having been with the revolution, or if not directly to any of them, to other Spanish military officers: if necessary, *they had every means to check*; whilst we know that, of course, Rizal must have been very careful in declaring such things before them in court because, precisely, he was declaring them in court and not only his life hanged in the balance, but, what was more important to him, as proved several critical times before then, also his reputation as a most devoted son of Mother Spain, as a most dedicated Spanish patriot, and as a ready-to-die-for Spain-anytime defender of Spanish colonialism. (He had refused to escape or be rescued from Dapitan several times because being a "runaway" would stain that reputation (see his Letter to Dr. Lorenzo Marquez below), he had offered to go to a possible death as Spanish military doctoral patriot and hero in Cuba in order (as he wrote his friend Blumentritt in that infamous September 28, 1896 letter from aboard the *Isla de Panay* in the middle of the Mediterranean Sea) to redeem that reputation as it was sullied by his Dapitan exile (his exact wording in that letter was: "to make a name and undo calumnies"; when on August 19, 1896, the Katipunan was finally fully exposed through Patino and Fr. Mariano Gil and the shooting and hacking war broke out whilst he was still on board the *Castilla* waiting for the mail boat to Spain en route to Cuba, he offered in a letter to Gov. Gen. Blanco no less than his very life, all he "can do", and even his "very name", "to be used in whatever manner they might deem fit to stifle the rebellion" (and made sure even that the letter was duly witnessed in writing by the Spanish commander of the *Castilla*, Colonel Santalo!), and what else indeed but for securing and affirming that same reputation as Spanish hero and patriot?; and when, not caring a bit for the utter destruction of his reputation amongst his revolutionist countrymen for such reputation as a native patriot and revolutionary was what he was precisely at great pains to slay, he wrote his unspeakably evil and perfidious *December 15 Fort Santiago Manifesto* and submitted it to the military court for publication and for the Spaniards to use it to dissuade the Filipinos from joining the Revolution and to persuade those who were already in it to go home and keep their peace; and when in writing and during the trial he *reminded* the court that he had reported, that he had betrayed, to the Dapitan governor a Katipunan emissary in 1892, for them to torture and kill him, and did not care a whit that his entire family and his loving wife Josephine were in court and would surely in moral shock know; and when, once more in writing and in open court he declared that he had requested Blanco to hold him incommunicado aboard the *Castilla* for fear that the Katipuneros might try to get to him and ruin or in any way sully by such contact that very same reputation of his as a most loyal and devoted son of Mother Spain?; and when in that same document and on that same occasion he *announced to the court* that in that abovementioned letter which he took great care that it should be duly witnessed by no less than the commander of the Spanish warship *Castilla,* namely, Col. Santalo, he had offered his life, his name, his all for the Spaniards to use in whatever manner they might deem fit to stifle the rebellion?; and when in the afternoon of the day before he was shot he made absolutely certain that his family and his friend Blumentritt would know that he would be dying as an *assimilationist redeemer and patriot* and ***not as a separatist and revolutionary fighter for his native land's independence*** by writing his friend Blumentritt and his brother Paciano that he was dying tomorrow "innocent of the crime of rebellion", even assuring Paciano that if, against his wishes, his "writings might have contributed" to it, then he thought that he had already "atoned" for such possible contribution to that evil "criminal", "savage", "absurd", "dishonourable" cause (as he described it in his December 15 Manifesto)—expressing great and heartfelt regret thereby that he had written the *Noli* and the *Fili* at all!?; and when, finally, finally, finally, he made the request to the Spanish officer of the death squad for him to be shot facing the bullets and not from behind for only traitors *to Spain* were shot thus?; and when, finally, finally, finally, finally, but finally, his last request having been denied, he with mighty effort wheeled around to face his executioners as he heard the order "fuego!"?; for it was true, Rizal was brave, very brave, and was not afraid to die for his principles and convictions which however happened to be *assimilationist* and thus counter-revolutionary, anti-separatist, anti-independence, anti-Filipino, colonialist and *Spanish patriotic*, and those who allege, imagining no doubt their cowardly selves in Rizal's condemned shoes, that he among other things wrote that unspeakable *December 15 Fort Santiago Manifesto* to save his own skin are insulting him and his memory by thus pronouncing him as cowardly and pigly and insectile as themselves.)} We now know moreover, and from the same court records and other documents and corroborative testimonies, that Valenzuela indeed surrendered thus to the authorities and even betrayed other Katipuneros, and was able thus to buy his life: he was jailed but not executed. One more thing to complete the destruction of this pernicious traitor: It was also this double-tongued doctor of fructiferous confabulatory imagination who coined the story that in their conference in Dapitan on that same day of July 1, 1896, Rizal answered upon being queried by him why he was going to Cuba that he wanted to go there in order to be able to study the revolution there firsthand so that he could then do it better here when the time comes! And do we even need to point out that this story must be a lie because to make such a joke was simply so out of character for Rizal? But there is something else that just now lights up in Rizal's declaration concerning Valenzuela's cowardly and traitorous act of asking the Spaniards to forgive him; Rizal writes that he tried to convince Valenzuela against the "uprising": "Mr. Valenzuela separated from me seemingly convinced, so much so that instead of taking part later in the rebellion, he *presented himself* to the authorities *for forgiveness*." It was Valenzuela himself who told the story that Rizal was actually for revolution but that he advised them to wait and make preparations; this would jibe with that coda to the same story that Rizal supposedly told him that he was going to Cuba to study the revolution there so that he could do it better here when the time comes. If these details were true, and it was concerning them that Rizal was supposed to have convinced Valenzuela, why then did the latter surrender at once to the authorities and ask their forgiveness? If Rizal was able to convince him to merely lie low and wait for the proper time, why did he not just make himself inconspicuous somewhere and wait for Rizal to come back for the proper time? If it was not to reject the however that it was in fact Rizal, because of his foolish and hallucinatory assimilationist idea and project of launching the *Liga* thus, who had caused them to be exposed to such mortal danger and thus caused their torture and death, we have more than mere hearsay or testimonies by liars like Pio Valenzuela. The fact of the *Liga* was not hearsay. Whilst it was of course automatic for the Spaniards liberal or friar or in-between, to take it for a subversive organization: in the Philippines of that time, for an Indio to merely open his mouth in a determined way was filibusterism. And we can cite the court records in which this fact of the arrest of *Liga* members *because* they were *Liga* members *was several times brought out.* One of the main charges against Rizal was his being the founder of the *Liga.* Which even then he impotently denied, owning only that he it was who framed its by-laws.

Joe Blue: And you are establishing a connection between this attempt at *assimilationist martyrdom* and filial piety on one hand and what happened and did not happen to him in his four years in Dapitan?

---

revolution itself finally and forever *that Rizal was able to convince Valenzuela*, why did he have to surrender at once and prostrate himself before the Spaniards to ask their forgiveness? In other words, *it must have been to reject and even abhor the revolution per se, totally, completely, uncompromisingly and in its very idea itself, that Rizal was able to convince Valenzuela.* Which was but to be expected: for such extreme fear and abhorrence of revolution is everywhere in Rizal's writings and was of course the very presupposition and implication of all his propaganda activities; whilst never in his writings did he speak of revolution except as such object of fear and abhorrence, and almost always as a fearful and horrible eventuality with which to scare the liberal Spaniards in the Madrid government to grant their anti-revolutionary, counter-revolutionary, revolution-preventing and revolution-countering *assimilationist* demands.

Ingoo: That's right. And his Cuba escapade too which made him an international (if aborted) counterrevolutionary and an ultra-conservative non-European defender of Europe in being during that time perhaps the most dedicated defender of Western-Christian Capitalist Global Colonialism...

Joe Blue: To Dapitan then, and then to Cuba... He did not write anything political in Dapitan. He had been saying, even while still in Europe, that they should all go home and pursue the fight there, citing that the doctor should stay where the patient is.

Ingoo: And that, among other things, was why, under the widespread misconception, lying issue and malefic spawn of more than a hundred years of brainwashing in school and media to the effect that he was a disguised revolutionary, we tend to immediately conclude that what he was then declaring was revolution already. Even then he was convinced that, at least as far as his own role in the assimilationist movement was concerned, enough had already been done and accomplished the *propaganda way*. He must also have been of the opinion that nothing more could be done by the movement as a whole to achieve assimilationist success—the only kind of success Rizal cared for at all (and he showed it by religiously refraining from doing anything for it, and thereby withdrawing totally from politics, as he himself many times put it, from the time of his arrest and exile to his death four years and five months later.). Something spectacular has to be done, something dramatic (indeed melodramatic). And for that, he has to go home. To dramatize himself as was his wont, he at times generalized his self-invented case: they should *all* go home because the fight is there! But he did not really mean that *all*; just as he alone was, according to him himself in these two letters, that singular one around whom "the future of my country gravitates" (!), he alone could do it, and he alone was going home—"to show them...etc., etc..." The fellow was certifiably vainglorious and a pious exhibitionist. He meant only himself—that he had done everything he could--and in the abovementioned letters he had emphasized that he was right in everything he had done thus, and that there was nothing for him to repent or atone for, and that should time repeat itself he would do exactly the same things that he did exactly as he did them—and that it was time to do *something else*, namely, for him to "put the finishing touch", and a victorious touch he meant it to be, to all that he had done. Besides, he knew that at least until the glorious culmination of his *assimilationist martyrdom,* the Filipino propagandists should be there in Spain to chorus the outrage.[106] He was deluded of course. For no outcry was heard when he was arrested and exiled; and no one amongst the Filipino reformers was outraged when news about his deportation reached them. Or else, the outrage was impotent. The *martyrdom act* was a flop. The self-styled giant was a pygmy or else an ordinary mortal, in any case nothing so very special to those liberal politicians in Spain whom he thought would raise hell because the great assimilationist writer and lover of Spain, Don Jose Protacio Rizal Mercado y Alonso, was arrested at the instigation of the super-piranha and cormorant shark Dominican landgrabbers and rapists of Calamba. He had made sure he would be jailed and tried and executed: that's why he launched the inutile *Liga* with its cooperativist assimilationistically anaclitic by-laws which he formulated

---

[106]He was in fact extra-concerned that the Spaniards, especially those liberal ones in the Peninsula who were perceived by him to be supportive of their assimilationist aspirations, should not make the mistake of suspecting the assimilationist movement of being anything else, of being hiddenly separatist, of being "filibusterist", as can be seen in his many letters to Plaridel and also to De Lete and Mariano Ponce, excerpted in this volume. He even wrote Plaridel at exactly this time (and he repeated this to De Lete and Ponce) that he made Simoun a dark figure in order to show the Spaniards what a real *filibustero* looked like so that by contrast he could demonstrate to them that the assimilationist movement was not filibusterist, not separatist, not revolutionist at all and was in fact, against Simoun's blackness, white, very white…

with infinite care so that in any case his liberal Peninsular friends in particular and the Spaniards in general would not mistake it for a separatist organization. But Despujol, himself comparatively liberal-leaning, was too solicitous for his life and he had him smuggled to Dapitan in the dead of night, so that when the friars learned about his disappearance he was already out of their carbuncled and hirsute reach in that Jesuit-priested Zamboanga town (he requested for his own comfort this Jesuit feature from Despujol, too, and got it). Would the assimilationist *martyrdom act* have been successful had not Despujol snatched him away from the maws of those evilest of creatures the friars? I don't think so. He simply was never that important or big to the Spaniards for them to mind too much his very skewering. Neither did anyone of his Peninsular friends make a stir when he was finally executed in 1896…

Joe Blue: And you are saying that it dismayed him greatly that he was so to speak spurned by his liberal Peninsular friends and his *martyrdom act* was treated as a non-event by them and was almost completely ignored by the Filipino propagandists in Spain?

Ingoo: Exactly…

Joe Blue: And that confirmed him in his withdrawal from the assimilationist movement…

Ingoo: Yes… And hardened his decision to stop doing anything political whatsoever, to "withdraw from politics altogether", as he repeatedly put it in his pleadings during his trial and even before that in letters which we have also excerpted in the new book. Which is logical, because to him the only kind of politics worth engaging in was assimilationist propaganda. As for revolution, separatism, independence, he hated and feared it from his very guts…

Joe Blue: And that was why he refused to escape from his Dapitan exile…

Ingoo: Exactly! To the point of putting in an awkward position those relatives and friends of his who were plotting his escape…

Joe Blue: And now to the breakthrough on his Cuban misadventure… In our history textbooks and in the writings of all or almost all of our historians on the matter, we read that Rizal's chief aim in going to Cuba as a Spanish military doctor was, as Dr. Pio Valenzuela testified, to study firsthand the revolution there so that he could do it better here when the proper time comes. In other words, it was as a revolutionary that Rizal wanted to go there. As proof of this revolutionary intention, it has often been cited by the same writers and repeated by history teachers in colleges and universities that Rizal could have disembarked and escaped when the mail boat docked in Singapore for a stopover, as supposedly other Filipinos fleeing from the revolution in the Philippines did. What can you say about this argument?

Ingoo: Only in the Philippines, my dear Sir, only in the Philippines…!

Joe Blue: Yes, only in the Philippines—though you said it first here and I merely approvingly—and how else indeed?—repeat you, for aside from you I have many Filipino friends who might get hurt somewhere in their lungs hearing such a thing especially from strangers like me.

Ingoo: Only in the Philippines is Gloria Macapagal Arroyo possible and her electoral-cheating machine and mass-media mass-murderer and backhoe gravedigger, the *evil thing* called ***Ampatuan***[107] whose arsenal of high-powered arms included

---

[107] This **evil thing**, whom one must hesitate to name with words that suggest any trace of humanity (this is for the benefit of the Spanish and the French and other non-Filipino readers), massacred in one fell swoop 57 journalists and the relatives of the other private army chief in that province called Maguindanao (a name forever dedicated now to the memory of an unspeakable evil

tanks supplied by the AFP (Armed Forces of the Philippines) itself... and Virgilio Garcillano without whose renowned expertise in electoral cheating Gloria Macapagal Arroyo would not have been able to steal Malacanang—his crime, his *GloriahellOGarci* crime, which of course would not have been possible without Gloriahellya herself, making of our democracy, i.e., our very souls, our very humanity a massmurderous comedy, was actually incomparably worse, immeasurably more malevolent, more anti-human, more cruel, more destructive, more *nihilistic* than the Ampatuans': in fact, in view of the daily massmurder through politically cultured and inflicted mass-poverty premised on that crime of crimes—five thousand murders every day, say?—Virgilio Garcillano *as murderer* dwarfs to near-invisibility the certainly already unthinkably evil Ampatuans, and seven years after that

---

spawned by Gloria Macapagal Arroyo herself whom an *evil lieutenant* who got a salary of 55 million pesos a month, one named Romulo Neri, in a Senate hearing understatedly called an ***evil person***), and all those who happened at that moment to pass by that portion of the national highway, raped some of the women, and buried everybody including their cars and vans (unique detail!) in a mass-grave—with that same backhoe used to dig the instant cemetery, yes: the ***evil thing*** planned all of it over lunch: of course they ate human beings there, and ate them live, whilst two of their own children were copulating on the huge table; and with what else but human blood from freshly opened breasts of virgin girls did they wash the menu of still warm hearts and liver chunks and young and tender breasts and scrota and labias majoras and labias minoras and clitorises?, whilst for dessert, a salad of freshly gouged eyes of children garnished with imported Lennon-McCartney strawberries (the same which used to be raised by African slaves which made Liverpool world-historically famous for being that 400-year Atlantic Slave Trade's biggest European trading centre) were served in your imagination of the clan feast, dear reader, isn't it?

crime of crimes and even today with a new president supposedly zealous in prosecuting the gang of super-criminals who constituted the previous government (there is not a single exception among them—and this Tiglao, this other **thing incapable of compunction and shame** named Tiglao, ugh ugh puke puke), Virgilio Garcillano walks free and prosperous for his reward was great, is grand—in the Philippines, only in the Philippines... And, just recently, you will not believe this—Oh, but yes, you will, knowing already that the Philippines is the Philippines , that is to say, the world's most corrupt country—the *retired* president of the biggest state university there, the Polytechnic University of the Philippines (population 55,000), a certain Dante Guevarra, age 66, *whose 6-year term provided by law had lapsed a month ago*, quite simply refused to retire last year (65 is the compulsory retirement age for all public officials in the Philippines) and again quite simply refuses to leave the president's office now, and the uncaring, toothless, and inaccessible president of the Philippines to whom I have written an open letter about this man cannot do anything to protect the law, let alone the university, the students, the part time teachers[108] there, and the young boys, and the butterflies...

Joe Blue: The butterflies—and the young boys?

Ingoo: His favourite dish is live butterfly salad served by naked young boys in huge Chinese gold cuspidors...

Joe Blue: In *my* imagination...?

Ingoo: In *your* blessed imagination yes... But back to Rizal's Cuban international counter-revolutionary project now...It's

---

108 Who up to now have not received a cent of their wages since the semester began because the DBM (Department of Budget Management) does not honor Dante Guevarra's signature anymore, whilst this same Guevarra is preventing the OIC assigned by law as interim president from entering PUP!

as simple as simple honesty and commonsense: If Rizal merely wanted to study a revolution firsthand so that he could do it better here when the time ripens, as they put it, a revolution was happening at exactly that time right here where he was supposed to want to apply the wisdom of his projected field research and Cuban OJT (On the Job Training); in fact, the revolution was exposed through the craven Patino and the archangelic Fr. Mariano Gil (August 19, 1896) 16 days before he sailed for Spain, and five days before that departure, hostilities broke out. Moreover, he knew from Valenzuela as early as July 1 of that year that the revolution was due to explode anytime. In short, no better revolutionary OJT can be had by such as he than here in his own country and than joining his own people in making one. In view of which it would have been utterly capricious of him to prefer a Cuban OJT. Of course, the merest suggestion of such a wish or objective on Rizal's part would have been ridiculous to say the least. And we have no doubt that Rizal never said such a thing, and that it was a mere invention by the liar and traitor Valenzuela.

Joe Blue: Now that you say it, yes! It's plain and obvious...And the storyteller Valenzuela... But perhaps Rizal was joking when he told him so?

Ingoo: No, I don't think so. It's not like Rizal to make such a joke. But to pursue this thing further, do you know why Rizal did not even imagine escaping on the Singapore stop-over like some rich Filipinos, notably Pedro Roxas, did?

Joe Blue: No, because you have not told me yet!

Ingoo: Alright then, I'll tell you. It's because, unlike them, he was not afraid of being arrested on board or upon reaching Spain. And do you know why, even when, arrested on board and shipped back and straight into his prison cell in Fort Santiago, he was, according to reports, not worried at all, and seemed even to not take very seriously the apprehensions of his relatives over the possibility of his getting convicted and shot? Because he had an ace, indeed four aces, a *quadra de alas* suite, which he had entrusted to no less than Governor General Blanco before his departure, *just in case…*

Joe Blue: And that *quadra de alas* suite was…

Ingoo: Why, of course, the letter he wrote Gen. Blanco, *witnessed by the Spanish commander* of the cruiser *Castilla* on board which by his own request he was held incommunicado all those 28 days he had had to wait on Manila Bay for the next mail-boat to Spain... Rizal wrote that unwordably shameless letter, fruit of a most absurd kind of moral-political-historical ignorance, something like an insane stupidity, in which, instigated to the ignominious deed by the discovery of the Katipunan by Fr. Mariano Gil on August 19, 1896, and by the irrepressible desire to demonstrate to Governor General Blanco, and to all Spaniards, and to all the world, the kind of love and devotion in which he held his Mother Spain, and the unfathomable contempt and disgust in which he held his own native countrymen and women, he offered to the Spaniards, as he himself put it in the reference he made to this letter in his equally malefic and vicious *December 15, 1896 Fort Santiago Manifesto*, "not alone my good offices, but my very life, and even my name, to be used in whatever manner they might deem fit to suppress the rebellion".

Joe Blue: And have you gotten hold of that letter and…

Ingoo: No, I haven't; not yet… And it is not unlikely that that letter no longer exists. But that it existed, and that it contained the unspeakable perfidies spoken of there by Rizal himself and to the existence of which there Rizal testified thus in court, in writing and in speech, cannot be doubted. For he himself referred to this letter in three documents he submitted to the military court, namely, in that odious *December 15 Manifesto*, in his *Data For My Defense* which he wrote earlier, on December 12, and in his *Additional Data for my Defense* which he composed on December 26–documents innocently included in the state-sponsored publications of his historical and political writings, but which no Philippine historian-- and certainly no Rizalist, no Quibuyen or Pangilinan or Jose David Lapiz--has read until quite recently.[109]

---

[109] It was in the December 12 *Data For My Defense* that he spilled the beans on himself, indeed splurged them, mentioning that it was in a personal letter that he did make that heinous offer, and that that letter was duly witnessed by Col. Santalo, the commander of the warship *Castilla.* Here is the relevant passage: "Nay, when the uprising broke out, I was on board the *Castilla*, incommunicado, and I offered myself unconditionally to His Excellency (a thing I had never done before) to suppress the rebellion. **But this was a personal letter and it was witnessed by Colonel Santalo. This cannot be used without the permission of His Excellency.**" Three days later, he wrote the *Manifesto* in which he mentioned what kind of "unconditional" offer it was that he made in that letter, namely, that: "When later, despite my counsels, the uprising broke out, I offered spontaneously, not only my services, but also my life, and even my name so that they might use them in the way they deem opportune to quench the rebellion…" (I reproduce here the translation in the anthology *Rizal's Political and Historical Writings*, NHI 2007, p 348; I have also used other versions, like that of Zaide in his Rizal course textbook, and that of Horacio dela Costa in his translation of selected portions of the court records culled from Retana's book *Vida y Escritos de Dr. Jose Rizal;* they show that no matter how you spell out the evil thing, the same vicious and unhinged treason shines through). When exactly did he write that letter which, exposed thus in the clear light of day now, is more than enough to destroy him completely by reversing his supposedly grand heroism into villainy of the most contemptible kind? In his *Additional Data for my Defense*, we find the following details pertinent to this question: "When the movement started, I was on board the *Castilla* and I placed myself at His Excellency's service unconditionally.

Joblo: That he had that *quadra de alas* suite cannot be doubted now. You have fully documented it. However, he still got

---

Twelve or fourteen days later I sailed for Europe, and had I an uneasy conscience, I would have tried to slip away at any seaport, especially Singapore where I went ashore and where other passengers who had passports for the Peninsula remained. My conscience was clear and I expected to go to Cuba." (ibidem, 351) Rizal's last letter to his mother before he left for Spain was dated September 2, from aboard the *Castilla*, which he wrote precisely to say goodbye to her and the family (there was no mention of Josephine of whom as we know the entire family except for his father and his sister Narcisa puritanically disapproved). Rizal must have sailed on the 3rd or the 4th of September, "twelve or fourteen days" he said, after he wrote the perfidious letter. He must then have written it sometime on August 22 or 23 or 24, three or four days after Patino exposed the revolution. And this piece of intelligence must lead us unstoppably to a most sinister thing—namely, that Rizal had had plenty of time to inform against Katipunan leaders about whom Valenzuela must have told him things in their July 1 conference. Whilst, having offered his very life, his name, his everything to be used by the Spaniards to suppress the "rebellion", do you think Blanco, who was of course a military man and expectably military-minded, would not have seized the opportunity to at least use him as such an informer? In short, we have to conclude that Rizal must have informed against and betrayed all the Katipunan leaders he knew. Rizal cannot do such a thing? But he had offered them to do infinitely more than that; as per his offer of his all to suppress the rebellion, Blanco could have assigned him for instance to plot a way to deceive and entrap Bonifacio; or he could have ordered him to head a division of Spanish soldiers, or to campaign house to house against the revolution, etc.

arrested despite it, and convicted despite it, and shot despite it...

Ingoo: The friars—they pressured the Madrid government to pressure Blanco to have Rizal arrested for trial; and in the deranged circumstances of the insurrection and the reign of terror, they got what they wanted. In fact, this pressure from the friars went all the way to effectuate the removal from office of Gov. Gen. Blanco who was perceived, not without reason, as Rizal's friend. And that was the tragic stroke of fate that did in Rizal. On December 13, 1896, Polavieja arrived from Spain to replace Blanco. Rizal must have been alerted by Blanco himself about the impending developments. Note that Rizal wrote *Data For My Defense*, where he specifically and pointedly referred to the evil letter, on December 12; he must have known earlier that Blanco was due to be replaced. And indeed, the very next day, his replacement arrived. This must have made him hysterical. His direct reference to Blanco in his *Data For My Defense* was already a forthright dragging of the then still Governor General into the trial. It was tantamount to a summons for him to testify together with the letter of evil. Nor could there have been any doubt that had he testified thus, even merely as a former Governor General, Rizal would have been acquitted: there was no way for those military men to ignore such testimony by and from such as Blanco. But, hell-bent on judicially murdering him, now that Blanco was no longer Governor General, there was a very great likelihood that they would ignore the reference to the evil letter and pass over in silence what in effect was Rizal's plea to have Blanco testify with the letter. Rizal had to make sure that all-important letter would not be ignored. He had to force the court to make Blanco testify. And that must have been what prompted him to write that despicable *December 15 Manifesto* with the request that it be published and disseminated amongst the native population, it being also shrewdly written as a denunciation of the revolution and its leaders and a plea to those who were in it because (as he put it) they were "deceived" by those "savage" leaders, to quit the revolution and go home, and live in peace with their families, and to those who have not yet joined it to desist from joining it. He composed it in such a way that it would not be easy for those military men to justify their not publishing and disseminating it. Whilst such publication and dissemination would catapult the evil letter to central prominence and make it a matter of course for Blanco to testify with it. But evidently, those military judges had already made up their minds to do away with Rizal and therefore had to refuse to publish and disseminate the *Manifesto*. Gen. Nicolas dela Pena who was Judge Advocate General was tasked to write the recommendation (to Polavieja) not to have it published and disseminated. His reason was absolutely fantastic:--he alleged that publication of it and dissemination amongst the native population would make those who are already in the revolution even more zealous revolutionaries and those who have not yet joined it to flock to it! Polavieja who was one of them did not need any convincing; it was a mere matter of form and he gave his formal concurrence. The *Manifesto* was not published, the letter and together with it its addressee, Blanco, were ignored, and Rizal was convicted and duly executed.

ii

Ingoo: Before we go to Dr. Pangilinan's fallacious *retrospective fallacy*, allow me to expose something which I am almost certain to forget if I do not say it right away. This is about a case of intellectual irresponsibility and slapdash scholarship, in fact of zero or below zero scholarship, which I just caught Dr. Pangilinan's master, Dr. Floro Quibuyen in the act of perpetrating. This concerns his absolutely unargued claim that "...the author who influenced him (Rizal) most profoundly, as far as the study of culture and history was concerned, was Herder... Herder's influence on Rizal's cultural concept of the nation is unmistakable...", etc. (pages 167 *et seq.* of his absolutely futureless sophomoric book of pasyon-ately unargued allegations and hearsays, *A Nation Aborted*, etc.). This is how it happened. Quibuyen caught sight of a detail in a *May 26, 1890*[110] letter from Rizal to

110 "Strangely, no scholar has explored Herder's impact on Rizal", writes Quibuyen (168). Strangely, there was no

Blumentritt about the works of the father of German nationalism (the same that culminated in Nazism and the Holocaust—a thing of which Quibuyen seems to be absolutely unaware), Gottfried Herder. In this letter Rizal, who was then in Brussels, mentioned that he bought in a bookshop there all the 38 volumes of Herder's complete works "for a song", adding that, if he, Blumentritt, is interested in Herder, he will at once send him all of it[111]. Blumentritt replied in another letter (May 28, 1890) that he had all of Herder in his library

---

mention whatsoever of Herder in Rizal's works—only in this letter, and in a carefree offer to send all of him away to his friend Blumentritt at once without as much as opening a leaf of the 38 volumes—a most strange way to treat one's profoundest, *sine qua non*, intellectual influence! If we take Quibuyen's protestations on the profundity and completeness of such Herderian influence on Rizal's mind, on his thought, his soul, his spirit, which of course can only be palpably expressed in his works, we should be saying things like, *Without Herder, no Rizal*. You know how discipleship is: Without Socrates, no Plato; without Hegel, no Marx; without Confucius, no Mencius, without Nietzsche no Derrida or Hitler, without Rizal, no Quibuyen or Jose David Lapuz, without Quibuyen, no Antonio Pangilinan…without Januario Labios and his *Santong Boces* and without his *Tatang* Valentin delos Santos, no Reynaldo Clemena Ileto… And then, we should be asking this insidious question:--Why then did Rizal never mention Herder in any of his works? Was he hiding his sources? And was he a cheat also, like more than one Rizalist pasyonist-voodoist we know?

111 Here are Rizal's words: "Recently I acquired the following works: Raffles, *Java*, and Beauvoir, *Voyage Around the World*. If you need such works, write me. I also have *The Complete Works of Herder*, which I bought for a song. If you like Herder, I will send you his 38 volumes. (Letter 144 in *Rizal's Correspondence with Blumentritt*, p 355).

too, and proceeded to lecture Rizal on the great virtues of that proto-fascist patriarch and prophet of German national greatness. From this, and without showing any textual proof of whatever kind, Quibuyen promptly concluded that Herder had most profoundly influenced Rizal! He cited among other works the *Noli* (*published in March, 1887*) and the "landmark" essay *The Philippines A Century Hence* (*published in a series in La Solidaridad from September 1889 to February 1890*) as proof of such profound influence! Unfortunately for him, Rizal had already published the *Noli* three years, and that mediocre and politically wrong and evil essay several months, *before* he "bought the complete works of Herder for a song"! And that indeed is a shining example of Filipino scholarship for you! Nor is there any whatever theoretical or conceptual explication of what Herder was about in his works which supposedly influenced Rizal ***even before he read them***! But not only that. There was also no discussion whatsoever of what really Rizal's supposed nationalism was about. All there was were bold assertions absolutely without explicative proof. Like his master Ileto, Quibuyen used the *identical spelling hermeneutic method*, a specialized branch of the general approach known as the *speleological-troglodytian voodoo historiographic method* which requires that everything be done in the labyrinthine secrecy of caves preferably subterranean ones, and, just in case we need to say it, with, of course, an assortment of dolls and other effigies and the needles to match, salamander shit, fermented fetus, and the absolutely indispensable *Santong Boces* from, of course, the *Santong Labios, Labios Majora* and *Labios Minora* (androgynous as you can see), etc..., etc. Which in this case meant that Quibuyen simply relied on the occurrence of some English (not even German or Spanish) words in Herder and Rizal to be able most emphatically and bombastically to conclude that "Herder's influence on Rizal was unmistakable", "the most profound", etc. , etc. Just as Ileto in finding that Bonifacio also used the words "liwanag" and "katwiran" which can be found in pasyonistic texts concluded at once that Bonifacio and the KKK were pasyonist-millenarian[112]... Fantastic! And

---

[112] To be fair to Quibuyen and to indulge the reader's

craving for blood or burlesque or comedy, let us quote him here. According to Quibuyen "...the author who influenced him (Rizal) most profoundly, as far as the study of culture and history was concerned, was Herder..." (p167). This is a very forthright claim and we are therefore led by it to expect a thorough demonstration of how this *most profound* of all influences on Rizal by that German nationalist who was actually the direct ancestor of Hitler, happened; such demonstration must of course contain a coherent, in-depth, conceptual, theoretical, and certainly philosophical reconstruction and presentation of Herder's and Rizal's corresponding theories of nationalism, of nation, culture, and history—and on such theoretical-philosophical basis, a comparison of the two. However, all that Quibuyen was able and perfectly content to do here was an of course totally superficial and sophomoric juxtaposition of words in Rizal and in Herder which happened to sound alike and to have in the English translations, *the same spelling*! (In the end, perhaps Quibuyen cannot be blamed too much for such a lengthy parade of superficialities and preconceptual thinking at least as far as showing what Rizal has by way of a theory or philosophy of culture, history, nation, nationalism, etc., for the simple fact is there was no coherent theory or philosophy of such things in Rizal himself, even as it must certainly be counted as abuse of language to call him a theoretician or philosopher at all. If Rizal had a coherent view of such things, it was an *assimilationist* one and was as such delusional and, as such, of exceeding stupidity: it does not deserve the name *theory*. However, Herder was a different matter and it was incumbent on Quibuyen to have fully explicated Herder's theory/philosophy of culture and history. But how could he have done so when his intellectual capacities are sufficient only—as should be obvious to any normal reader of his book of teratological and comic abortions—for writing a grade three theme in a grade five themebook?). Quibuyen proceeds to wonder at his wondrous discovery: "Strangely, no scholar has explored Herder's impact on Rizal" (p. 168). We are hereby alerted therefore to the fact that here Quibuyen is attempting it for the first time! Quibuyen continues: "In his 26 May 1890 letter, Rizal informed Blumentritt that he had *The Complete Works of Herder*—all thirty-eight volumes—'which I bought for a song'." Quibuyen neglected to cite the fact that Rizal, in the next sentence, offered to send all of the 38 volumes to Blumentritt, or that Blumentritt in the reply letter lectured him on Herder in such a way as to make one conclude that that was the first time Herder ever cropped up between the two of them and that, as far as Blumentritt knew, Rizal did not know a thing about Herder. Quibuyen pushes on with his discovery of a Herderian Rizal: "Rizal's affinity with Herder's ideas is uncanny: the notion that the integrity of all peoples and historical epochs have intrinsic value and must be respected; the stress on the climatic and geographic factors, and historical circumstances in the development of cultures; the lifelong rejection of tyranny and the affirmation of human rights and all that fosters human freedom and dignity." Were these Herder's ideas? Quibuyen merely claimed they were; he did not show how. And were they Rizal's too? Again, Quibuyen merely alleged and did not show they were. Where did Quibuyen get the idea that Rizal believed in "the notion that the integrity of all peoples and historical epochs have intrinsic value and must be respected"? If Rizal held such an idea and adhered to it, he would never have been an assimilationist; for, of course, assimilation can only have one meaning here, namely, the dissolution of the *assimilated* people and the destruction of their culture; which was why Rizal in all his works had demanded the systematic teaching of Spanish to the natives, the systematic propagation of Spanish culture and in general of Western-European civilization through a colonial program of education, the promotion of, of course, capitalist industry and trade amongst the natives, the rationalization of the government bureaucracy in Weber's sense, the inculcation amongst the natives of a Western-European progressivist outlook, etc. The teaching of the lightning rod (Tasio), yes! The next sentence in this quote will give us the astounding method of Quibuyen which he inherited from his master Ileto like a grade one pupil inheriting from a grade one-and-a-half pupil, for such is the level of mentation they, master and slave, have in common. Which accounts for the fact that their supposed "books" are such comedies, brave, certainly, and shameless, inevitably and irremediably shameless. But to Quibuyen's and Ileto's method perfectly exemplified now: "Herderian notions crop up in Rizal's novels and essays. Consider, for example, this line from Herder:

"But the very moment their inherited national feeling awakens again, the fire, that for so long has been assiduously kept smouldering in the ashes, will burst out into open flames. (In FM Barnard 1965,286)

"Compare it with Tasio's exhortation to Ibarra in the *Noli*,

"When the light of day shows up the monsters of darkness, the frightful reaction will come. So many sighs suppressed, so much poison distilled drop by drop, so much force repressed for centuries, will come to light and burst! (*Social Cancer*, 161)

"Rizal employs the same Herderian tropes in his landmark essay, 'The Philippines A Century Hence', where he writes that the 'flame' of 'the spirit of the people' was spreading surely and fiercely' (*Political Writings,* 132), and that 'the national spirit has awakened' (140)."

There! And every arsonist then, but also every fire department, is a Herderian, and, but, every Japanese too, by virtue of the *Rising Sun*, a Herderian including of course Hideki Tojo and Miss Moshi Moshi Anoneh, who then are, by spelling and other speleological conductivity, Rizalists, too. And you too, dear reader, Herderian, Rizalist, Hidekist, Tojist, Moshist, Anonehist, and a pyromaniac for have you not somewhere there in some nook of your years and cranny of your nights used the voodoo words *inherited, national, feeling, awakens, again, the, fire, that, for, so, long, assiduously, kept, smouldering, ashes, burst, out, open, flames, light of day, monsters of darkness, repressed for centuries, spirit, people, national, awakened…liwanag, katuwiran, panata, lakaran, katubusan, katarantaduhan, kabugukan, ha? ha? ha*? Do we need to say more? But this verbal voodoo method launched full-scale first by, of course, the voodooist guru Ileto, in his voodoo book *Pasyon and Revolution* in which by the same *spelling voodoo* which must certainly be very deeply speleological and troglodytic he was able to prove that the Katipunan itself and Andres Bonifacio himself were *pasyonist*, i.e., millenarian, voodooistically insane, because Bonifacio too used the voodoo-pasyon words *liwanag, katwiran,etcetera bwahaha*—this method, sanctified and officialised by Ateneo and Cornell University's Southeast Asian Studies Department (and does one have to wonder what manner of intellectual troglodytes must they be who inhabit such intellectual caves?)—this method under the self-contradictory and dishonest and opportunist name "history from below", was zealously and slavishly embraced by Zeus Salazar, Prospero Covar, Francisco Nemenzo, Jr., Babaylan Queen Fe Mangahas, Juan Gatbonton, the Bathaluman of the UP English Department Duktora Con Solaciona Laras, Isagani Annie Cruz from the UPSCA and the University of Maryland (heart of the *Ku Klux Klan* and no wonder then!) and other Filipino Haitians (see back cover and blurbs of Ileto's

Pasyon and Revolution) including of course Quibuyen himself. It has become a movement of stupidity, of Philippine stupidity in general and a school for insulting and denigrating Bonifacio and the Katipunan in particular by imputing pasyon-voodoo to him, to it, to the Revolution itself. We have to say more. And nothing better than to repeat Quibuyen here in the shamelessness of the cheat and the herpes of his scholarship and rub right into his open eyes once more the siling palay or, wanting this, the Tabasco of his downfall and shame as scholar and professor, for this should be more than enough urgent reason for his university in Australia to terminate him and have him prosecuted for swindling them and their Australian students—and for the Ateneo Press to close shop for very shame. Actually, Quibuyen's sole warrant and the only one he puts forward at all, for his stupendous conclusion that Rizal was a thoroughgoing Herderian, that Herder was the most profound influence there was on Rizal, that "Herder's influence on Rizal's cultural concept of the nation is unmistakeable" (p169), is this ***May 26, 1890*** epistolary detail on the acquisition by Rizal of the 38 volumes of Herder's complete works "for a song". Being an agogged practitioner of the Iletist voodoo-pasyon or pasyon-voodoo method, he at once, *without looking at the relative dates or even thinking about such unvoodoo things*, jumped into applying sorcery upon supposed Herderian words from not even Herder's books but from mere, and of course English, secondary sources and other hearsays on one hand, and Rizal's Englished words on the other hand, seizing the unsuspecting words by the neck or the armpits or even by the pudenda and the vis a tergo of them, and bundling and trundling them and making them copulate tastelessly and without regard to the perimeters of their culture and the niceties of their sex, making them give birth to each other thus… And he did not notice that the *Noli* which came out in *March 1887* (the accompanying personally but more malefically nationally destructive even massmurderously injurious in its blank-idiot-grin stupidity, *evil—evil evil evil*. Another thing on Quibuyen's bold inability to think which in a doctor professor who lays claim to being a writer thus is really a skunk's imperious shamelessness: He maintains that the Spaniards decided not to publish Rizal's *December 15 Manifesto* because, according to him, they saw that rather than convince the Filipinos against the Revolution, it was likely to do the opposite, namely rally them to it. This, as we have already pointed out, was actually the reason given by Gen. Dela Pena in his recommendation to Polavieja to desist from publishing it. And, without even reading the *Manifesto*, Quibuyen simply agreed with him! Without reading it, I say, because anyone who reads it—except ones like Dela Pena who were intent to convict Rizal and have him executed—must, if he be of normal intelligence, see the opposite. And, this bears repeating because the Filipinos—effect of a century of brainwashing and a culture of dishonesty and lies—are very forgetful, we have shown why Dela Pena made that recommendation, and that was because he was certain that should it get published it was certain to

---

letter of Rizal's gift of a copy of it to Blumentritt was dated *Berlin, 21 March 1887*) and which must have been in the works then in *1885-86*, cannot possibly have borne croppings up or down or transversal of "Herderian notions" for having been written *2 months and 5 or 6 years before* Rizal could know any Herder. The same for the supposed fierce and rampant Herderianism of the flame of the spirit of the people spreading like e. coli or hi-ni of "*the landmark essay, The Philippines A Century Hence*", which came out as a series in *La Solidaridad* from *September 1889 to February 1890*. But that's enough for now for Quibuyen, for the mess and the stink of the puke. *Labios majora* and *Labios minora*, as we have seen, yes from Ileto's incensetuously beloved Januario Labios' *Santong Boces*, great-great grandfather of Ileto and Quibuyen. Let us now pause and wash our minds…

have such an effect as without fail to exonerate Rizal… Why? Because publication of it would surely call attention to *that detail in it of his offering of his life, his name, his everything to the Spanish authorities on August 22, 1896 or thereabouts, to be used by them in "whatever manner they deem fit", to " stifle the rebellion"*. Attention would have been focused on *who* he made the offer to and *how* he made it. And it would then be revealed that it was to Governor General Blanco no less that he made the offer, and that he made it *in a letter witnessed by Colonel Santalo* who was the commander of the Spanish cruiser *Castilla* docked in Manila Bay then, where he was, upon his own hysterical request held incommunicado while waiting for the next mailboat to Spain[113]. And then that revelation would constrain the judges to have the letter presented, and such presentation cannot have any other effect except Rizal's exoneration… For what that letter demonstrated was that Rizal could sell his very own mother *por kilo* if that would prove his loyalty to his Mother Spain and his undying love for her.

Joe Blue: Those are new insights and fresh lights indeed on some of the most disputed episodes of Rizal's greatly infamous and ignominious betrayal of the Revolution and of the Filipino people…

Ingoo: And newly and fully documented ones, Joblo!...

Joe Blue: Certainly one of the most important lessons you have already imparted to the Filipino historians and students is the need to properly document every historiographic claim—and how.

Ingoo: I mean to be as emphatic as possible on it…

---

113 On these details, see Rizal's *Data for my Defense*, and his *Additional Data for my Defense,* in the 2007 NHI edition of *Rizal's Political and Historical Writings*).

Joe Blue: And now, and by way of theoretical propaedeutic as you say, we can perhaps consider that fallacious invention by the famously disputatious Dr. Pangilinan from Balic-Balic University?... He meant to destroy the main thrust of your critique of Rizal by exposing it as theoretically misconceived, as wrong from the very concept of it, i.e., as fallacious...

Ingoo: Yes, like a category mistake...

Joe Blue: Category mistake, precisely!

Ingoo: *Fallacy*. It's not a question then of kindness or cruelty, of humane consideration or the lack of it, but of logic—an epistemological matter. He—whoever he may be who's saying it—is saying that it is logically wrong for me to castigate Rizal for being logically wrong about a question which such as it was, was logically—or which is the same thing, onto-logically—impossible *contemporaneously* to be logically right about[114]. *Onto*-logically. *For it concerns the being of knowledge itself in relation to the being of the knower and the being of the known, and specifically the time, the temporality--the contemporaneity and the retro of it--that determines everything here and which constitutes for knowledge a condition of its possibility or impossibility*. And in connection with this *contemporaneity and retrospectivity* of it, i.e., the *temporality* of it, what is being said here concerns the *being itself of history and its knowability*, and what it says is that history does not exist, is impossible, and is unknowable...

Joe Blue: You have immediately ontologized it, which is to say, radicalized it, and pushed the thing to the extreme limit.

---

[114]It happens that the thing, the question, the knowledge of which is here in question, is revolution, separation, independence from colonialism on one hand, and its/their exact opposite/s, counter-revolution, assimilation, perpetual or eternal colonialism on the other hand.

Ingoo: I have simply taken it as a philosophical question[115], and to philosophy all questions are immediately ontological or *existological*. By The latter term I mean to mark the difference which in a specific sense of the term *infinite*, is infinite, between being and existence or, more precisely, *ex*-istence, where the latter includes the infinite qualification of freedom or transcendence at, of course, both the individual and social-historical levels or dimensions, which is absent in the former. This distinction will also mark how the *power to die* happens in my radical re-thinking and re-construction of the social sciences and of philosophy in general.

Joe Blue: The *power to die*, yes. The, to you, apropos of Plato's *epekeina tes ousias*, true beyond of being!

Ingoo: Which nevertheless is not its ontological beyond...

Joe Blue: An ethical and a poetic beyond...

Ingoo: Which is really nothing but the irreducibility of freedom to being...

Joe Bue: Which exactly is what defines transcendence...

Ingoo: Yes, transcendence is the transcending of being by freedom...

---

115 And how else indeed? Quibuyen's amanuensis is here talking about a fallacy, and questions of fallacy are questions of logic, not of psychology, and such questions are of course properly, very properly, philosophical questions. It has moreover, in the conjunction, become an ontological question because it concerns the being of time in relation to the being of knowledge in relation to the being of the knower in relation to the being of the known... The problem of course is Quibuyen himself, let alone his devoted *escribiente*, does not even know what ontology, the word *ontology*, means.

Joe Blue: Which defines freedom onto-existologically...

Ingoo: Yes, that's how it is...

Joe Blue: But does not the philosopher also entertain particular questions? For, the way I understand it, ontological and (your new notion of) existological questions are the most general, in fact always universal, things and questions there are.

Ingoo: What the philosopher does, thinking philosophically, considering any question whatsoever in the properly philosophical way which is a way all its own, is all at once to plunge back with the thing or question to the deepest and most comprehensive level or dimension which is the ontological and which in the case of things historical is at once existological, and from there to interrogate and analyse and spell-out the particular thing or question[116]. For instance this

---

[116]A way all its own... Science, physics for instance, or psychology, or sociology, or indeed history, does not as a matter of principle interrogate itself or its concepts onto-existologically thus. The reason it is able to push ahead and produce results which are certifiably scientific is that it naively, automatically, quite unconsciously presupposes what we may term a fundamental praxiological realism which is at bottom the same as the naïve, universal realism of the everyday. Onto-existologically, all science, from physics to psychology to history and sociology and politics, is, yes, a species of naïve realism; the difference between the realism of the everyday, and that of the scientist doing science, e.g., the realism of the quantum physicist peering into the electron microscope or analyzing cloud chamber printouts, is *onto-existo-logically* within the same naïve realist range. And the fact that science is so successful proves, validates, this fundamental praxiological realism and with it that of which the latter is the core, naïve realism itself, the realism of the everyday. Spelled-out, this fundamental realism is possessed of the following self-evidentiating principles:

retrospective fallacy thing or question here...In this sense, the first question the philosopher asks of a thing or question is:--Can it be grounded onto-existo-logically? And how? This plunging back at once to the onto-existo-logical level is what we have done here, automatically as it were (philosophy having become a habit thus to one who has been doing it for many years now such that it can be said that it has become his life itself), to the term, the thing, the question called quite intriguingly, the *retrospective fallacy*. This plunging back of the thing, the question, to the onto-existo-logical level and its interrogation there is an attempt to configure it onto-existo-logically, and that means, interrogating it as to its ontological-existological conditions of possibility. It is a re-configuring in thought, a *re-construction* in thought on the basis of the thing's roots themselves which are its conditions

---

from nothing nothing comes: ex nihilo, nihil fit, which is also to say, nothing, no being, is without a cause; beings come from beings and from the whole; which is to say, there was no absolute, pure, simple beginning, for always already there were beings and being; always already being is beings and beings are being (our clarified notion of the ontological difference; so that there is no beginning and there is no end to this entire thing which is being/beings; being/beings is/are whether I think of it, of them, or not, i.e., the mind does not create the being/beings which are/is its ultimate referent/s, there is being, there are beings out there whether we like it or not, whether we are here to confirm it or not…Driving a car, I do not merely think I am driving a car…Quark cloud-chamber traces are traces of something, not of nothing at all, and are not mere mental products. Breaching this onto-existological barrier lands one into metaphysics, which is always a delusion because while one is "there", one nonetheless remains solidly here, eating and drinking and talking and drawing salaries even and fucking or being fucked even, here, here, here, where else?

of possibility. What it seeks to produce thereby is the *concept of the thing itself.*

Joe Blue: Radicalized thus—ontologized, existologized as you put it—why does it follow from the concept of this so-called retrospective fallacy that history is impossible, and that it does not exist and that it is unknowable?

Ingoo: "From the concept" of it, that's right! That is exactly how the thing should be put. We are considering this so-called *retrospective fallacy* according to its very concept—if it has any concept at all. And by this we mean, if it is a thinkable, coherent, and *true* thing at all. And what follows from this its very own concept is that there is no history, history is impossible, and there is no such thing as historical knowledge and such knowledge is impossible. And then, of course, it, itself, together with knowledge and truth is impossible:--it is a self-contradictory thing, and this reconstruction of the possible concept of it reveals that it is itself impossible and is thus itself without concept... In fact, what its impossible concept must presuppose and imply is that human beings themselves are impossible, and Dr. Antonio Pangilinan himself cannot possibly exist together with those who applauded this nonconcept of a concept, namely Dr. Jaime Veneracion, Dr. Obet Verzola, Quibuyen himself... I heard that Veneracion was very happy in saying that "Tony's intervention is good!" Whilst Dr. Verzola was very happy that Dr. Pangilinan was able to save Dr. Jose Rizal from the peril of the doubts and accusations Ingoo has been sowing and hurling everywhere.

Joe Blue: Dr. Antonio Pangilinan himself cannot exist? And Veneracion, and Verzola and Quibuyen himself. And therefore do not even now exist at all! Wow! I mean, that could be nice, I mean, no not exactly nice, only that I won't mind, really. But, how come?

Ingoo: Let us go back to the term *fallacy*. We are saying that if this thing called *retrospective fallacy* is a true and real fallacy then the inability to know revolution/separation/independence on one hand and the opposite terms or things namely reform or counter-revolution, assimilation, eternal colonialism on the other hand, being attributed to Rizal was not due merely to a contingent psychological, mental incapacity or any other accident or incident, but was rather *intrinsic to the things themselves* such that it was due ultimately to the being and *ex*-istence of time itself, of history itself, of society itself, of the individual human being herself/himself, of knowledge itself, and was therefore an inescapable, necessary, universal, yes ontological and existological condition. And then what the concept of this retrospective fallacy thing is saying about the things themselves here would be that their temporality is such that it impossibilizes the contemporaneous knowledge of any social-historical thing, event, state-of-affairs...You will at once see and at once agree however that our knowledge of the past (such as is attributed to himself and to Dr. Demigilio and generally to present human beings by Dr. Antonio Pangilinan) is possible only as a correlation between it and our knowledge of the present:--and how else indeed if the temporality of things and events, of onto-existo-logical things and events and beings, is a movement from within the things themselves? But the latter is absolutely, onto-existo-logically impossibilized by this *retrospective fallacy* thing. If, like Jose Rizal was in relation to his present, we are irreducibly ignorant of our present, then we must in fact be irreducibly ignorant too of our past because of course each moment of our past was a past moment of present irreducible ignorance! What all this leads up to is one very important insight. It is that a minimum of self-knowledge and therefore of truth is presupposed by any possible individual and socio-historical existence, failing which the human being ceases or fails to be a human being at all and society ceases to be a society of free beings, of transcendent beings, that is to say, of *human* beings at all, and history is not history but a merely thingly movement of a compound-complex *thing*[117]... I hope I am making myself clear...

---

117 An insight dawns here, which we badly need. History is possible only as, and on the basis of, a certain knowledge of history by the very people who make it. You will see at

once that this must be true when you ask the opposite question: Is history possible on the basis of the absolute ignorance of it of its supposed agents?

Of course Pangilinan said only that Rizal did not know enough and cannot know enough; he did not say Rizal was absolutely ignorant; but he concluded from this the existence of a fallacy and that is why we have the right to nail him on it, whilst this concept of fallacy epistemologizes, logicizes, ontologizes and existologizes the seemingly simple question of Rizal's not being able to know *enough* of that which was contemporaneous with him. How much is "enough" here? Enough for me or for anyone who was born later to fairly, justly, and validly judge him on the correctness, the rightness, the intelligence, of his view of himself and of his present. In question here is a kind of knowledge that is equally valid for contemporaries as for non-contemporaries and ultimately for all possible times (which is not the same as a timeless or non-temporal knowledge), on the basis of which my judgment of Rizal or of Bonifacio, or of Plato, or of Moses can be validated, criticized, compared, confirmed, improved or confuted. And first of all, and at its most basic, Pangilinan is saying by way of this *restrospective fallacy* thing of his that there is no such knowledge and there cannot be. Note, once more, that this knowledge which we claim to be possible and exists is not absolute knowledge such as metaphysics in its unconscious Goddism must always claim the only possible kind of knowledge to be (unconsciously elevating thus the claimant metaphysician to the delirium tremendum of Godhood which empowered and duly armed must make of him a practicing fascist and massmurderer). Now what I am saying is that this denial—ultimately a metaphysically motivated one—by such as Pangilinan of the very possibility of such knowledge must not only lead him to deny the very possibility of the social sciences and of the human sciences in general; it must also lead him straight into a kind of nativism, a temporalized nativism where the inevitable differences between knowabilities that are differently temporally located are absolutized, so that no two differently temporally located knowledges are comparable in such a way as to enable non-synchronous subjects or agents to fairly, justly, and intelligently evaluate and judge each other. The key term here is *incomparable*, where the *incomparability* is *absolutized* thus. It is this comparability that bespeaks the continuity of social existence into a sociality and a historicity which accounts for the very be-ing of society itself and of history itself, without which then neither society nor history is possible.

And then, but then, why stop at continuity-discontinuity/comparability-incomparability/knowability-unknowability, at the social-historical level? At any rate, stopping here will immediately metaphysically absolutize the social or the historical or both at once, into a veritable metaphysical substance: the tribe, the blood, the native land/soil, as mystical entities that among other things restricts all possible knowledge to self-knowledge inside the tribe: Nazism, metaphysical tribalism/racism, metaphysical xenophobism, metaphysical Chosen-Peopleism...But really, stopping here is unwarranted. It's a question of the temporality of being-knowledge, and there is absolutely no reason why it should be limited to historical periods and collective entities like tribes or clans. Since time absolutely separates units of being-knowledge from each other, there is no reason whatsoever why it must not absolutely separate my yesterday from today, and indeed, my instant now from my instant immediately before it. Every instant of me must then be absolutely ignorant of my past instant of being and so on, and I am not anymore, and cannot be. Atomized into impossibility here is the be-ing which is at once a be-ing of knowledge, of self-knowledge which is at once a knowledge of being, of beings, of other existents, of nature, of the world, namely the be-ing of the subject that makes possible the very existence of the subject as subject, that is to say, the very be-ing of the human being as human being: there are no subjects and there are no human beings—only multiple series of atomized instants of subjectivity; but even a series must have a principle of continuity to be able to be the series that it is and to distinguish it from other series:--what would this principle be? On the other hand, it is the same kind of comparability of instants of knowledge/s on the individual or micro level that constitutes one of the conditions of possibility of historical knowledge itself whose very possibility itself constitutes the condition of possibility of history itself.

From this inevitable radicalization to the level of the instant, it follows inescapably that it is ontologically-existologically impossible for anyone to know anything contemporaneous with her/him including of course and first of all her/his very own self. From which follows that there is no self there but only a thing, no history there but only a thingly, a natural, causality. And this because freedom/transcendence is possible only as a certain irreducible self-knowledge. This is not God's knowledge of himself, of course, there being no such thing in the first place (for if there is, then you must not be and are not), but self-knowledge rather than pure, absolute self-ignorance it is. In very truth, those who, like Nietzsche and Derrida, and generally the modernday or rather, as they themselves would have it, the postmodernday neo-Buddhists who are then capitalist neo-Buddhists, the so-called post-structuralists who cannot find any self in themselves for them to know or even to not know, in denying this self-knowledge are denying absolute self-knowledge, failing which they then declare that there is no such thing as self-knowledge, even as they do declare that there is no knowledge whatsoever at all, and for exactly the same reason, namely, there is only nothing there to be known and only nothing there to know. This is negative metaphysics which is of course but the inversion of positivist metaphysics. These negative metaphysicians are such God-addicts that, realizing that there is no God they then declare that in that case there is nothing but nothing. If you cannot know anything with God's omniscient knowledge, then you cannot know anything whatsoever, and there is no such thing as knowledge at all. It is God or nothing for them; but there is no God, ergo, there is nothing, nothing but nothing. Similarly, it is God's omniscient knowledge or absolute non-knowledge for them; but there is no such thing as omniscience, ergo, there absolutely is no such thing as knowledge. On the same negative metaphysical premises, either the self, yourself, for instance, is God, or there absolutely is no self; but the self, yourself, is not God, therefore there is no self and you do not exist. Derrida, following Nietzsche following Buddha, "discovered" that the self is differed/deferred, i.e., is different, harbours difference, is constituted differentially; but to Derrida, the only real reality, the only thing that genuinely *is*, is the absolutely undifferentiated, the absolute One of Parmenides; but the self of such mere humans as you and I (Derrida excepted of course, for how else would he be able to see and say all that he is seeing and saying here?) is not absolutely one, not the Parmenidean ONE, therefore, it, the self of you and I absolutely is not and you are not and I am not absolutely! Moreover, Derrida, following the same filiation, and having "discovered" that the only real reality is the absolutely one, i.e., the Parmenidean ONE, "discovered" also that every thing, every self, is many, and there is absolutely nothing that is not many, and the absolutely one, the ONE is not and cannot be; from which he of course concludes that, since there is no ONE, then there is only nothing, absolutely nothing but nothing but nothing.

Joe Blue: Whew! I lost myself and found myself and lost myself again at arduous passages in your discourse there... But please go ahead, I have not yet fully seen how thinking through or working out this impossible concept of the *retrospective fallacy* of Dr. Antonio Pangilinan makes Dr. Antonio Pangilinan impossible of existence and hence non-existent...and Quibuyen too, ha ha, and Veneracion, and Versola, and, but, why not Jose David Lapuz also, please?

Ingoo: What this *retrospective fallacy* thing says among other things is that it is fallacious, logically wrong, epistemologically prohibited and caput, to judge the judgment of actors, agents, of past periods as though they knew *enough* of what they should have known enough of their period if they were to be right about such judgments. And this because they must of necessity—of onto-existological necessity—be ignorant of all those things about their own period:--of all those things, namely of themselves, of their social-historical conditions, of being, of beings, of the world... This means that

---

Going back now to this irreducible self-knowledge after establishing the insanity and the absolute violence, the nihilistic violence, of those who deny it:—and of course, Dr. Antonio Pangilinan is one of them for this absolute violence is entailed by his very notion of *retrospective fallacy*... This irreducible self-knowledge is a *pre-reflective cogito* in Sartre's sense (as discovered and explicated by him in the first part of the great work, *Being and Nothingness*); in Heidegger, it is the pre-comprehension of being, in Kant, the *I think*... I call it the *nurr*, short for *nuclear ur-reflection.* The structural position that these terms name is the same. Why do I insist on my term *nurr?* Because, just as Sartre's, Heidegger's, and Kant's concepts differ substantially from each other, so does my own concept of that structural-existential position and agency differ from theirs. I hold that this pre-reflective cogito or pre-comprehension of being is already the *power to die which alone gives being.*

according to Dr. Antonio Pangilinan, there is an irreducible ignorance that pertains to every human being in relation to his/her own present; and therefore, that there is an irreducible unknowability about things to anyone who is contemporaneous with them. Now we have to radicalize this temporality of this unknowability or of this irreducible ignorance in accordance with the logical-epistemological notion or concept of fallacy which excludes from its definition everything merely psychological or empirical, everything merely contingent, accidental, incidental. A judgment, a conclusion, a reasoning is fallacious because it violates a logical rule and thereby transgresses an epistemological and not merely psychological requirement or necessity. Why is it fallacious of me, according to this *retrospective fallacy* thing to blame Rizal for not being a revolutionary in the 1890s? Because, so Dr. Antonio Pangilinan maintains, one of the indispensable things for such as Rizal to become a revolutionary during his time was knowing something which ontologically and existologically was impossible for him to know, *and this because no one can know that which is contemporaneous with himself/herself, because anybody's present is unknowable to him/her*. If, for instance it was possible for some Filipinos during that time to know that thing which Rizal failed to know such that they were able to become revolutionaries and Rizal was not, then Rizal's failure and ignorance would not be ontologically or existologically necessitated, and must thus be due to his simple lack of intelligence and perhaps humanity; and then it would not be a retrospective fallacy for me to point the failure out and diminish his popularity or entirely blot out his historical stature on account of it. It could perhaps be extra-cruel of me, but fallacious it would not be.

Joe Blue: Oh, but in fact, Andres Bonifacio and company were able to know that which Rizal failed to know and, knowing it thus, were able to become revolutionaries... Or, put another way, they became revolutionaries and therefore must have known *that* the failure to know which prevented Rizal from being revolutionary...

Ingoo: You are a philosopher, though you contrive always to hide it. You betray it in the phrasing... And yes of course, it's true, Andres Bonifacio and his multitude of true heroes knew what Rizal failed to know, and that's why the simplest and the humblest of those Katipunero ancestors of ours in the indubitable truth of their heroism and the unblemished brightness of their glory were more intelligent and were deeper and larger human beings than Dr. Jose Rizal in the deepest and truest sense of being intelligent and being deep and large in one's humanity. And yes, that Andres Bonifacio and company were there was a huge and multitudinous refutation of Dr. Antonio Pangilinan's *retrospective fallacy* thing. But at this point, that is not the point. It constitutes another route to showing up the stupidity and perversion of some people including those that are in the habit of applauding the stupidity and perversity of the former, but that is for later, for I mean to work that thing out too from inside the thing itself and exhibit it here to shame them and punish them for their shamelessness.

Joe Blue: You are not cruel at all, Senor Ingoo!

Ingoo: Of course I am not! As a person, I am even shy... Why, I even have stage fright...

Joe Blue: Stage fright, hmm...ahm... Ah...I, I, ah, I believe you, I think. And that no doubt is why you frighten a lot of speakers onstage and offstage. Yes, I can believe you there... You are not cruel at all, only thorough, logically thorough... extremely, pitilessly logically thorough, like you are now, for instance...

Ingoo: I am a logician...a dialectician...

Joe Blue: And mercy is not a logical attribute...

Ingoo: Even among the ancients, already, Zeno of Elea was the Prince of Dialecticians, but it was Plato whose debt to Zeno even more than to Socrates was immeasurable, who said that, and I quote, "the dialectic is no respecter of persons..."

Joe Blue: Where did he say that?

Ingoo: In the opening exchanges of the *Statesman*, if I remember right... What Plato calls *dialectic* is the essence of the thing itself working itself out, and what Hegel calls "the movement of the concept". They each have their own metaphysical tampering and meddling with the concept, the essence, the thing itself though, which pervert philosophy into its opposite and deadliest enemy, metaphysics...But this will take us too far afield...

Joe Blue: Indeed it will. Let's reserve that for a separate interview. Please resume your dialectically merciless demonstration of the nihilistic fallacies involved in Dr. Antonio Pangilinan's *retrospective fallacy*...

Ingoo: *Nihilistic fallacies*—bullseye! For they are logical, onto*logical*, existo*logical* , in fact *negative metaphysical* errors which, unbeknownst to the doctoral commissioners that commit and applaud them, must presuppose and imply the non-existence and impossibility of being itself, the non-existence of *existence* itself, the destruction of time itself, and with it of the time of the self itself which is tantamount to the destruction and impossibility of the self itself, of such as Dr. Antonio Pangilinan himself, and Drs. Quibuyen, Veneracion, Versola, and the other applauders of the *retrospective fallacy*...

Joe Blue: And Jose David Lapuz also...

Ingoo: And Jose David Lapuz also... I was saying that the movement of the concept itself which is the working out of the thing itself in the dialectical reconstruction of its possible or impossible essence must necessitate that we radicalize the concept of the *retro* and the concept of *fallacy*...

Joe Blue: Which radicalization will do away with, will impossibilize the existence of, Jose David Lapuz, and this without his understanding what thus befalls him as he gets nullified thus like a tampered ballot, for the fellow is without a touch of dialectic in his head.

Ingoo: What I have been saying is that if this so-called *retrospective fallacy* is truly a fallacy, Rizal's ignorance of what the revolution was about, and of what assimilation was about, of, in a word, his present when he was making his misinformed or uninformed decision to *not* make or join the revolution and to instead be, and remain, an assimilationist, must not be a merely contingent thing dependent on contingencies like his relative shortness, his great attachment to his mother, his colonial middle class upbringing, his father's having been mayor or capitan municipal of Calamba, his having been born and raised in a stone house, the stupidity of his professors in Ateneo and UST, Leonor Rivera's mother's not liking him for a future son-in-law, Marcelo del Pilar's curvaceous and well-oiled Papa Piccollino mustache, the weather, etc. Rather, such ignorance must be *necessary*—necessitated by ontological and existological factors and conditions. And what we have just shown is that the very concept of a retrospective fallacy is absurd and self-contradictory; that it leads directly into negative metaphysics, i.e., into a denial of being itself, of existence itself, of freedom, of the self, of society, of history—an ultimately nihilistic notion. We can however approach the matter and refute Pangilinan on his own expectably superficial level, although this time concerning merely his self-stultifications as a Rizalist and a Quibuyenist. What was it that again that Pangilinan was saying?

Joe Blue: This is what Dr. Pangilinan said: "We must place things in proper perspective. Gene (Dr. Eugenio Demigilio, formerly professor, Philosophy Department, UP Diliman) was raising a question, and the other points related to it, *with the full knowledge and certainty of things that happened a hundred years ago.* We now have definite information about the revolution, about Rizal and about the war against Spain. But at that time, Rizal's ideas about assimilationism *were the most progressive that the liberals could advocate*, and therefore looked radical rather than reformist from that vantage point.

Of course, today, those ideas may sound not revolutionary enough, that's true. Rizal did not have enough information at that time that could have led him to the realization that the Katipunan would be as potent as we now know it to be; so he could not have made so easy a decision to join the Katipunan. This lack of enough information on his part should caution us and restrain us from cursing him for not joining it in the end. To curse him so for it (as Ingoo did) would be to commit a *restrospective fallacy*."

Ingoo: Actually, what Dr. Pangilinan might have wanted to really say was that in taking Rizal to task, I was guilty of *retrospective cruelty*. For I could have been kinder to Rizal and more considerate since I am able to take advantage of what is called "historical hindsight" which in relation to Rizal's own time and place was of course denied him by the very fact of his contemporaneity with himself—and perhaps we should add, on account of his *collocality with himself*. Again, if we take the thing seriously in a philosophical way, which is to say, once more, ontologically-existologically, bearing in mind that the object of this reasoning is to exempt Rizal from being blamed for failing to see the (queer) "potency of the revolution", which, I suppose, is to say, its possibility, even its urgent possibility, and yes its necessity, even its glorious necessity, or, in a word, its *truth*, we shall have to generalize this "historical hindsight" thing as belonging to the human condition per se, such that by definition, that is to say, by nature, or by essence, or by virtue of being and of existence, i.e., ontologically-existologically, any human being's *present* knowledge of herself/himself and of his time and place, that is to say, of himself/herself in his/her *present* historicity and therefore of *present* history, that is to say, of this very real thing which is a thing of becoming which is historicity *in the present* of its *being-existing*, must of necessity *lack* that kind and amount of knowledge which is called *historical hindsight*. And since this *lack* is an ontological-existological condition of being human, i.e., of being historical, no one can be blamed, and no one should be blamed for the effects, the manifestations, the implications of it—such as for instance, in Rizal's case, *not* seeing the "potency of the revolution". In which case, and once more, blaming Rizal for failing to see the truth of the revolution and thus for failing to make or join it, becomes a fallacy, a retrospective fallacy. But this analytical re-construction is not exhaustive. For it remains to be proved that such so-called *historical hindsight* is *always* a necessary condition, and that is to say once more, an *ontological-existological condition* of (the possibility of) seeing the truth of such things as revolution (assuming, that is, that a certain specifiable degree of seeing and knowing of this truth is a necessary condition of joining and making a revolution). And here a curious thing comes up: If, in order to be able to join or make a revolution one has first to have historical hindsight in relation to it, then no one can join or make a revolution, for when finally one is ready to join or make it, it is no longer there! But if no one *can* join or make a revolution, then no one had joined or made any! And this indeed—and once more—exposes the fallacy behind this so-called *restrospective fallacy*. For, of course, there had been very many revolutions and countless many had joined and made them. In all this, of course, what is not noticed is the fact that Dr. Pangilinan's much-applauded feat[118] of extricating

[118] Its brilliance, as it struck Quibuyen's mind like a clot of mud on a bowl of gruel, was such that the master could not contain his explosive jubilation over his adoring apprentice and he duly jubilated in a holler over his boy thus: "And galing talaga ng batang ito!" (Oh, but this boy of mine is really good!); even as, unable to contain his happiness over the Herculean achievement of this *vis a tergo* Pangilinanian argument (that should be its proper name—*vis a tergo fallacy*), Dr. Veneracion callooh-callayed also at the spectacular salvation from Ingoo's talons of the great potter of Calamba, had had to share the glorious feeling of the eureka moment with eternal Pangilinan enthusiasts Alex and Mae Dacanay by interjecting around the party's terminus thus: "Tony's intervention was good!" Whilst Dr. Obet Versola, with tears of joy and everlasting gratitude threatening to surge forth from the back of his eyes deluviated with his whole soul that now at long last all

Rizal from the ignominy of failing to be a revolutionary at a time and a place where a hundred thousand, two hundred thousand, a million, three million human beings were doing it—for revolution, and especially an anti-colonial one such as Bonifacio's KKK, is in the mind, is first and last in the mind, is first and last and lastingly a revolutionization of the people's mind, soul, spirit, sensibility, humanity from out of which of course revolutionary deeds follow, flow, heroic deeds, deeds premised on the constant readiness to die for that which is always more important than life, *infinitely* more important than *mere* life which in the ultimate analysis is dignity, the dignity of the transcendent one/s, the dignity of the free one/s—is premised on the acknowledgment and the avowal that he indeed was *not* a revolutionary. But more of his own spit against the wind is coming back to infect his face:--for of course, that three million and more Filipinos under Bonifacio's leadership were then doing it was three million and more refutations of his premise that such so-called historical hindsight is a *conditio sine qua non* of knowing the truth or "potency" of a, the, revolution. They were three million and more expositions of the truth that singular stupidity was why Rizal failed to become the revolutionary he could, he should, have been—a singular instance (for Rizal was a real standout there) of a general darkness of mind which socially and historically determined and defined that group of colonial-upper-middle-class humbugs called (by them themselves!) *ilustrados*! Those *hijos de putas*, those wastrels of destiny who wasted, who missed out on the *historical opening* which was *in fact uniquely theirs*, and what else indeed but *the Revolution*! And chose instead, and fell as into a well of putrid water, into a septic tank even, into choosing, instead of *Revolution*, ***Ass-i-mi-****lation*, and thus becoming, instead of the great heroes they were destined to be, the never-seen-before, and never-to-be-seen again (except of

---

the doubts about Rizal being sown by the infernal Ingoo have been conquered and overthrown, and now at last, he understands...

course in the Philippines, only in the Philippines) ***Assholes of History***.

Joe Blue: Before I lose sight of the great insight which you just adumbrated a while ago—that thing about a minimum of self-knowledge and therefore of knowledge and therefore of truth which being a human being must presuppose, and which, presupposed thus in every member of the society of humans is presupposed thus therefore by the being human of human society and by the being there at all of society as human society, and by the being history of history..., failing which then there are no human beings, no societies, no history, and I suppose no *retrospective fallacy* either....

Ingoo: There must be time enough for being to be, for the same to be the same as itself, for selves to be themselves, for things, events, states of affairs to be themselves, for truth to be possible in knowing them as themselves in knowing them, across all possible changes, to be for that time of their knowing and of their truth thus, the same as themselves...This is the sameness of essence which is not a static but rather a dynamic being-the-same-in-difference.

iii

Joe Blue: You were actually banned, as some people have been murmuring, from the June 22-24 *Rizal Sesquicentennial Conference* held at the Asian Center in UP Diliman. How could such a barbarous thing happen this late in this supposedly postmodern world? After the death of God, and, topping it, the death of Nietzsche which is your singular handiwork, when apparently people could merely affect to believe in anything, for the only thing that can really possess them in their souls now (assuming they got any still) is that nothingness called money which disintegrates into nothingness the very hand that handles it and the soul of that hand--this passion of nothingness, for nothingness...

Ingoo: It's nasty nothingness, murderous, mass-murderous nothingness... I thank the murmurers hereby. It's inquisitorial, they say. It's fear, others say. And someone added—*abject fear*. A young UP professor who knows who Focillon is, likened them to a conference of rats, and how else but ban the cat? These people, Miclat, Almario, Michael Tan, Howie Severino, who push Rizal and the other assimilationist traitors and mental colonies like dope—I am very sorry, heartfeltly sorry for them;--they absolutely have no future; the future belongs to Rizal's erasure. Or yes they do have a future, one of pertinacious ignominy and enduring shame. The truth which is Rizal's erasure has been launched—the inevitable, inevadable, unstoppable truth. They cannot ban it just like that. Intellectual pygmies cannot ban it just like that. Indeed, even gigantic pygmies cannot ban it just like that (and who else but such oxidized morons would attempt to stop the truth?).

Joblo: Is it true that Virgilio Almario had something to do with it?

Ingoo: Very likely. There were three who ultimately must have made the official decision, Dean Mario Miclat of the Asian Center, Dean Michael Tan of CSSP, and the conference chair, Marot Flores…she's beautiful...there's something…you are haunted by it…a nostalgic beauty…

Joe Blue: Oh, but, is not every beauty nostalgic?

Ingoo: Beauty itself, yes. Always already it is lost.

Joe Blue: Always already *she* is lost…

Ingoo: It lingers, haunts…

Joe Blue: In *her* eyes…

Ingoo: Yes, in *her* eyes, a something that is also painful, an evanescence…

Joe Blue: And therefore a sadness…

Ingoo: Sweet sadness…

Joe Blue: In *her* eyes…

Ingoo: In *her* eyes…

Joe Blue: And Virgilio Almario?

Ingoo: Scabrous thought!...

Joe Blue: Scabbies of thought…

Ingoo: Leprous thought!

Joe Blue: Leprosy of thought…

Ingoo: ….

Joe Blue: Interrupting Marot…

Ingoo: Interrupting the rose…

Joe Blue: Did Virgilio Almario really pressure any or all of them to make sure you would not be there to terrorize him? Why is Almario so abjectly afraid of you? What is it he seems to be hysterical in hiding from the terrible hound—whose name is Ingoo Zman--of intellectual fakes and shams and venal operators of traduttorial enterprises? Why would he do anything to prevent you from being there to open your mouth about Jose Rizal? What was it that concerns Jose Rizal and him, Almario, Virgilio S, that he was mortally afraid you might talk about in that conference?

Ingoo: You mean *tradittorial enterprises*? I don't know that he had a hand in this. But it's very likely he had. The Filipino Department is his fiefdom. Someone insinuated something of that sort to me. Very likely…

Joe Blue: And he will be punished right now for the likelihood and the very…

Ingoo: As for his abject fear of me, it is going to be that immediately if it was not already that. It concerns his "translations" so-called of Rizal's two novels... He trembles!...

Joe Blue: Ah, that! I heard about it, fifteen or so years ago...People were whispering about a scandalous project, a commission, a scam...

Ingoo: "His" Tagalog version of the *Noli* came out in 1998, pushed and towed by a lot of money—a Centennial Commission commissioned book!

Joe Blue: Thirteen then, but it must have taken "him" at least a year or two to cobble it...

Ingoo: Cobblers are honest people made honest by the clarifying discipline of honest toil. I'm quite sure you are insulting them by metaphorically identifying them with Almario and Co. Cobblers are not thieves, at least not by profession, whilst those translations could be the work of....

Joe Blue: Leoncio Co? Leoncio Co had something to do with that dubious thing?

Ingoo: It's not just dubious. Or else, its being dubious is not dubious at all but a most certain thing... Certain beyond reasonable doubt as the lawyers say...

Joe Blue: Teka, teka...you were saying that those translations could be the work of...what?

Ingoo: Of professional thieves, of thieves by profession, whereas cobblers are not that; cobblers are cobblers by profession.

Joe Blue: Oh, I see... And Almario and Co are professional thieves?

Ingoo: And Leoncio Co has nothing to do with it, no! He's not a member of the *Virgilio S. Almario and Company Traduttorial Enterprises*... Although I think Almario had something to do with something which Leoncio Co did do, namely cut short the display for sale of my book *The Evil That Men Do* at his UP Faculty Center 2nd floor Canteen franchise. The book was on sale there for three months I think, when it was booted out, kicked out, yes; and my suspicion was that some influential somebody must have threatened Leoncio Co to do so or else he loses his franchise.

Joe Blue: And Almario and Company are professional thieves?

Ingoo: We all know that he does not speak Spanish. How did he become the translator of these two novels? The least we should ask of a translator of such works is mastery of the Spanish language, and it is nothing less than such mastery that s/he who attempts such a thing automatically presumes. Virgilio Almario, listen...: What has happened has happened. You are nailed upon it irremediably. In the eye, through your two eyes with five-inch nails rust-bloomed. And that was: *That the most important detail, the most important distinguishing mark, the most important positive or negative attribute, the singularly crucial positive or negative selling point of any translation whatsoever, but especially of such a historically famous literary work as the* Noli *was missing, was absent, was left out, was nowhere to be found in the first, 1998, Centennial Commission edition, and cannot still be found in the cheaper textbook editions afterwards, namely—the declaration of whether the Tagalog version thus produced is a translation from the Spanish original or from some English version or versions, or else a reconstruction from one or two existing Tagalog translations which were honestly and uncriminally and unthievingly and unshamelessly translated from the original Spanish, like that of Patricio Mariano and that of Maria Odulio de Guzman...* Or did Rizal himself dictate it to the, what's that na nga? fool, ehr, pool of swimming translators or to the ear itself of Rio Alma Coroza himself? Of course Almario Virgilio S forgot to have it printed there, and it indeed is a wonder then that he did not forget to have the title printed there too, so forgetful was he!: *Noli me tangere, salin mula sa orihinal na biyaheng Divisoria ni Virgilio S. Almario, Pambansang Alagad ng Kung Ano he he he*—there. Someone should go to jail for amnesia...larcenous amnesia...amnesiac larceny.... Blas Ople...! And Blas Ople who wrote a faceless preface in the usual blankness of humanity that he was since he licked Marcos' asp for twenty plus years, (ac)complicitiously forgot to notice that IT was NOT there. Yes, all the committers of the how many billions missing Centennial Commission had (ac)complicitously failed to remember that IT should be there. NAKALIMUTAN EH, HE HE HE...

Joe Blue: And Virgilio S. Almario & Co Traduttorial Enterprises are professional thieves?

Ingoo: I am not saying that. And, moreover, is it necessary for me to say it? Does there remain a need for anyone to say it at all? Meanwhile, Virgilio Almario S must know that he was utterly vulnerable there—***there*** *where the forgetting, the amnesia shouts*! He must do everything to make people forget the shouting forgetting—but in such a way that they would also at the same time forget that it was a case of forgetting, for, for them to still remember it to be some kind of forgetting is for them to be perpetually close to noticing that there must be something amiss in such forgetting namely that it simply cannot be possible that it was a case of forgetting and therefore that it must be a case of deliberate forgetting, of wakefully and strategically not forgetting to forget to put right on the front cover in bold letters beneath the very title *Noli me tangere*, ***SALIN MULA SA ORIHINAL NA ESPANYOL NI VIRGILIO S. ALMARIO, PAMBANSANG ALAGAD NG (EWAN) SINING (DAW)***, or else, the truth, if it be the truth they/he solely were/was able to manage in his well-known not being a speaker of Spanish, let alone a master, a literary master, of it, which is what such a translation project must when honest presuppose, the truth then in such a case, namely—***SALIN MULA SA INGLES NI DERBYSHIRE O NI GUERRERO O NI QUEPE O NG LAHAT NG ITO NI VIRGILIO S. ALMARIO, PAMBANSANG EWAN NG EWAN NG EWAN...*** People must not notice that it is very, very, noticeable that that inscription of from where the translation was made was not and cannot have been forgotten in its *not being there.* He, Almario Virgilio S must be infinitely careful not to accidentally or incidentally nudge them ever so lightly to the reflection that it was simply impossible that that inscription was not there because he, they, forgot to put it there. (It's like wearing a tuxedo to a Manila Hotel function and, in an apparent attack of brevity, i.e., brief-ness, forgetting to put on the pants!) Nor can Almario S Virgilio just simply, and all of a sudden, inscribe IT there, for, aside from very certainly calling attention to *its not being there before and for more than ten years now* (!), and therefore immediately and scandalously pricking and prising into existence *the raucous question of why it was not there from the start and all those years*, an even greater, certainly more terrible, danger will in such a case attack his nights with Durer's black mare and the castrating horse of Little Hans:--for, publicly imprinted and blazoned and claimed thus—***SALIN MULA SA ORIHINAL NA ESPANYOL (NG FACSIMILE DAW)...ETC***—he then lays himself open to the legal challenge by someone who remembers that they must have purposely forgotten to put it there before, to prove it in court, charging him thereby with perjury, plagiarism, literary larceny, intellectual dishonesty. Such a crime can send him in his old age to jail...

Joe Blue: And so what he did was, little by little, in seemingly innocuous, matter-of-course ways, indirectly to lay claim to having translated the novels (for he also "translated" the *Fili* afterwards) ***from the original Spanish,*** in fact, as he puts it in well-placed places, ***from the facsimile itself*** of the novel itself...

Ingoo: Yes, Joblo... I see that you have read from his book of Rizal advertisements and marketing strategies, titled *Si Rizal:Nobelista* which the UP Press published in 2008... And in order not to lay himself open to such charges before the court of law, he is there infinitely careful in a contrivedly naturally careless and nonchalant way, to not directly say it in saying it in those places either. On page one for instance of this ad-book that sells his translations daw, he writes: "Pinag-aralan ko rin ang facsimile ng manuskrito ni Rizal at napansin ang ilang pagkakaiba sa opisyal na edisyon sa Espanyol na ipinalimbag ng National Historical Institute, kaya't ipinasiya namin ni Roger[119] na ang facsimile ang higit na *titigan at pagbatayan* ng aming salin..." Note how careful he is here of not being able directly to say that he has translated the novel ***from*** the original Spanish of the facsimile, and in instead limiting himself to *claiming* that he has used the facsimile as *basis (batayan)* which could simply mean *ultimate authority* against which to check dubious renditions and nuances. Thus far, he has not categorically made the claim that he translated it *from the original Spanish*, on the basis of which claim he could then be haled to court; it is deadly important for him to not be caught making that claim for it

[119] Note how he even drags Rogelio Sikat's name here for effect; for, like him, everyone knows that Roger did not know any Spanish; and yet here he tells this apocryphal story of having originally planned his translation with Roger! Unfortunately for Roger and of course very, very fortunately for Almario Virgilio S, Roger is dead and cannot speak anymore to clear his name. For he has to clear his name here of the taint, the stain of the accusation of planning to translate a Spanish novel without knowing a word of Spanish...Roger and I were, along with Reuel Aguila and Jun Cruz Reyes, among the inaugural fellows of the *UP Creative Writing Center* (somebody changed it to *Institute* apparently to match the mental state of its permanent inmates who have clung to their desks there tooth and nail and have vowed to die inside it and to rather die than relinquish their cells to other mental cases who salivate so for the great privileges and distinction of being institutionalized thus...):--he would at least have mentioned in passing that he was secretly studying Spanish; moreover, Federico Licsi Espino, who was even then already master of Spanish enough to write poems in it (he later won first prize in a poetry contest in Spain in, of course, Spanish) was also there with us:--Roger would at least have attempted to practice it with him...

must always be left open as a possibility for him to be able to declare in court that he in fact had never claimed to have translated it from the original Spanish. So that then, just in case, he can declare in court that he simply forgot to put there from what language it was that he did the translation... He forgot it, eh, what can you do? Surely, it is not a crime to forget anything? In the only other place where claims concerning the provenance of the translations were in this same book made, the same infinite carefulness in view of the possibility of being nailed down to the commission of a crime has been exercised, namely in the advertisements on the back cover. Here, Almario VS is almost already claiming that he has translated the novels from the original Spanish, and he can be so bold here because such blurbs can always be disowned by the author of the book: one can simply impute such promotional avowals to some publishing house editor or marketing director. Almost—but still not quite in being almost almost; let us see how: "Hindi nababasa ng karamihan and buong nobela ni Jose Rizal. Halos lahat kasi ng ibinebentang 'salin' sa Filipino ng *Noli me tangere* at *El Filibusterismo* ay mga halaw lamang at sinulat *ng mga ni hindi rin nakabasa sa orihinal ng mga nobela sa wikang Espanyol* ng ating pambansang bayani. Ito ang nag-udyok kay National Artist Virgilio S. Almario para isalin ang mga nobela ni Rizal ***batay sa facsimile*** na inilathala ng National Historical Commission..." ***Unlike VS Almario***, those writers of mere extracts from the novels were not even able to read the novels in Rizal's original Spanish:--***VS Almario, unlike all of them, was able to read them in Rizal's original Spanish.*** And even this is very highly doubtful! Now, being able to read in a language is not the same as being able to translate from it; whilst being able to read Spanish thus could enable one to use as "batayan", basis, ultimate authority, the mss' original Spanish. Again, haled to court, this escape remains open in these all- important promotional salesman's declarations to the salesman VS Almario here. Virgilio S. Almario, I hereby dare you to categorically claim that you have translated Rizal's two novels ***from*** the original Spanish, like this : ***SALIN*** **NI VIRGILIO S. ALMARIO** ***MULA SA ORIHINAL NA ESPANYOL NI DR. JOSE RIZAL***

PART II:

THE AGUINALDO COUNTERREVOLUTION

Chapter 18

FROM THE RIZAL COUNTERREVOLUTION FROM OUTSIDE THE REVOLUTION TO THE AGUINALDO COUNTERREVOLUTION FROM WITHIN THE REVOLUTION

(this series is composed in preparation for 3 lectures for grade seven/first-year Philippine History students & the humanities faculty of the Philippine Science High School, Baguio)

I.

HOW I DISCOVERED PHILIPPINE HISTORY

Or how I discovered that there was no such thing as Philippine history, or that the Philippine history in all the history textbooks and by all the so-called Filipino historians without a single exception, and retailed and commented upon and referred to by 99.9999999% of Filipino intellectuals, fictionists, poets, journalists, supreme court justices, politicians, lawyers, professors of all sorts, etcetera, and enforced and propagated by every Philippine government since 1946, is so distorted, and in all important respects the direct, brutal, massmurderously criminal, anti-human and immoral opposite of what really happened that, in point of fact, it did not and does not exist...

Its very existence is a lie. That is to say, there was, there is, no such thing. It was certainly not the history of the Philippines. It was not the history of anything. It was not a history at all.

There absolutely was no such thing. And this then is how I discovered its non-existence and, in step with such discovery, discovered what really happened and how in the historical existence of the Filipino people—*and discovered thus Philippine history itself...*

History is like biography. What I call Philippine history here is the life-story of the living socio-political entity called *the Philippines*, or--which is the same thing--*the Filipino people*. The central drama in this life story was of course the Philippine Revolution. It is in and as this central drama that the people, here the Filipino people, makes its own history. This history which it makes thus is the people itself, in the accomplishment of its own essence. This essence is the achievement and proclamation of its truth as the people and the history it is; or, failing which, it fails to even have a history and, to that extent, fails to be a people, fails to be *the people*, i.e., the sovereign subject of its own historical existence.

The truth happening as the truth of a people is the fulfilment of the *democratic essence* of the social-historical existence of beings who speak, i.e., of beings whose *principle of existence* is freedom, namely, human beings. Indispensable in the being people of a people as such sovereign subject of its own existence is the pride it has in being itself. To realize that this is so, let us picture to ourselves what it would mean for a people to exist in the shamelessness of contented slavery or of rampant corruption...

Such contented slavery and rampant corruption was what Rizal and his ilustrado confraternity *in effect* envisioned and clamoured for with their *assimilationist reformism*. In terms of the *actual* racist, plundering, exploitative, tyrannical political economy of the colonial relationship, *assimilation, "the Philippines as a province of Spain, etc."*, really meant nothing but *that*. Had Bonifacio heeded Rizal's preachings of such shameless contentment in slavery and corruption, we would never have had our sole source of pride which was at the same time our birth and fullest emergence as a people, as the revolutionary Filipino people—the Revolution!

This pride consists above all in its passing the test of its existence as *the people*, i.e., the sovereign subject of its own existence, which in turn consists in proving to itself (and yes to the whole world) that freedom is infinitely more important to it than life itself, and that therefore it is ready always to put mere life totally on stake to defend and fulfil freedom in the truth of its essence.

It is indeed this capability to sacrifice life to achieve the fullness of freedom that chiefly distinguishes the human from the animal. We call it the *power to die* which is the power of heroic existence. For the power to die can only be the power to die for the others, for the social body. Not for the animal body but for the body of freedom which is precisely the social body, the body-social, which is precisely *the people*. The power to die is the power of absolute sacrifice which can only be the power to die so that the others may be, and be not the mere biological organisms that they also are, but the speaking, *ex-isting*, being-transcending, *absolutes*, i.e., *free* beings that they as human beings and not merely animal beings, are, for, of course, it is absurd to propose to oneself to die in order for oneself to be free. *The dead is nothing—neither free nor unfree.*

This then is why the Revolution was the central drama of our history as a people. And it is in reference to this central drama that I am here saying that it was only recently that Philippine history has been discovered. It was a discovery because before I unearthed it, what everybody thought was there for the last one hundred years and more was--worse than nothing in being in its nothingness invertedly perverted at every crucial juncture--actually its exacerbated opposite... A perverted, inverted, exacerbated nothingness then...

For instance, in the false story that was the non-history presented as the history of the Revolution in all the history textbooks, the infamous and execrable Dr. Jose Rizal who was actually the Philippines' foremost and deadliest counterrevolutionary leader and national traitor, is hailed and celebrated as its greatest hero and most ardent patriot.

In point of fact, this very same enemy number one of the Filipino people called Dr. Jose Rizal even managed to become the country's foremost international counterrevolutionary, and therewith enemy of humanity, through his Cuban Spanish military doctoral counterrevolutionary project. Rizal, as we know, was on his way to Cuba as a Spanish military doctor with the mission of helping the Spanish colonial army kill as many Cuban Katipuneros as possible and put down their revolution, when he was once more overtaken by his mortal enemies, the friars, who pressured the Madrid government to have him arrested on board and sent back to the Philippines for trial. To experience the evil meaning of this project through which Rizal had fondly hoped to become an internationally famous Spanish hero, you have to imagine it as a Cuban Katipunero getting wind of the coming of this evil brown Spanish military doctor to help kill all of you and put down your revolution!

Rizal's gargantuan crime against the Filipino people and their history was of course his pulling the colonial middle class away from, and setting it against, the Revolution as the great and powerful counterrevolutionary (i.e., reformist-assimilationist-propagandist) ilustrado leader that he was. This paved the way for Aguinaldo's hostaging and selling of the Revolution at Biyak na Bato, and later on to the colonial subjugation of the Filipino people by the Americans which entailed the murder of some two million Filipinos. (We have documented all this in the last two books we have published in 2012 and 2013.)

No less malefically, Rizal's great charismatic leadership of the Counterrevolution, by preventing the colonial middle-class from joining –and leading-- the Revolution, forfeited also the epochal chance of the same colonial middle-class to scuttle the *multicenturial culture of corruption* of which they, *as the multicenturial colonial collaborators they were*, were the native bearers--a feat they could otherwise have accomplished had they joined and led the Revolution.

This forfeiture of what otherwise would have been their truly glorious destiny was largely due to Rizal's charismatic influence as counterrevolutionary leader. There were conjunctures where many of his ilustrado assimilationist followers were not merely ready but were very eager to take the revolutionary leap in the mistaken supposition that he, their revered leader, was about to take it (this was immediately before his return home to Manila on June 26, 1892):--Rizal misled them; he let them down; he prevented them from making the leap; he eventually denounced and betrayed them! These were among others, Edilberto Evangelista, Antonio Luna, Jose Alejandrino, Graciano Lopez Jaena, Mariano Ponce... Whilst according to Evangelista, "the entire Barcelona colony" was with them in this impending eager leap into revolution and it only depended on Rizal to sound them off.! (Again these episodes have been fully documented in the two books.)

This forfeiture of the truly glorious destiny that awaited Rizal and the upper colonial middle-class stratum in the 1880s was unique to the Philippines. Unlike Jose Rizal and company, the colonial middle-class intellectuals in all the other parts of the colonial world (particularly in Simon Bolivar's Latin America), were intelligent enough, and deep enough and were true human beings enough to have been the conceivers and leaders of their own anti-colonial revolutions. Only in the Philippines were such obtuse and vicious, narrowminded and tiny-souled traitors as Rizal and his ilustrado company possible—only in the Philippines!

Instead of extirpating this culture of corruption (of which, as the upper stratum of the mental-colonial, collaborationist, venal, sycophantic, social climbing, colonial middleclass, they were the bearers in their very souls), and to that extent redeeming the criminality and corruption of their class-ancestors, by joining and leading the Revolution (and becoming truly great heroes thereby), they did the opposite: they joined the enemy in defending colonial tyranny against their own revolutionary countrymen! What they then were able to most successfully accomplish was the exponential aggravation of the virulence of the same culture of corruption in their very own persons and in their very own *class*.

Having collaborated with the Spaniards thus, they went on as a matter of course to collaborate with the Americans, and then with the Japanese. When finally this same Rizal-led class of national traitors ascended to the position of ruling class once more, they would already have become the ruling class bearers and implementors and enforcers of a galloping culture of corruption as the world's most corrupt ruling class, catapulting then as a matter of course the Philippines to the great and wondrous distinction of being the most corrupt country in the world.Thus, Rizal, more than anybody was the master architect and the perjured main source of this world famous culture of corruption which incidentally murders some two thousand babies and children every day by way of the poverty it inflicts on the Filipino masses.

Meanwhile, in accordance with the abovementioned perversion-inversion, all of Rizal's ilustrado colleagues and followers in this most deadly counterrevolutionary movement have been hailed and celebrated in this false story and perverted nothingness of a non-history, as the same "glorious" kind of heroes and patriots.

NOTES: 1.) To be exact, my discovery of this *new Philippine history* started in 1982-85 by way of my weekly Filipiniana columns in *WHO Magazine*; the process of discovery continued through my Malaya columns of 1987-89, in my monographic essays in the *Journal of Social History* (whose editor in chief I was, concurrently with my directorship of the Institute of Social History at the Polytechnic University of the Philippines, from 1986 to 1992), and in my extended essays published by Celina Cristobal's and Bonifacio Ilagan's *The Review* and in Pete Daroy's *The Progressive Review* (between 1983 and 1985); it pushed through via my Philippine Journal columns of 1992-98; it became a poem in my 53,000-line epic *FREEDOM! Andres Bonifacio & the Tragedy of the Philippine Revolution* (which lost in the Centennial Literary Contest; the only surviving copy of which is with Pepe Miranda: I delivered it to his UP Diliman house a few months after the Centennial loss, and it was his son Alex who received the 1500-page gigantic red, hardbound volume); finally, it achieved book form in 2010, 2011, 2013.

2.) We are saying that because utterly and even invertedly false, the supposed history in all the textbooks and taught in all the schools on all levels and commented and descanted upon in all the media and sponsored and ritually enforced by every Philippine government since 1946, is pure vicious fiction, is malevolent illusion, and is thus so completely *unreal* that it does not exist.

This textbook history is a form of nothingness, the nothingness we said of a pure but vicious fiction. The viciousness is a mode of false reference, the mode precisely of vicious misrepresentation and vicious mis-attribution, where, in this particular case, the false reference is so invertedly complete, is, so to speak, 360-degree false, that it completely cannot and does not refer at all to the real way the historical reality concerned actually happened.

Which is to say it never *really* happened as such. And it never really happened as such *so completely* that it does not exist *as a history, and specifically* not *as the history it is presented to be.* Which is to say that there is in every given case a specific, in fact unique, unfolding of events, acts, persons, institutions, individual and collective causalities, constitutive of the historical existence of a people, and this unique unfolding is this people's history.

One may want to call this view of ours of what may be termed the ontology-and-existology of history, *historical realism.* This is to say merely that *history really happens*, that there is such a thing as real history which then is the real and true referent of possible histories (i.e., historiographic accounts and narratives), just as a true biography must have a real person behind it whose life history is supposed to be presented thus by it. And that a history, i.e., a historiographic account or narrative, is a real and true history, and therefore to that extent *exists* as such a history, to the degree that it is true and faithful to its *real* referent which is the actual, real, history, the actual, real, unfolding of which, history (as historiography) attempts to retrace, comprehend, and retell. Now, this actual, real unfolding is an actual, real movement with its own internal causal configuration, logic, and coherence on the basis of which it determines by so much the internal causal configuration, the logic and the coherence of the present, and is thus in actual fact continuous with the present. This causal configurational, logical, and intelligible continuity with the present is what above all should underlie as reconstructive guidelines, grid or matrix, narrative demonstration and documentation. This is how, for instance, we were able to trace back the current exponential inflation of the present culture of corruption in the country to Rizal's charismatic leadership of the counterrevolutionary, anti-independence, and thus traitorous, villainous, anti-heroic assimilationist propaganda movement...

II.

How Aguinaldo proclaimed his own Government and Army barely two days after the outbreak of hostilities...

Let us demonstrate and document here why and how from the very start, what Aguinaldo was intent upon doing and was actually doing was not revolution but rather counterrevolution. And let us be mindful all the while that factionalism, sedition, treason, and in effect, counterrevolution, was what, as soon as Bonifacio set foot in Cavite, Aguinaldo and his band had charged him of doing, and that finally, it was for sedition, treason, and counterrevolution that he was arrested, tried, sentenced to death, and executed! And all the historians not only did not fail to take these charges seriously. They all believed them to be true, and had agreed with Aguinaldo that his murder of Bonifacio was justified because those accusations were true! This among other things is what we mean by saying that their textbook history is in its entirety not simply false or a simple lie:--it is the brutal opposite of what really happened, it is inverted!

From day 3 of the outbreak of hostilities, i.e., August 31, 1896, Aguinaldo in his first manifesto of that date had announced the absolutely seditious, treasonous, counterrevolutionary formation of his own national government and army and was recruiting his fellow Cavite municipal captains to join it.

THE AUGUST 31, 1896 MANIFESTO

Cavite el Viejo

August 31, 1896

Dear Municipal Captains and ***Countrymen****:*

I am very sorry to inform you that on August 30, 1896, Don Ramon Blanco, Captain General and Governor General of the Philippines, declared war against eight Tagalog provinces, namely, Manila, Bulacan, Pampanga, Tarlac, Nueva Ecija, Laguna, Batangas, and Cavite. Because of this I am inviting you to join ME in rising against Spain and break the chains of slavery that have bound us with her all these hundred years. As an answer to this declaration of war, we started to rebel against this tyrannical race, and I AM very glad to inform you that the towns of Cavite El Viejo, Noveleta, and San Francisco de Malabon are already free and the government is now in the hands of the Filipinos. Here in Cavite El Viejo, we succeeded in disarming the civil guards, and the provincial command at Noveleta is already in OUR HANDS.

So I AM inviting all of you to follow as soon as you get my letter. Do all you can to overpower the enemy. Remember that the strength of OUR ARMY will depend upon your cooperation.

I AM confident that your patriotic hearts will heed this call of our Motherland. Conquer your foes there, but try not to kill anyone, especially if he is a Filipino. I BELIEVE this is the only way by which our Mother Country can be freed from slavery.

Respectfully & cordially

EMILIO AGUINALDO (MAGDALO)

Flag Lieutenant of ***the Revolutionary Army***

In this his first politico-military manifesto, Aguinaldo y Famy already referred to his own "revolutionary army and government", to join which he was exhorting his fellow Caviteno municipal captains. There was no mention whatsoever of the *KKK Republic and National Revolutionary Army*! Nor a breath of Andres Bonifacio which otherwise would have been not merely formally proper but politically and even militarily imperative.

In the inverted-perverted textbook non-history narratives brainwashingly repeated in classrooms, forums and in the mass-media for more than a hundred years now, there is no mention whatsoever of even merely the possibility that Emilio Aguinaldo and his Magdalo Caviteno tribal group could be a *counter- revolutionary organization*. Nor is there any suggestion or hint whatever that Aguinaldo was ever seditious, divisive, factionalist, let alone a traitor to the Revolution and the Filipino people. And yet, though not yet forthrightly declared as such, this, his very first manifesto and political-military act, cannot be anything but blatantly counterrevolutionary in being not merely subversive but flagrantly seditious.

This horribly ominous act was not merely factionalist or divisive: he was not declaring here the establishment of a mere faction within the KKK organization which would as such divide it within itself:--rather, he was here announcing *his own* government and army which as such cannot possibly be mistaken with the *Katipunan Republic and National Revolutionary Army*, and which then, in not being part of the *KKK Republic and Army*, can only be against it—i.e., anti- and counter-revolutionary *and therefore a deadly enemy of the Filipino people*. This was no mere insubordination. This was absolute treason against the Revolution and the Filipino people.

We shall see in what follows that, doing it on the third day of the national outbreak of hostilities and in the afternoon of the very first day that he made his first military move, attacking his own municipal hall which he knew beforehand, less than an hour ago, to be undefended (for he was told by the Cavite governor himself and the Cavite Provincial Commander himself in conference less than an hour ago that Blanco had in fact pulled out all the Spanish soldiers from Cavite days before and transferred them to Manila to defend the capital against Andres Bonifacio), sedition, treason, counterrevolution, was really all that he wanted to do and there would be no respite for him in perpetrating it against the Revolution and the Filipino people until he was able to hostage the Revolutionary leadership and sell the Revolution for 800,000 pesos to the enemy at Biyak na Bato, surrendering it for pay thus!

Let us analyze this document.

1.) "*I am very sorry to inform you...*", he says. It's purely personal. The fellow is ambitioning something and is advertising himself. In this advertisement, he has included the Magdiwangs without naming them. He says that in their part of Cavite too, namely Noveleta and San Francisco de Malabon, they had risen and were now free, "and the government is now in the hands of the Filipinos". The occasion that prompted his manifesto cum self-advertisement was the illiterately worded (by him, Aguinaldo y Famy, here, right here in this manifesto) "declaration of war" by Blanco "against eight Tagalog provinces" including Cavite. All these details should have made it not only natural but *politically imperative,* and even literarily obligatory to put forward the name of the Katipunan and to speak not on his own but on the Katipunan National Revolutionary Government and Army's behalf, such that to fail to do so, to *not* do so, was already, and at once, seditious, treasonous, counterrevolutionary:--if, i.e., what he was intent in promoting thus was the Revolution itself, and not a purely personal agenda leading to, and in preparation for, counterrevolutionary sedition and treason, with, as obligatory deduction which we must make from a lifetime of insurpassably venal behaviour, the omnipresent horizon of trunks of money such as he got for instance as proceeds from the Biyak na Bato sale of the Revolution.

For here he wrote *as though the Katipunan did not exist*. And this when the very writing of his manifesto made it necessary and urgent to mention the national revolutionary *political body*, organism, organization, government, army, for the mention of the "declaration of war" against the "eight Tagalog provinces" must cry for immediate explanation, for this meant that there was a simultaneous uprising in those eight provinces which of course could not have been mere coincidence.

How did it happen that they had simultaneously risen in Kawit (Aguinaldo was actually *late* by almost two whole days!), in Noveleta, in San Fancisco de Malabon? How did it happen that the same simultaneous rising was possible in all those eight provinces? And the answer to these questions shouting and stamping their feet for it, was, of course, --*the Katipunan.* And if the Katipunan, then—*Bonifacio*! On behalf of which and of whom and in the name of which and of whom he, Emilio Aguinaldo y Famy, should be doing his recruiting instead!

2.) "...on August 30, 1896, Don Ramon Blanco, Captain General and Governor General of the Philippines, declared war against eight Tagalog provinces..." Blanco did not "declare war" against the 8 provinces; that would be impossible, insane, and absurd. What he did was declare that the 8 provinces were "in a state of war". But this semi-illiterate error was not without meaning here. For, if he were not already contemplating to subvert the KKK and to seditiously and treasonously and effectively counterrevolutionarily establish his own presidency of his own government right here, scarcely two days after the first Katipunan revolutionary attack on the 29th was launched, and less than five days after the Katipunan through its Supreme Council declared war against Spanish colonialism on the 26th, he would not have fallen into this crude and farcical mistake of inverted attribution.

3.) That Blanco declared a state of war over the 8 provinces meant that on the 29th and the 30th there were simultaneous attacks there as planned in the Tambobong , Caloocan KKK Supreme Council provincial district commanders meeting on Saint Bartholomew's Day. The telegraph reports from these provinces by the Spanish commands there about the attacks in their jurisdictions must have prompted that declaration. Which means that all the provincial SB commanders obeyed the KKK Supreme Council order, including the Magdiwangs who attacked on the 30th. All then obeyed the order, except Aguinaldo y Famy who attacked his own presidencia only upon learning on the 31st that there were no enemy soldiers to be encountered there or anywhere else in all of Cavite except the company of infantry guarding the powder depot at Binakayan. That, in addition to his being a pathological liar and his semi-illiteracy was why he could invert cause and effect and say that he and those at Noveleta and San Francisco de Malabon "started to rebel" "as an answer to Blanco's declaration of war" against them!—implying therewith that those in the 7 other provinces did the same for the same reason!

4.) "... Because of this I am inviting you to join ME..." Because Blanco "declared war against eight Tagalog provinces", therefore, Emilio Aguinaldo y Famy rose in arms against Spain, and, but, somehow, also, some other Cavitenos, in San Francisco de Malabon for example, and in Noveleta, rose in arms against Spain, and, but, also some people in seven other provinces, therefore, Emilio Aguinaldo y Famy is inviting you to join Emilio Aguinaldo y Famy, yes, Emilio Aguinaldo y Famy, but Emilio Aguinaldo y Famy only, not those in Noveleta, no, nor those in San Francisco de Malabon, no, no, no, but Emilio Aguinaldo y Famy, yes, yes, yes, Emilio Aguinaldo y Famy only, and most certainly not Andres

Bonifacio and the KKK; Aguinaldo y Famy then, who--see pages 14 and 15 of Aguinaldo y Famy's Memoirs of the Revolution--wrestled with a giant shark off Matuko point in Batangas in the deep night in the deep black of the sea, and, tying the giant shark up with a huge stout rope hauled the poor little gigantic thing onto his paraw singlehandedly, Emilio Aguinaldo y Famy, yes, outbiagging Lam-ang thus, see, see, pages 14 and 15 of Emilio Ilyong's Biag, the sheer windiness of it, the sheer windy hugeness of it and the wind, the super-typhoon wind of it, of the BIAG, THE BIAG NI ILYONG outbiagging LAM-ANG thus, outhumbugging, outwinding him in his BIAG! Reading him in his BIAG thus, can't you see how utterly credible the fellow was—the great general and el presidente…who is inviting you here to join not the Katipunan Revolution but his "revolutionary army" not Andres Bonifacio but llyong Buktot…

5.) "Because of this I am inviting you to join ME in rising against Spain and break the chains of slavery that have bound us with her all these hundred years..." The poor wretch did not even know when colonialism arrived and the chains of slavery were forged...

III.

How Aguinaldo proclaimed his own Government and Army barely two days after the outbreak of hostilities... *(cont'd)*

THE AUGUST 31, 1896 MANIFESTO

Domingo DC De Guzman

Cavite el Viejo

August 31, 1896

Dear Municipal Captains and ***Countrymen****:*

I am very sorry to inform you that on August 30, 1896, Don Ramon Blanco, Captain General and Governor General of the Philippines, declared war against eight Tagalog provinces, namely, Manila, Bulacan, Pampanga, Tarlac, Nueva Ecija, Laguna, Batangas, and Cavite. Because of this I am inviting you to join ME in rising against Spain and break the chains of slavery that have bound us with her all these hundred years. As an answer to this declaration of war, we started to rebel against this tyrannical race, and I AM very glad to inform you that the towns of Cavite El Viejo, Noveleta, and San Francisco de Malabon are already free and the government is now in the hands of the Filipinos. Here in Cavite El Viejo, we succeeded in disarming the civil guards, and the provincial command at Noveleta is already in OUR HANDS.

So I AM inviting all of you to follow as soon as you get my letter. Do all you can to overpower the enemy. Remember that the strength of OUR ARMY will depend upon your cooperation.

I AM confident that your patriotic hearts will heed this call of our Motherland. Conquer your foes there, but try not to kill anyone, especially if he is a Filipino. I BELIEVE this is the only way by which our Mother Country can be freed from slavery.

Respectfully & cordially

EMILIO AGUINALDO (MAGDALO)

Flag Lieutenant of ***the Revolutionary Army***

6.) "As an answer to this declaration of war, we started to rebel against this tyrannical race, and I AM very glad..." Feeling no doubt the urgency of answering the silent but powerfully nagging question of how there must be a simultaneous or single regional provocation that compelled Blanco to (as Aguinaldo y Famy illiterately puts it) "declare war against the eight provinces", Aguinaldo y Famy answers it here by saying that they "started to rebel against this tyrannical race" "as an answer to" Blanco's "declaration of war"! Inverted, yes. This inverted reasoning would have been impossible had Aguinaldo began by announcing the Katipunan Revolution and himself as a Katipunan provincial chapter commander. It would then have been clear at once and a matter of course that a revolution of national and archipelagic intent and scope founded, cultivated and ragingly established across a number of years now (which number y Famy could then, and should then specify—and how would he be able to do that without at once mentioning the great founder's name and the current Supremo, Andres Bonifacio?) was why there were simultaneous risings in the eight provinces; and it would then have become needless to mention in its obviousness that by thus joining and making this revolution it was in fact they, Andres Bonifacio and his Katipuneros, who had declared war against Blanco and Spanish colonialism, and, that was why, the revolution having been exposed for being the declaration of war to death against Spanish colonialism that it was, Blanco declared not war against the eight provinces but that the eight provinces were thenceforth in a state of war.

7.) "... and I AM very glad to inform you that the towns of Cavite El Viejo, Noveleta, and San Francisco de Malabon are already free and the government is now in the hands of the Filipinos. Here in Cavite El Viejo, we succeeded in disarming the civil guards, and the provincial command at Noveleta is already in OUR HANDS..." "...our hands"—whose? If he had not already contemplated sedition, and in a most insidious way committed that counterrevolutionary crime, he would have been saying "in Katipunan hands".

8.) So I AM inviting... OUR ARMY... I AM confident... but try not to kill anyone..." There is a subtext to this without which this seeming humanitarianism of this mass-murderer and killer of at least ten generals of the Revolution (all for reasons of necessarily counterrevolutionary ambition, insecurity, cowardice and greed) would be unthinkable and his counsel of kindness to your enemies insane: although his "countrymen" in the salutation gestures toward the real imperative extent of his ambitions which was archipelagic and national, at this specific juncture he must be thinking more specifically of the Cavite municipal captains he was recruitingly addressing, and the subtext is this: he knew that only a company of Spanish soldiers remained in all of Cavite, assigned to secure the Binakayan powder depot, and that the "enemy" he was instigating his fellow municipal captains to "overpower" and "conquer" consisted of one or two creaky civil guards:--in his own municipality of Cavite el Viejo, there were only two whom after one of them was shot by one of his forty plus cuadrilleros, they were –O mighty victory of the great general!—able to disarm. For of course, in the face of the battalions of Spanish soldiers such as were confronted by Bonifacio and company in Manila, such a humanitarian counsel to try not to kill anyone would be perfectly insane.

This astounding detail which constitutes another case of direct and vicious inversion, which we now fully know and have fully documented, namely, that there were absolutely no battles for the liberation of any Cavite town, and that Cavite was not a liberated zone but an ABANDONED ZONE, was however never directly owned and only circumstantially acknowledged thus by Aguinaldo. Whilst the exact opposite have without qualification been trumpeted by all the Caviteno historians, and indeed by all the historians and writers who wrote about the Revolution in Cavite—all, except Mabini and myself (even as Mabini was rather vague about it, saying only that there were only very few civil guards left to secure every town in Cavite).

9."I believe this is the only way..." How did you come to believe so? All by yourself? And since when? Just now, after you and your 147 and a half soldiers engaged in a great and most bloody battle for the liberation of Kawit about which you are so cantankerously proud now, TWO, two, 2, TWO, yes, 2, dos, dalawa, oo dalawang walang kahinahinalang, aanga-angang, unsuspecting civil guards? Would Blanco have declared Cavite and the other provinces to be in a state of war if Andres Bonifacio had not founded the KKK more than four years ago? Would Blanco have pulled out all the Spanish soldiers in Cavite and transferred them to Manila thereby "liberating" Aguinaldo's Kawit and all of Cavite had not Andres Bonifacio founded the KKK more than four years ago and across four deadly dangerous years spread the fire of revolution virtually archipelagically, and, in the Tagalog region as well as in Pampanga and Tarlac with such intensity that when suddenly hostilities broke out because of the untimely exposure of the revolutionary movement, Blanco had had to, at a moment's notice, declare those 8 provinces to be in a state of war? And by the way, that Blanco had had to declare a state of war in the 8 provinces the day after the August 29 attack by Bonifacio of the San Juan Del Monte polvorin can only mean one thing, namely that, as planned by the national revolutionary command in Tambobong on St. Bartholomew's Day, the simultaneous attacks in all the KKK SB districts in those provinces were successfully carried out—except, that is, in the 6 towns that belonged to the Magdalo district in Cavite; the Magdiwangs, late by half a day, staged their attack in San Francisco de Malabon and Noveleta on the 30th whilst, as should be expected from the coward and opportunist vendor Emilio Aguinaldo y Famy, he tarried for another day and attacked on the 31st , and that only upon learning from the Spanish governor of Cavite and the Spanish provincial commander of Cavite that except for a company of infantry assigned to secure the polvorin in Binakayan, all the Spanish soldiers had been evacuated from Cavite to secure and defend Manila against Andres Bonifacio.

10.
"Respectfully & cordially

EMILIO AGUINALDO (MAGDALO)

Flag Lieutenant of the Revolutionary Army"

Of what "Revolutionary Army"? "Revolutionary Army" of WHAT? "Army" of WHAT REVOLUTION? Aguinaldo has here already mentioned somewhat illiterately of course that "Blanco has declared war" on the 8 provinces—in one fell swoop. From the tone of this insidious, creepingly criminal, counterrevolutionarily seditious manifesto, those Aguinaldo was addressing did not yet know anything about the KKK and must thus have been anticipated by him to fall into wondering how it could happen that simultaneously as it were there was war against the Spaniards in those 8 provinces; which means that Aguinaldo must himself have felt the necessity of informing, and enlightening them about it, namely, of telling them that this war was the Katipunan Revolution happening in one fell swoop upon the 8 provinces now. But he did not say it. He forbore to say it. He stopped himself, he prevented himself, from saying it. That is to say, he suppressed it, he suppressed the fact that it was the Katipunan happening, whilst because of this suppression and the tireless and indeed shameless insinuation of his I, I, I, me, me, me, my, my, my, he succeeded only in projecting the impression that he was speaking on his sole behalf, or on the sole behalf of his Cavite band, his Cavite Revolutionary Army of which he was flag lieutenant...

IV

Two months after the outbreak of hostilities Aguinaldo commits his second and third acts of treason by declaring his own Republic and national revolutionary army...

11.) The simultaneous August 29, 1896 uprising in the 8 provinces the swift reaction to which being Blanco's August

30 declaration of a state of war encompassing them was the first glorious fruit of the four years of Bonifacio's and the Katipunan's deadly-dangerous underground labours of theorizing, organizing, and propagating the anti-colonial Revolution.

How if he was not already the counterrevolutionary he was, and not the crude braggart he was, should he be composing this recruitment letter? First of all, he would announce the Katipunan, and, with it, Andres Bonifacio. And he would then recruit them to join NOT him but the Katipunan and Andres Bonifacio. Telling them of course about what they were able to do in Kawit and the Magdiwang in San Francisco de Malabon and Noveleta, and the state of war declared by Blanco over the 8 provinces in *simultaneous revolt*, he would at once give the reason for the state or war declaration, namely that the 8 provinces have risen in *simultaneous revolt* and that was why Blanco has had to make that declaration. He, however, the legendary coward, liar and traitor and opportunist Running Man of Asia, did not attack on the 29th and 30th as planned and ordered by the KKK Supreme Council, *and that was why he could not bear to say that the 8 provinces launched their simultaneous attacks and their explosive declarations of war against the Spanish colonial government on the 29th and the 30th in response to which Blanco had had to declare all of those provinces in a state of war.*

Moreover, he was subconsciously constrained to not declare that those 8 provinces launched their simultaneous attacks on the 29th and 30thbecause he then would have to explain or say something about how such simultaneity could happen; whilst he knew of course that such simultaneity could not have been pure chance, and that there must be an organized and systematic thing behind it, and therefore a political body, a politico-military body, a politico-military organization, behind it, and therefore a chief of that political body, of that organization, which would of course be the Katipunan and Andres Bonifacio respectively, and he must not even mention either and both of them because his express intention was to advertise himself and to recruit for himself, his own government and his own army *and therefore against the Katipunan and Andres Bonifacio:--to advertise then, and recruit for his own counterrevolutionary self and his own counterrevolutionary government and army...*

And then of course, obedient to the necessity to explain how such a wondrous case of simultaneous rising by the 8 provinces could be possible, he then would be constrained to tell them the most salient things about the Revolution, about the Katipunan, about Andres Bonifacio; and he would then situate their tiny victory disarming two or three decrepit civil guards in their town presidencias as, precisely, the counterparts of those other risers in the other provinces doing what the Supreme Council and the assembly of provincial commanders had agreed upon, namely precisely that simultaneous attack that prompted the Blanco declaration of the state of war. In making that situating, he would of course have to tell them that there were those disarmings and no battles at all in their taking possession of "the government" because Blanco more than a week ago had had all the soldiers in Cavite pulled out and transferred to Manila (to be tremendously added to the enemy force Bonifacio has had to face).

Here incidentally the bragging chief counterrevolutionary liar forgot to be extra careful and had owned in passing that they had merely disarmed and not really fought the enemy, which would make his municipal captains and "countrymen" suspect that the disarmed ones must not be very many. And, but, really, he should in real honesty tell them the truth about the evaporated soldiers and arms from Cavite (to be reconstituted in Manila against Bonifacio) because he was inciting them to do as they did in Kawit and Noveleta and San Francisco de Malabon, namely, NOT to engage the nonexistent enemy soldiers in real, honest-to-goodness battles, but to take precautions to safely disarm the two or three sleeping guardia civil policemen in their own presidencias.

Did he, Aguinaldo y Famy, know that it was only in Cavite that the Spanish soldiers were pulled out? Perhaps he did not. But now we know: in all the seven other provinces, there were no such pull-outs; if at all, the transfer of the Cavite regiments would have enabled the enemy to send reinforcements against the seven other provinces. And in those seven other provinces the battles were of course real ones, gory ones; nor did the Spaniards let up until they had driven the revolutionists to the mountains from where they would now and then re-emerge to wage guerrilla war against the enemy...But in the "history" written by four generations of exceptionally dull and unprincipled "historians", journalists, barbershop and talipapa rumourmongers—Epifanio de los Santos, Jose P. Santos, Carlos Quirino, Teodoro M. Kalaw, Teodoro Agoncillo, Onofre D. Corpuz, Abraham Sarmiento, Nick Joaquin, Carlos P. Romulo, Ambeth Ocampo, the malicious Jesuit researchers Achutegui and Bernad, etc.—great battles were fought by Aguinaldo and the Cavitenos to liberate Cavite, and they were such great warriors that they were able in a twinkling to thus pulverize the enemy and liberate Cavite, and they were the only ones in all the eight provinces who were able to liberate their province, whilst according to the extraordinarily malignant and extraordinarily unintelligent Jesuit duo Achutegui and Bernad, it was the greatness of the greatest general ever, Emilio Aguinaldo y Famy, that made all the difference!!! Whilst all these lies were directly traceable to the greatest general ever, Aguinaldo y Famy himself, who according to him himself in his *Memoirs of the Revolution* (see pp14-15) wrestled with a giant shark biting the same to death after tying it up and pummelling it with ninja chops to the kidney and the liver of it after which he extracted a kalamba (it was made in Kalamba, Laguna together with Dr. Jose Protacio Rizal Mercado y Alonso de Realonda) of shark liver oil from half the liver of the autistic shark whose extreme fondness for Baby Ruth ruined all its teeth and that's why!!! And indeed, liberating the entire Cavite against nonexistent Spanish soldiers in nonexistent battles is no sweat for such a giant shark killer!!! By the way, his wrestling bout with the giant shark happened at night. And not on land either (cf. *Note* below).

Achutegui and Bernad wrote in their Chapter I introductory commentary to their 1972 book, *Aguinaldo and the Revolution of 1896, a Documentary History*: "But an attack did occur, as was learned later. Andres Bonifacio and Emilio Jacinto led their men (several hundreds, we are told) from the Marikina region towards San Juan Del Monte with the intention of capturing the powder storage. But it was a futile attack doomed to fail. The rebels were brave but ignorant and untrained, and they were armed only with bolos. They were no match for the government soldiers who routed them easily. The rebels fled from the field, leaving behind some 80 dead. *It was the first of Bonifacio's failures, a failure reflected also in some of the other provinces of central Luzon.*

"But in Cavite the situation was different, *and the difference was due largely to Aguinaldo.* As one writer has pointed out, Bonifacio's band was a proletarian rabble, trying with puny weapons to strike at an entrenched Establishment. But in Cavite, the leaders of the rebellion were the social and economic leaders of the province. They were the landed gentry. They were the educated aristocracy; or, if not greatly educated (as Aguinaldo was not), they held responsible positions. Emilio Aguinaldo was the municipal captain of his own town. It is not surprising that *his first manifesto* (my italics: this manifesto precisely that we are analyzing) should have been addressed to the municipal captains of the other towns in the province."

Here, the Jesuit duo are saying that Bonifacio and all the other Katipuneros in the other provinces failed in their first attacks, and only the Cavitenos were successful—alluding no doubt to the allegation, claim, and unanimous conclusion of Philippine historiography that they were able, as the Katipuneros in the 7 other provinces were not, to "liberate" their province. And in this work of "liberation", the Jesuit comedians were saying, "the difference" between Cavite's great success and the miserable failure of the other provinces "was due largely to Aguinaldo". To which they blithely and quite innocently added the following words which absolutely belie what they just said here about that great difference that was due largely to Aguinaldo, namely that the Cavitenos were able to "liberate" all of Cavite, because the Cavitenos, and Aguinaldo in particular, could not find any Spanish soldiers in all of Cavite from whom and against whom they could "liberate" Cavite:

"Puzzled over the failure of the expected attack on Manila, Aguinaldo *waited a day*; and then, on the morning of Monday, 31 August, he went to the provincial capital (the newer town of Cavite) to see the Spanish provincial governor. On the pretext that they were needed to protect the town of Cavite el Viejo from bandits, Aguinaldo asked for a detachment of soldiers. (The plan, apparently was, later to ambush these soldiers and strip them of their much needed guns.) He was informed that no men were available *as all the infantry (with the exception of one company) had been sent to Manila on the urgent summons of the Governor of the Islands, General Ramon Blanco.* Aguinaldo then asked for arms—at least a hundred guns. These too were not available. Although he did not get the arms he needed, Aguinaldo learned two important facts: a) The Cavite garrison consisted only of one company, with no reserves to send out to the rest of the province; b) General Blanco on the previous day had declared a state of emergency, placing 8 provinces (including Cavite) under martial law..."

There. And Cavite was liberated by the Spaniards by abandoning it, and, of course, Aguinaldo had absolutely nothing to do with it, and could not have added an iota of "difference" to that unique "situation in Cavite". And if I now declare that these Jesuit Cavitenos were exceedingly stupid in their evil intent and evil deed and evil fact, and exceedingly evil in their wanton stupidity and that they deserve not an iota of respect, can anyone blame me, can anyone disagree with me without joining them, without having already joined them in their evil stupidity? Whilst, in this hefty volume, this is not necessarily the most stupid of their numberless evils nor the evilest of their multifarious stupidities.

Note: Here then is Aguinaldo y Famy's own account of how he defeated and killed in single combat at the bottom of the sea the unnamed giant shark who unfortunately cannot testify here on its own behalf. Dead sharks tell no tail.

"In one of our trips on the paraw San Bartolome bound for Tablas Island, we noticed the slackening of the wind as we passed Point Matuko off Batangas. It must be expected that without the favourable wind the paraw could not sail, so we decided to pass the time lying on deck, waiting for better wind. I lay at the end of the deck and watched the twinkling stars. While in such reverie, I felt something pulling the rope tied to my thigh. As I was nearly carried overboard, I shouted for help. My seven companions came to my rescue, and we pulled the rope back with all our might. We found out that a huge fish was pulling our rope. It was two yards long, and we could not make out what kind of fish it was. Our old pilot Cornelio tried to solve our problem by following a superstition regarding situations like this. He chewed buyo and afterwards wiped this on the rope in the belief that this procedure would weaken the fish. But the fish was as strong as ever.

"When it was finally brought near the paraw, I asked one of my companions to jump into the water to tie a rope around its head. My man hesitated. Fearing that the fish might escape, I jumped into the water myself. The fish struggled to free itself and, in the battle, I was carried into the depths of the sea. The struggle did not last long, however, for I succeeded in tying the rope around its head. I called my companions who by now were ready to give me assistance. In no time, the fish was secured to the side of the paraw. We had to use the mast rope to haul it on board. It was so heavy that the boat veered to one side. Imagine our surprise when we learned that our catch was a huge shark! We discovered that I wounded the fish at the s

tomach, so it succumbed. We had a big feast prepared by Patricio Solis, our able cook. We also had three big buckets of dried shark meat which we gave to friends in Tablas. *Believe it or not*, from just one half of the liver of this fish, we got a big jar of oil. We even threw some meat to the sea because we could not cook all of it." (pp 14-15)

(And most truly, this singular feat from the great Cavite epic Biag ni Il-yong, tops anything in Ripley's!)

V.

Two months after the outbreak of hostilities Aguinaldo commits his second and third acts of treason by declaring his own Republic and national revolutionary army...

Then in a second manifesto dated October 31, 1896, Aguinaldo announced the establishment of another national revolutionary government and army, namely, his *Imus Republic.* At the same time, in

yet another manifesto of the same date (October 31, 1896), purportedly denouncing the massacre by Spanish soldiers of innocent civilians in Lemery and Nasugbu, Aguinaldo firmed up his claim that already he had established a "new Revolutionary government" which as such, as far as he was concerned, had displaced the KKK and was thus a government, and indeed a Republic—precisely the same *Imus Republic* announced on the same day in the other manifesto--separate from the KKK...

The October 31, 1896 Seditious-Treasonous COUNTERREVOLUTIONARY MANIFESTO

To the Philippine People

Liberty, Equality and Fraternity

The Philippines present today a spectacle without precedent in their history, the conquest of their liberty and their independence, the most noble and lofty of their rights—a heroism, which will place them on the same level as civilized nations, inspires them. We know that real progress in a people is based upon liberty and independence. Hence, this right inspires the most noble and sublime emotions which a citizen can feel—feeling them, he should not yield to the fear that our interests or our families may suffer, nor should he tremble at shedding blood to break the chains of slavery, which we have dragged for three hundred years of tyranny and abuse.

A proof of this truth is this, that the revolution is founded on justice and right, is shown by all civilized nations, for none of them will permit the slightest encroachment upon the merest hand's breadth of their domain without pouring out the last drop of blood in defence of the integrity of the nation.

Citizens of the Philippines, we are no savage people; let us try to follow the example of the civilized nations of Europe and America; the time has come to shed the last drop of our blood to conquer our beloved liberty.

The Spaniards, conquerors of this our adored land, accuse us of ingratitude and tell us that we should repay them for opening our eyes by placing their yoke upon our neck. It is a false argument by which they desire to deceive us. For the civilization introduced by Spain during her three centuries in these lands is superficial, and at the bottom a mere fraud, since her effort has been to keep the masses in ignorance, destroying or quenching the centre of real light which has slowly begun to burn in the hearts of a handful of Filipinos, who merely on account of their intelligence are now victims of the persecutions of the government. The results of this are deportations, decrees of exile and the other acts of tyranny which for some years have been carried on here. Tell me,--have we not paid full measure for our great advancement during the three centuries which Spain has used our blood and our sweat? Spain, who, not satisfied with her shameful exploitation of us, spits in our face and calls us carabaos, lazy creatures, apes, and other shameful names!

People of the Philippines: the hour has come to shed our blood to conquer our right and liberty. Let us band ourselves about the flag of the revolution, whose motto is Liberty, Equality, and Fraternity!

A central committee of the revolution composed of six members and a President, will be charged with the continuation of the war, (sic) will organize an army of thirty thousand men, with rifles and cannon, for the defense of the pueblos ***and provinces*** *which adhere to the* ***new Republican Government*** *which will establish order while the revolution spreads* through all the islands of the Philippines. *The form of the government will be like that of the United States of America, founded upon the most rigid principles of liberty, fraternity and equality. Every town* which adheres to the cause *of the revolution will be defended and protected by the revolutionary army against any attack of the enemy.*

Every town will choose by vote a Municipal Committee, composed of a President, a Vice-President, a Treasurer and a Secretary, a judge and two associates, who will carry on the government and administration of justice, and these committees will be completely independent of the Central Committee, but will be obliged to provide for it a contingent of men, food and contribution of war for the support of the army. Every municipal Committee will appoint a delegate to represent it at meetings of the Central Committee (which will deliberate. (sic))

The body of delegates will form a congress in union with the President, and members of the Central Committee, which will deliberate upon sending contingents of troops, food and contributions of war.

The revolutionary army will be composed of three corps of ten thousand men under the command of three generals and a general-in-chief. The central committee will be composed of a President, a Vice-President, and as members it will have the General-in-Chief, a Treasurer, an Intendente, an Auditor and a Secretary.

Each Municipal Committee, as soon as organized, will appoint a captain to form a civil guard in which all citizens will be required to enrol themselves. This body in conjunction with the guard assigned by the General-in-Chief will serve for the protection of the town.

In the name of the Revolutionary Committee I have the honour to beg you to cause the contents of this manifesto to be promulgated by the means which you may find proper. This is a service which we ask of you for the liberty of our beloved country.

Magdalo, (Cauit) [Cavite Viejo] October 31, 1896.

EMILIO AGUINALDO, Magdalo

1.) That it was in fact Edilberto Evangelista who ghostwrote this manifesto must mean that he was an accomplice in the seditious, absolutely treasonous counterrevolutionary conspiracy and was indeed among its major plotters. Used as decoy by Aguinaldo who propped him up as his candidate for the presidency of the *"new Republican government"*, he was destined to be its first victim—with a bullet in the forehead, Aguinaldo had him assassinated on February 17, 1897, a month before Tejeros, no doubt because he must have begun to show proof that he was taken in by the ploy and was enthusiastic in ambitioning that post which of course Aguinaldo y Famy had absolutely exclusively reserved for himself.

2. One of the most absurdly stupid or stupidly absurd justifications for the Aguinaldo sedition-treason of establishing his own "national revolutionary government" put forward by counterrevolutionary writers like the Caviteno "historian" Carlos Quirino was this: that the old national revolutionary government of the Katipunan was nothing but a conspiracy, a conspiratorial organization which had become obsolete because of the open war, so that it now became necessary to establish a new government to manage the open war, etc!!!

The formerly seemingly honourable Supreme Court justice Abraham Sarmiento, also from Cavite, repeated this malevolent betise with absolute glee in his book *The Trial of Andres Bonifacio: The Appeal*, which seals his intellectual fate in this nation's history thus like a five-inch concrete nail endlessly being planted securely through his forehead—Emilio Aguinaldo's enterprising apologists and ghostwriters invariably got it in the forehead, and this one too, which of course is not from me, no no no no no, but from Kapitan Emilio for Abraham gets it here as ultimate repercussion and bountiful harvest for doing it for Kapitan Emilio, assassinating the dead Bonifacio thus for the eternal propping up and holification of his dearly beloved Kapitan Emilio.

Why should people who had nothing or next to nothing to do with the theorization, founding, organization, and four-year long archipelagic-national propagation of the idea and practice of the Revolution be allowed to take over and control, and manage and decide the fate of the Revolution a few months after the outbreak of hostilities, or a year or two years or four or ten years after that?

According to General Apoy or the coward Santiago Alvarez himself in his *Memoirs*, both the Magdiwang and Magdalo factions were officially created by Bonifacio himself and Supreme Council members Emilio Jacinto and Pio Valenzuela *only* on Holy Friday of 1896, a mere five months before the discovery and exposure of the KKK by Fr. Mariano Gil of Tondo and the ensuing outbreak of hostilities, and were thus among the very last and the very very late to join the Revolution.

Why should such Johnny-come-latelies with a wellknown history of piratical and brigandaging cowardice and treachery and overwhelming money-greed (cowards, liars, traitors, rapists and sneaks and pigly rapacious operators belong together and are invariably one and the same persons)—evil traits they most stupendously confirmed to be possessed by in their subsequent acts which culminated in the perfidious and craven murder of ten generals and the sale of the honor and the glory of the Motherland itself, of the Revolution, and thus of the Motherland herself—why, instead of being expelled and forcibly eliminated from the ranks of the Revolution should they be allowed to elect themselves as the leaders and controllers of it?

Even as a mere idea which would not necessarily involve the total or near-total elimination of the *mere* "conspirators" and the takeover of the supposedly *professional* "warmakers", the thing was an arrant and bulbous absurdity. Emilio Aguinaldo whose peculiar way of simpleminded reasoning was absolutely original, invented it to justify his counterrevolution, to justify his murder of the founder of the Revolution and therewith of the Filipino nation and the Philippine state, Andres Bonifacio, to justify his hostaging of the Philippine Revolution and his selling of it at Biyak na Bato for 800,000 pesos... And Abraham Sarmiento believed it in togaed solemnity...

3. "... nor should he tremble at shedding blood to break the chains of slavery, which we have dragged for *three hundred years* of tyranny and abuse". In his August 31 seditious manifesto and self-advertisement, Aguinaldo says it's only a hundred years, and that was a distinct sign that he was the one who wrestled with the pen/cil to produce it. Now he says it's three hundred years, and that was a distinct sign that someone more literate and better informed must have written (that is to say, ghostwritten) it, namely, precisely, the ilustrado engineer friend and erstwhile counterrevolutionary assimilationist co-propagandist of Rizal's, Edilberto Evangelista.

We have seen him, along with Jose Alejandrino and Antonio Luna, and yes, Graciano Lopez Jaena, and even Mariano

Ponce in their letters pushing Rizal towards revolution and even concluding that Rizal was already a convinced revolutionary and that was why he was going home in late June 1892; but Rizal, of course, did not launch a revolution but aspired instead, in uttermost perversity, to stage a one-man show, namely his *Assimilationist Matyrdom plot*, which he insanely contemplated would spectacularly pre-empt the Revolution, coup d'etating it even before it was born, and when he was finally executed in Bagumbayan in 1896 still fighting desperately against the Revolution even up to the last seconds of his evil life (his last request was to be shot facing the bullets arguing farcically with his farcical Spanish murderers--for they did not know that the man they were about to kill was the greatest non-Spanish Spanish hero of all time, defending Spanish colonialism against the Revolution thus to very death--that he was no traitor to Mother Spain and was thus not one of those criminal revolutionaries: up to the last seconds of his evil life he rejected the very idea of any kind of oneness with the Revolution and refused in utter abhorrence thus to be identified with *them*) , he had already done so much for the ultimate triumph of the counterrevolution in fighting for which he indeed died. Later on, and in their own belated ways, Edilberto Evangelista, Jose Alejandrino, and Antonio Luna would come home and join the Revolution which even at the time when Evangelista did so in mid-October 1896 was already being actively undermined by the Aguinaldo *counterrevolution from inside the Revolution*, so that they all, at different periods, in making the grievous mistake of joining the Revolution by joining Aguinaldo, had actually joined the Counterrevolution! Evangelista, who like another misguided ilustrado ghostwriter of the Chief of the Caviteno Counterrevolution Ilyong Buktot, namely Mamerto Natividad of Nueva Ecija, would be farcically given the rank of Lieutenant-General, next in command only to him, Aguinaldo y Famy, the *General en Jefe* or, in colonial Spanish style, the Captain General, would be murdered by this same Counterrevolution with a bullet in his forehead just like the same Mamerto Natividad. Luna who also was Aguinaldo y Famy's Lieutenant-General would suffer the same fate except that in lieu of the proverbial bullet in the forehead, he would get it by way of 57 or 67 dagger thrusts. As for Jose Alejandrino, he would stay with Aguinaldo y Famy's Counterrevolution to the very end and defend to the very end

Aguinaldo y Famy's Counterrevolution in his *Memoirs* in which, among other massmurderous things he would go on slandering Andres Bonifacio rantingly without end.

VI.

Two months after the outbreak of hostilities Aguinaldo commits his second and third acts of treason by declaring his own Republic and national revolutionary army...

The October 31, 1896 Manifesto (cont'd.)

4."Citizens of the Philippines..."—and surely, that makes the Philippines, with, as its center of stateness now the eight provinces in simultaneous revolt, a veritable *state*, a veritable *nation-state!* And being so brandnew it must still sound a bit anachronistic and incongruous thus, Engineer Edilberto Evangelista alias Emilio y Famy A, was nonetheless perfectly right in calling the Filipinos at that most crucial juncture of the Filipino people's political-historical existence, *citizens*. Which also means that what Aguinaldo and his all-Caviteno Counterrevolutionary conspiracy perpetrated in Tejeros on March 22-23, 1897, was illegal, unconstitutional, anti-democratic, and the supposed government they conjured up there was a fake government, illegal, unconstitutional, anti-democratic, criminal, and above all, counterrevolutionary.

In arguing for the fact that the KKK on the eve of the outbreak of hostilities simultaneously in the eight provinces was in the fullest sense of the term a state with its own government, with its own written constitution and certainly with its own unwritten constitution (of which every state, and certainly every nation-state, is in possession, and there is no genuine state that is not primordially and historically founded on it, with its written constitution being also, if it is authentic at all, founded on that unwritten one:--the legality of customary laws or of common law which precedes and underlies all the written and officially-formally legislated laws of any nation or state derives from this unwritten constitution, whilst this unwritten constitution itself derives its lawful and rightful element and character from the *primordial democracy and the continuous practice of this primordial democracy that in every human society, in every city state or nation state, underlies the being-people of the people*), we zero-in on the fact of the being people of the people, here the being people of the Filipino people, which was created, constituted, made to crystallize, and allowed to emerge and at once activated, nay catalyzed into explosive activity and epochal creativity by the Revolution itself. At that juncture in the creation and actualization of the Revolution by Bonifacio and the Katipuneros which at precisely that point had already become the entire Filipino people (we can take the *assent* and active *ratification* of it by the Katipunan vanguard and the rank and file soldiery of the Revolutionary Army simultaneously in the eight provinces as legally and democratically and rightfully *representative of the assent and active ratification by all, by all the people*) the Katipunan emergently metamorphosed into a state, into the nation-state which it still is today.

And whence this continuity then when the *Aguinaldo Counterrevolution from within the Revolution*, thanks to the great impetus bestowed on it by the *Rizalian Counterrevolution from outside the Revolution*, had hostaged the Revolution in Tejeros and sold it at Biyak na Bato and had prostituted it to the Americans, and destroyed its army with the murder of Antonio Luna who opposed this prostitution and the shameful and massmurderous pimping of it by Emilio Pedro Aguinaldo Famy y Paterno? It is the continuity of the being people of this same Bonifacio-Katipunan *revolutionized people* itself which *being revolutionized* although damaged by the Aguinaldo counterrevolutionary vendoration and subsequent pimping and prostitution was itself not sold and was only relatively superficially and only in some parts prostituted. The *revolutionized Filipino people* sheltered that stateness within themselves, in their being the *Bonifacio-Katipunan revolutionized people* that they were, falling back thus upon their being the people's, and thus their own, unwritten constitution *in their being their own primordial democracy revolutionized and fulfilled thus*. That is to say, in their revolutionarily assuming and gloriously accomplishing that primordial democracy that (as primordial substructural relations amongst free beings constitutive of the foundation and condition of possibility itself of any possible society of free beings)subtended their being the people that they were.

5. "...her (Spain's) effort has been to keep the masses in ignorance, destroying or quenching the centre of real light which has slowly begun to burn in the hearts of a handful of Filipinos, who merely on account of their intelligence are now victims of the persecutions of the government". This "centre of real light" was of course the ilustrados, Rizal and company, who as such should have, like their counterparts all throughout the colonial world, conceived and organized and led the revolution, except that they here lacked the heart and fell short of the requisite intelligence to do so, and founded instead the assimilationist counterrevolutionary *Propaganda Movement*! This sentence proves beyond doubt, even as Aguinaldo did not really make a secret of it, for in his *November 9, 1907 Statement on the Revolution in Cavite and the Death of Andres Bonifacio* and elsewhere, he mentioned that Evangelista wrote the constitution of the "Imus Republic" of his wanton fakery, that it was indeed Evangelista who wrote this manifesto and the summary constitution basted onto it. Of course, the seditious-treasonous counterrevolutionary idea must belong to Ilyong Buktot himself, whilst Evangelista's willing and even quite eloquent ghostwriting of it must entitle us to conclude that he agreed wholeheartedly buktotly with it and was thenceforth a major accomplice in the plot.

6. "People of the Philippines: the hour has come to shed our blood to conquer our right and liberty. Let us band ourselves about the flag of the revolution, whose motto is *Liberty, Equality, & Fraternity!*" This flag then was *not* the *Katipunan* flag, not Bonifacio's flag, not the Revolution's flag. For although Bonifacio did not oppose and must certainly have

been enthusiastic in approving that motto of the French Revolution, he, as far as we know, never used it as his or the Katipunan's own.

7. "A central committee of the revolution composed of six members and a President, will be charged with the continuation of the war (*sic*), will organize an army of thirty thousand men, with rifles and cannon, for the defence of the pueblos and provinces which adhere to the *new Republican Government* which will establish order while the revolution spreads through all the islands of the Philippines..." And what about those provinces which do not *adhere*? What about those generals of the KKK which do not adhere to this "new" government of yours? Here Emilio Buktot Evangelisto Famy y Aguinaldo had even anticipated, and could not help but anticipate, that there would be provinces, i.e., leaders of--of course--the KKK, generals of the KKK, and Bonifacio first of all, who would vehemently disagree to adhere to his buktotical *counterrevolution*. Aside from Bonifacio and his two brothers, Aguinaldo had sentenced to death Gen. Emilio Jacinto and Gen. Julio Nakpil for having opposed the Tejeros coup d'etat. And for being against the Biyak na Bato Deed of Sale, he had had Gen. Mamerto Natividad, Gen. Feliciano Jocson, and Gen. Julian dela Cruz assassinated. Whilst, of course, Gen. Antonio Luna was stabbed 57 times by Emilio Kalawit y Famy for having opposed the vendoration of the same Revolution to the Americans. *That* was what must in his hands await those who would not adhere…

And how does it happen that Abraham Sarmiento, in his scandalously anti-democratic, fascistic, might-is-right book *The Trial of Andres Bonifacio: the Appeal*, did not see this aspect of the question which falls directly under his supposed juridical-theoretical expertise? How does it happen that Onofre D. Corpuz, the Caviteno from Camiling, Tarlac, failed, in his contribution to the abovementioned book titled "Separate Opinion", to even hint at the possibility of the likelihood of the massmurderous criminality and the wanton sedition, the irredeemable treason, the rabid unprincipledness and rightlessness of this act? And even Constantino who was normally honest and intelligent (the rest are normally dishonest and stupid)...Was it because, as the saying goes, having murdered Bonifacio and grabbed power, the crime ultimately succeeded?

An additional bluff was necessary here however, namely, the unthinkable lie that the same crime was not only crowned with personal success for Aguinaldo the powermad and moneymad criminal, but for the Revolution itself and thus for the country, the people!!! That Aguinaldo perpetrated all those atrocities in order to save the Revolution!!! And then, but then, how could the sale of the Revolution at Biyak na Bato and the disintegration of the revolutionary army with the murder of Antonio Luna be reckoned as "saving the Revolution"? What kind of stupidity is it that presides over this reckoning? What kind of insanity, what kind of insane stupidity and stupid insanity is it?

8. "In the name of the Revolutionary Committee... I have the honor... *Magdalo, (Cauit) Cavite Viejo October 31, 1896."* There. The ideas, the concepts, the ideals, the legal formalities presented in this manifesto were all absolutely beyond Emilio Aguinaldo y Famy's criminally vulgar mind. Employed—and abused—as such in this criminal instrument, they are absolutely worthless and are only words, nothing but words. What was concrete and seditiously, treasonously, counter-revolutionarily efficacious, was the presentation itself, the rhetoric of evil, which was evil itself, swaying the evil mind and leaning upon it, and it upon it, as it assumed and merged into the historico-political project, which was at once, and at this level of efficacy, a politico-ideological body, the politico-ideological body of the Aguinaldo counterrevolution, responsibility and guilt for which Edilberto Evangelista the writer of this evil manifesto must perforce share.

For if Edilberto Evangelista were himself more upright, more intelligent, and less powerfully determined in his unconscious by ideological class forces to slight and treat as virtually nonexistent the largely working-class constituted Katipunan nation-state (*forced to be so by main force of the Rizalian colonial middle-class rejection of, and opposition to, the Revolution and the Filipino people*), and with it treat as nothing at all Andres Bonifacio also and his four years of underground leadership of the people's revolutionary project, he, Edilberto Evangelista, should with all his might have resisted and rejected Aguinaldo's patently seditious, treasonous, counterrevolutionary project, of which in the littleness of his mind and the shallowness of his humanity he instead became here a chief exponent and scribiential, intellectual-traitor advocate, one of the first such in this nation's history...

VII.

Two months after the outbreak of hostilities Aguinaldo commits his second and third acts of treason by declaring his own Republic and national revolutionary army...

The October 31, 1896 Manifesto on the Nasugbu & Lemery Slaughter

The Savagery committed by the Spanish troops, on orders from their officers, within the church in Nasugbu and in Lemery, are proof of the bitter hatred, the contempt, and the savagery of these so-called 'Fathers of Civilization'. What the soldiers did in Nasugbu was hailed in bold headlines in the newspapers in Manila: they called it a 'complete victory'. But this is what actually happened:

The Filipino patriot army had succeeded in dislodging the Spanish soldiers from Nasugbu. Then, leaving behind some twenty men to garrison the town the Filipino troops then went elsewhere. In their absence the Spanish forces returned to attack Nasugbu. The small Filipino garrison put up a brief resistance from the convento, but finding themselves outnumbered, they withdrew. In the meantime, the women and children and the defenceless populace were in the church, hearing Mass. They had fled to the church, thinking that its walls would give them sanctuary. But an incredible thing happened. The Spanish troops, finding no more Filipino soldiers to fight, went into the church and vented their fury on the women, the children, and the defenceless men. They slaughtered everyone, except for a few women whom they used for their lust. That was what happened at Nasugbu. We leave it to the judgment of the people.

In Lemery, a similar massacre took place. They slaughtered some 200 persons: women, children, unarmed men...

After condemning thus the savagery of the Spanish soldiers in slaughtering defenceless civilians in Nasugbu and Lemery, Aguinaldo through the prose of the traitor ghostwriter of his, Edilberto Evangelista, whom in mid-February of the following year, he, Aguinaldo y Famy, would murder with a bullet in the forehead, forthwith announced his brand-new government to the "Citizens of the Philippines" and campaigned to them for its recognition thus:

"...Citizens of the Philippines! We have established a provisional Government in the towns that have been pacified. Its principles are: Liberty, Equality and Fraternity. This Government consists of the following:

A Revolutionary Committee whose task is to carry on the war until all the islands are freed.

A Congress of Deputies from every town.

Municipal Committees, enjoying absolute autonomy, in charge of the administration of justice within the territory of each town.

There are now in existence two revolutionary armies engaged in attacking the Spanish forces in every town.

The safety of each town shall be preserved by the Citizens' Guard, composed of local citizens capable of bearing arms.

At present, the progress of the new Revolutionary Government is three times better than that of the Government of Spanish Tyranny.

The Revolutionary Committee calls upon all Filipino citizens who love their land: to rise up in arms; to proclaim the liberty and independence of the Philippines as a right to which they are entitled in justice; and to recognize the new Government of the Revolution, *which has been established by the blood of its sons.*

Magdalo (Cauit) 31October 1896.

EMILIO AGUINALDO

Magdalo

1. "Citizens of the Philippines! We have established a provisional government in the towns..." Note how carefully Aguinaldo y Famy alias Edilberto Evangelista failed here to specify that those towns were in fact Cavite towns only, and how he carefully neglected to say that those towns were not pacified at all but were rather abandoned by the Spanish forces upon orders from Governor General Blanco days before the outbreak of hostilities.

2. "We have established a provisional government in the towns *that have been pacified"* Again, and we should not tire repeating this in order never again to forget the lesson, and in order never again to forget how all of Philippine historiography lied about the thing and used the lie to justify the Tejeros coup d'etat of the Katipunan and of Andres Bonifacio and the murder of Bonifacio and his brothers, and the sale of the Revolution at Biyak na Bato:--*there was no work of "pacification" or "reconquest" or "liberation"* that Aguinaldo in particular and the Cavitenos in general had had to do in the entire province of Cavite because Blanco, days before the first Katipunan attack on the 29th and 30th August in Manila and in all the other 7 Luzon provinces including the Magdiwang side of Cavite *and excluding only Aguinaldo's Magdalo side of it,* had ordered the pull out of the Spanish forces in Cavite and transferred the same to Manila to face Andres Bonifacio there. Cavite was not a liberated zone—it was rather an ABANDONED ZONE. Every time therefore that Aguinaldo and the Caviteno historians so-called and the aguinaldically perverted Filipino historians so-called—fascist hacks like Epifanio de los Santos, Teodoro Agoncillo, Carlos Quirino, Carlos P. Romulo, Onofre Corpuz, Zaide, Gualberto Moron, Ambeth Ocampo...—referred to this thing as pacification, liberation, conquest, instead of *abandonment by the enemy,* they were lying...

3. "A Revolutionary Committee whose task is to carry on the war until *all the islands are freed..."* Apart from the glowering fact that there was in this document absolutely no mention nor even hint of the presence and reality and antecedence of the Katipunan; here, in the lying face of the supposed mere "provisionality" of this *new Revolutionary Government for the recognition of which by all the Citizens of the Philippines who were all the Filipino inhabitants of "all the islands" Aguinaldo was here campaigning*, this liberation of *all the islands* as the task and *ambition* of this "new Government of the Revolution" gives the seditious, counterrevolutionary thing away.

4. Meanwhile, it is not yet clear what really happened there, in Nasugbu and Lemery. One of the very first things we have to ask—and try to answer—when confronted with documents such as this is why its author should write and publish such a thing. What is he trying to say, and what does he hope to accomplish by saying and publishing it? The author, Aguinaldo y Famy (who had a co-author, a ghostwriter, in the person of Engr. Edilberto Evangelista), had caused to be written and published on the same day the *October 31, 1896 Manifesto* which as we have seen was nothing less than the promulgation of a constitution of a new republic, a new government, a new army, and indeed a new state. This was to become known in a little while as Aguinaldo y Famy's "Imus Republic".

In other words, the author was the self-proclaimed, nay, self-decreed, leader of a by now forthrightly declared *counterrevolution.* More than that, this *counterrevolution* was now a "state", a "republic", a "national government" with its own, brand-new "constitution", a new "army", and of course a brand-new "president" in the person of yours truly, Aguinaldo y Famy; and not only that:--this *counterrevolution* in the first as in this second document, was supposed to be "revolutionary"; hence it was the "new Revolutionary Republic", the "new National Revolutionary Government", with its "new Revolutionary Constitution", and its "new National Revolutionary Army", whose "new Revolutionary President" was of course, yours truly, Aguinaldo y Famy. But that is not yet all of that:--for there was, right there and then, of course, a revolution, namely the KKK, antedating that Aguinaldic "revolution" by at least four years and 3 months, and, as we all know, the Magdalo and the Magdiwang of Cavite were provincial districts, chapters, commands of it; whilst, of course, this Katipunan Revolution was a, in fact the, first, the original, Revolutionary Republic, Government, Army, with its Revolutionary Constitution, and at the time of the promulgation of Aguinaldo's "New Revolutionary Republic", etcetera, its National Revolutionary President, Andres Bonifacio, the *Supremo.* And Aguinaldo's "New Revolutionary Republic", etcetera, was *not* the same as Bonifacio's KKK! And therefore, lo, and behold!—we discover right here right now that what Aguinaldo y Famy promulgates in these documents was a *Counterrevolutionary Republic, Government, Army, Constitution, President*, and that indeed and truly truly, Aguinaldo and cohorts were counterrevolutionaries and what they were doing was *Counterrevolution*!!! And I am very very sorry dear editor, but it has to be this painstaking because the thing is so obvious that everybody's neck has to be twisted 360 or even 720 or 1080 degrees for us Filipinos to see it for what it *was*/is. *Counterrevolution*! Declared as such less than two days after the outbreak of the war (in the *August 31 Manifesto)*, and simultaneously now for the second and third time in these two documents two months afterwards....

Counterrevolution! –the distinctive characteristic of which, *as determined by its personally designed purpose, namely to be able to hostage the Revolution in order to sell it to the enemy,* was that it had to be able to pass itself off as the true and better managed revolution. *For which then it was imperative that he murder Andres Bonifacio. Which he did.*

5.) The author/fabricator of this manifesto then was the self-elected President of a *counterrevolutionary "Republic",* which, in the other manifesto of the same date has just been promulgated! It goes without saying that his being so must have something to do with the fabrication and contents of this document. And indeed, we see that the greater half of the manifesto was overtaken by the advertisement of this *counterrevolutionary "Republic", "Constitution", "Army" etc.*, and its instant accomplishments. So to the question why a Caviteno *capo* of one of two provincial factions of what supposedly was the Katipunan--(both of which were able to garrison their corresponding towns and claim them as their territory without fighting for them because the Spaniards had had to abandon them by order of the Governor General; whilst both of them had ceaselessly bragged that they had

fought the Spaniards for those towns, that they had defeated them and booted them out of those towns, that they spilled their blood to conquer them, that they severally died to oust the Spaniards from them—see for instance the stentorian boast of General "Apoy" alias Santiago Alvarez, whipping his pistol and threatening to shoot Antonio Montenegro during a dramatic episode in the staging of the all-Caviteno, Magdiwang-Magdalo Conspiracy and coup d'etat at Tejeros, on page 84 of his *The Katipunan & the Revolution, Memoirs of a General*)--should be denouncing Spanish atrocities outside of Cavite, the broad answer is he, Aguinaldo y Famy, was acting it out as the "President" of the "Republic": and therefore of all the islands. That, however, was not the whole story.

From what we know from historical hindsight of what wanton evil this Kapitan Ilyong was capable of perpetrating with not a tinge of compunction, and of how all he cared for was money and the power necessary to get at the money and to get more and more of it, that to lay his hands upon bundles of such he had murdered at least ten generals of the Revolution, we can be absolutely certain it was not at all because he cared for the Batangueno victims of those Spanish atrocities that he was now denouncing them in this manifesto. (It was well-known for instance that, even within Cavite, Aguinaldo y Famy's soldiers were dreaded rapists—and of course thieves—and that Aguinaldo y Famy was tolerating them, saying that the people should be more patient with his soldiers because "after all they were not being paid"—see report on the matter by General Julio Nakpil in his memoirs, *Julio Nakpil & the Philippine Revolution*, part iii, pp 59 et seq.; whilst, during the siege of Limbon where Ciriaco Bonifacio was shot point blank while being held by Aguinaldo y Famy's men, and where the Supremo was treacherously shot and then knifed in the throat, during the night, Aguinaldo y Famy's men abducted all the women in the Supremo's camp and raped them, stole everything there they could lay their hands on, including, according to Gregoria de Jesus, their "utensils"!, and in the morning, the commanding officer, Col. Agapito Bonson manhandled and raped Gregoria de Jesus herself, and Aguinaldo y Famy was very happy about it, no one was prosecuted, everybody was promoted, and Col. Intong remained with him on his bedside in his Hong Kong exile and was there like a bedpost till death did them part...Question: Do we have to suspect or imagine what Aguinaldo y Famy's men must have done to the people of their Batangas territory, namely Talisay, by way of lust and thievery?—since even in their own hometowns they were doing it?)

What then, aside from acting-out the caring "president of all the islands", was it that lay behind this show of outrage at the Spanish atrocities?

This:--he wanted to denounce and expose the gross ineptitude and criminal cowardice of his rival Magdiwang faction who abandoned Nasugbu and failed to defend it when *real* Spanish soldiers from Spain attacked it, leaving the Nasugbu people to the racist fury and schizoid lust of those European hoboes. *For Nasugbu was a Magdiwang town!* And Lemery? We cannot find it in the list of Magdiwang towns available to us through the extant documents, but perhaps it was to Lemery that the Magdiwang forces fled and where they were scuttled by the same *real* Spanish soldiers. These *real* Spanish soldiers arrived in batches from Spain only during the first two weeks of October. The October 18 Rape & Massacre of Nasugbu was one of their first fieldworks. Lemery on October 23 was their second.

By the way, the Magdalos too were no better defending the Batangas town under their "jurisdiction", namely Talisay, and the same kind of abandonment befell the townspeople there when, 3 weeks later, on November 8, 1896, it was attacked and sacked by the same *real* Spanish soldiers from Spain under Gen. Ernesto de Aguirre.

VIII.

Domingo DC De Guzman

Two months after the outbreak of hostilities Aguinaldo commits his second and third acts of treason by declaring his own Republic and national revolutionary army...

The October 31, 1896 Manifesto on the Nasugbu & Lemery Slaughter (ii)

This is what, by way of introducing this document, the unthinkable Jesuit duo whose great distinction is to be found in the peculiar way by which they do not betray all throughout even merely a suggestion of a hint of a shadow of intellectual conscience, Pedro de Achutegui and Miguel Bernad, wrote about the massacres and the insurpassable greatness of Aguinaldo y Famy in their book, *Aguinaldo & the Revolution of 1896, A Documentary History:*

"Although there was rebel activity in other provinces (we are told that on 3 September some 3,000 rebels converged upon San Isidro, Nueva Ecija, and besieged it for a day), *it was in Cavite where the rebellion was most successful; and* except for the capital city situated in a peninsula, the entire province was in rebel hands. *It was therefore to Cavite that the major expeditions were sent.*

"At the outbreak of the revolt, the Spanish government had at its disposal only a very limited force. There were two squadrons of cavalry, 1 battalion of engineers, 1 artillery regiment, and 7 regiments of infantry, but 6 of them were in Mindanao. Some of these were immediately recalled, and one contingent, arriving in Manila on 6 September, was immediately shipped up the Pasig into the Laguna de Bay. They landed at Binan and marched southwestward towards Silang, a rebel-held town at the foot of the Tagaytay Ridge.

Unable to reach Silang and not having enough rations, they turned back, the withdrawal being reported in Manila as a brilliant 'retreat'.

"But in October the reenforcements which Governor Blanco had urgently requested from Spain began to arrive. Over 800 soldiers arrived on 1 October, over a thousand arrived on the 6th, some 700 arrived on the 13th. *Most of these troops were deployed towards Cavite, or to the south of Cavite, to Batangas. Successful in Batangas, the Spanish troops were repulsed in Cavite, their biggest effort and biggest defeat being an attempted landing at Noveleta and Binakayan on November 8, 9, and 10....*

"It was on 18 October that the Spaniards attacked Nasugbu. That town is on the West coast of Batangas, protected on the north and the east by hills, but open to attack from the sea on the west and to a land attack from the south. A brigade under General Nicolas Jaramillo attacked Nasugbu, supported by gunfire from two Spanish gunboats in the harbour. The rebel soldiers had taken refuge in some farm buildings owned by Don Pedro Roxas. There they were overcome and some 100 Filipinos were killed. In the meantime, the civilian population (women, children, and male non-combatants) had taken refuge in the church. But the Spanish army did not respect that sanctuary. The church doors were battered down, the soldiers entered and slaughtered the refugees. They then set fire to church and *convento*. None were spared except some women who were taken 'to satisfy the soldiers' lust'. The massacre of Nasugbu was hailed by the Manila papers as a great 'victory'. But news of the outrage filtered through to Aguinaldo, and on 31 October he issued his second manifesto, condemning the slaughter.

"In the same manifesto, he also condemned what General Jaramillo's men did in Lemery on 23 October. Pushed by Jaramillo from Balayan and by General Aguirre from

Banadero, the rebel forces converged upon Lemery where they were attacked by Jaramillo's troops with great loss of life.

"Aguinaldo's manifesto may have been originally written in Tagalog. What we possess is the Spanish text, quoted in full by a Spanish historian, Jose del Castillo y Jimenez, whose book, *El Katipunan o el filibusterismo en Filipinas* was published in Madrid in 1897. The English translation is ours." (pp. 28-29)

i.) "Although there was rebel activity in other provinces..., *it was in Cavite where the rebellion was most successful... It was therefore to Cavite that the major expeditions were sent."*

If on September 3, 1896, a force of 3,000 Katipunan fighters laid siege to the Spanish provincial command in San Isidro, Nueva Ecija for a whole day and they failed to take it, whilst with forty cuadrilleros Aguinaldo y Famy in 3 seconds flat was able to conquer 2 sleepy civil guards, then indeed the Caviteno warriors must be the greatest in the world! And this even when an *expedition* of 500 Spanish regulars pulled out of Cavite had actually been sent to San Isidro two days ago to reinforce the Spanish forces there.

What the Jesuit duo are regaling us here are of course but some of the *inversions* that make up this inverted "history". It is going to be repetitious of us, but we have to denounce them wherever we encounter them. It will now be fully appreciated perhaps that we have thus far been excessively polite dealing with these "historians". But really it is not easy to be perfectly calm reading things like this and especially from such holy beings like them.

If there were some kind of "unsuccessful or not so successful" "rebel activities" in other provinces like Nueva Ecija, in Cavite there was practically *none*. Zero. With but a shadow of a shadow of *almost*. "Rebel activities" must refer *mainly* to fighting the enemy, and as we now know there were no Spanish soldiers in Cavite from the time Blanco pulled all of them out a few days after Fr. Mariano Gil exposed the Katipunan on August 19, 1896 (except, i.e., for a company of infantry to guard the powder depot in Binakayan), to February 14, 1897, when, finally, after driving the Katipunan forces to the mountains in all the other provinces, the Spaniards launched their assault on Cavite. There were thus practically no battles with the enemy in Cavite from day one, August 29, 1896, to February 14, 1897. And during those five and a half months, the Cavitenos were able to do two things: make some deadly fortifications as they awaited the coming of the Spaniards, and plot and consolidate the *counterrevolution.*

The first overt act in this *counterrevolution* was Aguinaldo y Famy's refusal to abide by the Katipunan Supreme Council order to attack his own presidencia on the night of the 29th or at dawn or early in the morning of the 30th. As evidenced by Blanco's August 30 decree placing the 8 provinces in a state of war, all the other field commanders obeyed the order. The Magdiwangs attacked in the morning of the 30th. Only Aguinaldo y Famy failed to attack. When queried later, he advanced lack of arms as the, of course, lying reason for his failure which in official military terms was a case of insubordination. Depending on the gravity of the situation, this contumacy or cravenness or plain cowardice could be tantamount to treason. Coincidentally—and now we should be more than merely suspicious that there was more to it than mere coincidence—this kind of treason was what Lt. Gen. Vicente Fernandez incurred when he failed to attack from a designated side at a given hour during the historic first armed Katipunan assault against Spanish colonialism at the San Juan del Monte polvorin, precisely on the night of August 29. Fernandez and his men were not there at all! The Katipunan strategy, capitalizing on what the rebels had in great abundance, namely numbers, was to overwhelm the polvorin defenders from all sides at once. As could be expected, this massive absence of Fernandez and his men led to the collapse of the attack and the massacre of an estimated 80 Katipuneros. Fernandez disappeared. A warrant of arrest—for *treason*—was issued against him by the Katipunan Supreme Council. And where did Fernandez go to report on a mission satisfactorily accomplished thus? To Aguinaldo y Famy whose adjutant he was! It turned out that Fernandez was Aguinaldo y Famy's spy who must have been commissioned by him to sabotage Andres Bonifacio and the Supreme Council preparatory to what from historical hindsight we now know he was intent on doing, namely, undermine Bonifacio's leadership, oust and murder him, hostage the Revolution, and sell it to the enemy (we are documenting this in the next issue).

The second public, political-military act by Aguinaldo y Famy in this long-range vendorial project of counterrevolution was precisely the issuance of his *August 31, 1896 Manifesto* which we have just *exposed as such*:--for the first time yes, for we are the first ever to see counterrevolution in it.

Hence, it was in Cavite where the revolution was *most unsuccessful.* For, strictly speaking, and to the very considerable extent that Emilio Aguinaldo y Famy's evil intent and vendorial-treasonous design was preeminent there all-throughout, from August 31, 1896 when he first declared in published form his *counterrevolution,* to May 10, 1897 when he murdered Andres Bonifacio and ordered the burning of the Cavite towns as in fear and trembling he fled Cavite, THERE WAS NO REVOLUTION IN CAVITE.

For taking over their towns abandoned by the soldiers of colonialism cannot be considered *revolution.* It was, to be sure, an *effect of revolution* that those soldiers of colonial tyranny were pulled out en masse and sent to Manila to defend the Spaniards there against Andres Bonifacio. And it was therefore an *effect of revolution* too that after the soldiers of colonial tyranny departed, the Cavitenos were *able without a fight* to take over their towns. But it was hardly *revolution* on their part that they did so. A band of robbers and rapists would have done the same upon perceiving the absolutely unique opportunity. *And it turned out that way indeed in the province of Cavite.*

For, due to the singular peculiarity of the abandoned situation in Cavite, everything depended upon the *intent and design of those who took over* what was to become of that *effect of revolution* there. Whilst the preponderant intent and design was, from the very start, *not* revolution but its opposite, namely, *counterrevolution*, and, with it, thievery and rape.

In fact, we can now be perfectly certain that, had there not been that absolutely unique opportunity of taking over their towns from the Spaniards *without a fight*, and without any enemies appearing in sight except for two widely-spaced perfunctory and singularly inept probings, one in the first week of September and another in the second week of November, 1896, the vendorial project of counterrevolution would never have been able to jell enough in Aguinaldo y Famy's cowardly mind. For then, if, for instance, 3,000-strong Magdalos had had to assault his own Kawit presidencia for one whole day and fail to take it, Aguinaldo y Famy would have lost heart from the very beginning and quit. For Aguinaldo y Famy was an eminently certifiable coward. Which certification he himself zealously provided.

Aguinaldo y Famy was such a timorous titmouse of a general that, when he was running away from the Spaniards on the last day of the victorious Spanish retaking of Cavite, he ordered the burning of the Cavite towns in order to impede the progress of the pursuing enemy! And he was so shameless that he even boasted about it to the Spanish correspondent Jose Barrozo of the Madrid newspaper, *El Imparcial* , during an ambush interview in Calumpit, Bulacan, on December 27, 1897, en route to their prepaid exile to Hong Kong and

Aguinaldo y Famy's rendezvous in a bank there with his 400,000-peso check which according to him was solely his as *personal payment* for his services to Mother Spain in hostaging the Revolution thus, murdering its founder, and surrendering it for pay! He even told this reporter that he decided to sell the Revolution to the Spaniards because he was nearly killed in Naic while fleeing from the Spaniards. Let us quote his scandalous words: "The burning of the towns was the plan of defence which we had arranged to delay for a short time the entrance of the Spaniards, and thus give us time to get away with our families and save our lives, going to the nearest towns which had not been taken. *In Naic I found myself very near the Spanish lines and thought I would be killed or captured. These great and serious events prepared my mind for the cessation of the revolution*, but we had no easy way—I of communicating my desire, and the others of explaining theirs to me..." (pp. 422-427, volume I, *The Philippine Insurrection Against the United States*, JRM Taylor, ed.; italics supplied.)

From the confession itself we can deduce that that must have been the *very first time* he found himself very near the Spanish lines and abreast of the thought that he could get killed or captured, and that was quite enough to make him resolve right there and then to quit. The timorous titmouse was never in a fight!

Meanwhile, there must always be a stormy cloud of doubt overhanging and enveloping the *revolutionariness* of the Magdiwangs during the initial stages from the day of their recruitment and establishment to the March 22, 1897 Magdiwang-Magdalo Tejeros conspiracy & *coup d'etat,* in which it of course ceased to be doubtful that they were with the *Aguinaldo Counterrevolution*: they were the ones who "invited" Bonifacio to Cavite.

Revolution came to Cavite with the arrival there of Andres Bonifacio of course, but from beginning to end, Aguinaldo y

Famy's *counterrevolution was able very successfully* to thwart him and the Revolution he brought with him there.

In short, it is not only that there was no revolution there where Achutegui and Bernad say "*the revolution was most successful*". It is that the *counterrevolution from inside the revolution* was hatched and worked out there and was *most successful* there. And it was so successful there that it was there that the Cavitenos were able to hostage the Revolution, or rather the leadership of the Revolution (at Tejeros, yes, and via an all-Caviteno Magdiwang-Magdalo Conspiracy), and murder its founder, en route to its culmination in the Biak na Bato Deed of Sale.

Concerning the *deadly fortifications:* they dug up kilometres-long trenches to await the technically and materially superior enemy and engage them in a war of positions when they should have prepared instead for guerrilla war. Result:--those kilometres-long trenches became their kilometres-long mass-graves.

And where did this *most successful* hostager and vendor of the Revolution flee to save his own neck? To Bulacan and Nueva Ecija—to Biyak na Bato, the mountain fort of the General from San Isidro, Nueva Ecija, Mamerto Natividad, who took care of him and whom not long thereafter he murdered with a bullet in the forehead because he, Mamerto, opposed the Biyak na Bato Sale.

ii.) 3,000 Katipuneros besieging the *provincial command* of the Spanish forces in San Isidro, Nueva Ecija for a whole day on September 3, 1896, was to Achutegui and Bernad nothing remarkable. In Aguinaldo's own town of Kawit, in the afternoon of August 31, 1896, and after learning from the Cavite Governor himself that all the Spanish soldiers had been evacuated from Cavite and transferred to Manila, Aguinaldo y Famy with his forty cuadrilleros *besieged* the town hall in absolute daring: they shot one civil guard and disarmed another in 3 seconds flat:—*most successful!* More or less the same scene was repeated in all the Cavite towns:--*most successful!*

iii.) "It was therefore to Cavite that the major expeditions were sent". *He he he...*

(to be cont'd.)

Chapter 19

REFUTING GLENN ANTHONY MAY

& PROVING THE AUTHENTICITY OF ANDRES BONIFACIO'S LETTERS TO EMILIO JACINTO,

THE DECALOGUE, THE POEMS, THE POLITICAL TRACTS…

1.0.) Towards getting at the truth or the facts of the Revolution and the Counterrevolution in Cavite, no testimony is clearer, more exact, more trustworthy and more discerning, more intelligent, more knowing, than Andres Bonifacio's letters to Emilio Jacinto and the long narrative eyewitness and participant account by Gregoria de Jesus on the abduction, incarceration, trial and execution of the Supremo in the form of a letter also to Emilio Jacinto.

When Andres Bonifacio was writing those letters, he was not denouncing Aguinaldo and his counterrevolutionary gang to a superior authority or any kind of Court of Appeals or Supreme Court (that would have been the case had Emilio Jacinto been the one making those reports and observations to Andres Bonifacio who as Supremo was also the President of the Supreme Council of the Katipunan National Revolutionary Government); nor was he trying to rouse his indignation at the treacheries and venalities and greeds and massmurderous ambitions of the Cavitenos because he was asking his help to extricate him from that snakepit and cavity of evil and veritable asshole of Philippine History that was Emilio Aguinaldo y Famy's Cavite: he was not thinking he could be entrapped and killed there:--in one of the later letters, he was even telling Jacinto about his plans of either going to Nueva Ecija and Bulacan to personally supervise revolutionary activities there, or else to Bicol with Malvar and his men to oversee the Revolution there (entry XXXVIII dated May 30,

1895, of the MINUTES OF THE KATIPUNAN records the Supreme President Andres Bonifacio's appointment of Mr. Simon Ibarra to the office of Director for the Province of Camarines Norte and Sur..). Nor could one imagine any other motive for Bonifacio to lie about those events and conditions in Cavite to his subaltern officer and closest friend; whilst it was of course not in his character to so lie or exaggerate things. In other words, Bonifacio was writing those letters merely to let Jacinto know what was happening in Cavite and of course to warn and alert him about many things there—like the Novo Ecijano Magdalo agent Mamerto Natividad, or the Magdalized traitor Vicente Fernandez, or the embezzler of Katipunan money Nicolas de Lara... In short, the testimony of those letters was such that we can find no credible reason why we should not trust them, nor even why we should not wholly trust them as we should their author's honesty, integrity and great human wisdom.

1.1. By the starkest of contrasts, Aguinaldo was a compulsive liar, a pathological liar, a pathogenic liar and exaggerator—i.e. an incomparable, insurpassable braggart (which as always is characteristic of cowards): he bragged in his own *Memoirs of the Revolution* (Ch. 3, pp. 14-15) how in the dead of night he wrestled with a huge shark and succeeded to tie a rope around its head without being eaten by it—whilst that did not happen on dry land but rather in the depths of the sea off Matuko point near Batangas. After reading such a chapter, one is impelled to ask: Can anyone possibly believe anything such a phantasmagorical liar said in that book or elsewhere anywhere?

2.) According to Glenn Anthony May in his 1989 book *Inventing a Hero: the Posthumous Re-Creation of Andres Bonifacio,* there was no real hero called Andres Bonifacio. The Filipinos, nay, some Filipino "historians" and memoirists merely invented him. And because a very real hero by the name of Andres Bonifacio would emerge from the *Bonifacio Letters to Emilio Jacinto*, the poems, and the political tracts if they were really authored by the same Andres Bonifacio, therefore Glenn Anthony May concluded that none of them were written by Andres Bonifacio. All of them were forgeries, according to him! In fact, according to Glenn Anthony May, Andres Bonifacio himself was a forgery. Writes Glenn May:

"In effect, Bonifacio has been posthumously re-created. He has been given a new personality and a childhood that may bear little resemblance to his real one. Literary compositions have been attributed to him that he *almost certainly* did not write. Key events in his life have been altered *beyond recognition*. The national hero who has emerged from this process of re-creation—the Bonifacio celebrated in history textbooks and memorialized in statues around the Philippines—is, in reality, something closer to a national myth... In the pages that follow, I demonstrate that almost every line of poetry heretofore thought to have been written by Bonifacio *cannot be shown* to be his literary product. Indeed, most of his personal correspondence is probably forged. Perhaps the single most astonishing fact about the Philippine national hero is that most of what we will ever know about him must be refracted through the lenses of his contemporaries. Furthermore, I argue that the historians and the one memoirist who were largely responsible for producing the image of Bonifacio we have today often adopted questionable methods. More than one consciously dissembled. More than one altered evidence. More than one interpreted the evidence at their disposal in very strange ways. One placed into circulation a small collection of seemingly bogus documents. I have entitled this book *Inventing A Hero* because that is precisely what those people did."

2.1. According to Glenn May, he was not able to push through with his original project of writing a biography of Andres Bonifacio because he could not find any reliable sources—in other words, according to him, Bonifacio's life cannot be reliably known from the extant sources. This must of course include his "personality and...childhood". What the unfortunate Glenn Anthony May does not seem to notice however is that if as he says this personality and that childhood were unknowable from the sources—because there were no sources, or because the extant ones severally contradict each other—then it must also be unknowable whether the personality and the childhood given him by the mythmaking Filipino "nationalist" historians does not match "his real one".

2.2. "Literary compositions have been attributed to him that he almost certainly did not write"... If he, Glenn Anthony May, was *almost certain* Andres Bonifacio did not write those poems/literary compositions, must he not equivalently be *almost certain* who their real author was? Must there not be other claimants to their authorship? Or is Glenn May insinuating that Emilio Jacinto was Bonifacio's ghostwriter and he it was who wrote those poems? This is malicious. In any case, this is something that requires proof of which Glenn May has not offered any.

Since the letters and the works are there, somebody must have written them. To prove that it was not Bonifacio who did so, Glenn May has to prove either that somebody else did, or that it was *impossible* for Bonifacio to have written them. This latter sense of *impossibility* cannot in this case be material, spatial, temporal; it concerns and can solely concern Bonifacio's soul, spirit, intelligence, humanity; and what this vulgar and uncouth American data scrounger and pigly rumourmonger is saying here is that it was impossible for Bonifacio to have written those works because something in his soul, spirit, intellligence, humanity was, were, in severe lack—for, after all, Andres Bonifacio who did not have a diploma was *only THE FOUNDER OF A REVOLUTION*! For Glenn May forgot to doubt and neglected to deny of Andres Bonifacio this greatest of all feats of intellectual power, wisdom, human depth and largeness, indeed genius, no doubt because in the skimpiness of his humanity and the sheer inexistence of his intelligence he was quite simply incapable of realizing what being such a founder of a revolution presupposes and implies.

Why is it only of Bonifacio's authorship that Glenn May—and only Glenn May thus far—requires proof? In the ultimate analysis, his answer to this question is—Because it is reasonable to doubt that Bonifacio did write those works and it is reasonable to doubt this because Bonifacio did not have a diploma—in fact, he never had any kind of education at all!

In one of the letters, Bonifacio mentions that he is sending with it a manifesto written in English which he wants him, Jacinto, to edit. He says it's rather long for publication, "sa'yo ko ipinapaubaya ang pagsasaayos nito". Who could have written it if not Andres Bonifacio himself? But of course Glenn May will say—'To the precise contrary, Bonifacio cannot have written that letter and therefore cannot have written that English manifesto mentioned in it, because Bonifacio cannot write or speak English! But Glenn May has, obviously enough, no proof to show. Which simply means that he has determined on the basis of non-existent sources and contradictory accounts and thus out of thin air that Andres Bonifacio was incapable of writing all those works and of thinking those ideas. But according to him, himself, there is no way of determining *that*. Is he God then who can get inside the minds of even such god-eating men as this man who could and did found no less than a revolution?

2.3. "...and, as a consequence, he has been credited with ideas he did not have." How does one go about knowing that a person did not have the ideas he did not have? Must not Glenn Anthony May no longer be Glenn Anthony May but some sort of God to know that? For does that not require knowing all the ideas Bonifacio did have and subtracting them from the infinity of all possible ideas, checking each one of them against the infinitely many possible ideas, and counterchecking each of the infinitely many possible ideas against every one of those ideas that Bonifacio did have?

2.4. "Key events in his life have been altered beyond recognition"... There is very little logic in this miserable writer from the University of Wisconsin. If he had seen how such "key events" in Bonifacio's life had been "altered beyond recognition", then he must have seen and known *the recognizable truth* behind those key events in the light of which he now could no longer recognize anything of that *recognizable truth*. And yet this wretched researcher is telling us everywhere here that he came to write this book about the unknowable Andres Bonifacio because on the basis of all the possible sources he was forced to conclude that the true Andres Bonifacio was unknowable. The poor wretch will flunk in my Intro to Logic class:--I have to send him back to grade three. Pwede nang grade four? Hmmm, depende sa mood...baka sakali...mabait naman ako *talaga*, at maawain!.

2.5 "The national hero who has emerged from this process of re-creation—the Bonifacio celebrated in history textbooks and memorialized in statues around the Philippines—is, in reality, something closer to a national myth..." This historian so-called, specialist so-called, on the Philippines, does not seem to know that in this country, and thanks to the American imperialists who ordered their colonial middle class Filipino collaborators to invent and prop up the traitor and anti-Filipino supercriminal Jose Rizal to be such, the distinction "national hero" is a unique and official and even a formally legislated one; and that unique one being Rizal, no one else is spoken of as "national hero" in this thought-forsaken country, which happens to be the most corrupt in the world for having the world's most corrupt ruling class and with it the world most corrupt, most venal and most porcine writers and intellectuals. On the other hand, however, namely, Glenn Anthony May's other, prestidigitous, hand, the mistake of imprecise categorization is not unmotivated—it suppresses the fact that not only is Andres Bonifacio not *the* national hero here, he is in absurd and dastardly truth *discriminated against* here, and *that* by this country's "leading nationalists" because the so-called "nationalists" in this country are all of them brainwashed believers in Jose Rizal or else in Jose Rizal *and* Aguinaldo or—as in the case of the *relativist* historian so-called, Teodoro Agoncillo who was the *relative* of his *Tio*

Emilio—in Aguinaldo first and in Rizal second, and you cannot be that or that without being a brainwashed disbeliever in and guffawing maligner of Andres Bonifacio. But Glenn May has had to supermagnify the love and devotion of the Filipinos in general and of the so-called nationalist writers/historians in particular for Andres Bonifacio because he needed a motive for the supposed *invention* of the good and wise and heroic and even a non-illiterate Andres Bonifacio by, who else but such Bonifacio-loving, Bonifacio hagiographizing because "nationalist" writers/historians who, since they did not exist, Glenn Anthony May has had to himself *invent*! Nor did this blind and insensate professor from Wisconsin notice that the "nationalist" "historians" (historians nga ba ang mga ito?) he has singled out as the manufacturers of the "Bonifacio myth" were the worst defamers of Andres Bonifacio, were in fact the heedless, conscienceless, venal. cowardly and malignant destroyers of the personal and historical image of Andres Bonifacio. This is especially true of Epifanio de los Santos, Teodoro Agoncillo, and Reynaldo Ileto..

2.6. Since Glenn May cannot prove that the poems were *not* written by Bonifacio, his malicious conclusion that "almost every line" of those poems "cannot be shown to be his literary product" is otiose if offensively, nay infuriatingly so like a fart of his mind. Who can *prove* that any of the unsigned plays by Shakespeare were by Shakespeare? And Homer… I have not seen a copy of *Kalayaan* in which *Agapito Bagumbayan's* poem *Pag-ibig Sa Tinubuang Lupa* and his political tract, *Ang Dapat Mabatid ng mga Tagalog*, were published; *Agapito Bagumbayan* was widely known to be Andres Bonifacio's *nom de plume*. That was what all the Katipuneros, especially the ones closest to Bonifacio knew, namely, Gregoria de Jesus, Emilio Jacinto, Julio Nakpil…It seems to me that the integrity of at least these three equally pure hearted revolutionaries were such that if they knew it to be untrue that Agapito Bagumbayan was Bonifacio and that therefore it was not Bonifacio who wrote the abovementioned "literary products", they would have spontaneously said so the moment they encountered the erroneous attribution.

According to Gregoria de Jesus, Andres Bonifacio had already written a "Decalogue" and had apparently been making use of it when Jacinto came up with his own; whereupon he withdrew it and endorsed Jacinto's. What this tells us is this: that Bonifacio would die of shame to own as his any "literary product" of another—and would thus rather die than do it. We cannot imagine this great individual using a ghostwriter! (Here also, Aguinaldo was his polar opposite: the Running Man of Asia who was semi-illiterate had had among others Edilberto Evangelista, Mamerto Natividad, Felipe Buencamino as his ghostly writers (he killed the first two *by planting a bullet each in their foreheads*). As for Emilio Jacinto—he also was the sort of man who would lose all respect for ghostwriter-users or plagiarists.

2.7. " I have entitled this book INVENTING A HERO because that is precisely what those people did." What about Bonifacio himself? Why did not Glenn May consult the image of Bonifacio produced by himself—as, for instance, the (even by him) undoubted founder of the Philippine Revolution and the immensely successful leader of its archipelagic propagation across four deadly dangerous years?

3.0.) But here meanwhile is very strong, circumstantial, definitive corroborative proof that it was indeed Andres Bonifacio who translated into Tagalog Rizal's *Mi Ultimo Adios*: In his 1935 edition of *Si Andres Bonifacio At Ang Himagsikan,* Jose P. Santos cited a note (ulat) sent him by Gen. Artemio Ricarte which included a map which Ricarte himself had drawn and which he had annotated, and which incidentally, circumstantially mentioned that it was in a certain house marked by Ricarte himself that Bonifacio translated the poem into Tagalog. Let us quote the pertinent passages here: "Kung ano ang ayos ng asyenda sa Teheros nang panahong yaon (nang maganap ang sabwatan at kudetang Magdiwang-Magdalo laban kay Bonifacio at kriminal at traidor na yumurak-pumalis sa Pambansang Pamahalaang

Rebolusyonaryong noon ay si Andres Bonifacio ang Supremo at Kataastaasang Pangulo), na lubhang naging makasaysayan, dahil sa magulong kapulungang idinaos doon ng pinaglakip na Sangguniang Magdiwang at Magdalo, at dahil sa bantog na Akta sa Teheros na siyang nangunguna sa talaan ng sampung lalong mahahalagang kasulatan ng himagsikan, alinsunod sa kuro-kuro nina Heneral Artemio Ricarte Vibora, Emilio Aguinaldo at Cecilio Apostol, ang bagay na ito'y siyang isinaysay ni Hen. Ricarte na siyang naging kalihim ng kapulungan at isa sa mga nakalagda sa Akta sa Teheros na tumututol sa pagkakahalal ni Hen. Aguinaldo sa pagka-Pangulo ng Gobierno Rebolusyonaryo, sa isang ulat na ipinadala sa akin noong ika-16 ng Pebrero ng 1931, at nilakipan ng isang munting mapang may iba't ibang palatandaan at paliwanag." J Santos then quotes Ricarte's "ulat" with map: "Ang sulok na may palatandaan sa ilalim ng blg. 12 ay siyang tapat ng bulwagang pinagdausan ng pulong noong ika-22 ng Marso ng 1897"—ang paliwang ni Hen. Ricarte sa sa kanyang ulat na kinakaharap ko ngayon—"at yaon naming may palatandaan sa panulok na blg 15 ay siya namang tapat ng bulwagang pinagdausan ng pagsumpa sa pagtanggap ng tungkulin…" and so on for more than a full page. Then, towards the end of the next page (28), we read: "Ang blg. 8 ay siyang liwasang bayan at sa tapat noon natatayo ang bahay na tinirhan ni Andres Bonifacio. *Sa nasabing bahay isinatagalog ni Andres Bonifacio ang Huling Paalam ni Dr. Jose Rizal.*" There. And Ricarte mentioned the thing here as a matter of course, like it was then common knowledge that Andres Bonifacio was indeed that Spanish poem's Tagalog translator:--as it was common knowledge since then, and up to now, whilst it was solely and uniquely Glenn Anthony May from Wisconsin who ever thought or said otherwise. This should shut him up. And may he never open it again. And then, but then…:--if only malicious, lazy, and lousy foreign researchers bamboozled and brainwashed by necessarily malevolent Aguinaldistas can doubt that it was Bonifacio who translated that Rizal poem (whilst the translation is far better as a poem than the original), what must that fact tell us concerning Glenn May's viragogical doubt about Bonifacio's authorship of those other poems of his, especially the hugely magnificent and powerful Pagibig Sa Tinubuang Lupa? Repeatedly Glenn May perorated that those poems were "almost certainly" not Bonifacio's work. And this again when everybody else, then as now, has attributed them to Bonifacio, and it was only this Doctor researcher (and see how lousy he is at it!) from Wisconsin who ever expressed any doubt about it, let alone concluded they cannot possibly be his at all. Translating a poem as big as that overnight—and let us not even mention that the translation is better by far than the original—is feat, a huge feat, a powerful accomplishment; only an extremely few of the highest calibre poets in the world are capable of it. And that was why people like Ricarte could remember it like that and not neglect to thus mention it.

4.0.) Corroborative proof that Bonifacio wrote the "Decalogue" which everyone except Glenn Anthony May attributes to him: "Si Andres ang unang sumulat ng palatuntunan at sampung utos at saka pa lamang si Emilio Jacinto kaya't masasabing ito'y munukalang tunay ni Andres, ngunit dahil sa kanyang pagmamahal at pagbibigay kay Emilio Jacinto ay ang Kartilyang sinulat nito ang siya nilang pinairal at ginamit ng mga katipunan. Ang orihinal ng sampung utos na sinulat ni Andres Bonifacio at hindi pa nahahayag ay nasa pagiingat ni G. Pepe Santos na anak ni Don Panyong Santos". (Gregoria de Jesus, Mga Tala ng Aking Buhay, 5 Nobyembre, 1928; National Library; p. 13.)

4.1.) It's a pity that Gregoria de Jesus is no longer around to bear witness to Andres Bonifacio's authorship of the poems too, and of the other documents, especially the letters to Jacinto. It happened that Jacinto had a Decalogue and Bonifacio too had his own which as it happened was written first, and prior to the publication of Bonifacio's it became necessary and significant for Gregoria to bear witness to the fact. During that time, however, and until recently, no one ever even imagined doubting the Bonifacio authorship of those poems and the letters, otherwise, Gregoria would have given the same kind of testimony. What this detail of Bonifacio's high sense of honour and his exemplary solicitude for his younger friend Jacinto however is that he would be the first to most vehemently object to the idea of his owning as his poems or any literary work written by Jacinto or by anyone else. And by the way, this most high sense of honour is but the most natural thing to expect from someone who, like Andres Bonifacio, was the founder of nothing less than a revolution. Someone like Glenn Anthony May however does not and can never know such nuances and distinctions. Glenn Anthony May has doubted everything about Bonifacio including his existence, but what he has never doubted was that Andres Bonifacio founded the Revolution, organized it, led it to its archipelagic propagation across four long utterly dangerous years; this greatest of all feats, this highest and deepest and most powerful of all conceivable achievements which Glenn May does not question, although he seems absolutely to have no sense in him of the greatness, the height, the depth, the power of such a feat and achievement, should have immediately informed Glenn May what kind of mind, spirit, soul, person, human being, Andres Bonifacio must have been—but it did not. In other words, Glenn May does not question that Bonifacio founded the Revolution and propagated it archipelagically across four years; but he has no sense or notion whatever of what kind of greatness, intelligence, depth, high honourableness and glorious largeness such a feat and achievement presupposes and implies. The fellow is simply too excruciatingly vulgar and tiny tiny tiny for that…

5.0) Today, August 1, 2013, between 11:30 and 12 midnight, I discovered the unimpeachable document/testimony that establishes beyond any but insane doubt the authenticity of Bonifacio's letters to Emilio Jacinto:--

5.1. On page 59 of the book *Julio Nakpil and the Philippine Revolution*, part III, Miscellaneous Notes, section 2, Julio Nakpil wrote:

"*For the National Library of the Philippines*

"Find out who has Andres Bonifacio's letter dated March 1897 addressed to Emilio Jacinto which was (about) the origin of the quarrel with Emilio Aguinaldo. In the said letter, among other things, he says: 'The heads of the Magdalo are already bowed.' At that time several towns under the control of Magdalo had been taken by the troops of General C. Polavieja.

"Another letter: 'In order to end the whole Revolution', refers to the series of conferences of the emissaries of the Jesuit Father Pio Pi with E. Aguinaldo to conclude peace behind the back of A. Bonifacio who was opposed and very much disgusted, similar to the disgust of General A. Luna when the Revolutionary Government wanted to accept autonomy from the Americans.

"Year 1942—*Another Act Of E. Aguinaldo:* He suggested to General MacArthur the surrender of the American and Philippine Forces to the Japanese Army."

"JULIO NAKPIL

2 February 1942"

There. And we can now be sure that another evil thing had befallen the documents: either this, that at least one of the letters is missing, for we cannot find that letter first mentioned by him where we are supposed to find the sentence, "The heads of the Magdalos are already bowed"; or someone had deleted those words from one of the extant letters, the way Agoncillo and Epistola had deleted the Tagalog equivalent of the abovementioned phrase, "in order to end the whole Revolution" in their translation of Epifanio de los Santos' English version of the letters.

We have found the other letter and with this the material corroboration of the authenticity of the letters is complete: in Epifanio delos Santos', book, *The Revolutionists*, the passage can be found on page 118, first three lines, where the line receives the translation: 'in order to put down the whole Revolution'; in Agoncillo's edition of *The Writings & Trial of Andres Bonifacio* (Manila, 1963. Publication Data: "Prepared and published under the auspices of Mayor Antonio J. Villegas and the Manila Bonifacio Centennial Commission in cooperation with the University of the Philippines), the passage is on page 21, last paragraph, and is rendered exactly as in Epifanio delos Santos' because those letters were merely reproduced from E. delos Santos' 1918 Philippine Review English translations.

What Julio Nakpil's note to the National Library (through its director, TM Kalaw) tells us is that he was not aware of E. delos Santos' transcription and translation into Spanish and publication of the same in 1917 by The Philippine Review and of the publication of an English translation of the same in 1918 also by The Philippine Review.

5.2. On page 47 of the same book, under the same heading, Notes on Teodoro M. Kalaw's *The Philippine Revolution*, written in 1925, we read: "The third invasion of, or battle in San Mateo was led by Emilio Jacinto and J. Giliw for the purpose of drawing away the attention of the Spanish forces toward other points and prevent their concentration at Kawit, Cavite, for, toward the end of February or March, *Andres Bonifacio* entreating us with urgency to make this move, inasmuch as the continuous rapid fire day and night of the Spaniards did not let them rest, and they feared that their munitions would be exhausted, although Remington and Mauser capsules were being made in Cavite, among the labourers being Manila silversmiths. In these encounters were present Generals Hermogenes Bautista and Francisco de los Santos."

"Andres Bonifacio wrote us...":--here's what Andres Bonifacio wrote "with urgency" for Emilio Jacinto and Julio Nakpil alias J. Giliw, "to make this move", in what turns out here to be the March 8, 1897 Letter :--"The trouble with which you speak, which occurred in Manila on account of the proclamation of the carabineers and engineers, has greatly helped our brethren here. However, our enemies here are not growing less and these pueblos are still in danger, *so we ask you there not to let up, and we will not rest, either, until we have rescued the pueblos they have taken from us*, as you already know". ("J. Giliw" was the *nom de guerre* of General Julio Nakpil. Hey, Glenn May, pay attention, baka mamaya eh hanapan mo na naman ng pruweba ito!) Since this is the earliest dated letter, there must be a number of letters prior to the bunch which were lost or destroyed by the elements, by white ants or by the Aguinaldo counterrevolutionary assassins and literary vandals.

5.3. The first paragraph of the earliest extant Bonifacio letter to Emilio Jacinto, dated March 8, 1897, reads: "Dear Brother:--I have received all your letters and with them the money, powder, and saltpetre. Our brethren here are congratulating themselves and are grateful for what you have sent, which is of peremptory necessity in the battles, and for the aid which you say you have rendered". And the fifth paragraph reads: "I also received a letter from Brother M. Rogelio, who asks me to send implements and experts for making cartridges. I have thought of this necessity a long time ago, so I had the implements mentioned prepared at the same time as the things I sent you together with the workmen." And the sixth paragraph reads: "Here, there is a lack of empty cartridges, because the enemies have already found out, too, that these were useful to us (nabatid na-man din na ito'y ating nagagamit); hence they pick them up again (pinupulot); *send us whatever you can spare there.*" Meanwhile, paragraph 2 of the Naik, April 16, 1897 letter, reads: "I received what you sent me: two cans of powder, a bayon of cartridge shells, and thirty pesos. The letter says 50, but only 30 were delivered to me, as I am informed that Brother Nakpil took the 20 pesos again". On page 15 of the same book of Nakpil's, the translator and editor, Encarnacion Alzona relates from her interview notes how Andres "Bonifacio entrusted to him the dangerous and delicate mission" "of procuring arms and ammunitions" and sending these to Cavite for use in the defense of Cavite: General Julio Nakpil "...during the months of December 1896 through March 1897...was able to send safely to Tejeros, San Francisco de Malabon (now a barrio of General Trias, Province of Cavite) some 30 or 40 copper boxes containing gunpowder which had been stolen little by little in the dead of night by the revolutionists from the Polvorin de San Guillermo (Powder Magazine of San Guillermo) in Binangonan, Morong." And on page 63 of the same book, Julio Nakpil, under the heading, *Notes for La Revolucion Filipina by TM Kalaw* wrote: "About February 1897 I made a suggestion to the barrio lieutenants of Pasig to take down the bells of the chapels or shrines at dawn and send them to Tejeros, Kabite, for melting and manufacture into falconets and cannons, inasmuch as there was a shortage of firearms and the Spanish soldiers were firing at them incessantly day and night".

On paragraph 13 of the same *March 8, 1897 letter*, Bonifacio tells Jacinto: "There is a brass foundry here and better cannon is cast than on the other side; neither melting-pot nor coke is necessary; *a resident of Manila makes them very well*. Hunt up some brass there and I shall send you cannons and *lantakas* immediately." And in paragraph 17, we read: "Only ten pesos were sent to your mother; the balance was used by me for rewards and other expenses here. It is necessary that you send me more for rewards *to the person who makes cannon and other implements, such as arrows and others.* I paid the expenses of the bearer of this letter and those of the families of the two *cartridge makers*."

5.4. Paragraph 17 of the March 8, 1897 letter reads: "Luciano is already strong and able to walk; his repeating rifle is in his possession and I have not yet taken it up. The Mauser you will receive from the bearer; take good care of it, because it is the first weapon we used in the war. *Only ten pesos were sent to your mother; the balance was used by me for rewards and our expenses here..."*

And in paragraph 18, we read: "...As for *Nonay*, who has remained there, I ask you to look after her for the time being; I have not considered it prudent to have her come here on account of the great danger here."

If anybody had forged this letter—as Glenn May is dead certain this and the other letters were "almost certainly" forged and were thus "bogus"—he must have been such in his knowledge of intimate details of the family life of Andres Bonifacio and of his relationship with Emilio Jacinto as to know that the "mother" referred to here as Jacinto's "mother" was no other than Bonifacio's wife and the Treasurer and Lakambini of the KKK, Gregoria de Jesus who as attested to by these same letters and as was common knowledge then amongst the Cavite Katipuneros (turned counterrevolutionaries, though in these letters and even at the instant he was shot whilst running towards the assaulting counterrevolutionary soldiers shouting to them not to shoot their own brothers, he still called them thus—brothers) was staying with her maternal relatives, the Alvarezes, in Maragondon. He must also have been in the know that the Nonay referred to here was Bonifacio's youngest sister, Espiridiona. And, but, we must mark out here this rivetingly momentous detail of the ten pesos sent to Gregoria de Jesus thus: The kangaroo court records, almost all the memoirs—by Ricarte, Santiago Alvarez, Carreon, and Gregoria de Jesus' own letter to Jacinto cited herewith—attest to the thievery by the rapist Agapito Bonson of Gregoria de Jesus' *ten pesos*, in addition to her revolver, 11 bullets, her wedding ring, and her fountain pen and nailcutter! It must have been the same *ten pesos* mentioned in this same letter.

Here and in the other parts of this section, we demonstrate among other things that the jibe or correspondence between the objective conditions, situations, circumstances, events, relations and relationships between people and between forces then obtaining in Cavite, in Morong and elsewhere in the Philippines at the time on one hand, and what the letter writer was writing about on the other hand was such that this letter writer was virtually indistinguishable from Andres Bonifacio himself, such that, if he was not Bonifacio himself, then he must have been such in his knowledge of Andres Bonifacio as to be able to *invent* Bonifacio himself and project him as the writer of these letters himself!

How's that then, Doctor Professor Glenn Anthony May? You happened to have said a number of times that those letters, "More graphically than any other source of the revolutionary period...made the case for Bonifacio and against Emilio Aguinaldo and his Magdalo followers". According to you: "The Bonifacio that emerged from those letters was honorable and patriotic; he was, in other words, very similar to the idealized prerevolutionary Bonifacio created by the mythmakers. The Magdalo men, on the other hand, were pictured as dishonest, dangerous, greedy for power, guilty of shady political tactics, and willing to compromise with the enemy. In Bonifacio's eyes, they alone were responsible for the growing dissension in the revolutionary ranks and the declining fortunes of the Filipino forces on the battlefield. By promoting conflict between the factions in Cavite, Aguinaldo and his supporters had made it virtually impossible for the revolutionaries to resist the Spanish advance" (p 59). Those letters then shows us, incidentally and circumstantially and all the more believably, an "honourable and patriotic" Andres Bonifacio:--which actually he must have been:--for how, if he were not the very honourable and utmostly patriotic human being he was could he possibly have founded a revolution, guided it and spread it into a national thing across four deadly-dangerous years of underground work?

6.0.) Those letters then contained the "honourable and patriotic" Andres Bonifacio's firsthand, on the spot, analysis and appraisal of the imperilled and fouled-up revolutionary situation in Cavite, and of the imperillers and foul-playing Magdalo traitors-politicians-intriguers-factionalists, and long-standingly seditious, treasonous, ultimately counter-revolutionary Caviteno agents and even Novo Ecijano traitors like Mamerto Natividad…

7.0.) In the Philippines, the Rizalian Counterrevolution was born before the Revolution. Eight months and a week into the fighting, the Aguinaldo Counterrevolution succeeded in hostaging the leadership of the Revolution, murdered its theoretician-founder and supremo, burned down and facilitated the retaking by the Spaniards of the abandoned province of Cavite which from late August 1896 to February 14, 1897 (the onset of the reconquest) became a free and warless zone because Blanco pulled out all the Spanish soldiers from Cavite and transferred them to Manila (all, except for a company of infantry to guard the gunpowder depot at Binakayan: which was exactly why, as related by Aguinaldo and Santiago Alvarez themselves there were no real battles for the liberation of Cavite in which the supposedly great general Aguinaldo could have distinguished himself prior to the consistent massacres and scampering away sustained by him and his great Caviteno army during the swift re-conquest. Incidentally, and for the record, Bonifacio could have many times died in those battles for the defense of Cavite: both Ricarte and Santiago Alvarez in their respective memoirs had ambivalently testified how one half of his men perished in those battles. Nor was it true that he had refused to fight in defense of the Magdalo towns, and the proof of it was incidentally provided by the insurpassable liar Emilio y Famy himself: How could he have accused Bonifacio of planting that murderous bullet in the forehead of Edilberto Evangelista during the battle of Zapote bridge on February 17, 1897, if he and his men were not there?

8.0.) In the Philippines of the last two decades of the 19th and the first decade of the 20th century, the anticolonial revolution was born, fought, hostaged, sold, and resold, and lost twice thus militarily and politically, and heavily damaged thereby culturally--ethically-morally, aesthetically-poetically, epistemically-intellectually--at which level of social-historical existence it is still being fought today, right here for instance, in this work which I am dedicating to the eternal destruction of all those writers, historians so-called, or whatever they might have been or are being called, starting with Rizal himself, and Del Pilar and Jaena, and Aguinaldo and his hackwriters like Edilberto Evangelista, Carlos Ronquillo, Santiago Alvarez, Epifanio delos Santos, TM Kalaw, Teodoro Agoncillo, Carlos Quirino…It was born on February 19, 1892, when Andres Bonifacio formally as it were, founded it. The distinct misfortune of the Filipino people however lay in the fact that in this country and in this alone of all the countries colonized and stung with a peculiar kind of evil by the Europeans and their white descendants, the counterrevolution was born, was already there, by a full decade, before the revolution…

9.0.) The historiography of the Philippine Revolution is split into two unavoidably bitter and acrimonious camps by the absurd and painful accident of the absurd and painful existence of a man whose exceeding evil was unfortunately exacerbated by a weak and cowardly and therefore necessarily treacherous and lying character, murderously envious, semi-illiterate, boundlessly ambitious and of unlimited greed. His name is—no, not Jose Rizal who was his closest rival in the profession of public, national, and yes in Rizal's case even international evil[120] —not Jose Protacio Rizal Mercado y

---

[120]His Cuba project through which he sought Spanish heroism as, of course, a Spanish international counterrevolutionary: he was on his way to Cuba, so he wrote his best and most loyal assimilationist friend and co-defender with him of Spanish colonialism in the Philippines and everywhere else, Ferdinand Blumentritt, "to win a name" as such a heedlessly brave lover and defender of Spanish colonialism, i.e., of his ever beloved *Mother Spain*, "and undo calumnies"—the calumnies namely that clung to his person in his having been declared an enemy of his ever-beloved Mother Spain and a traitor

Alonzo de Realonda, but,--Emilio Aguinaldo y Famy; split into two then by, among other disputes, how to read and analyze the absurd and

painful question of Aguinaldo's, or rather the Aguinaldo-led Magdalo-Magdiwang all-Caviteno Conspiracy and Electoral Coup d'etat, the ensuing murder of Andres Bonifacio and his two brothers and its logical culmination in the sale of the Revolution for 800,000 pesos at Biyak na Bato to consummate which Aguinaldo had murdered Gen. Julian dela Cruz[121], Gen.

---

to her in the shame and scandal of his Dapitan exile, and the even worse calumnies to come and which he knew then were swiftly coming through Andres Bonifacio's adamant and relentless recruiting efforts and the KKK's unauthorized use of his name which to him constituted the worse, indeed, from his words of hellhounding excoriations later on, the worst kind of calumnies conceivable that stained and barnacled his pure Spanish name.

121 In his *Memoirs*, Ricarte had lengthily exposed the particulars of this malefic murder by Emilio Aguinaldo through the instrumentality of his attack dog, Antonio Montenegro. Of course the Aguinaldistas will deny everything about it, and alien, innocent, or ignoramuous Aguinaldistas (Glenn Anthony May comes instantly to mind) will second the commotion; they will accuse Ricarte of partiality, or even of having invented the whole thing, even of being insane—Agoncillo in that liars' handbook, *Revolt of the Masses*, did this to Bonifacio in order to rationalize the latter's murder by his Tio Emilio, declaring that Bonifacio "lost his mind" or "his head" the moment he stepped into Cavite territory. And because Ricarte himself had proved to be many times a liar and dissimulator if but a trickier because, compared to Aguinaldo, subtler by a great deal because more intelligent by as much than the Biyak na Bato vendor, it is very difficult to establish any conclusive thing on the basis of

this testimony. What is required is a circumstantial corroboration of the kind that, for instance, Julio Nakpil's miscellaneous notes afforded us in connection with the authenticity of Bonifacio's letters to Jacinto and the bunch of documents mentioned in one of those letters as being also sent to the latter (in *Julio Nakpil & the Revolution*), or Ricarte's "ulat" (narrative report) with map as presented by Jose P. Santos in his *Si Andres Bonifacio At Ang Himagsikan* circumstantially corroborating Bonifacio's authorship of the first Tagalog version of Rizal's *Ultimo Adios* . Which miraculously we do *have*! Here then is the incontrovertible testimonial evidence—a miraculously preserved letter by Gen. Julian dela Cruz's widow, Juana Aguilar-dela Cruz, dated October 25, 1898, and addressed to "the Director of War" of the Aguinaldo Cabinet (the "Malolos Republic's" cabinet which was constituted on January 2, 1899, had Baldomero Aguinaldo as Secretary of War and Public Works, a position which he also held in the preceding Kawit Dictatorial Government; he then was the one addressed in this letter). Capt. JRM Taylor of the US Army selected it from tons of confiscated "insurrectionary" papers during the Philippine-American War for publication in his five mammoth volumes of such documents (see pp. 407-408, vol. I). We are quoting the letter here whole and entire.

"To the Director of War.

"Juana Aguilar, a native of Sampaloc, widow of the unfortunate Brigadier General Julian dela Cruz; of the town of Marikina (Manila), appears before you with consideration and respect and states: That trusting in your sense of justice, that you would never tolerate a criminal act which should and will be prosecuted to the fullest extent of the law, I appeal to your high

authority demanding justice for the same act, which I herewith describe.

"The question is of a murder, the commission of which is a notorious public matter, in Marikina, committed in a vile and inhuman manner, by Sr. Montenegro, at the present time Chief of the 3rd Zone, Sr. Calixto Santos, local president of the said town of Marikina, and a resident of the latter calling himself Captain and Aide-de-Camp of the said zone, named Agapito de Leon, formerly a stonecutter by trade, upon the person of my husband, Julian dela Cruz, Brigadier General, appointed by the Revolutionary Government of Biak-na-Bato. This murder took place in the barrio of Barranca (Marikina, in the month of November, 1897, his life being taken during a retreat, for the purpose, probably, of satisfying the unjust ambition of taking the high place that my husband occupied.

"I did not expect, Sr. Director, that so ardent a servant of the revolution should receive as a reward so base and brutal an act of cowardice, justice being taken in his own hands by a Sr. Montenegro and his followers, especially as my husband was the protector of his murderers.

"The crime of murder was tried in Puray camp under the Chief Licerio Geronimo, in order to punish the delinquent or delinquents, Sr. Montenegro being taken prisoner and his followers also, excepting Sr. Calixto Santos, who when about to be caught, sought refuge in the barracks of the Spanish Infantry, stating that he had been attacked by tulisanes; and when they were sent to the Government in Biak-na-Bato, it was just at the time that peace was being declared with the Spanish Government, and perhaps no one could consider the case on account of the very speedy departure of the Committee to Hong Kong" (Aguinaldo and his gang of thieves boarded the steamer to Hong Kong on December 28, 1897, more than a full month after Gen. Feliciano Jocson elevated the case to Biak-na-Bato, so this could not have been the real reason, about which we do not have to guess:--for what Aguinaldo did to reward Montenegro for a job well, because brutally and inhumanly, done,

---

was to appoint him Secretary of Foreign Affairs of the newly invented phony government called the "Biyak na Bato Republic"! Moreover, the same Montenegro with whom he, Emilio Aguinaldo y Famy was madly in love, had had to remain by his side day and night alongside two other great loves of his, Andres and Procopio Bonifacio's physical assassin, Lazaro Macapagal, and the rapist Agapito Bonzon: he would rather be dead than be separated from this hoodlum Antonio Montenegro and that obligatorily meant that he had to board the steamer "Uranus" enchained to the bedpost of Emilio Aguinaldo y Famy. They had a hell of a good time together in Hong Kong.), "and since then the matter has not been taken up; for which reason I again bring it up, having confidence that you, with your honest and just spirit, will prosecute such an inhuman act, and that the public opinion will never countenance silence.

"I will take the liberty of calling your attention to the biography and history of the celebrated Montenegro. This gentleman went to Mariquina to avoid arrests which were being made in Manila, without being captured. He did nothing but play the mandolin and took no part in the Camp situated in Pantayanin (Marikina) under the command of General Hermogenes Bautista and of Councillor Ponciano T. de la Paz, because he was an unknown man and had no prestige in that town, and he was known only as I do not know what of Lalaari's, a 'fondero' (restaurant or saloon keeper) and clerk of a tobacco factory.

"When the town of Marikina was infested by Flying Columns, he sought refuge from fear in Cavite, returning again later to Marikina, where for a time he was Civil Governor of Manila and then he took advantage of the opportunity to continue to Hong Kong, returning as Colonel without as yet been in action. Such is the history of the merits of this gentleman.

"Indeed, I can tell you many things of this gentleman, but I will not take your time. I have confined myself to what I have said, believing that it will be sufficient for his prosecution under the wise law of the Republic.

Mamerto Natividad, Gen. Feliciano Jocson, and (as prelude to the whole unwordably evil project, and by way of eliminating a very strong contender and expectable obstacle), Gen. Edilberto Evangelista; this absurd and excruciating question would extend further to include Aguinaldo's attempt, assisted once more by the skunk traitor Pedro Paterno of Biyak na Bato Deed of Sale fame and by another ilustrado pig, Felipe Buencamino, to sell the Revolution once more, under the name of autonomy this time (in Biyak na Bato the ideological alibi to make money-greed sound a bit less indecent and less criminal was a repeat of Rizalian Assimilationist Reforms), and this time to the Americans:--to pave the way to the dreamt-of millions of North American dollars, Aguinaldo fired his secretary, Mabini, and replaced him with, who else but, the skunk traitor salesman and vendorial negotiator Pedro Paterno, and, faced with the expectably unswerving opposition of Gen. Antonio Luna, he murdered Luna and thereby lost all chance to bag the loot, for, with his murder of Luna, he had caused the revolutionary army to instantly collapse and disintegrate, leaving him absolutely nothing to sell to the Americans but his petticoat (after the murder of Luna, his army disappeared, leaving him alone with Her Royal Highness his queen mother, and Her Royal Higherness and Queen Consort, his wife, and the rest of the Royal Family, his favourite dog which was also a general (a three-headed chihuahua), and his bodyguards, and once more, he, the Running Man of Asia, staged his second Long Run—then the Japanese came and how else?:--he, the Super Ilyong who killed a giant shark in single combat and using only his teeth one starless and moonless night

---

"And therefore, I humbly pray that considering this application presented, you deign to act as you may think proper. Justice is what I implore, and I swear what is necessary.

"God preserve you many years.

"Sampaloc, October 25, 1898.

(Signed) JUANA AGUILAR."

somewhere off Batangas, was a 72-year-old collaborator!:--and it goes without saying that, though at a rather severely reduced rate, he, the most venal man who ever lived, got paid). Now, all the Philippine historians—with only two exceptions who are known to me—have taken the side of Aguinaldo here. They justify all those crimes and even saw them as great deeds by their hero; or else they deny them; or else, taking Aguinaldo's cue, attribute them to Bonifacio himself and to his other victims, for Aguinaldo who was a pathological liar was a compulsive projector of his own criminal deeds, motives and designs. All the Philippine historians with but two known exceptions were, are, Aguinaldistas. The two exceptions are Mabini and myself.

10.0.) Glenn May is a convinced Aguinaldista. And from the looks of it, he doesn't even know he is. His participation in this central ideological, political, theory-and-methodology determining controversy carries with it a ring of perfect innocence that, had it not at the same time been so infuriatingly pernicious in his having written the criminally ignorant book *Inventing A Hero: The Posthumous Re-Creation of Andres Bonifacio*, one would be inclined with a tiny smile to just brush the presumptuous foreigner aside--such a babe-in-the-woods otherwise is he in the enviable bliss of his biological, nay, igneous, ignorance. He believed every lie, every gossip, every slander, every calumny invented by Aguinaldo and his hack writers against Bonifacio and the Katipunan and taken up and amplified and added upon by all or almost all the historians so-called, indeed by almost all the Filipino writers, journalists, politicians, presidents, UN officials and their ghostwriters[122], schoolmarms, etc., who wrote or uttered a word on the matter across a hundred and ten years now (starting in the first place with that staggeringly stupid and massmurderous petty bourgeois writer, Epifanio

[122] Like former UN General Assembly president Carlos P Romulo and his ghostwriter Petronilo Bn Daroy:--see the author's *Matakot Sa Kasaysayan Sapagkat sa Kasaysayan Ay Walang Mailililhim—Andres Bonifacio*, Gegeh Presss, 2013, Ch 13, pp 137-145.

delos Santos who was brainwashed by his Caviteno drinking buddy Clemente Jose Zulueta who lyingly told him he was a participant in the deliberations during Bonifacio's "trial", and even had the temerity to concoct the certainly shamelessly braggingly lying detail that he was present during Bonifacio's

execution—and Epifanio believed him! [123]). This is the textbook version of the history of the Revolution the two chief

---

[123] See page 133 of his book *The Revolutionists* (National Historical Institute, Third Printing, 2000) where he wrote: "In fact, Clemente J. Zulueta, who participated in the deliberations of the court which sentenced Andres Bonifacio to be shot, and was present in his execution, has told us that the people forced Aguinaldo to have him put to death; *that Aguinaldo was anxious to pardon Andres Bonifacio*, but nobody advised him to do so, as the popular masses demanded their victim." And Epifanio then quoted this liar Zulueta from Cavite thus: "Would you believe it, they (the people) attributed our defeats to the wrath of God on account of the impiety of Andres Bonifacio" (((whose Decalogue's duty number one was "Love God with all thy heart…"!))). "His death was inevitable because of the several circumstances and, *especially, for the salvation of the Revolution*". Which prompted Agoncillo to interject in the footnote of the same page: "Clemente Jose Zulueta was never a participant in the investigation and trial of Andres Bonifacio. His name does not appear in the documents of the trial." This pathological liar and windbag Ilyong who was scarcely a man had already desired Bonifacio's death when he began seditiously to form his own "revolutionary government" less than two months after the exposure of the KKK, the existence of which new government "complete with a constitution" was by this malevolent Ilyong boldly orated in his *October 31, 1896 Manifesto* whose author was of course his ghostwriter of the time who happened to have been the unfortunate Edilberto Evangelista (see Aguinaldo's *Statement Concerning the*

Revolution in Cavite and the Death of Andres Bonifacio in the Watson Collection):--Evangelista, an ilustrado engineer from the University of Ghent plagiarized said "constitution" from the Maura Law and from other ingredients of deceit, intrigue, usurpation and forthright treason; not long thereafter, he, just like the other victims of Emilio Aguinaldo's temerarious envy and boundlessly greedy ambition, was himself murdered with a precisely planted bullet in the forehead during the battle of Zapote river in late February 1897:--the exact replication of this bullet's situation was to be found in the forehead of that other ilustrado, Mamerto Natividad, who chose to side with Aguinaldo because Bonifacio was not a capitan municipal like the former; Mamerto Natividad who owned the fortress of Biyak na Bato to hide himself in which Aguinaldo was by him invited there:--having adamantly refused to sign the Biyak na Bato Deed of Sale, he was found dead with a bullet in the forehead, supposedly ambushed on the road to his of course *Aguinaldo-assigned* mission to attack the Spanish detachment in Cabiao, Nueva Ecija, during the *truce* for the peace-and-sales talks:--two days later, in the afternoon of the noon of his burial, the Deed of Sale was concluded with the signing of the so-called Second Protocol of Peace; the Imus Assembly *coup d'etat* of December 30, 1896 was thus already his second attempt; he finally succeeded in the Tejeros *coup d'etat*). In his interview by the correspondent of the *El Imparcial* Madrid paper, Jose Barrozo on December 27, 1897 while he was ecstatically fingering the bundles of the 400, 000 pesos in the delirium tremendum of his psychopathological imagination, which according to him in a *Free Press* letter was his sole, personal payment as stipulated in the Biyak na Bato Deed of Sale, he even bragged to the Spanish reporter that, and how, he "ordered him (Andres Bonifacio) shot"! And this *pardoning, compassionate Aguinaldo* has become a national myth which determinants of which are: 1.) the imperative to justify and even convert into virtues and heroic works all the crimes of the man who murdered Andres Bonifacio and his brothers (and four or five generals more including Edilberto Evangelista, Mamerto Natividad, Julian dela Cruz, Feliciano Jocson, and of course Antonio Luna and Col. Francisco Roman...[124]), sold the Revolution at Biyak na Bato, and

---

this uldog Glenn May from Wisconsin swallowed hog and all including the pig sty.

[124] Ciriaco Bonifacio was seized without a fight by the rapists and assassins Bonson and Paua and shot in front of his comrades—as Gregoria de Jesus-Bonifacio related in her letter to Emilio Jacinto to whom she cannot be imagined to have had any motives to lie about such a matter, for she was then merely making a grief-stricken and horrified report to a faraway comrade and very close friend; and this Bonson shot Andres Bonifacio and hit him in the left arm as the latter emerged from the house running and shouting, with both arms upraised not to shoot for they were all brothers there and should not be killing each other; and when Bonifacio fell, this Intsik Paua jumped down upon him and slit open his throat with a dagger; and as the Supremo lay bleeding on the ground, this Bonson pulled his wife Gregoria up the house and took from her everything including her revolver, eleven bullets, ten pesos, her wedding ring, and a nailcutter/ fountain pen, and, on the way to the Indang municipal hall again pulled up Gregoria into another house after ordering all its occupants out, and in the municipal hall was about to do the same thing to her and would have succeeded the third time had not Gen. Mascardo arrived to contain his lust:--and this Epifanio de los Santos believed totally in the sincerity of this Bonson when with seemingly kindly words of conciliation he supposedly invited in the morning of the previous day not to go away and settle peacefully wherever in Naik or Maragondon he might wish to settle—whilst

attempted to resell it to the Americans (which was why he ordered to have Luna stabbed 57 times down the stairway of the Cabanatuan Immaculate Conception convent: as Luna lay dying on the street outside, Ilyong's Rasputina mother, reputed to be such that her influence upon her son was rumoured to be absolute, shouted from the window to ask if her son's victim who was obstructing her delirious hugging to herself of the dreamt of millions from the resell of the Revolution to the Americans, was still breathing[125]...), and, evidently panting for more treason-for-pay income, had insinuated himself too into the list of outstanding Japanese collaborators which included Claro M. Recto, Benigno Simeon Aquino I, Manuel Roxas...[126]; and 2.) the ruling-class enforced ideological-legitimizing need to project their colonial middle-class ancestors as the true patriots and heroes, so that, because they were in fact anti-revolutionary or counterrevolutionary and collaborationist traitors, it is their "heroism" that was in fact pure and lying invention.

11.0.) Writes Glenn May (p.54): "...In the course of my research on the life of Andres Bonifacio, I have been confronted time and again with highly problematic

---

only these two towns then remained for the Spaniards to reconquer, which they would in exactly 13 days!

125 Julio Nakpil wrote in his *Additional Notes for Teodoro M. Kalaw's REVOLUCION FILIPINA*: "When General A. Luna was dastardly assassinated on the stairs of the Convent of Kabanatuan and already fallen on the ground, the mother of Aguinaldo looked out the window and asked: *'Is he still breathing?'*" And one does not have to look very far in figuring out the provenance of the son's unspeakable criminality. (See *Julio Nakpil and the Philippine Revolution, with the Autobiography of Gregoria de Jesus*; edited and translated by Encarnacion Alzona; Manila 1964; p. 55)

126 See footnote to page 34 of Hernando J. Abaya's *Betrayal in the Philippines...*

texts—poems supposedly written by the supremo but were almost certainly composed by other people and memoirs seemingly intended to cover up more than they reveal. But none is as patently untrustworthy as the famous Bonifacio letters."

--"Almost certainly"—why? On the basis of what premises could Glenn May have arrived at the almostness of this certainty of Bonifacio's not being the real author of those poems? Were the poems too good for a mere peon like Bonifacio to have written?

Bonifacio was actually never a mere peon; he was at least a self-made intellectual of the lower middle class. But should he had even been such a mere peon, why should it be necessarily impossible for a mere peon to be a genius, to be a prodigy; whilst, if he were a mere peon, a mere peon would have conceived, thought-out, theorized, organized, and created-propagated across four long gloriously deadly dangerous years a national, an archipelagic revolution?

And, but, is Glenn May--is such a certifiably scrimpily minded and self-blazonedly ill-educated ill-willed academic like Glenn Anthony May, capable in the stringent contingency of the demonstrated (by him, in this book) necessity of his Anglo-American anti-thought prosaism, of imagining that an undiplomaed, let alone a non-PhDd fellow like Bonifacio could write any poem at all, let alone one so huge and deep and beautiful and powerful—powerfully liberating--as *Pag-ibig sa Tinubuang Lupa*?

But on the other hand, could Glenn May, could this great-great grandson of white refugees who genocided 200 and more Indian tribes and some two million Filipino natives to be able to produce him, could Glenn Anthony May who was helplessly swindled by his Santiago Rillo and other aguinaldically perverted Cavite informants (he did not bother to check—and how could he when he was absolutely convinced of it already in his wide-eyed brainwashing?—Rillo's oratorical declaration that 2000 Batanguenos were led by him into the Tejeros "Convention", swallowing the patent lie whole and entire and the liar Rillo therewith, and was enabled by that freeload of slime to conclude that the coup d'etat or "Convention" was not an all-Caviteno affair for Rillo and his Batanguenos were there by the thousands!:--and he was not led to wonder that Malvar and Diokno and Fenoy who were the true Batanguenos with their true Batangueno thousands were not there at all![127])–

[127] Rillo was a 25 year-old native of Maragondon when he married a girl from Tuy and was by her matrimonially sequestered and tansplanted to that Batangas town. Bonifacio had pointed out many times the real and unexceptionable reason why everything that transpired there by way of resolutions and elections was null and void—actually null and void *ab initio*—namely, *that the other districts of the Katipunan jurisdiction, which by definition was the rest of the archipelago, were not represented.* In pointing this out, he of course also silently acknowledged his error, his illegal, undemocratic, unconstitutional political mistake of having consented to being thus dragged and trapped into participating in that well-orchestrated Polavieja-origined all-Caviteno, Magdalo-Magdiwang conspiratorial plot:--for, of course, Bonifacio, supremo that he was, cannot legally, constitutionally, democratically, all by himself commit the KKK to such a scrapping and erasure of itself, just as the president of the Philippines or of the USA cannot by himself decide to scrap the constitution and therewith the republic; in pointing this actually elementary requirement and fact, Bonifacio had also at once expressed acknowledgment of the fact that only a constitutional convention in which all the districts in the entire archipelago are properly democratically represented can decide on such a thing.

could he, Glenn Anthony May ,have had anything except such class-snobbish criteria for arriving at such certain almostness or almost certainness of Andres Bonifacio's being impossibly the poet of these poems? And to this last question, the only answer possible is—no, he could not, no, he did not...

12.0.) Snobbery--class-based snobbery, and, but, also the unwordably squalid vulgarity and anachronistic stink of colonial snobbery, colonially impelled academic snobbery, colonially resurgent doctorial snobbery, colonially laced and toxined and intoxicated drunk drunk drunk and creeping and tunnelling through septic mud and luga silt stupidity of diplomadic mackinleyist white-man's-burden-bluff and yes yes yes rizalistical snobbery undeclared as such--is in this other but now foreign attempt at erasing Andres Bonifacio not only as a hero but as an existence the one and only argument deployed by this pedestrian intellectual trudger from Wisconsin—and did it fail to convince his likes in local academia, a certain Luis Dery for instance who like some surreal mummy hardly emerged from three full layers of mental sarcophagi all of a sudden blurted out to me in delirious eureka the indubitable the apodictic the absolute certainty of this erasure gesticulating vigorously and waving or rather brushing out of existence like that like that yes yes Andres Bonifacio's very existence with both his upper forelimbs simultaneously:--"wala na si bonifacio...he was not the author of those poems...he was not the author of those letters...he was not the author of those essays, manifestoes, polyetows...he was not agap-ito bagum-bayan because rizal was that...or rather jacinto or no no mabini yes yes no such thing as andres bonifacio a myth an invention a posthumous invention said aguedo del rosario said doroteo cortes read read read the minutes of the katipunan kra kra kra!" But what is going to immortalize this Dery without the da is his revelation that Bonifacio was not even the founder of the Katipunan, for, through a letter sent through Deodato Arellano, Marcelo del Pilar was that! Nak ng tutah...Which erases Bonifacio's brain, for what Dery says here is that Bonifacio was not even capable of thinking the idea of revolution for himself, of having the thought of it through his own mind's agency in his mind...

13.0.) Bonifacio had founded the Revolution; must he not have theorized it? And if he had theorized it, must that not make him a theoretician, indeed a philosopher, of it? The theory of that Revolution is most powerfully embodied and most beautifully expressed in the long poem *Pagibig sa Tinubuang Bayan.* Why should there be an incongruity in the author of the Revolution's being the author of the theory of it—of the poem of it? Why should there not instead be a perfect fit, a perfect naturalness in their being one and the same person, in their being one and the same genius? For the only argument Glenn May surreptitiously bludgeons us with here in denying the very possibility of Bonifacio's authorship of those poems, and specifically of this one poem, the greatest that ever was written by a Filipino, was the disingenuously unspoken one of such class-structural class-origined or class-of-origin incongruity.

14.0.) This unutterably malicious descendant of necessarily evil evil evil genociders of 200 and more Indian tribes who also genocided one or two million and perhaps more Filipinos during the invasive Philippine-American War says it was impossible that Andres Bonifacio could have written those poems and letters and political tracts and manifestoes:--no, he does not exactly say it's impossible, he implies it, he insinuates it, he suggests it, he deduces it obliquely, and that aggravates the malice and the calculated, premeditated, and sniggering evil of it…:--he says everyone merely believed and no one has proved Bonifacio had written them, and no one can now prove he had written them, therefore he (and here is the insinuative operation towards the logical conclusion) almost certainly did not write them. From here and similar seemingly subjunctive passages, the book's very title jumps to the total certainty of its obscene and shameless thesis: *Inventing A Hero: The Posthumous Re-Creation of Andres Bonifacio*; a wink and a half and Bonifacio's being a fake hero, a bogus existent, a non-existent existent, i.e., a myth, becomes a matter of fact: "Before proceeding to my account of Bonifacio's posthumous re-creation, I need first to provide a modicum…" (p. 11). A modicum…He and his friend Ambeth Ocampo have plenty of that in their heads. Mang Kepweng who is a famous modic and a doctor of modicine from the University of Wisconsin was their great mentor and inspiration in the culture and manufacture and application of it in their books and newspaper columns.

15.0.) The most serious of the many scurrilous "almost certain" stories made up by Doctor Professor Glenn Anthony May of the University of Wisconsin concerning the authenticity of the Bonifacio letters was that in that one of them was "almost certainly" penned by a different hand, therefore it, and with it the whole lot, was a fabrication, a forgery perpetrated by "nationalists" who were out to manufacture national heroes, and specifically this national hero called "Andres Bonifacio". This connects with yet another bizarre detail, namely, that Jose P. Santos had edited and done some rewriting on one of the letters. Were they the same letter?

All the letters and the accompanying *Tejeros Magdalo-Magdiwang Coup d'etat Papers* had been published in Spanish translation by Epifanio delos Santos in 1917 in *The Philippine Review.*

Let us grant, for the sake of argument, that a different hand penned that one letter, and concede on the basis of May's citations that Jose P. Santos had indeed done some editing in his transcription of it. Does it necessarily follow that it was a forgery? Or that wanting to create a national hero out of Bonifacio, Jose P. Santos deliberately altered some words in it? Concerning the different hand:--Perhaps the same letter which May found to have been perhaps penned by a different hand, was severely damaged somewhere sometime in the collection's mortally threatened (by Aguinaldo witness killers and evidence-and-evidence-keeper obliterators) odyssey, and its present keeper saw fit to copy it. In fact, that keeper and copier could have been Emilio Jacinto himself, or any of those who in mortal fear of being assassinated by the Aguinaldo killers had been the keepers of the lot, and, indeed, it could have been Epifanio delos Santos himself, or Jose P. Santos himself. Or perhaps, that same letter was entirely destroyed or even lost sometime after Epifanio delos Santos published the transcriptions of the (partly coded) documents in his 1917 Spanish article, and Jose P. Santos or even his father Epifanio delos Santos saw fit to reconstitute it based on the Spanish version. Concerning the editing, perhaps Jose P. Santos was himself the restorer of that severely damaged letter who then had supplied many guesswork words into the restoration; or else, perhaps the letter was totally destroyed or lost sometime after the 1917 publication (of the transcripts/translation) of the collection by Epifanio delos Santos, and it was Jose P. Santos himself who reconstructed the whole thing from memory and, but, aided too here by his father's Spanish translations; or perhaps, it was the father himself who did the restoration, and the son knew he did. In both cases, Jose P. Santos would tend not to be exactingly meticulous and faithful in making his transcription, for he would know that the "original" though still essentially the same letter was materially not identical with the destroyed or lost original and was thus an unavoidably edited version. These possibilities and likelihoods are not only kinder to the father and to the son to whom after all history owes so much for having been the necessarily anxious-for-their-and-their-families' lives armed-to-the-teeth terminal keepers and preservers and ultimate exposers and explicators of them:--they are also likelier and incomparably more possible than Glenn May's malevolent tale.

16.0.) One more thing about the conceded editing by Jose P. Santos of his published transcription: Doctor Professor and up-to-date footnoter-bibliographer and meticulous documenter Glenn Anthony May had had already not altogether unmany chances of feeling utterly superior to those first-half of the 20th century Filipino "historians" who failed, as a matter of course, almost, to properly cite, or even to at all cite, let alone properly document their sources, and he mightily thumped with his two forepaws his windful chest windily howlingly many times each time: could not this Santos case of editing or, as May also puts it, "styling" a transcription be charged on such traditional "loosemindedness"?

17.0.) Concerning the uncorroborated and weird detail supplied by Agoncillo of Epifanio's discovery of the collection in a hen's nest, we can at once conclude that it was his, Agoncillo's, shrewd way of insinuating that the papers were of dubious provenance. For the historian so-called who was responsible for inflicting the greatest and most malicious damage on the historical image of Andres Bonifacio (and therefore would be furthest from being consciously or unconsciously motivated to invent or reinvent or fabricate or manufacture a "nationalist" hero out of Andres Bonifacio—to the precise contrary!) was most certainly this Agoncillo who shamelessly perverted everything that pertained to Bonifacio and consciencelessly invented malignant lies about him and against him in order to show that the father of the Revolution and thus of the Filipino nation, the founder of the Katipunan and its chief propagator for four deadly dangerous years was himself a pervert of sorts in addition to being an irascible fool and a complete nonentity and even a coward, yes, a fearful and trembling, tear-gushing, kneelingly supplicating coward!—and all this in order to justify his murder by his Tio Emilio and prop up as the greatest Filipino hero this Tio Ilyong of his who killed not only a giant shark in single combat once upon a night in a mammoth battle that churned and harrowed the very depths of the sea somewhere off Batangas [128] as he, Aguinaldo himself alias Super Ilyong matter-of-factly related in his *Memoirs*, but also ten generals including his "intimate friend" Edilberto Evangelista and his even more "intimate friend" Mamerto Natividad (each of them with a single bullet hole in the forehead) in order to hostage and sell the Revolution and the Filipino people twice—to the Spaniards and the Americans--and had attempted the vendoration of at least his rotten soul a third time as a Japanese collaborator[129]. In this lifetime project of diminishing

---

128 The harumpaging and hagucking altercation between the Caviteno Lam-ang and the Giant Shark produced a tsunami that engulfed the Asian mainland submerging Mount Everest and melting all its snow:--Noah's God's Great Flood was a tiny incident compared to it!

129 UP Professor, veteran journalist and brilliant historiographer Hernando Abaya in what must certainly be one of the 2 or 3 greatest historiographic works written by a Filipino, *Betrayal In The Philippines*, which chronicled the crimes of such oozy, slimy, helliously and heaven-houndingly stinking pukes as Claro M. Recto, Manuel Roxas, Benigno Simeon Aquino I, Jose P. Laurel, Jose Yulo, Camilo Osias, Jorge Vargas, has provided us with a list of (the usual kind of Filipino colonial middle class venal opportunist traitors) Japanese collaborators under the rubric of members of the so-called "Preparatory Committee on Philippine Independence" whose chairman was no less than the Filipino Japanese President of the Philippines, Jose P. Laurel thus: "Members of the Preparatory Committee were Ramon Avancena, Jorge B. Vargas, Teofilo Sison, Claro M. Recto, Jose Yulo, Miguel Unson, Vicente Madrigal, Pedro Sabido, Emiliano T. Tirona, Benigno S. Aquino, Rafael Alunan, Antonio de las Alas, Quintin Paredes, Melecio Arranz, Camilo Osias,

and erasing Andres Bonifacio and consequently boosting and inventing the heroic stocks and historiographic capital of his Tio Emilio, his greatest rival was Jose P. Santos' father, Epifanio delos Santos whose name is due to be eradicated from the road that bears it now as soon as this account of the truth of the history of the Revolution triumphs at last over the lies of all the historians who ever wrote about it, including this officious Glenn Anthony May from Alaska…

And Glenn May accuses the trio of being nationalist and of being thus moved and impelled by nationalist sentiments in inventing Andres Bonifacio as a nationalist hero! Is it possible that this Glenn Anthony May knows how to read? Epifanio delos Santos was the Filipino historian chiefly responsible for destroying Andres Bonifacio as a hero and a man, and this evil project of blatant lies and crafty tergiversation powered by a staggering amount of stupidity he pioneeringly accomplished in the same 1917-18 *Philippine Review* article where for the first time those letters and the accompanying documents were publicly exposed. And together with a long excerpt from Gregoria de Jesus' letter to Emilio Jacinto recounting the criminal and perfidious details of the capture, wounding, incarceration and final assassination of Andres Bonifacio by Emilio Aguinaldo and his cowardly, treacherous and rapist henchmen, he, Epifanio, actually used those letters and the other documents to vindicate the Biyak na Bato vendor of the Revolution Emilio Aguinaldo's murder of Andres Bonifacio and to thus destroy the heroic reputation and image of Bonifacio. Whilst, as I have demonstrated and exhaustively documented repeatedly and very lengthily in books and magazine and newspaper columns from 1983 to just a few days ago, Agoncillo was a conscienceless historiographic props-man of his Tio Emilio. His massive output, starting with Bonifacio's supposed biography, *Revolt of the Masses*, was all written to destroy Bonifacio and prop up his Tio Emilio.

Manuel C. Briones, Manuel Roxas, *EMILIO AGUINALDO*, Aloya Alonto (Sultan Sa Ramain)."

On the other hand, to explain Epifanio's staggering stupidity, his truculent malice towards Bonifacio and his altogether tergiversant existence as manifested in these evil labours of his, one is reduced to falling back on class-prejudice, actually colonial middle-class prejudice, the same as his unthinking idol's, Dr. Jose Rizal's. Aside from being an absolutely unthinking Rizal idolist, Epifanio who no doubt fancied himself a somewhat belated ilustrado, provided the first and the most influential set of lies and mythologies justifying the murders committed by Emilio Aguinaldo including and first of all his murder of Andres Bonifacio, and his consequent vendoration of the Revolution and of the Motherland for 800,000 pesos at Biyak na Bato (we shall demonstrate this charge right here in a little while). Going back to Teodoro Agoncillo, the first honest and intelligent reading of his 1948 Revolt of the Masses was made by the present writer in a booklength series in the now long-defunct *WHO Magazine* under the fiery editorship of the brilliant (and lovely) Cielo Buenaventura throughout 1983. (The illustrations were by the gifted painter Bogie Ruiz.) In the same *Who* column and later in the *Journal of Social History* which the present writer himself edited, this writer was also the first to have exposed the of course anti-nationalist, anti-Bonifacio, anti-Katipunan, anti-science, anti-reason, anti-thought, millenarianizing voodoistic philological swindle that Reynaldo Ileto's Cornell PhD book *Pasyon & Revolution* was. Ileto's criminal intent was to dishonour, diminish, and ultimately destroy Bonifacio by reducing him (and Emilio Jacinto with him!) into a prophet of millenarian doomsday and the Last Judgment, malevolently imputing to Andres Bonifacio and his Katipunan comrades thus the lowest form of religious torpor and superstitious insanity. This to Glenn May makes Ileto a nationalist historian dishonestly tricking out a "nationalist" national hero called Andres Bonifacio from his philologically voodooized material. The tricking-out was dishonest to be sure, and a remarkable sort of quasi-postmodern form of intellectual idiocy is very strongly evident in the extractive process; but to accuse Ileto thus of harbouring nationalist motives and to deem his invention a kind of national hero and thus a hero at all and not a thick and vaporous idiot is to this writer an intellectual idiocy that overturns and overtops Ileto's very own.

Why did Glenn May fail to even merely take a cue from those early documentary investigations and revelations of Domingo (de) Castro de Guzman which were already published and were the subject of raging national controversies across ten to fourteen years before he published this maliciously stupid book of his?[130] I thought the Philippines is his chosen area of specialization? Is it because Domingo (de) Castro de Guzman is not an academic historian, and is widely known as a UP dropout, and therefore utterly bereft of diplomadic distinction, and is therefore, to such diploma-obsessed, PhDeed mediocrities of his ilk, not a historian at all? Or was Glenn Anthony quite simply lazy and negligent? That or this or both, he now is going to pay for it—and dearly, very dearly!

18.0.) Concerning the charge and imputed motive of "nationalist prejudice" then... Glenn May accuses E. de los Santos and his son J Santos of deliberately and maliciously inventing Bonifacio as a hero, imputing to them as their most powerful motive for their perversion their supposed "nationalism". It was, he says, their overwhelming desire to make Bonifacio look great, noble, intelligent, etc., as befits the "national hero" they wanted to make of him, that they either themselves forged those letters and all the other momentously important documents mentioned in them by Bonifacio and

---

130 Sometime towards the end of 1983, and on account precisely of those scandalous series which happened to include a critique of his irresponsible and ill-educated pronouncements and rumouristic views on the matter—it was he who published the since-then ubiquitously quoted quip that Bonifacio had fought 29 battles all in all and lost every single one of them—Nick Joaquin in an interview by *The Daily Express*, even challenged this writer to a public debate at the Cultural Center of the Philippines. And because it was Nick Joaquin who hurled the challenge, the CCP officials arranged the show. I failed to come because I lived in Baguio then and I did not have enough money for the bus fare. I was, as usual, jobless then.

included in the collection, or else, forged by someone else before they got hold of them, they knowingly presented them as authentic, etc. Does Glenn May know how to read, seeing that not knowing how to think he hardly knows how to write? For he should have read but does not in the least appear to have, the works of the father and son tandem which he cites, and on the basis of which he was able to derive that singular motive behind the supposed perversion and slander them for their wanton intellectual criminality, for greedily soliciting literary and intellectual prestige through such deceitful means, etc. For if he could at all read--if he were not the semi-illiterate Anglo-Saxon academic flunkey and research swindler I most strongly suspect him to be--and did read, and read with the normal intelligence which the definition of reading presupposes, how did it happen that he failed to see that than the father, with the sole exception of the barbershop and talipapa relativist historian Teodoro Agoncillo[131], no history writer, talipapa or otherwise, had calumniated Andres Bonifacio more? As for the son, Jose P. Santos, who in his works appears to indeed be a believer in the greatness, the nobility, the heroism of Andres Bonifacio, I will cite only one gargantuan detail in his work which I deem more than sufficient to confute the error and expose the malevolence of Glenn May's accusation that he, Santos, was so overmastered by his nationalist prejudice and had forged or perverted those letters and the other documents because of his desire to create a national hero out of Bonifacio. This concerns something he did, and another thing he did not do, in his little booklet *Si Andres Bonifacio At Ang Himagsikan*, namely, his publication *without comment,* and indeed without directly denouncing as a hellious lie, of the chief assassin Lazaro Macapagal's letter narrative of how he murdered Andres Bonifacio and his brother Procopio on a foothill of Mt. Tala on the early afternoon of May 10, 1897. Here is the most malevolent part

[131] Agoncillo's bloody *relativism* was mediated by law: Aguinaldo was his uncle by marriage; this *relativist* connection determined completely that everything he wrote that touched on Bonifacio must assassinate him anew in order to prop up his Tio Emilio who was the husband of his Tia Emilia…

of that letter narrative. Macapagal had supposedly yielded to the request of the brothers for them to take a rest, and for him to read the order handed to him by Gen. Noriel:

"Nang marinig nila ang wikang 'barilin and magkapatid' ay napatigil ang pagbasa ko dahil sa ang Procopio ay napalukso sa upo sabay ang wikang "Naku, kuyang!" Ang Andres ay napaluhod na akmang ako'y yayapusin, sabay na napasigaw ang wikang "Kapatid, patawarin mo ako". Ako naman ay umigtad at ang minamatyagan ko ay ang kilos ng Procopio dahil sa mas malakas kaysa Andres ay baka ako maunahan. Kinabahan ako ng takot na baka lumaban o makawala at makapagtago sa kagubatan. Awa sa kanila at takot sa nag-utos ang naghari sa akin. Paano ako? At ako'y sumigaw ng 'Peloton, preparen! Cargen, armas! Nang marinig nilang naglalagitikan na ang mga gatilyo ng pusil sa pagkakarga, sila ay tumahimik na. Nang makargahan ang mga pusil, hinarap ko ang Procopio, sinabi kong: 'Defrenten, Mar!' Itinuro ko ang dinaanan, isang landas na munti patungo sa loob ng gubat. Sa loob ng gubat ay tinupad namin ang utos ng Consejo de Guerra. Pagkatapos ay binalikan ko ang Andres na binabantayan ng dalawang kawal. Nang ako'y makita niya ay paluhod na sinabi sa aking 'Kapatid, patawarin mo ako!' Ako noon ay nasa panganib din na gaya niya. Nagdaramdam siya ay nagdaramdam din ako, ngunit 'Wala akong magagawa' and naging sagot ko sa kanya. Nang makita niyang hindi siya makapapamanhik sa akin ay biglang tumakbo. Tinungo ang kagubatan, kaya hinabol namin. Inabot namin sa tabi ng ilog, pinakasulok ng isang ilog na munti. Sa malaki siya naroon at ang munting ilog ay pinakasanga. Doon namin siya binaril. Pagkatapos ay tinangka naming ibaon, bilang paggalang, datapatwat wala kaming panghukay. Gayon man ay nakagawa kami ng kaunti sa bayoneta, tinabunan ng kaunti na mga sanga ng kahoy ang pangdagdag..." (Si Andres Bonifacio at ang Himagsikan; Manila 1935; p 32).

There. If you care a bit for the image, the memory, the reputation of Andres Bonifacio, either you refuse to publish such utterly destructive lies about him, or, having published them denounce in the most forthright way the account for the malevolent lie that it must most certainly be. In the first place, Santos should not even have requested such an account from the assassin himself, for, if the object of such request was not to slander Bonifacio himself, then the thing requested was absolutely worthless. Lazaro Macapagal was himself the secretary of the fake trial; he knew that, as in the sham trial, everything must be done to destroy the heroic image and reputation of Bonifacio in order to justify his inevitable murder and exculpate Aguinaldo and his cohorts including himself.

19.0) Addendum. In 1983-84, in my Filipiniana column in WHO Magazine, I published in a "kilometric" series of "kilometric[132]" articles a booklength expose' and critique of

---

[132] "kilometric" was the term of obloquy employed by Nick Joaquin buddy Jose F. Lacaba to journalistically denounce to the journalistic establishment my ideas, my sentences, my columns and my series in his aggravated replies to my critique of Nick Joaquin's mental-colonial, fascistic, and altogether sophomoric historiography which I published in the same WHO column (the skunk traitor Paterno was "magnifico" to him; he wanted to lick the "dashing" Emilio Aguinaldo y Famy from big toe to crewcut; he it was who invented the malevolent quip that Bonifacio lost all his battles, 29 of them daw: nakalimutan o di kayang isipin o simpleng di alam ng istupidang bakla—maraming magagaling at matitinong bakla, tulad ni Da Vinci, at iginagalang ko at hinahangaan sila sapagkat sila'y kagalanggalang at kahangahanga—ang sumusunod: 1.) the greatest, the hugest, the most dangerous, the most difficult battle in a revolution, and especially in such an anti-colonial one was the founding of it, first of all, of course, in the head of him who conceived it, who thought-out all of it, i.e., who theorized it, in which the theoretician of it had had to battle against and vanquish his old self and, with that old colonized self of his, a

Agoncillo's *Revolt of the Masses*. That was the first time I came across the Bonifacio letters which Agoncillo and Epistola compiled and edited along with other primary sources on Bonifacio and published in 1963.

---

multi-centurial world-straddling , world-conquering, and world dominating colonial ideology; 2.) and then the battle for the concretization of that intellectual-theoretical and as it were, spiritual, triumph which was the theory of the revolution, which battle was the battle for the *revolutionization* of the hearts and souls of the people which in the case of Bonifacio took all of the four underground years of the KKK to wage—inspiring and instigating and *intellectually* convincing them and making each of them decide for himself/herself that death is preferable to unfreedom—and win; having thus won which, and only after his having won which, it then first became possible for anyone else to win—or lose—revolutionary battles at all; 3.) in a word, what Bonifacio thus won was the mother of all battles which all at once was the drawn-out, four-year long occasion of the founding, the foundation, the origination, the birth, of the Filipino nation (and what absurd farcicality and hideous comedy that this founding was credited to the father of Filipino counterrevolution Jose Rizal for the alleged linguistical-philological "feat" of having been the first to use the term "Filipino" to refer to himself and his counterrevolutionary "Indios Bravos"!)...

Chapter 20

THE FASCIST SUPREME COURT ASSOCIATE JUSTICE ABRAHAM SARMIENTO

IN HIS BOOK "THE TRIAL OF ANDRES BONIFACIO:THE APPEAL" IS A CHARLATAN…?

1.0.) *"Charlatan: False expert; somebody who falsely claims to have special skill or expertise."* Thus does my Encarta Dictionary define "charlatan".

1.1.) And Supreme Court Associate Justice Abraham Sarmiento was so absolutely accustomed to being unjust, partial, irrational, and fascistic--and fascistic and unprincipled to unconsciousness, fascistic and unprincipled to the bone marrows, in always being biased in favour of might as against right--that he did not seem to even notice the absolute anomaly, nay the absolute absurdity, of the fact that in this massmurderous farce which he along with all the other historians who wrote anything on it triumphantly announced and exalted as a *national election* which supposedly elected president, supposedly in fullest legality, constitutionality, and legitimacy, of, supposedly, the Republic of the Philippines (and not merely of Cavite) Emilio Aguinaldo y Famy, *ALL THE VOTERS WERE CAVITENOS!*

1.2.) And, but, Bonifacio was not Magdiwang, was as little a Magdiwang as he was a Magdalo--for he was Supremo, Supreme President of the National Democratic Revolutionary Republic of the Philippines! And we of course know why they must insist on this reductionism, on this absurd and contradictory absolute downgrading of Andres Bonifacio:--If Bonifacio was a mere Magdiwang, and knew and acknowledged in thus acquiescing to the election that he was merely so, then, the absolute absurdity of a national presidential election in which all the voters were Magdiwangs and Magdalos--or which is the same thing, in which absolutely all the other provinces and Katipunan districts were NOT represented, were excluded, were disallowed from representing themselves by definition, by decree, and by fact--could seem somehow to be a little bit less contrary to reason, justice, fair-dealing, honesty, sanity, acceptable or decent behaviour, could seem somehow to be a bit less absurd, less insane, or less dishonest, skewed, perverted, distorted, idiotizing, idiotic, idiotical…And yes, could seem a little bit less fascistic, less tribalistic, less totemistic, less gangsteristic…Also, it would somehow serve to deflect some of the blame, the nastiness,the perversion, the distortedness, the twistedness, the twisted pigliness, the pigugly twistedness, from the chief conspirator and organizer of the whole thing, Emilio Aguinaldo y Famy. For of all who have written on the matter thus who are all the socalled historians in or on the Philippines who have written about the Philippine Revolution, the chief anxiety is to exonerate Emilio Aguinaldo, to justify, even to glorify, the hijacking of the Revolution in Tejeros, and thus its surrender for pay and in pursuit of counterrevolutionary colonial-collaborationist middleclass interests, ultimately the same as in Rizal's and the ilustrado counterrevolutionists' case, its sale, its vendoration at Biyak na Bato and its eventual political and military destruction and cultural-moral, let us even say spiritual, deflection and eventual diminishment in and as the now world-famous Philippine culture of corruption--in and as Abraham Sarmiento's legal-political-historiographic charlatanry for instance…

1.2.1.) Seemingly less absurd, less fascistic, but more absurd for being more contradictory in that this very conspiratorial plot and act of coup d'etat, of electoral coup d'etat, yes, and as was already attempted three months before on December 30, 1896 by way of the so-called Imus Assembly which was Emilio Aguinaldo y Famy's first such attempt, must presuppose in purposing to scrap the Katipunan National Democratic Revolutionary Republic the preexistence of the National Democratic Revolutionary Republic and therewith the preexistence of its Constitution most grandly ratified by the very fact of the archipelagic expanse of the Revolution itself, and therefore the preexistence of its duly constituted National Government whose duly elected and presently incumbent president was President Andres Bonifacio…

1.2.2.) But, in fairness, and in kindness to him, Abraham Sarmiento defends and justifies Aguinaldo's murder of Andres Bonifacio, taking thus Aguinaldo's side *against* the Revolution, *against* the Filipino People, *against* History, *against* Humanity, and lapses thus into fascism, i.e., into his secret self; defends *counterrevolution*, defends *the Aguinaldo Counterrevolution*, defends *the Aguinaldo Colonial Middleclass Counterrevolution which was the middle-middleclass and lower middleclass* counterpart and twin of the *Rizal-Ilustrado Upper Colonial Middleclass Counterrevolution (whilst these two counterrevolutions of actually the same venal , grasping, greedy colonial collaborationist class-inspiration eventually merged and became one during the successful perpetration of the Biyak na Bato Sale of the Revolution for 800,000 pesos,* defends counterrevolution and genocide without, so it seems, in his arrant stupidity, quite realizing it was counterrevolution and genocide. Which mitigates somewhat his crime against the Filipino people and against Humanity in being less evil and demoniacal by a full-fledged commination thus--unlike the hallucinatorily sadistic breed of fascists, like Nietzsche and the Nietzscheites Hitler, Heidegger, Deleuze, Foucault, Guatarri, Derrida…and here Tom Agulto who could exult somewhat plagiarizingly and with swelling heart and moist eyes in bended-knee homage to his metaphysical and therefore fascist idol Ubermensch Superman Zarathustra-Nietzsche and shout like alleluiah, "DAHIL BANAL ANG DIGMA"

--BECAUSE WAR IS HOLY…

2.0.) THE ALL-CAVITENO MAGDALO-MAGDIWANG TEJEROS CONSPIRACY & COUP D'ETAT. A not small book can be written exposing this hitherto unsuspected conspiracy. A future movie or a huge part of a historical novel must someday be devoted to its impassioned analytical exhibiting. Let us for the first time present the major pieces of evidence, material, factual, documentary, circumstantial, reconstructive, argumentative, showing this ultimately genocidal conspiracy as a fact, as well as clues indicating, suggesting, pointing to the staging of the evil thing.

2.1.) Genocidal, yes, and there is nothing extravagant in the use of this word here. For it was this conspiracy that, successful as it was in murdering Bonifacio and hostaging the Revolution for eventual sale, constituted the turning point in the struggle between revolution and counter-revolution inside the revolution in favour of counter-revolution. The Filipino intellectuals had had to be uniquely idiotic, indeed the most idiotic in world history, and most perfidious and invidious and treacherous and anti-people, in fact the most such in world history, to have failed to see it as such. Successful thus to the ultimate point of vendorial consummation (at Biak na Bato), it was thus most hugely responsible for weakening and delaying the Revolution, which weakening and delay allowed the Americans to, so to speak, catch-up with it (it was overtaken by the Spanish-American War; moreover, it was also Aguinaldo who, vendorially motivated once more in his insurpassable pigliness and stupidity, fully cooperated with the Americans in the latter's efforts to land an entire army and consolidate overwhelming power in the islands, instead of resolutely blocking and countering—as would any real and not exceptionally stupid patriot, let alone revolutionary, indeed, as would any nationalist with something like commonsense—every military move of the Americans and from the very start declaring war against them, and doing everything thus to expel them from Philippine territory), in which catching-up with it, some 2 million Filipinos were murdered by the fair-skinned and dark-minded Americans. This genocide then was as much the handiwork of Aguinaldo and the all-Caviteno conspirators at Tejeros (sharing it thus with the traitor-worm in their minds and character, namely, Dr. Jose P. Rizal), and the Gringos who did the actual killings. Another such turning-point in the same—resumed—struggle between revolution and counter-revolution in the second, anti-American, phase, although less conspiratorial this time, for Aguinaldo was in full control and had had merely to give orders to subalterns, was heinously effected by the same Aguinaldo and his vendorial gang in the murder of Antonio Luna, with something like an added finishing touch in the murder of Gregorio del Pilar (Aguinaldo ordered him to suicide himself at Tirad Pass). That also successful counter-revolution inside the revolution was likewise crowned with vendorial success, although less spectacular this time, for this time the Great Vendor had had only his *Oath of Allegiance* and his influence upon the still actively fighting revolutionists to sell. The price? One thousand hectares of prime Cavite real estate…

2.2.) The hard evidence, the material evidence and conclusive proof, beyond reasonable doubt, beyond any but insane doubt, of this counter-revolutionary all-Caviteno, Magdiwang-Magdalo conspiracy, is the fatefully preserved original of a letter dated March 21, 1897 from Magdalo president Baldomero Aguinaldo addressed to Magdalo generals, Felix Cuenca and Mariano Noriel, informing them that he had just received, at 12 o'clock midnight, a letter from Magdiwang president Mariano Alvarez inviting the Magdalos to a meeting at Tejeros on the following day, for the purpose of electing the officials of a new revolutionary government at the national and provincial levels. Baldomero Aguinaldo adjoined the two generals to prepare for such elections by choosing carefully from amongst themselves their best possible bets. He also told them to inform the heads of the other towns about the meeting and the elections ("Pagsabihan mo po ang mga G. Plo ng taga ibang bayan diyan, at ipagpauna na huwag magkulang...") This original document has been reproduced in Achutegui and Bernad's compilation, *Aguinaldo and the Revolution* (p. 343). The original can be found in the Dominican Archives in Quezon City. Let us quote the letter in its entirety.

"Sanguniang Bayan

Magdalo

Kgg G. Felix Cuenca at G. Mariano Noriel Gargano.

Kapagtanggap ninyo po niyaring kalatas ay mangyaring isaisip ang kung sino ang mga maginoong nararapat sa Kgg na Kapulungang Naghihimagsik (Gobierno Revolucionario) at pulungan din namang naghihimagsik sa bawat hukuman (Gobierno Provincial) alang alang sa isang kalatas ng G. Presidente ng Magdiwang na tinanggap ko po ng may alas 12 nitong gabi, at doon ay tayo'y inaanyayahan na mangyaring makarating bukas 22 ng lumalakad na buwan sa Hacienda ng Tejeros upang doo'y magawa ang tinatawag na sabing botohan sa paghahalal ng mga punong nasambit sa itaas.

Kaya po sa bagay na ito ay inaasahan ko na ang inyong mga Kamahalan ay haharap dito sa bahay Hacienda (kung walang malaking panganib) datapwat maglalagay ka po ng sukat makatawan sa pamamahala ng inyong tungkulin diyan sa panguluhan, sa alas seis ng umaga nang nasabing araw.

Haligue 21 ng Marso 1897

Ang Plo.

(signed) B. AGUINALDO

H.K.: Pagsabihan mo po ang mga G. Plo ng taga ibang bayan diyan at ipagsauna na huwag magkulang

Kasama".

The following is our English translation of the body of this all-important, history-reversing letter:

"As soon as you receive this letter, you are enjoined to consider who are the gentlemen who deserve to become officials of the Supreme Revolutionary Council (Revolutionary Government) and also those of the revolutionary councils of each local jurisdiction (Provincial Government) in view of a letter from the Gentleman President of Magdiwang which I received at around twelve tonight, where we are being invited to be present tomorrow the 22nd of the current month at the Estate House of Tejeros in order to hold there the said elections for the officials we have mentioned above.

So that, in this regard, I expect your lordships to be present at the Estate House (barring great peril), but you should designate responsible deputies to take care of your duties as presidents, at six in the morning of the abovementioned day.

Haligue 21 March 1897

The Pres.
(Signed) B. AGUINALDO

P.S.: Inform the Presidents of the other towns and impress on them that they should not be remiss."

It is highly significant that the letter from Mariano Alvarez reached Baldomero Aguinaldo at 12 midnight. Everything was being done in great haste and secrecy. They had 36 hours to finalize preparations. I say *finalize*, because the two letters must merely have been confirmatory of negotiations and agreements which were being cooked-up since Emilio Aguinaldo received Pio Pi's letter of 14 March, to which he replied on 17 March, 1897. The Tejeros Conspiracy was a response to the letter of Pio Pi, and also to that of Rafael Comenge, and, of course, to the conference entailed by the former to which, as can be seen in Aguinaldo's reply, the latter had agreed and had even laid down certain conditions in some detail, including the color of the flag to be waved by the Jesuit Superior upon approaching the Magdalo capital of Imus.

2.2.1. The resounding Caviteno, Magdiwang-Magdalo silence concerning these two letters, and about the fact exhibited by these letters, namely, that the *coup d'etat*, i.e., the supposed elections and the presupposed overthrow of the Katipunan government and its replacement with the conspiratorial *government-for-surrender* one, was planned, that in fact, there was no other objective for the assembly except *that coup d'etat* (it was the only purpose mentioned in Baldomero Aguinaldo's letter), further confirms the solidity of this conspiracy.

A valuable clue was accidentally given by the brutal Aguinaldo hagiographers, the shameless excusers of Aguinaldo's crimes, the intellectual murderers of Andres Bonifacio, the continuators of the counter-revolution and the massmurders perpetrated by Aguinaldo and his Caviteno gang, Archutegui and Bernad, SJs, in their compilatory and commentarical opus, *Aguinaldo and the Revolution of 1896*, when they speculated that it was Polavieja himself who must have ordered Gen. dela Pena to write to Pio Pi, SJ to write to Aguinaldo to ask for a meeting toward a possible surrender on terms, and that Polavieja was prompted to do so by the death of Gen. Zabala during the March 12, 1897 battle at Anabo, which the Spaniards did take but at such great costs. Polavieja was set to attack the Magdalo capital, Imus itself, on the 24th of March. It is important to remember that Aguinaldo must have been made aware of this planned attack, or was in any case told that there would be such an attack, before or during the ensuing meeting with Pio Pi, SJ. Polavieja, appalled at Zabala's death and the great loss of Spanish lives entailed by their victory must have thought that perhaps they had terrorized Aguinaldo and yes the Magdiwangs enough to make them bite the offer of peaceful surrender on terms, even as they were poised to assault Imus itself on the 24th. A very strange and curious thing: Aguinaldo granted the request for a meeting, but there never occurred anywhere after that any mention whatsoever of such a meeting taking or *not* taking place. Which can only mean one thing, namely, that it did take place. Whilst the resolutions made in that meeting must have been such that everybody who knew about them was guilty of the series of crimes in which that meeting was an all-important link, such that everybody was struck dumb by such guilt and shame. And that means everybody who would be in the know—namely, Magdalo and Magdiwang alike. Why the universal silence about the meeting? Was it because the most shameless part of the deal was a certain payoff? Or that in any case, there was an offer too of such a payoff and that was *also* why the Magdiwangs were finally persuaded to give Bonifacio's head? *Also*: because fear of the Spanish juggernaut—in a word, cowardice-- was most certainly the main motivation behind the conspiracy to do away with Bonifacio, "constitute" themselves into a new government so that they could negotiate "on equal terms" and therefore could demand more money. The wrangle for the posts was also only comprehensible as a wrangling for greater payment i.e., for a bigger share of the pay. Speculating about this payoff, or the hankering for a payoff is too much? But that was how it all ended before the year ended. Moreover, the manufacture of many other such "republics" whilst Aguinaldo was running away and hiding and meanwhile sending signals for negotiation-for-pay is revealed thus as a strategy—which, again, is comprehensible only as such! *Nagpapataas ng presyo si Aguinaldo tuwing iimbento ng Republika!* And as such a price-upping device also should we view his hasty June 12, 1898 declaration of that dictatorial "republic" which idiotically Filipinos have been commemorating for their Independence Day, and the Malolos Republic after that (whose promulgation, no less idiotically, Bulakenyo historian Jaime Veneracion has been insisting for 40 years now should be made the Independence Day instead). For if he really wanted anything other than such price-upping retreat, running away and hide and seek, if he really wanted, at least that time (for there is no question as to what he really wanted to do with the vendorated Biak na Bato "republic") to fight as a revolutionary a truly revolutionary war and not run away run away run away as a counter-revolutionary in a vendorating war, he should not have murdered Antonio Luna and Gregorio del Pilar, and should have disciplined his PSG, i.e., his Kawit Company (whose superstar officers included the rapist who tied to a tree and manhandled Gregoria de Jesus and held her up and robbed her of her revolver, eleven bullets, ten pesos and her wedding ring, and even, as Gen. Francisco Carreon (who was there) testified, a fountain pen and nailcutter in one, and twice raped her, Gregoria de Jesus, in Limbon, Agapito Bonzon, the coward Agapito Bonzon who treacherously shot Andres Bonifacio in Limbon, the coward who loved to fight duels from behind, the lustful and concupiscent *vis a tergo* adjutant who was ever by his, Emilio Aguinaldo y Famy's, side, indeed at his bedside, and coming from behind, always, even in Hong Kong, yes, yes, and in Palanan and thereafter, and the coward Ignacio Paua who, upon seeing the Supremo fall from Bonzon's utterly brave bullet, jumped down on him with a shrieking dagger and slashed open his throat, and of course the cowardly assassin Lazaro Macapagal who sneakily "executed" Andres Bonifacio and Procopio Bonifacio upon a hill on Mt. Buntis), and his Caviteno generals. Concerning the latter group of bulldogs and chihuahuas, one could raise the question of whether such bandits, rapists and hoodlums could be disciplined at all for a revolutionary war; and perhaps they were indeed such as to be past disciplining thus; so that their being such must be such as to disallow Aguinaldo himself to think of fighting with them a real revolutionary war in a really revolutionary, and not rather counter-revolutionary, way. And the answer is indeed a resounding no.

2.2.2.) Nor was Gregoria de Jesus the only one raped by those hoodlums from Kawit, that execrable day of Y Famy's infamies in Limbon when the Caviteno counter-revolutionary conspirators murdered Ciriaco Bonifacio and together with his younger brother, Procopio, kidnapped the Supremo Andres Bonifacio. Gregoria de Jesus herself testified in her letter to Emilio Jacinto about that absurd and evil day that on the night of the siege, as the hoodlums were waiting for reenforcements, they had abducted the women—apparently all the women with the fleeing group, except of course Gregoria de Jesus herself—who were stationed outside the ramparts. In her account of the event, Gregoria de Jesus mentioned that one of those women was able to escape and report to them what happened.

Concerning what really happened during the kidnapping, the attendant shooting, knifing, and mauling of Andres Bonifacio, his days of wounded, starved, and humiliated captivity, and his hurried and stealthy assassination, the most reliable and authoritative reports were of course those made by Gregoria de Jesus herself who, except for the few hours during which the brothers Andres and Procopio were taken out of their improvised prison cell in Maragondon and brought to Mount Tala and assassinated there, was a participant eyewitness, although cruelly separated from her husband and brother in law during the thirteen days of captivity. Of the events of the kidnapping, she and the original circle Katipunero Francisco Carreon were the only participant eyewitnesses who were able to write a narrative; concerning this episode, Ricarte's and Santiago Alvarez's accounts were pure hearsay. All the accounts, starting with these two, were hearsay. Whilst the abovementioned liars were fully, upsurgingly motivated to lie about the event.

2.3.) Which then boils down to the same thing now, namely, that it was possible for Aguinaldo only to be a vendorating counter-revolutionary, and that was what he still was in his hide-and-seek with the Americans. When finally he was captured, the great vendor, the never-say-die vendorator, was nonetheless able to still vendorate that much of the revolution when he vendorated his surrender and his oath of allegiance to the new imperators, and most importantly, his order, declaration, manifesto, to all the Filipinos who were still fighting it out, to give up now and with him embrace the new imperators. For how much? He did not get cash this time. It was barter, reflective of his somewhat reduced circumstances. And the price was—1000 hectares of prime Cavite real estate.

2.4.). The Magdiwangs were supposed to be staunch Bonifacio and Katipunan allies; they demonstrated that they still indeed were so when they overwhelmingly voted down the first Aguinaldo proposal to scrap the Katipunan, form a new revolutionary government, adopt his readymade constitution (which at his instance Edilberto Evangelista made by plagiarizing the Maura Law) and elect the officials of the new government at the Imus Assembly on December 29, 1896. They could outvote them then because, to begin with, they were more numerous, even as they were in control of more Cavite towns (Cavite had 22 towns only 6 of which belonged to Magdalo). They could still have outvoted them in Tejeros a mere three months later. Why then, did they not vote there against everything that they voted against three months ago in Imus? The answer to this question is because the All-Caviteno, Magdiwang-Magdalo counter-revolutionary conspiracy was not yet on in Imus. It was now, in Tejeros.

2.4.1.) A sidelight on this “constitution”: it was made by the plagiarist Edilberto Evangelista as early as October, 1896, i.e., three months before the December 30 Imus Assembly: for even as it was a plagiarism of the Maura Law, it must have taken sometime to do the copying, and the organizing of the government which during the pre-Christmas meeting between Bonifacio and Aguinaldo in the yard of Juan Castaneda in Imus, Aguinaldo could already cite as accomplished fact, invoking this plagiarized constitution as proof that “we already have a new government here, complete with a Constitution”, in view of which, so he told Bonifacio, he, the Supremo had no *jurisdiction there anymore*, and could therefore order the arrest of the traitor Vicente Fernandez only as a comedy. According to Ricarte, the Magdalos sniggered and guffawed as the Supremo ordered Fernandez’s arrest. What this means, rightaway, is that the first thing Aguinaldo did as the Magdalos were able to boot out the extremely few Spanish civil guards assigned to the different Cavite towns (and thanks also to a change in Spanish strategy whereby the Spanish forces, after some initial skirmishes, withdrew completely from Cavite and assaulted for retaking first all other provinces—Nueva Ecija, Bulacan, Tarlac, Laguna, Morong...--except Cavite), was repudiate the authority of the Katipunan as the national revolutionary government, destroy revolutionary unity, seditiously and treasonously and counter-revolutionarily crown himself dictator dictating a new government by decree, creating a new constitution by decree, making himself president of the Republic of the Philippines by decree....

2.5.) The cowardly Gen. Apoy alias Santiago Alvarez, had himself confessed to the conspiracy in the following sentences from his *Memoirs of a General*, pp 100-101: *“In the evening of 29 April 1897, some Magdiwang leaders met at the invitation of the Secretary of War Ariston Villanueva and Secretary of*

Finance Diego Mojica in a house in the village of Malainin in Naic. The purpose of the meeting was to discuss a plan to rescue the Supremo Bonifacio and his brother, who were then held prisoners by the Magdalo. The organizers purposely did not invite General-in-Chief Mariano Alvarez and his son General Apoy, because the former was then with the Magdalo sponsored "Philippine Republic" as director of Welfare, while the latter was patently opposed to any move that would lead to a civil war." {Mark how the use of the term "civil war" must presuppose that Cavite was all of the Philippines, and that the Cavitenos, specifically the Magdiwangs and the Magdalos were the only Filipinos there were; and, of course, that the entire Philippines, namely Cavite was now legitimately governed by the newly "elected" government...} "Those present resolutely approved of a plan to organize a bolo regiment that was to pretend to reinforce the infantry contingent guarding the Naic estate house. At a given signal, it was to make a sudden and simultaneous attack and then capture the guns and the fortifications. That was how they envisioned they would liberate the Supremo and his brother. However the plan never materialized because of an unexpected attack by the Spaniards which led to the capture of Naic and Indang

"The next day, Gen. Luciano San Miguel visited General Apoy at Indang to report to him what had transpired at the meeting. The latter advised against such a plan as was approved because he thought it would lead the country to perdition.

"'What will happen if a small number of comrades split and engage each other in armed struggle?' General Apoy asked. 'Should that happen, the enemy horde will ride triumphantly over us and we will not be able to effectively defend ourselves against them. This will come about because of our arrogance, and avarice will prod us to betray our own brothers despite our commitment to the common goal of freedom for the Motherland..

"In the course of his briefing, Gen. San Miguel told of the news circulating among top military echelon of the 'Philippine Republic', to the effect that many of the chiefs of the government and the Army of the 'Philippine Republic' objected to the arrest of Andres Bonifacio and his followers and instead favored a grace period for them.

"'I am thankful that the plan did not materialize', Gen. Apoy reiterated. 'However, we should be reminded that in order for us to achieve our goal of freedom, to which we dedicate our blood and our lives, we should first be united. I wholeheartedly acknowledge the existence of the 'Philippine Republic', although on principle I was against its establishment. I am hoping that from the new government of the 'Philippine Republic' will come the deliverance of our country, which is at present still in the clutches of the Spanish enemy.

"'I hail the well-deserved promotion of Gen. Artemio Ricarte to captain general. Likewise, Magdiwang Pres. Mariano Alvarez welcomes his appointment as minister of welfare in the 'Philippine Republic'. This office he is serving well, and only a disabling arthritis prevents him from going to his office. As you can see, I continue to serve even if I am not the captain general of the 'Philippine Republic'(hu hu hu)... (etcetera)...The listener(Gen. Luciano San Miguel) found these statements very convincing."

This was his confession. We of course know now, thanks to the publication by Achutegui and Bernad of the Baldomero Aguinaldo letter (Document 100 in their compilatory history written and composed to exculpate Emilio Aguinaldo and hold him up as the greatest Filipino hero and savior of the native land) to Cuenca and Noriel telling them of the letter he received from Mariano Alvarez "at 12 midnight"(!) of March 21, 1897, that the secret negotiations indefatigably made by Emilio Aguinaldo bore the expected salivating fruit.

Santiago Alvarez was a typical colonial middle-class provincial principalia quasi-illiterate scion of a local political family, with the capital and decisive addition that he was

Caviteno: his father, Mariano Alvarez who instead of the food, the arms, and the escort of "loyal soldiers of the Motherland" he promised to Bonifacio as the latter sought his help towards expediting his hasty flight to Manila, sent assassins instead, informing them exactly where in Indang he was...Santiago the son was dying of envy that the post he dyingly coveted belonged to another, Ricarte the superdooper chameleon from Batac, Ilocos Norte. Dying of envy thus, he would kill anybody, or in any case—for the fellow must have been a frightful coward—would have anybody killed who might deprive him of the delirium of dreaming to someday grab that post.

The all-Caviteno conspiracy was not absolutely solid. There were a few, notably Diego Mojica, Santos Nocon, whose conspiring against the Supremo and the Katipunan did not include the idea of his death. If this incident was true, and perhaps it was, what a great tragedy that it—the plot to spring Bonifacio to freedom and ultimately to Manila-- failed. And why in any case was it not resumed? That leads us to realize that the desire to save him from the treacherous and rapacious Aguinaldo was quite lukewarm.

3.0.) ...and Abraham Sarmiento was happy and even proud that Aguinaldo had "outsmarted" and "legitimately" tricked and set-up Bonifacio and that was why he had no right to protest the elections and why his elimination by Aguinaldo was justified....

But Aguinaldo was the leader of the Cavite counterrevolution itself, and his "legitimate" triumph and "just" murder of Bonifacio was the triumph of counterrevolution...

Abraham Sarmiento was happy that the Aguinaldo counterrevolution triumphed and was able to put down Bonifacio's Katipunan Revolution. He was happy that Aguinaldo was able to murder Bonifacio and sell the

Revolution for 800,000 pesos at Biyak na Bato; and without a doubt, he was happy too that Aguinaldo was able to hostage the Revolution a second time and was almost successful in selling it once more, this time to the Americans—happy that Antonio Luna was murdered by him by way of 57 dagger thrusts because he discovered the ongoing negotiations with Otis for another surrender-for-pay and opposed it mightily...

Fascists, with the sole exception of Plato, are pre-eminently stupid. Hence, Aguinaldo; or, indeed, Jose Rizal...

3.1.) Humanity have become so debased and idiotized by global-intimate capitalism or the pigly religion of money, of material greed and material utility (to the level of technological slavishness) that an uncompromising enemy and destroyer and betrayer of his own people's revolution like Jose Rizal, or a successful vendor of his own people's revolution as Emilo Aguinaldo y Famy, must unfailingly be regarded as super-intelligent (or a super-general)—a superpig to common pigs. We will not argue with them. At this level of consideration, the difference is so massive and categorical that one's stand resolves itself into a matter of taste:--quite apart from the question whether there can at all be an intelligent pig, an intelligent pig is, well, a--pig...

3.2.) Of Rizal and Aguinaldo, the former was the more authentic and, as it were, intrinsic fascist. Fascism happens when one draws or implements (or draws implicitly, densely, unconsciously) the political implications of a theological or metaphysical absolutism. Hence, racism in essentializing a merely contingent difference like skin colour into a metaphysical difference, absolutizing it thereby and thereby metaphysizing it, making of it a metaphysical attribute, and thus ultimately making a religion of it, and in at the same time turning such difference into a criterion of metaphysical superiority, becomes fascism and is fascism in thus politicizing it and in thus infecting, polluting, perverting politics with metaphysics or religion/theology, and in thus making politics metaphysical or religious/theological: fascism is metaphysical politics, is political metaphysics, is political religion or religious politics, where the primordially democratic/communistic, the essentially democratic, the essentially communistic, the essentially-primordially egalitarian nature of power (which is always political power so that *political power* is already redundant) is infringed upon, violated, infected, polluted, perverted, contradicted, destroyed. The very humanity of the human which is different but inseparable from the sociality of the human being and of the human species, is founded upon this primordial democracy/communism, this primordially democratic/communist essence which then is primordially political, which is the primordiality of power and the primordiality of freedom and the primordial inseparability *in difference* of power and freedom, which is the primordial sociality of freedom, the primordial impossibility of freedom outside society, and thus the primordial impossibility of humanity outside society, outside the social relationship, which social relationship is, then, primordially political—and *free*! That is to say, primordially democratic/communistic.

4.0.) Abraham Sarmiento, formerly Associate Justice of the Supreme Court damaged severely his own reputation as a mind and a human being with this flukey book, *The Trial of Andres Bonifacio: the Appeal,* in which, in an expectably legalistic roundabout way, he argued for the justice and the rightness of the counter- revolutionary overthrow and murder of Andres Bonifacio, and the counter- revolutionary destruction of the Katipunan national revolutionary government by way of the March 22, 1897 Tejeros Coup d'Etat, and the counterrevolutionary hostaging and sale of the Revolution (at Biyak na Bato, for 800,000 pesos) by the vicious and counterrevolutionary traitor Emilio Aguinaldo y Famy, who must certainly be considered *one of the most successful counterrevolutionary traitors and the most successful counterrevolutionary hoodlum in the world's history.*

{Although Rizal was not a hoodlum nor a coward like Aguinaldo he was most certainly the longest reigning top one fake patriot in world history. In terms of counterrevolutionary havoc wrought and therefore counterrevolutionary success achieved, he is the only one to beat his fellow colonial middleclass traitor and fake patriot Emilio Aguinaldo y Famy…}

4.1.) *"The first question is: Did Aguinaldo have the right, as president of the Philippines, to try the accused? It is an inquiry, of course, that implicates Aguinaldo's very claim to the presidency, because if he was not the legitimate President, he would not have had the right to try accused persons…The Court does not believe that the petitioners are challenging the legitimacy of Emilio Aguinaldo's eventual Presidency of the First Philippine Republic. There seems to be no question that Emilio Aguinaldo, as a matter of historical fact, was the Republic's first President.*

"The first question is: Did Aguinaldo have the right, as president of the Philippines, to try the accused? It is an inquiry, of course, that implicates Aguinaldo's very claim to the presidency, because if he was not the legitimate President, he would not have had the right to try accused persons…"

If he had the right to try Bonifacio for treason right then and there, then it must be because--as Abraham Sarmiento here rather wishy-washily assumes--because his supposed election at Tejeros was valid, constitutional, legal, legitimate.

That he, Abraham Sarmiento, could write this book at all, presupposes that according to Abraham Sarmiento, Aguinaldo had the right to try accused persons in his capacity as President of the Philippine Republic, for if he did not have such right and was thus not any kind of legitimate President (except perhaps of Cavite, since except perhaps for two or three exceptions—and it was not even certain nor likely, the counterrevolutionary conspiracy being the Magdalo-Magdiwang affair that it was, that such non-Cavitenos like Pio del Pilar or Mamerto Natividad had voted at all--all the Tejeros voters were Cavitenos), then everything here that he could as such a legal commentator talk about was void and null *ab initio*. The stand then and the conclusion were foregone: this work from its very concept was to be an apology for the Aguinaldo counterrevolution which at the very least began with the seditious *October 31, 1896 Manifesto* and through it the formation of the *Imus Republic* so-called, "complete with a constitution", and "recognized as such even in Europe", "and which was already exercising its prerogatives" when Bonifacio arrived in Imus in December 1896, enabling Aguinaldo thus to mock the Supremo and refuse pointblank to obey his order to have the traitor Vicente Fernandez arrested for trial, telling him in absolutely seditious terms that "we are no longer under your orders here". Sarmiento was of course aware of the pre-existence of this absolutely seditious manifesto, although more haphazard, and unforgivably haphazard for thus being ultimately *criminally* haphazard, even *heinously* criminally haphazard about that which it purported to establish, namely the "Imus Republic complete with a constitution" --six words which in the ultimate analysis meant massmurder, a long chain of counter-revolutionary betrayals and atrocities including the murder of some ten generals of the Revolution culminating in the genocide of some 2 million Filipinos by the American imperialists. He who could omit discursive reference to, or fail to be able to be markedly and argumentatively aware of, so capital a thing has no right to write such a book as this. And which Manifesto he has also referred to in this his first and only sally into political theory and historiography. He however was able to pretend to be able to have forgotten its absolutely seditious and thus counterrevolutionary, anti-revolutionary nature, otherwise, he would not be able to write this ignorant and dirty book for he would then have to acknowledge that the Tejeros Convention was merely the penultimate culmination of a long series of Aguinaldo's seditious counter-revolutionary plots to wrest the Revolutionary leadership away from Bonifacio (which could of course be effectuated only by, among other things, murdering Bonifacio), hostage it by hostaging its leadership, and whose ultimate aim *as the fact of the sale showed it was*, was the *surrender-for-pay, the sale, of the Revolution*—at Biyak na Bato, yes.

In other words, the *Tejeros all-Caviteno, Magdiwang-Magdalo Conspiracy and Coup d'etat* was already Aguinaldo's fourth attempt at sedition, absolute treason, the overthrow of the Katipunan National Revolutionary Government and of Bonifacio—i.e., (and what else indeed but) *counterrevolution*. According to the talipapa and kwentong barbero "historian" Teodoro Agoncillo, who was moreover Aguinaldo's nephew in law, for having rejected the results of the Tejeros conspiracy and coup d'etat and for having afterwards "organized" a "seditious" government of his own in Indang, Aguinaldo "could have shot Bonifacio outright"! For any of those four blatant seditions, treasons, and counterrevolutionary crimes, Bonifacio *should* have shot Aguinaldo outright—and then Agoncillo would not have had the moronic and salivating opportunity to indite that singular stupidity and unique mindlessness of his, or to be a historian at all—for it is clear that had not Aguinaldo been his Tio, he would never have been able to anticipate the lucracy of scribbling his first book which still remains the dirtiest, or one of the three dirtiest, on Philippine history: the other two are Epifanio de los Santos' 1917-18 monograph on Bonifacio which formed part of the volume *The Revolutionists*, and Glenn Anthony May's *Re-inventing a Hero: the Posthumous Invention of Andres Bonifacio*. (For the quoted phrases above, see Aguinaldo's *Statement Concerning the Revolution in Cavite and the Death of Andres Bonifacio* which we have also analyzed and exposed in another documentary essay which appeared in volume 2 of this six-volume project.).

4.2.) And in order to let the Spaniards in general, and Gov. Gen. Primo de Rivera in particular, know that he, y Famy Aguinaldo E, was not that uncompromising at all between independence and money, between revolution and vendoration, he, Emilio Aguinaldo y Famy, released the Spanish prisoners captured in the Battle of Puray, and after a while issued his *Rizalian-Assimilationist anti-revolutionary Malabar Manifesto!* Whilst to make it appear that he was negotiating on an equal footing with Primo de Rivera and could therefore demand more money, he FROM THE VERY START contrived the so-called *Biyak na Bato Republic which lasted for only two days*! For, two days after its so-called constitution was promulgated (during the deliberations for which the skunkman Pedro Paterno was even present!), Lt. Gen. Mamerto Natividad who with his armed thousands stood against the Biyak na Bato sale, was fortuitously assassinated WITH A BULLET IN HIS FOREHEAD *JUST LIKE THE UNF0RTUNATE EDILBERTO EVANGELISTA WHO ON FEBRUARY 17, 1897 STOOD IN THE SAME WAY BETWEEN Y FAMY AGUINALDO E & HIS COUNTERREVOLUTIONARY GREED AND AMBITION (OR INDEED IN THE SAME WAY THAT GEN. ANTONIO LUNA DID ON JUNE 5, 1901)*... so that the Deed of Sale in the form of the Second Protocol of Peace could then already be safely signed and was duly signed by all the supertraitors concerned (for which they got paid, of course:--Makabulos 14k, Paciano Rizal 350, Malvar 8k, Pio del Pilar 11k, Lacuna 11k...etc. (I stumbled upon the receipt in volume 2 of JRM Taylor's five volume compilation of Katipunan and Aguinaldo Counterrevolutionary documents *The Philippine Insurrection Against the United States* and have since exposed the thing in my Facebook column, MATAKOT SA KASAYSAYAN; the receipt was in the original Spanish.)

4.3.) "*The Court does not believe that the petitioners are challenging the legitimacy of Emilio Aguinaldo's eventual Presidency of the First Philippine Republic. There seems to be no question that Emilio Aguinaldo, as a matter of historical fact, was the Republic's first President.*"

There seems to be no question...? His having become president at any other time after Tejeros is in fact absolutely irrelevant to the "appeal" they would be making. Meanwhile, that he, Aguinaldo, did not become president at Tejeros is absolutely decisive in making it impossible for him to become president after Tejeros. For if the Tejeros "Elections" was the counterrevolutionary coup d'etat that it most obviously was, and therefore was absolutely illegal, unconstitutional, illegitimate and absolutely unrightful, then the chief perpetrator of it cannot on its basis possibly become a true and real president of the fake and criminal successor governments founded on it as the perpetuation of the necessarily fake "Republic" of which such fake government would be a perpetuation. That is to say, Aguinaldo would have been able to be president at all had he legitimately succeeded the *first President of the Philippine (Revolutionary) Republic who of course was Andres Bonifacio* (Deodato Arellano was not that, nor Roman Basa, because, as I have discovered and documented, it is certain that Deodato Arellano was never even a Katipunan member, and highly uncertain whether Roman Basa was at least that:--it looks like these two rich middleclass agents have been insinuated there by the historians of the ruling class as part of the wholesale move to steal the glory of the Revolution from the lower classes, from the masses, and attribute the same to the ruling class, this move being the fundamental and comprehensive, all-determining ideological prejudice and bias of all of Philippine historiography from which only the present writer thus far has succeeded to liberate himself.).

The Philippine nation-state became fully such during the four years of its underground existence as the Katipunan Revolution under, of course, Bonifacio's presidency, when it grew into an archipelagic movement, which fullest deepening and expansion constituted the actual and most glorious ratification of its constitution by, of course, the revolutionary Filipino people! Otherwise, he, Aguinaldo y Famy would have merely been an illegitimate president and hence no president at all. Such a succession would have been Tejeros—if, that is, it was legal, legitimate, constitutional democratic, rightful. Which, however, it was most patently and most brutally and nakedly and obscenely criminally and counterrevolutionarily ***not***. And only an idiot, a political theory idiot, a human rights idiot, a commonsense idiot, an ordinary idiot, and thus an idiotic idiot such as Abraham Sarmiento *must be*, can possibly believe it to be otherwise. Of course, in this idiocy, he is one with the great majority of the Filipinos of the last 100 or so years, and one with almost all the historians, almost all the intellectuals so-called, of this country who ever wrote or thought anything about the matter—proving thereby that the colonial-middle-class-turned-ruling-class national brainwashing concerning the thing in particular and the history of the Revolution in general, was super-effective. That this omnivorous idiocy need not always abide however has here been very brightly shown by Haydee Yorac in her separate, and, lone dissenting opinion. The other two are quite simply otiose, especially the presumptuous historian so-called, Onofre D. Corpuz from Columbia and Harvard and Marcos' zombie Cabinet who would have gotten a flat 5 in my Philippine History class for failing to do his research homework.

4.4.) It has never been pointed out and its theoretical import and legal-constitutional implications taken into account (let alone full account), that all the charlatanic attempts to argue for and shore up the legitimacy of Emilio Aguinaldo's presidency, and thus his presidency per se, his being president at all, as purportedly established at precisely the Tejeros "Convention" cum All-Caviteno Conspiracy and Coup d'etat of Andres Bonifacio and the Katipunan National Revolutionary Government--as for instance this lousy one by this lousy Justice of the Philippine Supreme Court--willy nilly presuppose, and must theoretically, legally, and as a matter of constitutional law presuppose, that the Law of the State, and indeed of the Nation-State, and specifically of the Democratic Nation-State, i.e., (and as attested to by the (mis)use and (ab)use of the electoral legitimation function/process) the Law of the Republic, preexisted this conspiratorial convention and coup d'etat and what it falsely claimed to have established, namely the Aguinaldo presidency and government. And this nation-state, this democratic nation-state, this *Republic,* was of course, and can only be, and cannot be anything else but the revolutionary entity called the KKKNMANB, Kataastaasan Kagalanggalangang Katipunan Ng Mga Anak Ng Bayan--the Sovereign and Most Revered Association of the Daughters and Sons of the People, whose Sovereignty was of course the Sovereignty of the People, and whose Government was of course the duly constituted Katipunan National Democratic

Revolutionary Government whose Supreme President was of course none other than Andres Bonifacio. And these charlatans, and specifically this Supreme Court charlatan Abraham Sarmiento, must not point it out and must not even mention it, and must never think about it, because they would thus be realizing and pointing out and making egregiously blazoned that the Tejeros Convention was an all-Caviteno Conspiracy and Coup d'etat of Bonifacio and the Katipunan National Democratic Revolutionary Government, and the government it supposedly established there was a fake government (in fact a counterrevolutionary "government") and its president a bogus president, an illegitimate, treasonous, counterrevolutionary, vendorious, massmurderous gangster very much like Digong Duterte, including the nauseating braggadocious semi-illiteracy…

4.4.1.) In other words, what preeminently preexisted and cannot but be presupposed by that Counterrevolutionary Coup d'etat was *the People,* that primary element of the democratic/communist state that is *the People*, preconstituted as such by Bonifacio and his comrades across four deadly-dangerous years of underground recruitment into *peoplehood, nay, into revolutionary peoplehood,* from out of the disparate prerevolutionary tribes conquered and divided against each other by the colonial brutes…

4.4..2.) Hence these inverted human beings with inverted minds and souls who are all the historians who ever wrote on the matter must invert everything here and tag Andres Bonifacio and comrades who constituted the Filipino people into their peoplehood by constituting them into the revolutionary Filipino people, as the mere conspirators; and the greedy Caviteno pigs mottled with migrant devils like Ricarte, Pio del Pilar, Mamerto Natividad, as the true and authentic revolutionary, "no mere conspirators", *professionals*!!!

4.4.3.) These conspirators who organized no revolution but rather, from within the Revolution, their own vendorious ,pigly, counterrevolution…

4.5.) "*The petitioners, the Court believes, are objecting to Aguinaldo's presidency as a result of the Tejeros Convention, that is, he did not become president as a result of the convention. The argument seems to be that Aguinaldo assumed the presidency through other means, possibly because of Bonifacio's death...*" This Supreme Court Justice is confused. Or is purposely muddling the issue in order to underscore the of course false claim/thesis that Emilio Aguinaldo y Famy was the first president of the Philippine Republic (and thus was president at all). Aguinaldo was never president; he certainly did not become so in Tejeros which was the work of a band of tribalistic, perfidious, treasonous, counterrevolutionary thieves and vendors of the motherland and backstabbers of the Sovereign Revolutionary Filipino People--where they heinously and massmurderingly disregarded all the rights and prerogatives and interests of the Filipino People in order to subvert the Filipino People's will which was at that epochal juncture a revolutionary will. And if not in Tejeros, then nowhere and nowhen else--certainly not in the ensuing so-called Biyak na Bato Republic, nor in the so-called Kawit Republic of June 12, 1898, nor in the so-called Malolos Republic in all of which the same band of counterrevolutionary thieves and vendors of the Revolution merely tactically reaffirmed their counterrevolutionary vendorating project in the desperate endeavour to be able to sell the motherland at a higher price…But here, whether Aguinaldo became rightfully president after Tejeros was not the issue, but only whether he became so at Tejeros. For if he did not become so at Tejeros, then he, Abraham Sarmiento of the Supreme Court, would not have a case to mock-try; for if Aguinaldo was not president then he would not have the right to try and sentence anyone to death or community service. And the heirs of Bonifacio would then be, should then be, contesting first and foremost the rightfulness, the legality, the constitutionality, the democraticalness, the legitimacy, of his supposed presidency.

Note that his, Aguinaldo's, claim to being legitimate president and thus to being president at all rather than the mere chieftain of a band of robbers, rapists, and massmurdering vendors of the Revolution has as its singular indispensable and irreducible premise *the legality, the legitimacy, the constitutionality, the democraticalness of the transition from the Katipunan National Democratic Revolutionary Republic and Government to the supposed Republic which was the result of the all-Caviteno Magdiwang-Magdalo Conspiracy and Coup d'etat.* That is to say, the legality, legitimacy, constitutionality, democraticalness of the Coup d'etat, of the electoral coup d'etat, yes:--which was why they had to do it "electorally" rather than simply "shooting Bonifacio outright" (tanginang Agoncillo yan!) and declaring themselves the new, de novo, sui generis Philippine Republic. Which must then of necessity acknowledge and affirm the being people of the people, the being the Revolutionary Filipino People of the Revolutionary Filipino People, and thus the Sovereignty of the People, of this, the Filipino, People. And therewith acknowledge and affirm the being Supremo, the being Supreme President of Andres Bonifacio of this preexisting Philippine Revolutionary Republic. (Which was why, as we have already pointed out, their of course understandable sleight of hand attempt to reduce Andres Bonifacio into a mere Magdiwang was doubly absurd in also being self-contradictory...)

There of course was also this inexplicit claim that what legitimized the "take-over of leadership of the Revolution" (this phrase has to be put in quotes because it contains a duplictous claim which masks, dissimulates, and denies the being counterrevolution of that coup d'etat) was the victoriousness of Aguinaldo and the Cavitenos and the supposed ineptitude and inutility of Andres Bonifacio and the Katipunan National Government and military command. And that is why this supposed stark contrast was a constant refrain starting with Aguinaldo in his memoirs, letters and interviews, and without a single exception, amongst all the Philippine historians (Aguinaldo had even gone to the extent of declaring in his 1907 Statement Concerning the Revolution In Cavite And the Death of Andres Bonifacio, that he had to kill Andres Bonifacio and replace him with himself because he was apprehensive that "Andres Bonifacio might lose the Revolution itself in a single battle"--that's how truly stupid this Aguinaldo was!) --including even Renato Constantino who was one of the historian-respondents and consultants in this dirty and ignorant book, who rued Bonifacio's entrapment by the Cavitenos saying that he should not have gone there in the first place because whilst he was losing all his battles, "the Cavitenos were very victorious" as though their being (supposedly) so was any kind of de facto justification for what the Cavitenos did in Tejeros and Bonifacio's ouster and eventual death. But we have already demonstrated with absolute certainty that this Aguinaldo-Caviteno "victoriousness" was a wormy lie: Cavite was not a liberated zone or province but rather an abandoned zone (Gov. Gen. Blanco had pulled out all the Spanish soldiers from Cavite and transferred them to Manila right after the discovery of the Katipunan by Fray Mariano Gil of Tondo on August 19, 1896, except for a company of marines to guard the powder depot at Binakayan); the Cavitenos did not lose any battle because they did not fight any...Whilst this, this wormy lie of Agunaldo's and the Cavitenos' "great victoriousness" and "might" was, in the ultimate analysis, and as Abraham Sarmiento himself shamelessly declared, Abraham Sarmiento's ultimate argument justifying the coup d'etat and the murder of Bonifacio.

The only remaining possibility of an argument justifying Tejeros is anarchy-- Aguinaldo and his band were taking over and establishing a new, de novo, sui generis government and Republic during a period of anarchy. But this is nonsense.

"It is to be observed that Bonifacio himself had accused the Magdalos of 'rigging' the Tejeros Convention, an accusation contained in his letter to Emilio Jacinto...The Court believes, however, that Bonifacio's charges of fraud ('bad practices')

have never been historically proven. The Court agrees with Quirino, as follows:

xxx

xxx xxx

"Consider the fact that the two rivals for the presidency were Andres Bonifacio and Emilio Aguinaldo."

But they could not have been, except illegally, against all sense of law, constitutionality, right, and democracy, rivals in an election which had anything to do with the conduct of the Revolution in the entire Philippines, in the Philippine state as a whole as established by the KKK, or any part of it!

4.6.) "*As there were more Magdiwang members present, it was a foregone conclusion that the former would win easily. But what actually happened? The candidacy of Mariano Trias was presented by some astute Magdalo leader—possibly Baldomero Aguinaldo. Now Trias had been known as a Magdiwang stalwart and had a following among the members of that group, but not generally known is the fact that a few weeks earlier he had joined the Magdalos, because of a personal disagreement with some of the Magdiwang leaders, and had been given the rank of lieutenant general held by the late Edilberto Evangelista; he was therefore not averse to wresting the presidency from the Magdiwang candidate, Bonifacio.*"

But Supreme Court Associate Justice Abraham Sarmiento, like all the other Philippine historians without a single exception (and this includes Britishers like Jim Richardson, and Americans like Culinane and Glenn Anthony May, and a German Jesuit called Schumacher, and an Australian from Balic Balic, Floro Quibuyen), knows absolutely nothing about, not only the Rizal-ilustrado-colonial middleclass Counterrevolution, but the less occulted, more exposed to commonsense and normal intelligence Aguinaldo Gangsterist Vendorial Counterrevolution. Consequently, he, along with all of them, did not know anything about the otherwise egregiously obvious all-Caviteno Magdalo-Magdiwang Tejeros Conspiracy which there effectuated an "electoral" coup d'etat of Andres Bonifacio and the Katipunan National Revolutionary Government:--for this Conspiracy constituted the critical consolidation of this Aguinaldo-led Counterrevolution in all of Cavite. Before Tejeros, the Aguinaldo Counterrevolution which Aguinaldo launched formally as early as August 31, 1896, with his Manifesto of that date recruiting all the mayors or municipal captains of Cavite to join *him and his army to fight the then actually nonexistent enemy in all of Cavite* (for, as we have already documentarily shown, Gov. Gen. Blanco evacuated all the Spanish forces from Cavite and transferred them to Manila a few days after the Katipunan was exposed on August 19, 1896).

The Baldomero Aguinaldo letter to Cuenca and Noriel demonstrates beyond any but insane doubt that Mariano Alvarez himself was into the conspiracy. Did he know about the treachery of two of his maffiosi generals, Trias and Riego de Dios? If not, then we have to speak of a conspiracy within the conspiracy, and Mariano Alvarez himself and his son Santiago fell victim to it: for the former must have been expecting to win the Presidency, whilst Santiago was salivating for, and thinking to win, the captain general's post which went instead to that other major conspirator, the great actor Ricarte. Mariano Alvarez and the other two Alvarezes and those Magdiwangs loyal to them were thus themselves conspiratorially double-crossed by Aguinaldo with the help of the Magdiwang traitors Trias and Riego de Dios on one hand and Ricarte, the Ilocano-Caviteno Ricarte, on the other hand. This conspiracy within the conspiracy of the counterrevolutionaries within the Revolution in Cavite would explain the actuations of the Alvarezes in the repudiatory protest called ACTA DE TEJEROS. Pio del Pilar of Makati, we can safely assume, was not into those conspiracies. That would explain his prominent role in the ACTA DE TEJEROS and the NAIC COVENANT. Eventually of course, tribal and opportunist pressures would line up all these traitors behind Aguinaldo and against Bonifacio, on the way to the eventual murder of the Supremo which was the main strategic presupposition and inevitable implication of the Tejeros coup d'etat.

What was the result of this three-cornered fight? The Magdalos voted solidly for Kapitan Miong, while the Magdiwangs split their votes between Bonifacio and Trias, and Aguinaldo emerged the victor.

"When the balloting for Vice-President followed, four Magdiwang leaders were candidates: Bonifacio, Trias, Mariano Alvarez, and Severino de las Alas. Again the Magdiwang votes were split among the four, but this time the Magdalo faction voted in favour of Trias, who emerged triumphant. By a simple political maneuver, the Magdiwangs had been outwitted. Clearly they had not prepared for the political aspect of the convention, and they lost badly to the numerically inferior Magdalos. There was no need for fraud and chicanery to obtain desired results".

4.7.) This is stupid. They were supposed to be fighting for the highest positions in the supposed republic and they did not even know that nominating more than one candidate from their group would split their votes and make them lose? Of course they were not that stupid! And of course it was Quirino who was stupid for believing them to be so stupid; and of course Abraham Sarmiento was stupider still in believing the stupid Quirino. Which means that that supposed "simple political maneuver" was scripted, and that the main objective of the script was to "electorally" coup d'etat Andres Bonifacio and hostage thereby the Revolution:--this must logically lead to the murder of Bonifacio. That was the script of the grand conspiracy. The initial protests by the Magdiwangs can only mean that there was a conspiracy within the conspiracy involving Trias and Riego de Dios but also Ricarte.

4.8.) This is marvellous! You set a race between two horses by taking care to first cut off a foot of one of them, and indeed, you would not need any "fraud and chicanery" to ensure that the unmaimed one would win. And, but, of course, maiming the other horse thus is fraud, and it is not bright at all to suggest it isn't, in fact, it is absolutely stupid and, when insisted upon, shameless and criminal. And here you have an august jurist agreeing with the victorious horse that the race was run "according to the rules of the game" and that cutting off a foot here and a foot there of the other horse is "legitimate" although such tactic might be considered by some to constitute a bending of the rules, just the same, the maiming tactic meant that the unmaimed horse beat the maimed one "fair and square".

"Disappointed by the turn of event, Bonifacio quickly called for another convention at the same place on the following day. March 23, attended by his followers and the Magdiwang group, with the Magdalo faction naturally excluded, and they had signed an agreement—the misleadingly called Acta de Tejeros—which repudiated the results of the assembly held on the preceding day. 'We cannot accept the result thereof because the same lacks legality', the document reads in part; 'we have learned that actual pressure has been brought to bear upon our presidency; and that ballots have been prepared by one sole person and have been issued to unqualified persons in order to secure a majority; and we have learned that they have conspired there. For this reason we deny the validity of the action taken, the unlawfulness whereof is proved by the fact that they have been unable to prepare a formal minute record for our signatures, aside from the capital defect that our brother officers were not present there and were outside.

"Clearly, the reasons for invalidating the elections were flimsy; were not the minute-records kept by Magdiwang men at an assembly presided by them?"

4.9.) Oh, but oh ho ho ho, the actual presider, organizer, chief, chairman, president of the counterrevolutionary conspiracy was the counterrevolutionary traitor who was contacted by Polavieja through Gen. Nicolas de la Pena and Pio Pi SJ and Rafael Comenge for his wellknown amenability to such treachery and counterrevolutionary vendoration, y Famy Aguinaldo E., as proven by all the available documents and testimonies and causalities pertaining to the odious thing.

"Were not the absent officers from the Magdalo rather than the Magdiwang faction? If the Magdalo followers had 'quietly spread the statement that it was not advisable that they be governed by men from other pueblos', this was legitimate political propaganda that could not be claimed as 'dirty'. The charge that the ballots had been prepared by one individual and given to unqualified persons might stand if that individual had been a Magdalo official—but did not the Magdiwangs supervise the entire affair? In all likelihood this charge probably arose from the fact that the ballots given to the Magdalo members were filled out in accordance with a prepared form, in order to ensure the impact of a uniform slate—but there is nothing reprehensible or unethical about that, for it is a procedure followed by political parties everywhere. What Bonifacio and the Magdiwangs could not understand was that they had been neatly outmaneuvered. Having lost, they refused to accept the verdict, and blamed the outsome on 'bad practices' supposedly perpetrated during the balloting."

"The Court agrees that the Magdalos 'outmaneuvered' the Magdiwangs (and Bonifacio), plainly and simply, at Tejeros, but the latter could not have validly protested the results of the Convention for the latter's political acumen and

ambitions...The Court is agreed though, that Aguinaldo (or the Magdalos) probably 'set up' Bonifacio to yield the leadership of the revolutionary movement to the Magdalos. It is noteworthy that Aguinaldo had, as early as October 31, 1896, called for the establishment of a 'Revolutionary Committee' with apparent authority all over the archipelago. As Constantino would remark:

"The simple Bonifacio had been badly outmaneuvered. Although it was his duty to mediate quarrels within his organization, his going to Cavite may be termed a tactical error especially at a time when he had been suffering military reverses while the Cavitenos had been winning victories. Bonifacio had few friends in Cavite. On the other hand, the victories of the Cavite rebels were bound to arouse strong feelings of regionalism and pride in their local champion, General Aguinaldo."

4.9.1.) And here we see the simpleminded Renato Constantino displaying his own historiographic illiteracy, his documentary illiteracy and his being but a witless victim of the same massive and comprehensive and deep brainwashing inflicted upon the Filipino people by the Rizalian-Aguinaldian-ilustrado-cacique-US imperialist instigated counterrevolutionary and ruling-class enforced and textbook embodied ideological hegemony. For, again, here is one supposed historian who failed to do any real research, who did not read all the pertinent documents, and consequently was not able to properly document his own supposedly historiographic narrative, which then must of necessity fall into the category of tsismis, rumour, salivating lies. And consequently did not know that there were absolutely no victories won by the Cavitenos in Cavite, for there were in fact no real battles that happened there prior to the February 14, 1897 start of the Spanish reconquest of the Cavite they abandoned in the third week of August 1896. (The November 9-10 bombardment from the sea was not a battle; they bombarded Cavite and then withdrew when they realized it would take a huge overland force to retake it.) And of course,

Constantino did not know that what happened in Tejeros was a coup d'etat perpetrated by an all-Caviteno Magdalo-Magdiwang conspiracy--and this, again, because in his brainwashed dotage he neither researched nor read.

*"But Bonifacio's biggest error lay in his failure to insist that representatives from other provinces be present to participate in such a crucial decision. His suspicions should have been aroused by the unexpected agitation for the formation of a central government to supersede the Katipunan, but he was too naïve and trusting and perhaps also too secure in his preeminent position in the movement to think that anyone could be planning to wrest the leadership from his hands."*Bonifacio, as he himself told us in his letters to Emilio Jacinto, had voiced out that objection. He yielded to the clamor however when he saw that all the Magdiwangs were for it. In this sense he failed to *insist enough.* For to insist enough in such a situation can only mean walking out of it. In so yielding despite his better knowledge, he showed himself still completely innocent of the all-Caviteno Conspiracy; he did not yet know that the owerwhelmingly more numerous Magdiwangs had already betrayed him and the Katipunan Revolution. It was easy for him to acquiesce in the thought that anyway, with the Magdiwangs on his and the Revolution's side, the exercise would simply reaffirm him and the Katipunan government--as it transpired in the Imus Assembly of December 30, 1896. He could have imagined too that this unswerving result was going to consolidate his leadership of the Revolution. It must be pointed out that when they set Bonifacio up at Tejeros thus, only three of the eight Magdalo towns have not yet been reconquered by the Spaniards; Bonifacio of course knew this, and knew with it that in a short while Aguinaldo would cease to be a chieftain of anything--how could the Magdiwangs possibly recognize him as their leader, their president, their supremo, then? How could such a betrayal happen? Cowardice plus money. Money must have been offered by Polavieja through Pio Pi SJ and Rafael Comenge. A foretaste of it too must have been granted to the Magdiwangs as earnest money. Whilst the same Magdiwangs saw the devastating power of the Spanish army taking town after Magdalo town as a matter of course. Whilst

these Cavitenos had never fought any real battle at all before then. And, but, then, what happened to the money? The Spaniards might have reneged on the promise thinking that they could overrun without any real fight the whole of Cavite by then. Or else, Aguinaldo might have doublecrossed the Magdiwangs, running away thus with the first instalment...And getting a sharp foretaste from it of what he would later gorge his pigly self with in the Biyak na Bato Deed of Sale.

Sarmiento, Abraham: "and as Quirino pointed out, 'the events at Tejeros followed a pattern which has been repeated time and again in many a political struggle for supremacy...Surely, however, and to be fair, Bonifacio could not have had any cause for complaint in a contest otherwise played by the rules, although the rules might have had been bent in favour of Aguinaldo...

4.10.) Anong klaseng moronic ox ito? How could the contest have been played by the rules when the rules had been bent in favour of Aguinaldo? Anong katangahan at kagaguhan ito?

"As the Court said, there was no sufficient evidence to justify conviction, and the accused should have been acquitted. However, to condemn the Revolutionary Government outright for a bad verdict is to ignore the supremo's own shortcomings".

4.11.) Ha? "Revolutionary Government"? But only brainwashed idiots like you can make the mistake of calling such a completely and wantonly anti-revolutionary and shamelessly vendorial "government" a "Revolutionary Government", if government at all rather than a thieves' syndicate. Utterly prejudicial against the Revolution and utterly destructive of the Revolution's organization and government (which were of course not the same as the Revolution itself, for the Revolution itself was precisely that thing which can never be defeated, for the Revolution was the *revolutionization* of the psyche, the soul, the spirit of the people and only genocide can defeat such a thing…), whatever other things Aguinaldo's government might also be, it certainly must be a *COUNTER-REVOLUTIONARY GOVERNMENT.*

"There is no dispute, after all, concerning the Acta de Tejeros and the Naik Military Agreement, in which Bonifacio rejected the results of the Tejeros Convention and proclaimed his own right to leadership. There is no historical argument either, that Bonifacio established his headquarters at Indang, a 'regional government' (according to Agoncillo and Quirino), and that he named General Miguel Malvar Commander-in-Chief, Lorenzo Fenoy Vice President, Ananias Diokno Secretary of War, and Santiago Rillo Secretary of Interior.

"As Agoncillo pointed out, Aguinaldo could have shot Bonifacio outright for such an act of sedition."

4.12.) Aguinaldo was voted president by an assembly of Cavitenos inside Cavite *and absolutely without the rest of the Philippines having anything to do with that "election"*. If he was president of anything, it could then only be of Cavite. How could the President of the Philippines be guilty of sedition against the president of Cavite and his supposed government? And this for supposedly appointing officers of a certain "regional government"? Bonifacio should have shot Aguinaldo outright for those seditious acts of inventing that absurd situation and gossiping about such absurdity—and Agoncillo too, if that were possible, for the seditious act of suggesting that Bonifacio, the President of the Republic of the Philippines be shot outright by the president of Cavite for thus deeming the President of the Philippines subordinate to the president of Cavite which was tantamount to a subversion of the Constitution of the National Revolutionary Government and of the Republic which of course was none other than Bonifacio's Katipunan.

"Historians, of course, have expressed varying opinions on the meaning of Bonifacio's death. According to Constantino, there was no underlying reason behind the execution (and trial) of Bonifacio other than the burning ambition of the Magdalos to steal the Revolution from the 'masses', which Bonifacio had of course represented. Constantino said, 'Bonifacio could not have been dangerous to the Revolution as a whole for he remained resolved to continue the anti-Spanish struggle.'

4.13.) Anak ng putah! How could Constantino even have put forth this "defense" of Bonifacio's not being a danger to the Revolution as a whole? –and this against the egregiously counter-revolutionary essence, actuality, tendency, trajectory of Aguinaldo's leadership, "government", gang? But in his as in that of any other historian's case, the *SALE* of the Revolution at Biyak na Bato, failed to register as a sale—and that was why they must fail to recognize and categorize this so-called "government" of Aguinaldo as *counter-revolution, as the Counter-revolutionary organization itself that led precisely to such vendoration, to such surrender for pay...*

"Quirino has expressed the opinion, on the other hand, that the Revolution had simply peaked into a full military war in which 'conspirators' were no longer needed, but in which generals were indispensable. The death of Bonifacio, said Quirino, signalled that transition..."

4.14.) This is an absurd idea; but it is even more absurd that people like Abraham Sarmiento could take it seriously, let alone believe it and use it as an argument for the murder of Bonifacio by a gangster like Aguinaldo. But the worst thing is that in that Aguinaldo was in fact a thoroughgoing counterrevolutionary saboteur and destroyer of the Revolution (hostaging it and surrendering it for pay was, surely, sabotage and destruction?), this absurd idea coined by a hack whose pages demonstrate an obscene mindlessness and a singular incapacity for honesty (surpassed only, in both incapacities, by his Kawit idol) has now become an argument justifying the takeover via the Tejeros coup d'etat, of the Katipunan Revolution by the Aguinaldo Counterrevolution. How did it happen that founders of revolutions must as the revolutionary war begins turn into mere conspirators who must then be supplanted by true generals? Before the true generals entered the scene, they were not yet generals nor true. Were they mere conspirators too, to begin with? How in hell does it happen that founders of revolutions are nothing but mere conspirators--who then must be murdered by the true generals in order correctly to make the revolution? We have demonstrated repeatedly that from the very start it was Aguinaldo and his goony, hudloomy band that had been conspiring to gain control of the Revolution (with, it turned out, the ultimate aim of making money out of it, of selling it), that is to say, to eliminate, ultimately to murder, Bonifacio; and that later and at Tejeros precisely, he was able to recruit the entire Magdiwang into the conspiracy. They called themselves "generals" before that; and now they were nothing but conspirators. In actual fact, none of them had done anything to make themselves generals before that conspiracy either, since, as we have documented and even over-documented, and this through the circumstantial testimonies themselves of the two foremost fake generals of that all-Caviteno conspiracy, Emilio Aguinaldo himself and General Apoy alias Santiago Alvarez in their respective memoirs, they had not fought any real battles at all to liberate Cavite for there were no Spanish soldiers left to fight there after Blanco, even before the outbreak of hostilities, ordered the pull-out of all the Spanish soldiers from Cavite and their transfer to Manila to defend the capital against Bonifacio, and hence had never in actual fact become real generals. From the very start then, they were nothing but real conspirators—counterrevolutionary conspirators. Did they become, through the Tejeros Conspiracy less fake generals? Did they start winning battles after Tejeros? Were the Cavitenos less massacred by the Spaniards after Tejeros? Did they win a single battle after Tejeros? In Cavite, no. In fact they lost all their battles from day one on February 14, 1896 when finally the Spaniards attacked Cavite for the reconquest, to the day in May, right after Aguinaldo had murdered Bonifacio, on which Aguinaldo had to flee Cavite for his life who in cowardly and shivering panic had ordered the burning of the Cavite towns in order to impede his Spanish pursuers, such a perfect and exemplary coward was he! Thus, without having won a single, significant battle (for, as we have now perfectly memorized, Cavite was an abandoned and not a liberated zone, and there were no real battles for the liberation of Cavite at all), from before Tejeros and after Tejeros, the great Caviteno general who wrestled to death a giant shark in the deep night in the dark Batangas sea according to him himself!, was ignominiously chased out of Cavite by the returning, reconquering Spaniards. The only known victory that might have involved Aguinaldo or his cowardly and treacherous Kawit hoodlums was the so-called Battle of Puray in which however, the Katipunan Army of the South under the leadership of Emilio Jacinto and Julio Nakpil and non-Caviteno generals Hermogenes Bautista, General Kalentong, General Julian dela Cruz, and others from Marikina, Montalban and San Mateo were the main protagonists (Julio Nakpil in his memoirs of 1925, testified that Jacinto, who of course wanted to avenge Bonifacio against Aguinaldo, had with utter patience and forbearance desisted from doing so for the sake of provisional unity against the common enemy; his men were there in Puray but he was not, and this in order to avoid a confrontation...). On August 11, 1897, as we know from a document which we will duly cite below, the Spanish prisoners captured in this battle were liberated by Aguinaldo in order to entice Primo de Rivera to negotiate a surrender-for-pay with him. Finally then, Aguinaldo and his generals sold the Revolution for 800,000 pesos at Biyak na Bato after murdering all the generals that did not agree to the sale. And did that make them true generals at last and not mere conspirators?

4.15.) We have already demonstrated repeatedly, and documented exhaustively, that Cavite was not a liberated zone but rather an abandoned zone, and that there was not a single decent battle in the so-called liberation of Cavite, and that the so-called victories of the Cavitenos were a lie, and that at the very bottom, at the middle, and at the very top of that multifarious lie was the lie of lies that was the father and the mother and even the uncle of all those lies, namely the lie of Emilio Aguinaldo y Famy's great and victorious military generalship. The first occasion of the possibility of Aguinaldo's enactment of his supposed great military generalship came with the first attack launched by the Spanish army under Polavieja on February 14, 1897. From that time on, it was straight losses and massacres for the Cavitenos and their generals until May 10, 1897 when Andres Bonifacio and his brother Procopio were assassinated and Aguinaldo fled Cavite. A great Vendor rather than a great General was of course necessary to consummate the Biyak na Bato Deed of Sale.Towed back by Dewey, Aguinaldo once more never really fought a single real battle against the Spaniards who were surrendering *en masse* after Dewey sunk the entire Spanish fleet on May 1, 1898, and later on, as proved by the *mock battle* for Manila, because of secret negotiations between the Spaniards and the Americans culminating as everyone knows in the sale of the Philippines for 20 million dollars by way of the Treaty of Paris. Once again then, Aguinaldo's military generalship was an otiose claim; whilst during the Fil-Am War, if at all Aguinaldo was never really anywhere near any battle to be general about, it was straight rout and disaster for him until his ignominious surrender to Funston at Palanan.

Made in the USA
Lexington, KY
25 May 2018